WHERE ARE YOUR BOYS TONIGHT?

WHERE ARE YOUR BOYS TONIGHT?

THE ORAL HISTORY OF EMO'S MAINSTREAM EXPLOSION 1999–2008

CHRIS PAYNE

DEYST.

An Imprint of WILLIAM MORROW

DEYST.

HarperCollins books may be purchased for educational, business, or sales promotional use. For information, please email the Special Markets Department at SPsales@harpercollins.com.

FIRST EDITION

Designed by Jennifer Chung
Black texture background © Ivan Popovych/ Shutterstock
White distressed background © Inkura/Shutterstock

Library of Congress Cataloging-in-Publication Data has been applied for.

ISBN 978-0-06-325128-1

23 24 25 26 27 LBC 6 5 4 3 2

FOR MOM AND DAD

CONTENTS

INTRODUCTION

Emo was never supposed to be cool, so when Gerard Way saw the chance to manifest his comic book fantasies, he went all in. The black marching band uniforms, the skeleton costumes, the broken, the beaten, and the damned—it's all part of the lore now, but it wasn't until one night in August 2006: the night My Chemical Romance introduced the world to the Black Parade. MTV had provided six full minutes during the Video Music Awards for the band to unveil its new single on live television, which in the days of *TRL* and MySpace was kind of like getting your own Super Bowl commercial. North Jersey's biggest dreamers answered the call. Looking like a zombie *Sgt. Pepper's* brigade, My Chemical Romance ascended 30 Rockefeller Plaza and rocked out "Welcome to the Black Parade" on a strip atop the skyscraper just wide enough to hold the stage. They were warned not to jump, or else the wind could knock them off and down to the city streets below. The fading rays of sunlight had just dipped below the Manhattan skyline. After belting one last "We'll carry on," Way held out the mic and gazed into the great beyond, looking like a damn superhero.

Down inside the ceremony awaited some old acquaintances and some new ones. There was Fall Out Boy, who one year earlier slogged it out across the parking lots of America alongside My Chemical Romance on 2005's Warped Tour. While passing through Las Vegas, Fall Out Boy bassist Pete Wentz had introduced members of My Chemical Romance to a band he'd just discovered on the internet: four local teenagers who called themselves Panic! at the Disco. The recent high school graduates could have easily milled through the Warped crowd unrecognized; now, more than a year later, Panic! filed into Radio City Music Hall with dreams of winning all five VMAs they'd been nominated for, including Video of the Year. Fall Out Boy, whose "Dance, Dance" video was up for two awards of its own, was set to introduce Panic!'s in-show performance of "I Write Sins Not Tragedies." And at night's end, My Chemical Romance's opening spectacle would be matched by an upset for the ages: After losing their first four nominations, Panic! at the Disco beat out the likes of Madonna's "Hung Up" and Shakira's "Hips Don't Lie" for Video of the Year. Emo had not only reached the summit—it had conquered it.

Underground rock scenes had crashed the mainstream before, but with those—punk's class of '77; eighties indie rock and hardcore; and nineties grunge—there was a prevailing sense of self-detonation, of burning down the house party before the lights got flicked on. MySpace-era emo, on the other hand, not only had immense star power, but stars who weren't the least bit bashful about being the biggest band in the world. At the 1992 VMAs, Nirvana famously refused to perform "Smells Like Teen Spirit"; by 2006, My Chemical Romance's dramatic unveiling of "Welcome to the Black Parade" showed how much the barriers of showmanship and selling out had broken down. This generational shift was due to a lot of things: the rise of social media, a desperate, post-Napster music industry, the pull of hip-hop culture, and most of all, this eager new generation of bands. At any date along the 2005 Warped Tour, the kids in Panic!—or any other kid with about thirty bucks—could have caught Fall Out Boy and My Chemical Romance in their prime, and then seen a side-stage band of fellow high schoolers called Paramore, out on their first nationwide tour. It was all happening, all at once, and no one knew how far the moment could take them.

But in the scene Hayley Williams, Brendon Urie, Pete Wentz, and Gerard Way came from, bands didn't start out expecting to become rich and famous. The music this book is about, whatever you want to call it—[early] 2000s emo, emo-pop, third-wave emo, mall emo, MTVmo, *Steven's Untitled Rock Show*-core, fake punk bullshit for posers—can be traced back, somehow, someway, to hardcore punk, and thus, an outsider mentality. American hardcore—bands like Bad Brains, Black Flag, Minor Threat, and Dead Kennedys—started in the late seventies as a loosely connected community of scenes with no link to the mainstream music business. It thrived off-the-grid in LA and DC, but also in places like Austin, Texas, and Reno, Nevada. Fiercely independent, the American hardcore scene taught kids to self-book national tours and helped spread the gospel of straight edge, animal rights, and an array of leftist politics. It was also extremely violent. And since the only non-punks paying attention were often cops trying to kick the shit out of punks, the scene developed a pretty thick skin to strangers. A flyer for a hardcore show might've included a drawing of a bullet obliterating JFK's forehead, or Ronald Reagan holding up a Butthole Surfers shirt. There wasn't a lot of room for vulnerability here. So about eight years into the hardcore movement, when a few DC bands got tired of stage diving and built their identities around yearning, poetic lyrics, and performed like they were about to burst into flames, they stood out. People even thought of a word for it. The term "emocore" (short for "emotive hardcore" or "emotional hardcore") had been bouncing around the album review sections of publications like *Thrasher*, and with bands like Rites of Spring and Embrace, the term stuck.

These forerunner bands eventually saw their legacies grow as emo gained popularity, but it's hard to stress how localized their appeal was in their day. Rites of Spring, commonly cited as the "first" emo band, played only a handful of shows outside DC and broke up after about two years. Embrace's run was even briefer; they split in 1986, and vocalist Ian MacKaye formed the post-hardcore band Fugazi a year later.

The version of emo that blew up in the 2000s has little to no direct connection—sonically or aesthetically—to this first wave. Like most interesting genres, it evolved greatly over time. By the mid-nineties, emo's "second wave" had spread to college towns and medium-sized cities across America, and taken on a bit of indie rock melody. Grunge was exploding, but second-wave emo never caught on with normies like its distant, northwestern cousin. Some major labels and prominent indies tried to ride the post-Nirvana rush and break emo bands in the mainstream, but the moment wasn't right. Over the decades, records like

Sunny Day Real Estate's *Diary*, the Promise Ring's *Nothing Feels Good*, Jawbox's *For Your Own Special Sweetheart*, and Jawbreaker's *Dear You* have grown into underground classics, but upon release, they certainly weren't making anyone rich. The bands were largely unwilling to play the music industry game and their music, iconic as it was, was still too knotty and weird to log more than a few late-night plays on MTV's *120 Minutes*.

Enter emo's "third wave," the wave that got popular, and the subject of this book. *Where Are Your Boys Tonight?* is divided into five sections, each marking a crucial pivot point in third-wave emo's evolution. We start at the turn of the millennium, when a handful of overlooked scenes fostered a slew of promising groups who hardly dreamed of any sort of success, outside of filling basements and Elks Lodges (often with the help of five other bands). For Thursday, Midtown, and Saves the Day in New Jersey; Brand New and Taking Back Sunday on Long Island; Dashboard Confessional in Florida; and the hardcore kids who'd soon form Fall Out Boy in the Chicago burbs, local heroes were exactly that: local. On the music biz's late nineties radar, bridge-and-tunnel kids riffing on Lifetime and Silent Majority landed just south of nowhere. But with good looks, catchier songs, and a more advanced version of the internet on their side, glossy magazine covers and MTV stardom suddenly became realities for this new generation. Part two picks up in 2001, with Dashboard Confessional and Jimmy Eat World, a survivor of that post-Nirvana alt-rock bust, on the verge of taking emo to the masses. In 2002, the moment arrived.

Heartthrob Dashboard singer Chris Carrabba became an MTV star and Jimmy Eat World's "The Middle" cracked the top five of the *Billboard* Hot 100 and appeared in seemingly every teen movie soundtrack. Purists grabbed their pitchforks, but this was only the beginning. Part three follows the mass media feeding frenzy that ensued in 2003, but even more importantly, the social media revolution that began that year with the launch of MySpace. When the platform took off in 2004, soon-to-be stars like Fall Out Boy and My Chemical Romance flourished on its pixelated pages. The age of influencers had dawned, and emo was its choice aesthetic.

And then there's 2005, the only year to get its own section. This year was a unicorn, a collision of old media and new, of punk rock and pop stardom, that we're unlikely to see again. That summer, "Helena" and "Sugar, We're Goin Down" topped the *TRL* countdown while My Chemical Romance and Fall Out Boy spent the Warped Tour riding in vans with broken air-conditioning and showering with canned water. They played forty-eight shows in fifty-nine days, including stops in Nampa, Idaho, and Bozeman, Montana. One day in Detroit, My Chemical Romance sold $60,000 worth of CDs, T-shirts, hoodies, and skeleton gloves with cutoff fingers. Paramore arrived that summer, and anyone who heard Hayley Williams's voice—whether on Warped Tour's Shiragirl Stage or their feisty debut *All We Know Is Falling*—seemed to act like they'd been struck by an otherworldly force. And finally, across those twelve magical months, Panic! at the Disco went from Pete Wentz's blog buddies to a real-life freight train obliterating everything in its path. The same way rock historians talk about 1977 and 1991, 2005 was the lynchpin of emo, the big bang of the 2000s.

By 2006, there was no turning back. MySpace ruled the internet. Emo was popular culture. What did these bands do with all that power? Over section five, we'll ride the celebrity roller coaster through the triumphs of Paramore's *Riot!* and My Chemical Romance becoming the Black Parade, but also the commercial misfires and band breakdowns that led to the end of mainstream emo. Or at least, for a while . . .

Where Are Your Boys Tonight? contains material from more than three hundred hours of interviews with more than 150 people, ranging from artists to managers to critics to superfans. This book is not meant to be an encyclopedia of emo, but a narrative of a specific period in its history. Some seminal emo bands won't appear at all, and other bands that may not be called emo per se you'll hear from a lot, because the story of the genre's explosion would be impossible to tell without their voices. It's worth noting that approximately zero of the bands covered in this book—or the ones that came before them—owned up to the "emo" tag during the eighties, nineties, and the first decade of the twenty-first century. Back then, "punk" or "indie rock" were preferred, or if you were a little more tryhard, "post-hardcore." "Emo" was often used as an insult with homophobic undertones, mocking the vulnerability of the lyrics and performances. Even when it wasn't being used as a slur, bands found their reasons to reject the title. Some would get philosophical ("Isn't *all* music emotional?") and others got historical, agreeing, sure, Rites of Spring were emo, but since we sound nothing like them, how could that word possibly describe us? Plenty of bands would eventually grow to accept the term, but we're still about four hundred pages away from that.

Reexamining emo's pop years brought out many extremes: how young the participants were, how novel their fame was, how much cash was being thrown around. How the internet felt like a savior for music and social connection. How male-dominated the bands onstage were, while the audiences were often predominantly teenage girls.

This inequity dovetailed with rampant misogyny and abuse, which is still coming to light. In 2017, Brand New's Jesse Lacey was accused of sexual misconduct by multiple women, who described similar accounts of a twenty-something Lacey preying on them throughout the 2000s when they were as young as fifteen. Brand New subsequently canceled touring plans and Lacey issued an apology statement, though it did not address specifics of the of sexual misconduct accusations. In *Where Are Your Boys Tonight?*, I attempted to depict where and how Brand New drove the narrative of the 2000s emo boom, without glorifying Lacey himself. I realize that, at times, this bestriding may seem difficult, if not impossible: Brand New was arguably the most innovative and critically acclaimed band of their scene. Their appeal was so cultish and specific, it's hard to put into words. I truly hope I captured it in a way that feels accurate to the era, and brings no further pain to those Lacey hurt.

While the emo boom is inextricable from the internet, it's tied to physical space and a time I don't think could ever exist again. A time when the earliest recordings from bands like Thursday and Saves the Day felt like they could change the world, but you'd never heard anything like them on TV or radio before; when the internet was accessible enough to spread word of new demos and DIY shows, but pre-MySpace platforms like message boards and LiveJournal were still too analog and isolated to make anyone famous. This is the era in which the book begins, and within that era, no scene was more vital than New Jersey's. Before My Chemical Romance brought it to the Top of the Rock, emo's explosion began across the Hudson River, in the suburbs just out of view . . .

—Chris Payne, Brooklyn, New York, October 2022

PART 1

CLOSE TO HOME

1999–2000

CAST OF CHARACTERS

PART 1

HANIF ABDURRAQIB: author and poet (and Midwest native)
JOANNA ANGEL: adult film star; cofounder, BurningAngel.com; author (and New Jersey native)
JUSTIN BECK: guitarist, Glassjaw; cofounder, Merch Direct
DAN BONEBRAKE: bassist, Dashboard Confessional, Vacant Andys
CHRIS CARRABBA: front person, Dashboard Confessional, Further Seems Forever; vocalist-guitarist, Vacant Andys
VINNIE CARUANA: front person, the Movielife, I Am the Avalanche
TOMMY CORRIGAN: front person, Silent Majority; designer, Merch Direct
EBEN D'AMICO: bassist, Saves the Day
MIKE DOYLE: vocalist-bassist, Lanemeyer
MIKE DUBIN: photographer, videographer, radio host, tour manager (and Long Island native)
RICH EGAN: cofounder, Vagrant Records; manager, Dashboard Confessional, the Get Up Kids
FRED FELDMAN: founder, Triple Crown Records
GLENN GAMBOA: journalist, *Newsday*
CHRIS GETHARD: comedian (and late nineties punk kid and New Brunswick resident)
NICK GHANBARIAN: bassist, Silent Majority (and later, Bayside)
CHAD GILBERT: guitarist, New Found Glory; front person, Shai Hulud
AARON GILLESPIE: drummer-vocalist, Underoath
JIM GRIMES: Chicago hardcore show promoter; front person, Extinction
CHRIS GUTIERREZ: bassist, Arma Angelus; blogger and author
PAUL HANLY: New Brunswick basement show promoter
TARYN HICKEY: photographer
ROB HITT: drummer, Midtown (and later, manager, Crush Music)
BENNY HOROWITZ: New Jersey show promoter (and later, drummer, the Gaslight Anthem)
BEN JORGENSEN: drummer, Random Task (and later, front person, Armor for Sleep)
ARI KATZ: front person, Lifetime
MELISSA KUNDRATH: show promoter, the Bergenfield Girls
SARAH LEWITINN: journalist, blogger, DJ (alias, Ultragrrrl), cofounder/A&R, Stolen Transmission Records
JOLIE LINDHOLM: front person, the Rocking Horse Winner
AMY FLEISHER MADDEN: founder, Fiddler Records; zine maker, *Fiddler Jones*; author; photographer

STEPHANIE MARLOW: publicity, Victory Records

MIKE MARSH: drummer-vocalist, the Agency (and later, drummer, Dashboard Confessional)

CHRISTIAN MCKNIGHT: Long Island show promoter (and later, talent buyer, Bamboozle, Skate and Surf, This Island Earth festivals)

MANI MOSTOFI: front person, Racetraitor

BRYAN NEWMAN: drummer, Saves the Day

JOHN NOLAN: vocalist-guitarist, Taking Back Sunday (and later, vocalist-multi-instrumentalist, Straylight Run)

SEAN O'KEEFE: producer, Fall Out Boy, Arma Angelus

JENN PELLY: author and journalist (and Long Island native)

MATT PRYOR: front person, the Get Up Kids, the New Amsterdams

ANTHONY RANERI: front person, Bayside

TYLER RANN: vocalist-guitarist, Midtown

KATE REDDY: guitarist, 108; comanager, Equal Vision Records

SCOTTIE REDIX: drummer and guitarist, the Stryder

RICHARD REINES: cofounder, Drive-Thru Records

STEFANIE REINES: cofounder, Drive-Thru Records

ERIN RENDON: show promoter, the Bergenfield Girls

KATHY RENDON: show promoter, the Bergenfield Girls

EDDIE REYES: guitarist, Taking Back Sunday (and previously, Mind Over Matter, Clockwise, Inside, the Movielife, Runner Up)

GEOFF RICKLY: front person, Thursday; New Brunswick basement show promoter; producer, My Chemical Romance

NEIL RUBENSTEIN: front person, Sons of Abraham, This Year's Model (and later, comedian)

ALEX SAAVEDRA: cofounder, Eyeball Records

GABE SAPORTA: front person, Cobra Starship, Midtown (previously, bassist, Humble Beginnings)

RICKY SAPORTA: show promoter, Bomb Shelter Productions; photographer

HEATH SARACENO: vocalist-guitarist, Midtown (and later, Senses Fail)

TOM SCHLATTER: guitarist, You and I

WALTER SCHREIFELS: front person, Quicksand, Rival Schools; guitarist, Gorilla Biscuits, Youth of Today

ALEX SUAREZ: bassist, Cobra Starship; multi-instrumentalist-vocalist, Kite Flying Society (and Florida native)

MIKEY WAY: bassist, My Chemical Romance

PETE WENTZ: bassist, Fall Out Boy (and previously, bassist, Racetraitor; front person, Arma Angelus); founder, Decaydance Records, Clandestine Industries

JAMES PAUL WISNER: producer, Dashboard Confessional, Paramore, Underoath, The Academy Is . . .

DAN YEMIN: guitarist, Lifetime, Kid Dynamite

CHAPTER 1

JERSEY BASEMENTS & *THE* MANHATTAN SKYLINE

MIKEY WAY: In New Jersey, everyone's trying to get out of New Jersey, you know what I mean? Well . . . not everyone. But if you're an adolescent in New Jersey, there's this need to make something of yourself. That's the underlying theme of New Jersey. *I'm going to get out of this town . . .*

CHRIS GETHARD: There were a lot of people who felt . . . how would I put it? Nobody has time to worry about your fucking artistic dreams in New Jersey.

MIKEY WAY: Growing up in Belleville, certain parts weren't the safest, so you had to create escapes. You had to live in your head. Kids would ride bikes and play with friends, but that wasn't an everyday thing because the neighborhood my brother and I lived in was more dodgy. That's where the fantasy and world-building came into play. We were always massive fans of fantasy, sci-fi, comic books. Through that, we got into Dungeons & Dragons and all that stuff. Everything we were into was tailored to somebody who didn't like to go outside, anyway.

GEOFF RICKLY: I grew up in Dumont, New Jersey, in Bergen County. It's one square mile. My high school graduating class was maybe a hundred kids. One day during my freshman year a bunch of kids from my grade surrounded me, making fun of me for being a punk, spitting on me and stuff. And all the older kids that were punks fucking terrorized them—they made them sit on the ground and screamed at them and made me go around and spit in each one of their faces. I felt caught between a rock and a hard place because it was all these kids that I grew up with. I was like, "I don't wanna spit in their faces." But they were like, "Do it, tell him he's a fucking chump." I never got picked on again. But I don't think that made me beloved by the guys in my grade.

CHRIS GETHARD: It sounds like a cliché to say, "Man, we were so close to the city we could see it." No, you could—from my hometown [West Orange], if you walked out my front door and made a right you were walking uphill and if you go about halfway up the next block and turned around, you could see the New York City skyline, where everybody's dreams supposedly came true. And then here we are. All these people with working-class dads, a lot of people with drinking problems in their family, a lot of people who feel like they couldn't be further away from the idea of living your dream. I bet you feel better being on the outside looking in if you live a thousand miles away from New York, instead of twelve. When you feel like you can reach across and touch the Empire State Building.

GABE SAPORTA: I'm an immigrant who is the son of an immigrant, who is the son of an immigrant, who is the son of an immigrant. Four generations of Jewish families having to move around. The Holocaust happened to all of my grandparents, probably the worst for my father's side. My great-grandfather died fleeing the Nazis in the mountains of Yugoslavia. They finally settled in Uruguay, where my father, Diego, became a physician. Uruguay in the early eighties was under a military dictatorship, so I was born into that world. We came to America and stayed here illegally for three years, undocumented, on expired tourist visas until we became permanent residents. Just because you're a doctor in some third world country doesn't mean they're gonna let you practice medicine here, so my father had to go to med school all over again. We were living in a one-bedroom apartment in Queens while he was doing his residency. I shared a room with my brother and my parents had this vinyl thing separating their room from the living room. My father finally graduated [when] I was twelve. That's when we moved to Jersey, in 1991. Then my parents got divorced three years after that. It was a very nasty divorce.

RICKY SAPORTA: I was like fourteen, fifteen, having a shitty time in high school and our parents were going through a divorce. I think I moved four times in six months. I thought of school as the thing you had to get through to get to your weekend where you had this music and these shows. You had a place to go.

CHRIS GETHARD: Springsteen was not what us young kids were listening to. Springsteen was our dads' music.

DAN YEMIN: If you were a punk band saying you were influenced by Bruce Springsteen it would have been like saying you were influenced by Michael Jackson. People would either think it was funny or be like, "What?"

MIKEY WAY: There was a Ticketmaster in the video store that shared a parking lot with the A&P I pushed carts in. I would buy tickets to shows, lie to my parents about where I was going, and hop on the PATH train to Fourteenth Street in Manhattan. From there, you could walk to lots of venues.

RICH EGAN: 'Ninety-four was the first time I saw a punk rock show in New York. On the West Coast, because of the Bay Area scene, it was very inclusive of females, very PC, socially conscious. There was nothing socially conscious about New York hardcore. . . . All dudes. Many, many fights. It was a lot closer to the Black Flag scene, the LA shows I saw in the eighties.

DAN YEMIN: My first time at CB's I was baffled by how bloody it was.

GABE SAPORTA: We were at CBGB's and I don't remember why, but this kid just pulled a box cutter on me. Security found out—he just came up to the kid: "The choice is yours, either we take you outside and beat the crap out of you, or we call the cops." And he's like, "Call the cops."

GEOFF RICKLY: When I was around fifteen, I went to Coney Island High for the first time. It was one of those old hardcore matinee shows: Madball, Crown of Thornz, 25 ta Life. As I went to walk in the front door, Freddy Madball has a guy in his arms and yells, "YO, GET THE FUCK OUT OF THE WAY, HE JUST GOT STABBED!"

FRED FELDMAN: Just crazy violence. But it was the scene that showed people anybody can do this: anybody can pick up a guitar, anybody can book a show.

TARYN HICKEY: I grew up in Mount Vernon, in Westchester County, New York. So my experience of punk rock at a young age was very suburban. My parents wouldn't let me go to the city, but once I turned eighteen, I was like a little bitch: "You can't tell me, I'm eighteen!" So I started going to the city, shows at Brownies, Coney Island High, CBGB's, Wetlands. All these places that are now defunct.

WALTER SCHREIFELS: Giuliani came in, and he was this tough-on-crime dude, cleaning up all the homeless people.

RICKY SAPORTA: Giuliani was on a mission to shut down nightlife in New York. So Giuliani shut down all the places punk bands wanted to play in New York: Tramps, Wetlands, Coney Island High. So all the bands started hitting New Jersey harder.

RICH EGAN: It took punk shows out of the city and drove it into the suburbs, which will always skew younger.

KATE REDDY: From squatter kids and punk kids, it shifted to this cleaned up, emo-y post-hardcore music during that time. Similar ideals and aesthetics, but a kinder, gentler, more suburban version.

GABE SAPORTA: There were these metalhead bars [in New Jersey], but they were all twenty-one-plus and you'd have to sell tickets yourself and you'd get ripped off by the promoters. So we said fuck it, we'll do our own shows. If you had friends at high school who were like, "I'm going to a concert," they're not in the scene. If you're in the scene, you go to shows.

GEOFF RICKLY: If you were touring in vans on summer or winter breaks from school, there just wasn't a lot of time to travel around. In that Northeast Corridor area you could hit a bunch of places: Boston, New York, DC, Philadelphia. And the one place you could set up as a hub in the middle of that was New Jersey. And in the middle of New Jersey was New Brunswick.

ARI KATZ: The destination of New Brunswick probably goes back a hundred years. New Brunswick is an old college town and there is a huge Black population, so there used to be record stores everywhere downtown. It was a hub. They called it the Hub City.

CHRIS GETHARD: Kids in New Jersey felt very mobilized to go out and do it, so you had so many shows happening in people's basements, especially in New Brunswick.

GEOFF RICKLY: I don't think New Brunswick became the New Brunswick that we think of now until '94, at least.

PAUL HANLY: The first guy to mention is Chris Ross. Chris was doing shows in his own house, this place at 67 Handy Street, right around the corner from where the Bouncing Souls lived. It was a perfect basement for shows. You'd have Lifetime playing there, the Bouncing Souls playing there. I saw Ink & Dagger there with Eric Wareheim on bass.

GEOFF RICKLY: The basement shows really started with the Bouncing Souls and Lifetime. They were a huge reason New Jersey came up.

DAN YEMIN: Lifetime definitely got the emo tag a lot. We started in 1990 and the term "emo" by that point had been used to describe Embrace, Rites of Spring, and Dag Nasty. Bands that were really special and important for us. But by the mid-nineties it was being used to describe bands that we saw more as, like, rock bands. And by that point it didn't feel like a compliment. It felt like we were being misconstrued. And nobody likes being misunderstood. I'd rather be ignored than misunderstood.

ARI KATZ: The goal was to make two awesome albums, and then split. After that, it's so hard to make another good record.

CHRIS GETHARD: Lifetime was a band that flew under the radar during their existence, but a lot of bands that went on to really big things admired them: that blending of hardcore with lyrics about sitting next to a girl that you like at a basement show. I bet a lot of those musicians were like, all right, we gotta stop singing songs about eating cereal and watching cartoons.

PAUL HANLY: That house really inspired me. One of the reasons I wanted to go to Rutgers was because I loved the house shows, the music scene in New Brunswick. And I know it inspired Geoff Rickly and Clay Wiers, who did the shows over at 331 Somerset Street.

GEOFF RICKLY: Rutgers was a huge sprawl in New Brunswick: three separate campuses all smashed together and a big state school party school vibe. At my orientation, I met a bunch of hardcore kids: Clay and Louis, my two roommates I wound up living with in the dorms, and Steve, Thursday's guitar player. Our freshman year, Clay and I joined the Rutgers Student Arts Council, which put on shows. The first show I put on was They Might Be Giants, and I was like, this fucking sucks. We went to the first meeting and I remember the president of the Student Arts Council was like, "We'll never have bands like Lifetime and Ink & Dagger, ever." And we quit that day. Like, "Seriously, we've been going to basement shows, we can do them. We're gonna get a crew, we're gonna move off campus, we're gonna find a house together."

CHRIS GETHARD: I got to Rutgers and Lifetime had just broken up, but we all knew about the house shows they ran; we all knew about the basement shows.

GEOFF RICKLY: So our sophomore year, me, Clay, and Louis all moved to a house way down Somerset Street, pretty far from campus, where we could afford it. And then we started doing shows. We were this weird little vegan hardcore DIY house down at the edge of the street. Cops almost never hassled us because we were so far down. There was a murder in front of our house during one of the shows. People came out and found someone with a knife in their back. And the cops got there and were like, "Oh, there's a noose, it's okay." We're like, what do you mean? "There's a noose, it's a gang killing, it doesn't have to do with you guys." Really not reassuring.

ROB HITT: A basement show is the lowest barrier of entry for anyone to be able to play. The whole idea is to build a scene. No insurance, no approvals, no one's calling the landlord.

GEOFF RICKLY: The bands are calling themselves, they don't have agents at this point. I'd just call around and see who was looking for a show and get them to come to New Brunswick to play. It was like *Maximumrocknroll Book Your Own Fuckin' Life*: "We've got a place for you to stay, we'll fill your gas tank, we'll cook all of you dinner, we'll take you somewhere for breakfast. And whatever we get at the door as donations, you can just have it all. We'll get some local bands to play for free."

PAUL HANLY: I remember seeing the last You and I show in their basement.

GEOFF RICKLY: I lived with Tom from You and I, this hugely influential skramz band, which was what we used to call screamo.

TOM SCHLATTER: If you saw the size of that basement, it's not meant to hold that many kids. I pull up, bring my equipment down, and there's a line of kids in the driveway at noon. I'm like, "Oh shit, this is gonna be rough."

GEOFF RICKLY: When we did their last show, I think 275 people paid. People were outside lying down on the ground so they could look through the windows into the basement. It was the dead of summer and it got so hot with all those people. At one point, it was raining from the pipes because the sweat had evaporated and stuck to the colder pipes and just started raining down.

ALEX SAAVEDRA: Kids were coming up to the mic and talking about how much You and I meant to them. People were fucking sobbing that it was their last show. One thing I remember clearly was talking about how it's okay to cry.

TOM SCHLATTER: There was a turning point during the band where I was just like, I don't care if I look dumb and I don't care if this makes people uncomfortable. This is important to me. This is what's making me get through the day. For the hardcore scene, which is historically more masculine, a lot of people were uncomfortable. It just seemed like people wanted to talk about politics and stuff and it was like, don't get too deep into your emotional self. And that was restrictive. So when I was able to share a space with people, with men who had decided to forgo those societal restrictions of vulnerability, it was really powerful.

PAUL HANLY: People were emotional about the music. There were huge things to deal with coming out of the lyrics to their records. But at some points it felt contrived—like it's so emotional, people are gonna cry their eyes out.

TOM SCHLATTER: You're in that tumultuous, turbulent part of your life, where you fall in love for the first time, and then it doesn't work out, or you're going through those coming-of-age moments at home, where your parents and you aren't seeing eye to eye. I grew up in a domestic violence situation. Music for me was a place to channel that aggression that I didn't want to take on. I wanted to make a healthy expression.

ALEX SAAVEDRA: It's okay to be hurt. It's okay to be frustrated. It's okay to have your heart broken. The things that men don't normally talk about because we gotta be men, walk it off, and be tough.

GEOFF RICKLY: One night you'd play with Knapsack. Then Hot Water Music, then At the Drive-In. If you're a young local band opening shows in those basements, your idea of what it means to be good enough just goes up and up and up. And our local "we all love this band" was Saves the Day. Having a songwriter like Chris pushed us all to be better. Everybody knew Saves the Day were gonna be huge. Some people resented it, some people didn't. When that first record came out, people were like, "Okay. He's like seventeen years old. And they're from New Jersey." You know what I mean?

KATE REDDY: Their music was melodic, but I still think of them as a hardcore band. I thought they were this perfect expression of fiery innocence and beauty.

EBEN D'AMICO: I remember the early Saves the Day song "Handsome Boy," Chris was writing about either Dave or Bryan from Saves the Day, who were these beautiful, tall, statuesque young men. And Chris was this short, awkward kid with bad skin looking at his friend like, "Why can't I be beautiful like you?" That kind of shit is so real.

TARYN HICKEY: Saves the Day would play with Converge. If you think about that, it's insane: Saves the Day, this super melodic hardcore band with Converge, this brutal metal/hardcore band. That's just how it was back then.

BRYAN NEWMAN: We played Lifetime's last show at the Melody Bar [in New Brunswick]. We were seventeen-year-old kids and Lifetime were gods to us. The Melody Bar is tiny. Justin, our guitarist at the time, climbed up into the rafters and perched there for the entire Lifetime set. It was on a Saturday, and I remember coming back to high school on Monday morning feeling like a king. Everyone else is like, doing drama rehearsals or studying for the SATs, and we're opening for Lifetime's final show. Nobody in my high school knew who Lifetime was, but it didn't matter.

MIKE DOYLE: The first time I listened to [Saves the Day's] *Can't Slow Down* I was like, holy Christ, this band is ripping off Lifetime so bad. But the songs were so good, we couldn't dismiss them.

MELISSA KUNDRATH: We played the shit out of *Can't Slow Down* on cassette. Music Connection in Elmwood Park was where we went for tapes and CDs.

GABE SAPORTA: You would read *Maximumrocknroll* and *Punk Planet*. I remember staying up all night on my fucking Compaq on AOL punk chat rooms, bro. It was all about AOL chat rooms. It was a brand-new thing: I like punk rock, you like punk rock, I don't know anyone else who likes punk rock, let's talk about it on the internet. This was before MP3s, so I'd send a WAV file of my band's demo to the group and people were writing back to me like, "You fuckhead! This is like forty megabytes, this is destroying my inbox!"

RICKY SAPORTA: Google didn't even exist. I'd grab the phone book, take it to the copy machine at my high school, and xerox all the pages of places with halls you could put on shows in: Knights of Columbus, VFWs, American Legions, Elks Lodges.

BENNY HOROWITZ: Elks Lodges are these social clubs, fraternal orders for grown men and, a lot of times, vets. You pay in, there's a bar, and I think the impetus for most of these places is for these guys to have a place to sit around and drink fifty-cent beers, play bingo, rent halls for their daughters' weddings.

RICKY SAPORTA: So then it would become a question of: Okay, how much is it? Some places would want to charge $1,000. So you're looking for the ones charging a hundred dollars or less. And you never wanted to say, "Can we have a punk show at your hall?" I would say something like, "Oh we wanna maybe have some event, have a music thing, have people come by."

After the first two or three shows I learned what's worse than them saying no from the get-go is neighbors or cops shutting down the show, or the hall itself to be like, "Fuck this, get out of here, we didn't sign up for this." So I quickly learned the more upfront you could be, the better.

BENNY HOROWITZ: Seventy-five percent of them would just be like, no, we don't do that. So I decided to try Manville Elks Lodge because the guy who was head Elk, Dan Shields, ran a gymnastics studio that me, my brother, and my sister all went to when we were kids. So he knew my last name. And I didn't know it at the time, but him and his brother were in an eighties punk rock band called Detention. They were a fairly accomplished band that had played with the Ramones and Social Distortion. So I randomly stumbled upon the only hall in New Jersey that had an old punk rock guy who was willing to advocate for me with the other Elks.

TYLER RANN: It was the place to be. And Manville's never been the place to be.

CHRIS GETHARD: The only things you ever heard about Manville, New Jersey—if you weren't from Manville, New Jersey—was that there would be shows put on there and more legendarily, there was a strip club called Frank's Chicken House. It was known to have a pretty *skeevatz* reputation, as we would say in New Jersey with our Italian hybrid slag. You'd see a show advertised in Manville and be like, "Oh it's the Frank's Chicken House town."

BENNY HOROWITZ: Manville is not an easy town. It's a blue-collar, working-class, old-school Polish town. Even a little Jewish kid coming in there being mouthy was strange for them.

MIKE DOYLE: Benny was heavily involved, man. He was booking shows at Manville Elks when he was thirteen, fourteen.

BENNY HOROWITZ: Once I did a Less Than Jake/Weston show at Manville. And most of the bands I was doing were either straight edge or not twenty-one. So the Elks' bar usually wasn't a thing for anyone. But Less Than Jake were hell-bent on staying around and having some drinks. Somehow those guys were gregarious enough to make their own Elk friends. At a certain time of the evening they started closing the doors and dimming the lights. They rang this bell and there was this clock with an actual elk on it and they started doing this chant: *WE ARE THE ELKS, WE DO THIS, WE DO THAT.* The Less Than Jake guys were like, "What the fuck is going on, are we part of some ritual Elk suicide?"

TYLER RANN: Benny was like an adult in a kid's body. Such a baby face, but he would go in there and talk with these big tattooed scary guys about how he's not gonna be able to pay them.

BENNY HOROWITZ: I was working the door for a show once and these Nazi skinheads came in; it's like a school dance—the record skips and you could feel a palpable thing in the room. My first instinct was to try to get these guys out of there so my hall didn't get fucked up, make sure no one got killed. And bear in mind, I'm a chubby, sort of effeminate Jewish kid trying to deal with these three fucking grown-ass man Nazis. I had six earrings in my left ear, a high voice: "Listen, guys, I really don't think it's safe for you!" It was just instinct. "I'll give you your money back, just please get out of here." And they were pretty resistant. Before you know it, a group of guys are mobbing together on the other side of the room, pointing and starting to yell. The Nazis see it too and they decide to take me up on my offer, but now they're getting followed really closely by this mob of thirty, forty people. A guy I went to school with turned around and got knocked the second he turned. And then they started hustling, went across the street, hid out on some person's porch they knew and called the police! I wish I could say cops that were sympathetic to us showed up, but I'm not sure that was the case in Manville.

TARYN HICKEY: Being a female in that scene, you would notice the other girls and be like, "Oh okay, cool," you know? Growing up, girls were always taught to just be there. I think it had a lot to do with how our parents were raised. I think now kids are completely different. But back then girls were always taught to be seen and not heard. There were these terms that were a thing. Like, "Oh, she's a coat rack." The girl who would hold her boyfriend's stuff so he could go mosh. So I think as we became teenagers were like "No, fuck that, I don't wanna be the way my parents were. I want to be heard, too."

RICKY SAPORTA: The Bergenfield Girls would put on shows up in Bergen County, really awesome shows in VFW halls, American Legion halls.

ERIN RENDON: The Bergenfield Girls, that's a nickname other people gave us. Kathy and I are sisters and Melissa lived down the street.

KATHY RENDON: I've heard before that we were the first girls to ever do it in our area. And I take pride in that, because we did a damn good job. Our breakthrough show was October of 1997. Three hundred kids came in and shut down the Westwood American Legion. After that show, we just had more bands at our fingertips that wouldn't have played our shows. The first time Humble Beginnings played one of our shows was January 10, 1998.

CHRIS GETHARD: Humble Beginnings was the pop-punk band Gabe Saporta was in before he started Midtown.

KATHY RENDON: Gabe was always the one we had the most contact with—you called Gabe to book the shows.

MELISSA KUNDRATH: We all talked fast, we're from Jersey, you know? But Gabe talked really fast.

TARYN HICKEY: Gabe was famous before he was famous.

GEOFF RICKLY: He's a tall, good-looking kid who knows how smart he is. He would introduce everyone to everyone: hardcore kids, pop kids.

CHRIS GETHARD: There were a lot of people going, "Man, girls like him and he's not a real punk and he's bringing in all these outsiders," and "I'm going yeah, well guess what, you sold four more seven-inches tonight because of those girls."

MIKE DOYLE: Josh was the singer, Jeremy could sing, Gabe couldn't sing. He was really high-pitched, he had a lisp. He would do backup vocals but even then we were like, Jesus Christ.

GABE SAPORTA: I played bass and wasn't really the singer, but most people knew the band through me, which was a weird thing. And I think that caused some friction between the singer and I, and I was excused . . . kicked out of the band.

TYLER RANN: At these shows, it wasn't just about the performance of the band. It could be just spending forever looking at the merch table, or reading pamphlets from PETA or AK Press.

TARYN HICKEY: There were always zines for sale. You know, next to the Anti-Racist Action table.

RICKY SAPORTA: At the heart of zines is this DIY ethic, that anyone can do anything. If you have something to say, here's a platform, go out and say it. You photocopy it yourself. It doesn't have to be fancy. It doesn't have to be glossy. Whether your artistic talent is drawing, or writing, or photography, or you just have thoughts to share.

BENNY HOROWITZ: Animal rights and veganism was such a big part of the scene. I was already sort of a little hippie kid who was really into the World Wildlife Fund and things like that. I used to adopt a whale every year.

JOANNA ANGEL: In the back of the Rutgers dining hall, there was a mini line that was all-vegan. All the emo kids at Rutgers, we would congregate around the emo lunch line. So I would see Geoff there, and we were both in English classes together.

I was a little emo girl, a little punk rock girl. I bought two tickets to go see Elliott Smith and I remember working up the courage to go ask the cute emo boy in my English class to go with me. And it's funny, to this day . . . I think we're both waiting for the other one to decide if it was a date or not. We took the train to Irving Plaza together. We both were very shy so we just sat next to each other, like seventh graders at a movie: "Should I put my hand here?" We saw the show, whatever. On the way home, he said, "I'm starting a band and we're playing our first show soon." I was like, "What's the band called?" He said Thursday, but I thought he meant that's the day they were playing. "No, the band is called Thursday." I remember saying, "I think you should come up with a different name."

ROB HITT: The shows are doing well, so booking agents know there's something going on: "How did they get four hundred kids out to this market in New Jersey?" That might be a bigger show than they're gonna do in any venue in New York City. "When my band from, say, the Midwest, LA, or Florida, comes through this small town, I know there's gonna be four hundred kids there." That's how people started to book big shows.

BENNY HOROWITZ: By the time I was seventeen or eighteen, Ricky had popped up.

GABE SAPORTA: My brother really ran with that in Jersey. He started a collective called Bomb Shelter.

BENNY HOROWITZ: You couldn't go anywhere without seeing a Bomb Shelter flyer.

MIKEY WAY: The first time I saw a Bomb Shelter flyer was at this really cool record store in Montclair called Let It Rock. The flyer was for New Found

Glory and Saves the Day and it said, "Come to the show before these bands are on MTV."

RICKY SAPORTA: We would go to Staples because their machines didn't have counters the way Kinko's did. Frank Iero worked at Staples, he'd hook me up. He would be like, "Here's your box of one hundred flyers!" And it would be so heavy I could barely carry it out to the car.

ERIN RENDON: When Ricky started throwing bigger shows it was harder to get a good draw sometimes.

BENNY HOROWITZ: Bomb Shelter was doing good shows and Ricky would sometimes need an extra venue, so we started a relationship. I was a bit older than him and I had a deal worked out with the Manville Elks Lodge that I was the only one they would book to. So me and Ricky would do shows together. He would have a package of bands that he would get, I would book a couple bands and take care of the Elks, and he would work the door and take care of the money.

MELISSA KUNDRATH: When Saves the Day got big, we wanted them so bad. We would talk to the drummer Bryan, who was going to NYU. He was the contact person on their website so I called him and he was like, "Well, I would love to say yes to you girls, but I would have to find out from my agent, we might be playing a show the weekend before and we can't play New Jersey twice in one month." I'm like, "Huh, what is all that?" That's when it started to become a little more complicated.

GEOFF RICKLY: All my different roommates had different styles. Clay was very youth crew, and I was more like, "We should have DC bands like Q and Not U." And we would have places where we all agreed. We all wanted to do the Saves the Day New Year's show. That was one of the big, defining shows we played in our basement. Poison the Well came up from Florida and the Movielife came from Long Island. It ended up so stacked because every band that played that show was like, "Oh, we can play with Saves the Day? Yes."

RICKY SAPORTA: First of all, parking in New Brunswick fucking sucks. You could drive around Rutgers for a half hour just trying to find parking—a whole lot of the spots you'd either get towed or ticketed. So you eventually find a spot. And you can tell where the show is from far away because you have grubby punks just sitting outside.

GEOFF RICKLY: There'd be a bunch of people hanging out on the steps, just talking shit.

RICKY SAPORTA: That night, it was cold as fuck out.

GEOFF RICKLY: You couldn't go through the front door. So you'd go around to the back and there'd be a bunch of tables set up with zines and T-shirts, and whatever else was being sold, kind of like a little flea market. And there'd be that hatch door down to the stairs.

RICKY SAPORTA: You go down these stone steps, you'd probably bump your head if you're not careful, it's literally into the cellar of the house.

GEOFF RICKLY: You'd have to step around the hot water heater, and the band's just right there playing in your face. There's no hiding. People really didn't have cell phones when we were doing shows, but if you did, the band was gonna smack your shirt like, "Pay attention, you're not gonna stand here and look down if you're here." It was very confrontational.

BRYAN NEWMAN: The bands that would get bigger and bigger [eventually] got further away . . . This was the exact opposite of that. This was as close as you could be. Inches between the band standing there and you.

RICKY SAPORTA: If you're not within, like, the first twenty people in front, it's almost impossible to see anything. So you're just listening and feeling the energy—the energy's huge, you can't downplay that—and catching little glimpses of the band. The basement would span the entirety of the house and maybe twelve people would live in these New Brunswick houses. So it's not a small house. You could comfortably fit a hundred people in that basement.

BRYAN NEWMAN: These shows were such firetraps . . . basements with one flight of stairs going up and down.

ALEX SAAVEDRA: Saves the Day had laminates, tour laminates like, "ALL ACCESS." I remember talking to Geoff like, "What is all access? To get to the kitchen?"

GEOFF RICKLY: It was Thursday's first show.

PAUL HANLY: Geoff had never been a singer.

GEOFF RICKLY: I was pretty nervous. I didn't really drink but there was a bottle of Amaretto in the kitchen and I remember sitting on the steps to the upstairs apartment and pounding Amaretto because I was so nervous. It was the only thing to drink.

GABE SAPORTA: Geoff really just went into a different place live. You wouldn't expect it because he's such a smiley, mild-mannered, skinny kid. He'd just turn into this crazy thing live.

GEOFF RICKLY: We played our whole demo tape. So four songs, ten minutes. The crowd was so supportive of us. We've been doing shows for free in my basement for two years. Of course they're supportive!

PAUL HANLY: I mean, they were not really good at first. Geoff wasn't a great singer . . .

ALEX SAAVEDRA: But you could feel the emotion of his voice, which made up for it.

GEOFF RICKLY: That show was the first time Saves the Day played "Jodie," the last song on *Can't Slow Down*. It was a much mellower song than the rest of the record. It pointed where they were going next.

HEATH SARACENO: Saves the Day's crowd was hardcore kids who had a sensitive side. Kids who primarily went to hardcore shows, but every once in a while would put on the Smiths.

TARYN HICKEY: Chris wasn't like a hardcore dude shoving mics in people's faces. It was more swaying back and forth, like Morrissey.

BEN JORGENSEN: I remember I saw Gabe there. And I was screaming at the top of my lungs to *Can't Slow Down*.

BRYAN NEWMAN: We did a Bon Jovi cover, "Livin' on a Prayer." We'd never done that before or since. Sean, our original bass player, was still with us, and I remember there was this staccato bass line he had some trouble with. It wasn't very serious. It was because it was New Year's Eve and we were in New Jersey and we were eighteen years old. It was probably horrible . . . I think it went over pretty well.

RICKY SAPORTA: Inside you're sweating bullets; you couldn't really go outside that night because you'd be freezing.

TARYN HICKEY: I remember going outside afterward and it was snowing.

CHAPTER 2

THE FIRST FANCY TOUR BUS *TO* PULL UP *AT THE* MANVILLE ELKS LODGE

HEATH SARACENO: I have this memory of Gabe at an 88 Fingers Louie show in West Orange, New Jersey. After the show, everyone was leaving, and Gabe had this huge car. It was a Ford Crown Victoria, fifteen, twenty years old. It was gigantic, like an old detective car. I can't stress enough how big this car was. He got in the car with his girlfriend and he blasted the first Saves the Day record. At the time, pop-punk kids didn't listen to Saves the Day. If you liked 88 Fingers Louie, you didn't like Saves the Day. If you liked Lagwagon and had the most recent NOFX CD, you didn't like Saves the Day. I was like, "I fucking love *Can't Slow Down*, this guy listens to the same music I listen to!"

GABE SAPORTA: Let me give you the backstory on my relationship with Saves the Day. I was at an Ensign record release show at the Manville Elks Lodge; this is 1997, '98. Hardcore was really big. It was a little bro-y, everyone looked really tough, right? In comes this band of skinny, young kids in skinny jeans. And I remember so clearly there was a guy onstage setting up and he's wearing a puffy jacket that said POLO. Nobody in those days wore brands or logos from any mainstream brands. It was a faux pas, but also a little cool: What's this fashionable skinny jeans kid doing at a hardcore show? It was Bryan, the drummer of Saves the Day.

A few months later, after I'd been kicked out of Humble Beginnings, I'm in my dorm at Rutgers. I was in the shower. Like, dude, I remember this so vividly. I remember what shampoo I was using—this Garnier Fructis. And I'm like, "Man, I would really love to be in Saves the Day." That night, I went to go see Elliott at Coney Island High. I see a kid who I think looks familiar, like the drummer from Saves the Day I'd seen with the POLO jacket. I go up to him, like, "Hey, sorry if this is a weird question, but are you in Saves the Day?" And he's like, "Yeah, I am." We're talking and hanging outside the show; I remember playing him New Found Glory, because New Found Glory just had their first EP out, *It's All About the Girls*. I'm like, "This is like the Florida version of you guys." I ended up going to his apartment at NYU and we played *007* on N64. I told him the story about that morning and how I'd love to play in Saves the Day and he's like, "Oh, actually we're looking for a new guitar player."

I tried out to play guitar in Saves the Day, but I didn't have the dexterity to play guitar. I have fat fingers. My pinkie's super short. So I had to play bass. It was the only instrument I could get away with.

CHRIS GETHARD: And Gabe immediately tumbled into Midtown . . . Midtown is definitely a marker of when the pop-punk infatuation started to die out and the more emo-y stuff came up.

GABE SAPORTA: We formed at Rutgers. Rob was the oldest member and he went there first—it's kinda why we went there, honestly. Rob and I would talk a lot about starting a band.

ROB HITT: In your town, the good bands start to bubble to the top and are able to do shows with the good bands from other towns. That's what was happening with me, Tyler, Heath, and Gabe.

HEATH SARACENO: Tyler and I were in a punk rock band called Nowhere Fast, Rob was in a ska band called the Royalties, and Gabe was in Humble Beginnings. But none of us were really happy with the trajectory of our bands. Around the summer of 1998, the three of them came together at Rutgers. One night, I got a call from Tyler: "Why don't you come down to New Brunswick, I have something here that will change your life." I was like, "All right . . ." So I'm in New Brunswick on line at the Grease Trucks, ordering some kind of sandwich, like a Fat Cat or something.

TYLER RANN: Grease Trucks is this parking lot surrounded by food trucks that sold these big, greasy sandwiches with french fries in them.

HEATH SARACENO: And I see Rob Hitt in line. We started talking and then Tyler shows up. I introduced them, but they were like, "No, we already know each other. Why don't we go to Gabe's dorm?" I get there and the three of them are really chummy. I'm like, "Okay it's cool that these guys from different bands all know each other." Then all of a sudden, the needle comes off the record, and there's just a shift in the conversation. Gabe's like, "You know why we brought you here? We're a band, we have five songs, we're gonna record our EP next week, and we need a guitar player."

TYLER RANN: Gabe came in with this pitch strategy: If we want people to come to our shows and know the songs, they gotta have the music.

HEATH SARACENO: The *Sacrifice of Life* EP on a finished, printed, pressed CD. We didn't want to go through the thing of dubbing demos and selling tapes and selling CD-Rs. We wanted the final product.

TYLER RANN: That was not the norm. I don't remember anyone else doing that.

GABE SAPORTA: In the photo on the back of the EP, we were dressed really nice and wearing scarves. We got so much shit for that.

BENNY HOROWITZ: I was mad at them for getting so big so fast. And part of the reason was they had a good demo CD for their first show. And shirts. And that was fucking Gabe . . . maybe Rob, too. Bands like mine, we didn't do that. We would play first and be like, "Oh, people kind of like us, let's do a demo." And after ten shows it's like, "Now it's time for a shirt. We deserve a shirt!" Kind of this punk rock guilt that slowed the process. And Gabe's just a hustler, man. From the get with that band he was just like, "Yo, I'm trying to make this band big."

JOANNA ANGEL: I didn't understand why anybody would want to do anything other than play in Brunswick. And Gabe said something like, "There's no money in punk rock." I was like, "You're a *sellout*. GABE!"

HEATH SARACENO: We wanted to be more than the band that played the local VFW every Saturday or Sunday in New Jersey—we wanted to tour the world. We wanted to be the biggest band in the world. We felt we couldn't do it by keeping the same attitudes we had when we were playing hall shows. I think we were trying to be more professional and more worldly about it. I guess we developed big egos pretty quickly.

GABE SAPORTA: At the time, it was a thing where you had the two singers: Hot Water Music had that, Fugazi had that.

HEATH SARACENO: We knew that we had three singers, we thought that was special.

GABE SAPORTA: It was out of necessity. I was a good writer, but I couldn't fucking sing. Part of the problem I had in Humble Beginnings was I was involved in the writing in the beginning—the singer and I wrote the songs together—but then he was like, "I'm the fucking singer, you're not writing songs." And I was like, "Fuck!" And then I got kicked out. So I was like, "I'm never getting kicked out of a band again if I'm doing all the work. I'm gonna sing." But my voice wasn't strong enough to sing by itself, so we all sang together.

HEATH SARACENO: We wrote a lot of harmonies into songs. I thought it was such a powerful image, all three guys in the front singing at the same time.

GABE SAPORTA: And then my voice got a little better.

GEOFF RICKLY: Gabe was a diplomat to everybody: pop kids, hardcore kids—he got it.

MIKE DOYLE: Midtown, my band Lanemeyer was so close to them, so we watched their success and I was jealous of it. But Saves the Day . . . they were on a different fucking level.

ARI KATZ: I worked at a record store in New Brunswick [after Lifetime broke up] called Cheap Thrills. Chris Conley used to come in there. He was a Lifetime fan so he used to chat me up. This was before I knew he was playing music or anything . . . On—I think it was his prom—he drove to the store so we could see him. I think I have a picture of him and his girlfriend at the time.

Here's a funny story—I remember showing him this Devo record. And he's like, "Who's that?" I'm like, "This record's great, this song is awesome: 'Through Being Cool.'"

RICH EGAN: If you listen to Saves the Day's first record versus their second one, *Through Being Cool*, you can see it going hardcore influence then poppier, poppier, poppier.

TARYN HICKEY: David from Saves the Day was in Massachusetts going to college and when he would come back to Jersey to go home, he would stop at my parents' house because he drove right by the exit. So after they recorded *Through Being Cool*, he made me a cassette of it and came over to my house and we listened to it in my bedroom for the first time. It was so different from *Can't Slow Down*. I was like, "Oh my fucking god, this is so good." I wasn't supposed to play it for anyone, and I obviously didn't listen. I went right to SUNY Purchase and played it for my friend Meredith. They had these hardcore songs, but it was so melodic. Nothing sounded like that at the time.

MIKE DOYLE: In "Holly Hox, Forget Me Nots" there was this part where Chris sings, "Every skyline and every night spent alone are tearing me apart" with this *whoa* going on in the background. They added these little things where we were like, "Holy shit, we gotta start ripping them off."

EBEN D'AMICO: A band is a weird little human machine. Bryan had a very close relationship with Chris. He had Chris's ear in a way that other people didn't. I remember Bryan would just shut down song ideas. There was something Chris had written about like, going to the Bahamas with his girlfriend and I remember the sentence coming out of Bryan's mouth: "We can't have songs about you going on vacation."

TARYN HICKEY: I mean, I love the lyrics, especially now knowing some of them were just assignments for class at NYU. Like, "Let me take this awkward saw and run it against your thighs." Like, what the fuck, Chris? The lyrics were so different and out there.

EBEN D'AMICO: I remember the song "Through Being Cool" was about how Chris hated his NYU roommate. He says, "The next time you see Nick, tell him I'm gonna stick some needles in his face." Probably Nick was trying to party and be a college kid and Chris was studying quantum physics and writing songs because that's the kind of guy Chris was.

MIKEY WAY: I saw *Through Being Cool* at the record store Let It Rock and I remember looking at the album cover: Whoa, this is a total shift . . .

EBEN D'AMICO: We got made fun of so much when *Through Being Cool* came out. That album cover. We got absolutely cooked. The genesis of the idea probably came from David and Bryan, they were the art school kids at NYU. They were thinking David LaChapelle or something like that—colorful, hyper-real, ironic in a way. I was like, "Are you sure you want to do this? This is so corny." I hated the idea. But I was so new to the band so I got shut down pretty quickly.

TARYN HICKEY: Now it's such an iconic record, but at the time no one did anything like it before.

CHRISTIAN MCKNIGHT: That fucking cover, that iconic cover of the band sitting awkward, afraid to talk to girls at a party, could not better summarize awkward scene kids. It made so much sense. And that's who that band was.

EBEN D'AMICO: Those images were a statement of pop ambition. It was like, "Here we are, *ha, ha, ha,* we're making pop songs, *ha, ha*!" Because it was a radical thing at the time for a band like us coming out of the hardcore scene, on a label like Equal Vision, making a record with *songs* on it.

KATE REDDY: My sister had an apartment in Queens so they did the whole shoot at her house. It was my sister's roommate who was a New Jersey hardcore kid that took the photos. The pictures in the artwork of *Through Being Cool* are all at my sister's house.

TARYN HICKEY: We were all kids, and we'd never done anything like that before. It was like this weird adventure. That was the first photo shoot I ever did. I think I was nineteen.

EBEN D'AMICO: It was like a party. Being the age I was, it was this exotic, tantalizing thing I'd never tasted before.

KATE REDDY: All these emo kids kept ringing the doorbell, coming in and out of the apartment. They got in trouble with the landlord for having all those people in and out. Even though it's just supposed to look like they're having a party, they kind of actually had a real party.

SCOTTIE REDIX: It was superhot inside. It was an all-day thing. You have this feeling in the back of your head that this is some important shit we're all here for, you know?

EBEN D'AMICO: We had a real smorgasbord of people there. A bunch of Saves the Day's friends, a bunch of Jersey people, a couple of Long Island people.

SARAH LEWITINN: There were a lot of people I kind of knew from going out: *Oh, that guy, oh, that girl . . .*

SCOTTIE REDIX: At the time, Chris was having an issue with his skin. He was really bummed about it because he had to take pictures. I remember them really trying to make him feel comfortable and confident: "You look cool, don't even worry about it."

EBEN D'AMICO: My girlfriend at the time was there; I remember she got mad at me because she wasn't in enough shots. Who else do I remember being there? Sarah Lewitinn! Who went on to become Ultragrrrl. I feel like Sarah was the original influencer.

SARAH LEWITINN: I was interning at *Spin* at the time. *Spin* had thrown a party and I met Bryan from Saves the Day there. I was just so eager to make friends. I was like, "Hey, here's my phone number. I work at *Spin* as an intern, I always know a really cool party, I'll reach out to you if I hear of any fun things . . ."

TARYN HICKEY: We were at the age where we were doing things . . . and then they *became* things.

EBEN D'AMICO: There was Taryn, the redheaded girl who was like the focal point of the photo shoot.

TARYN HICKEY: I'm the girl on the cover, top right, that's seductively looking at David.

SARAH LEWITINN: I had a little crush on both David and Bryan at the time, so I remember thinking Taryn was so lucky. She was so pretty and so tall, and she was gonna be the one David was pining after.

TARYN HICKEY: The whole point was that I was supposed to have this crush on him. I found out after the fact that David did have a crush on me. David can clarify, but that's why he asked me to be the girl, because he had a secret crush on me.

EBEN D'AMICO: Yeah, that sounds like something David would do.

TARYN HICKEY: If you were a pretty girl, people didn't take you seriously and thought you were just there to date dudes in bands. I constantly had to stick up for myself and be like, "No, I fucking like this music like, I don't just want to have a boyfriend."

I didn't have a boyfriend when we shot the scene but when it came out, I was dating this guy, and all of his friends were like, "What the fuck's up with your girlfriend? Dude, what is she, *a slut*? How could she do this to you?" And he was like, "Bro, this was forever ago." But you know, I got shit.

TYLER RANN: Gabe is in the pictures, he's on the couch making out with his girlfriend from college.

SCOTTIE REDIX: That was Gabe. That was Gabe in a nutshell.

TYLER RANN: I would go to shows, kids would come up to Gabe and be like, "Are you that guy making out with that girl?" and he was, like, *stoked* on it for sure.

EBEN D'AMICO: There was P. J. Ransone, who you might know as Ziggy from *The Wire*.

TARYN HICKEY: P.J. is the guy passed out on the futon on the back cover.

EBEN D'AMICO: David and Bryan spent all this time at NYU, so they had all these artsy friends in their orbit. P.J. was definitely one of those kids.

KATE REDDY: I might still have that futon in my basement. It's really gross, though. People are like, "Can I have it?" I'm like, "You don't want it."

RICKY SAPORTA: Then it was like, "Hey, Saves the Day has a CD coming out, they really want to put together a show at Manville Elks."

PAUL HANLY: All these bands just one step removed from getting to that pinnacle. The New Jersey scene was so hungry for a show like that.

TARYN HICKEY: Vagrant was trying to sign Saves the Day.

RICH EGAN: I wasn't at the show, but I remember it because I was managing the Get Up Kids. I got an advance copy of *Through Being Cool* and was like, "Holy shit." So we called Saves the Day.

RICKY SAPORTA: Out of the blue one day I got a phone call—no wait, it was a pager. I got a page from a weird 917 number. Turns out it was their booking agent Andrew Ellis. And I'm like a seventeen-year-old kid, I have no idea who he is. He's like, I got a little band you might have heard of, called the Get Up Kids.

RICH EGAN: Saves the Day had seen what was going on with the Get Up Kids—they were blowing up, and that was the only reason anyone knew about my label, Vagrant. They put us on the map.

MATT PRYOR: We were on the tail end of a sixty-five-show, seventy-two-day tour. And the idea was when *Something to Write Home About* came out we were gonna go anywhere and everywhere that would have us. If we're gonna do a tour this long, we're gonna need to have a tour bus. And if we're going to have a tour bus, we're going to need to have to justify paying for the thing, so we're gonna need to play more shows, not take days off. When we left for the tour, we started at CMJ in New York in September and then we went all over the entire country. By the time we came back to the East Coast in November two months later, it was like a bomb had gone off.

RICH EGAN: As much as I love Dischord and those kinds of labels, I didn't want to be that exclusive, where we're only gonna sell ten thousand records. In indie rock, selling twenty thousand was massive. *Something to Write Home About* sold a hundred thousand in its first year. Most records have an immediate impact and tail off. This one had an immediate impact and kept growing.

TYLER RANN: The Get Up Kids had that look of what was to come with emo, with the hair and the glasses.

RICH EGAN: They got a lot of shit because they were poppier and cuter and they were getting bigger than all the bands they came up with.

TARYN HICKEY: And then the Get Up Kids rolled up to Manville Elks and it's just like, "Yo, look at us and our bus." We'd never really seen a tour bus.

RICH EGAN: They'd be a little embarrassed, like . . . could you park around the corner?

SCOTTIE REDIX: Back then the luxury was those long vans with the rows of seats—like how new was yours? I remember seeing that bus-trailer combo like, "Okay, next-level-type shit."

RICH EGAN: It was controversial at the time: they're sellouts, tour bus fuckin' rock stars, etcetera. But the band toured so much, it was really about safety.

MATT PRYOR: We just thought, "Okay, we're gonna go to New York, we're gonna go play Manhattan, we're gonna go play at CBGB's. That's what we're gonna do." And then we got into these peripheral areas like Jersey, and I'm like, "What is this? I don't even know who these people are. Why are there these kids in an Elks Lodge in New Jersey who know every lyric to every song?"

HEATH SARACENO: Saves the Day, the Get Up Kids, and At the Drive-In—three of the biggest bands in the scene at the time—playing *one* show. And I was so excited because Ricky was putting it together.

RICKY SAPORTA: The Get Up Kids were on tour with At the Drive-In, and then I added Saves the Day, Ultimate Fakebook, and Six Going on Seven. And of course Midtown, my brother's band. They were a really young band at the time and super psyched to be on that.

TYLER RANN: Isn't that lineup insane? For ten dollars!

HEATH SARACENO: I remember being very excited to see At the Drive-In. You heard all these stories about the lead singer, how he'd cover his whole face in duct tape, then duct-tape the microphone to himself, and hang upside down from bars in the ceiling, just causing all sorts of destruction.

BRYAN NEWMAN: They were from El Paso; that seemed like a million miles away. They didn't really fit the show, but that was the magic of that era. It's just kids putting on shows; it's not some big booking agency. It's just whoever they can find who's crossing paths through Jersey.

ROB HITT: To get all your favorite bands on one show to see . . . And to play alongside them . . .

PAUL HANLY: You drive in, the parking lot's in the back. And you walk up these stairs and there's this entrance hallway where they set up the table to take admission. Then the stage is immediately to your left. For a show like that it'd be hard to get into the room cause people would be immediately packed up next to the door.

RICKY SAPORTA: Eight hundred people. My favorite moment: as bands are setting up it's quiet, then mics start to turn on, they're testing instruments. Those few moments where there's a lot of tension in the air like, "What song are they gonna open with?"

And then the whole place explodes.

SCOTTIE REDIX: It was Napster days, so even though it was the record release show, we all had the Saves the Day album. I remember everyone singing that shit, word for word. And they played that whole album.

TYLER RANN: As soon as they started playing a song, as soon as anyone could recognize what it was, you couldn't hear anymore. Hundreds of teenagers screaming the words and cymbals resonating everywhere.

BRYAN NEWMAN: No bands sounded sonically great at these shows. It's a crappy rented PA from Guitar Center.

EBEN D'AMICO: There were guys in our band that were like, not the greatest musicians. Ted was an okay guitar player; he wasn't as good as Chris. Bryan had good ideas as a drummer, but he would fumble a lot when he played live. And I really fucking gave him shit for it.

HEATH SARACENO: I remember watching Saves the Day's guitarist Ted. I'd heard that Chris had forced down-picking of everything at all times for a heavier sound, like Metallica's *Master of Puppets*. It's such a tempo that your wrist is gonna give out because no one can do that, except for like, James Hetfield. I tried it at home, and I considered myself to have a pretty good right hand, but I couldn't play Saves the Day's shit. So I was paying a lot of attention to their guitarists' right hands, because I was a fucking nerd. I would watch them at a chugging, down-picking part. They fucking did it.

TARYN HICKEY: There was a lot of crowd-surfing, 'cause Manville was like, stage, and then crowd. There was no barrier.

SCOTTIE REDIX: I remember crowd-surfing, pulling Chris in, and singing the end of "The Choke."

MATT PRYOR: I remember we befriended a lot of the Elks because the only place you could drink was the Elks bar and we went in there and drank with these old-timers. They're like, "You guys are all right!"

BENNY HOROWITZ: All of a sudden, bands had tour managers who were protecting their backstage. At the time I was still helping broker the shows for Ricky, and I remember the Get Up Kids' booking agent kept asking me who I was and why I was around. And we got into it at that show. It wound up being a guy who became one of the bigger booking agents in America. I saw him fifteen years later when Gaslight Anthem was already successful; he was booking someone else and we totally recognized each other. "Yo, you were that little kid from the Get Up Kids show who had a big mouth." And I was like, "Yeah, you were the booking agent who was kind of a dick!"

TYLER RANN: I can close my eyes and picture that back room right now, with all those guys. It was Saves the Day, it was At the Drive-In, and it was the Get Up Kids. I feel eighteen-year-old me in that space right now. I can see what they're all wearing and where they are. At the Drive-In wore, like, the tightest clothes ever. And that was probably the first time that you saw that style. I talked to everybody, with the exception of At the Drive-In. They had this aura of really being out there, like in a scary, intimidating way.

HEATH SARACENO: One of the Get Up Kids was trying to use a pay phone in the lobby of the Elks Lodge and was getting so frustrated that he couldn't hear his girlfriend on the other end.

MATT PRYOR: That was definitely me.

TARYN HICKEY: Saves the Day dudes went on the Get Up Kids' bus and that was like, the *coooolest* thing.

MATT PRYOR: All of a sudden, your house is now the party house.

TARYN HICKEY: It was like, "Yo, this is . . . wow, you did it. You're on a bus."

BRYAN NEWMAN: "Oh wow, they have a bus, they're clearly on some other mission here." Which Saves the Day obviously bought into, and we tried to do all that. But at that time, I was nineteen years old. When I meet nineteen-year-olds now, it's like, "You're a child." Putting a child onstage is exciting, and also kinda fucks people up. This was before things started *really* going to our heads, but it started to. It's hard to let a show at the Manville Elks Lodge go to your head. At the end of the day, there's still the Korean War vets in the back drinking.

KATE REDDY: Saves the Day was the tipping point. The zeitgeist of that type of music was manifesting exactly in that moment.

MIKEY WAY: People were poking fun at *Through Being Cool* because it was more polished, but those people also memorized all the words, you know what I mean?

ROB HITT: It gave the local Jersey scene, in my opinion, our first real champion. When *Through Being Cool* came out, Saves the Day felt like a champion for New Jersey and beyond.

CHAPTER 3

LONG ISLAND & *THE* LAST SILENT MAJORITY SHOW

CHRISTIAN MCKNIGHT: What's important to remember, about Long Island, about our scene, is that everyone knew each other.

RICH EGAN: The thing that set Long Island apart? They literally were set apart. They were out there on the island, you know? So they were able to create their own biosphere where they nurtured their own bands, promoters, everything.

GLENN GAMBOA: Long Island is the two counties at the eastern end of the same island as Brooklyn—it goes Brooklyn, Queens, Nassau County, Suffolk County. Long Island is about thirty miles east of Manhattan, but it seems like a different world. It's where the first suburbs in America were. A lot of bands and people like Billy Joel came from Long Island in the sixties and seventies because they had garages and it was easier for them to practice, whereas in the city, you're all on top of each other.

DAN YEMIN: Long Island's in the shadow of New York City, the way where I'm from in New Jersey is, but because it's such a bottleneck and so hard to get to from everywhere, it's like its own country. We used to joke it would make more sense to book a show in Boston than Long Island. And usually that wasn't an exaggeration.

MATT PRYOR: There's this sibling rivalry between New Jersey and Long Island, that they kind of seem to hate each other, but are kind of exactly the same. Like Will Ferrell and John C. Reilly in *Step Brothers*.

GEOFF RICKLY: Long Island was very much more a New York scene than Jersey. The kids in indie rock or emo-y bands or whatever you wanna call it were way more like New York hardcore guys. They were tougher, they'd been on the streets more, most of them had been arrested for whatever reason. They were New York hardcore kids who happened to play *pretty stuff*, you know what I mean? Whereas New Jersey kids were way more like Midwestern, kinda plainspoken kids. In Long Island, they were just more streetwise.

VINNIE CARUANA: Me and my brothers got into rap music at first; that was our first number one. Rap was exploding and a lot of big artists were from close to where we lived. We were only a few miles away from where Public Enemy is from.

TOMMY CORRIGAN: Pretty much everyone I knew listened to rap. Breakdancing, graffiti, skateboarding—it was all mixed together for us. On Long Island public access there was a TV show called *Video Music Box*—we got to see all these people and realize they're all one town over from you. Five minutes from where I grew up in Lindenhurst was Amityville, which had tons of the most popular rappers in America at the time: De La Soul, one of the guys from Leaders of the New School. North of me is Wyandanch, that's where Rakim is from. Public Enemy's more like Nassau County, over where Beck from Glassjaw is from.

JUSTIN BECK: As you go from Nassau County to Suffolk County, farther east from the epicenter of Manhattan, it gets less diverse and cornier and whiter. And the North Shore of Long Island is much more affluent compared to [some of] the South Shore.

SCOTTIE REDIX: Its proximity to hip-hop culture made the scene unique. All the good Long Island bands had a hint of a bounce to their sound. It's that vibe. It's that air. It's that lifestyle.

RICKY SAPORTA: When you saw a band onstage, you could tell they were from Long Island.

MIKE DUBIN: Dancing in our scene wasn't just punching, kicking, moshing, fighting. There was rhythm and moves. From being on tour, I can say it was like nowhere else.

SCOTTIE REDIX: It was like, you can dance with a girl and also mosh with a girl, too. Because there were also girls doing the same thing in our pits. It's just the sound. People danced like they were at hip-hop shows.

EBEN D'AMICO: It was always a little bit high school, you know, people ostracizing each other and talking shit about each other, being the cool kids and the less cool kids.

SCOTTIE REDIX: You had to be a player. That's what kept you cool. How good you were at your instrument determined how cool you were in that scene. You could be a complete whatever . . . if you knew how to play, you're in. There wasn't a lot of it, but there would be skinheads, and bands that had that type of following.

There were a handful of us [people of color] at shows. The local Long Island scene, you would have a set cast of regulars. We see each other, give that little nod, like it's all good, good to see you. These are like my first shows—going and playing. And fifteen, sixteen, my only knowledge of skinheads was what I'd seen on TV or what I read. My friends would always tell me, "You gotta check the shoelaces, that's how you can tell if they're white supremacists. Red shoelaces meant they're cool; white shoelaces meant they're not cool." And even those lines would get blurred. When I would see them, I'd just lay low until it was time to play. We're talking mid-nineties—it wasn't as liberal as it is now. On Long Island, the closer you got to the city, you wouldn't see the racism as much. You would see that most at shows out east in Huntington, Merrick, or Levittown. Racist vibes, not exclusive to skinheads per se. The tough-guy, straight-edge types, they would always blur the lines with those old crews like DMS. And when you think of that white machismo thing, it had hip-hop elements. That always boggled my mind.

ANTHONY RANERI: Long Island bands weren't playing in the city because you couldn't get booked by a real promoter. Christian McKnight booking you on Long Island in some hall was pretty much the only show you could get.

FRED FELDMAN: What made those other scenes really work was there was that local promoter. Jersey had Ricky Saporta. On Long Island, Christian

McKnight was the guy. I would talk to Christian to try to get my bands booked. And then also just ask what was going on, what's happening?

CHRISTIAN MCKNIGHT: When I was a teenager, Long Island hardcore was my life. I decided that my school that I went to, West Hampton High School, was not for me. I dropped out so I could focus full time on being a scene kid. And I did nothing but book shows and go to shows; I was in a band for a little bit. I opened up a record store when I was nineteen. I opened up a venue when I was eighteen. And then when my band broke up when I was about twenty-two, I started booking shows full time again.

RICKY SAPORTA: Giuliani had shut down Manhattan, right? So I got to be close friends with Christian and we'd coordinate shows together: "Saturday this band will play New Jersey, Sunday they'll play Long Island."

TOMMY CORRIGAN: In our town, Lindenhurst, there was this spot called the PWAC, which was the People With AIDS Coalition. And that ended up being the best place for shows in the history of Long Island. We all volunteered there and ran it. We did a Fugazi show with over a thousand people. We were doing shows every week, so it turned into a scene where kids were showing up regardless of who was playing. I remember VOD [Vision of Disorder] played there in their height and three thousand people showed up. We were like, "Ho-ly shit."

MIKE DUBIN: The top three bands in the mid-nineties were VOD, Silent Majority, and Mind Over Matter. Silent Majority's earlier stuff was more punk and it became more melodic. VOD was straight-up screamy metal, and Mind Over Matter was that piece that fit in between.

CHRISTIAN MCKNIGHT: Silent Majority were the one band that nobody from Long Island would ever disparage, nobody would ever talk shit about, even though there was so many different scenes. There was the tough guy scene, like all the people that played beat-down hardcore. There were the people that played DIY hardcore, which was really socially conscious. But the one band everybody loved was Silent Majority.

EDDIE REYES: To me, they were Long Island. Those were my friends, we all lived together, we had the hardcore house. That was my crew.

TOMMY CORRIGAN: Silent Majority started in my high school, my friend Ryan on guitar, my brother Steve was on drums. We were all from age thirteen to sixteen when we first started, goofing around writing funny songs after school. And then a couple years later we figured out to play a little bit and started taking it more seriously. When we did our first demo tape, that's when it became real. That was a big deal back then. And then we did our first seven-inch, *This Island Earth* in 1994.

JUSTIN BECK: They could not have gotten off the stage if they didn't play "Knew Song," off *This Island Earth*. That was like their legacy song. It's a simple song, but a pop anthem. Everyone could be like, you gave your rocks up for this cool new rhythm you're doing, but could you please just play "Knew Song."

JOLIE LINDHOLM: Silent Majority was emo. That's what we called emo on Long Island.

GEOFF RICKLY: I thought they were criminally underrated. They were loved in Long Island, in New York, but the rest of the emo world looked at them as an anachronism, like a bunch of Long Island tough guys in an emo band. That was not a thing yet.

TOMMY CORRIGAN: I remember the first time I heard someone say "emo." I was at the More Than Music Festival in Ohio, like a big coming together of every hardcore scene on the East Coast. This was like, 1992. There was a band from Long Island called Fountainhead, right? The bassist ended up being in Texas Is the Reason. This girl said, "Oh, that singer was dressed so emo." And I was like, what the fuck? In the eighties there was a standup comedian called Emo Philips. He had these bangs, he was like a really weird, nerdy-looking dude. He'd be on like, *HBO Comedy Hour* and he had a very weird act. So when this chick was saying like, "Oh the singer of that band was dressed so emo and acting so emo," I thought he's walking around acting like the comedian.

GEOFF RICKLY: Silent Majority shows could be quite rough. Their fans were a lot bigger than a lot of the fans that were coming to see Thursday at the time, and usually old enough to drink. And they probably had a few to drink before the show.

VINNIE CARUANA: You would go see Silent Majority and the crowd would be filled with people who would become members of the next wave of bands that made a huge impact on the world of music: guys from Brand New, Taking Back Sunday, Glassjaw, Movielife, Crime in Stereo, all in the front row singing along.

GEOFF RICKLY: A lot of it really revolved around the singer Tommy's charisma. Just an incredibly magnetic guy. He's got really sharp, piercing eyes. He would be right there in the center, locked into the crowd. Total commitment to be in the moment.

TOMMY CORRIGAN: Our drummer, Ben Van Dyke, a lot of people copied the way he did his drum kit. We'd play with a band, then play with them six months later, and all of a sudden the guy would have his kit set up exactly the same way.

JUSTIN BECK: I remember Silent Majority wrote a song in a six-eighths time signature. Everyone was like what the fuck is six-eighths? And then, all of a sudden, every fucking shitty emo song on Long Island was in six-eighths.

GEOFF RICKLY: I remember my roommates in You and I telling me this story where they went to play and it ended up [that] the person who [had] put on the show I think was in Silent Majority. And they were like, "Oh yeah, you can stay with us. But you can't leave your van outside unattended, it'll get stolen. Somebody's gotta sleep in the van." And they were like, "Oh, that's weird. We have to sleep in the van even though it's dangerous and could get broken into?" And they were like, "Yeah, here, take this gun." They were like, "UHHHHHHH, what?"

TOMMY CORRIGAN: I lived in a really bad neighborhood. I can see me saying that to somebody. And we did have guns. I'm not sure it's true . . . it might not be . . . I can't confirm or deny it. Definitely sounds like something we woulda done.

TOM SCHLATTER: Okay, I can tell the story to the best of my subjective memory. On our first tour we got put on a show at a beach club in Long Island. After the show, we started to drive from this beach club in a pretty swanky part of Long Island, and after about fifteen minutes of driving, things started to look less swanky. We get to the basement apartment Tommy lived in with his friend, one of the guitar players for the Movielife. Tommy says, "Hey, you should have one person go sleep in the van, because the van's probably going to get broken into." We're weighing our pros and cons: If the van gets broken into and no one's there, some of our stuff will get stolen. If the van gets broken into and one of us is in there, our stuff will get stolen, and someone from our band will also probably get into a fight and get beat up or stabbed.

Then ten minutes later, Tommy comes out of his room dressed in all black. And he had two guns. And the guy from the Movielife is like, "All right, we're going out to shoot up some cars, mi casa, su casa." For all I know the guns could have been paintball guns and maybe there was some all-night paintball car shooting thing? I don't know. So these guys left. And we're like, I guess someone should sleep in the van.

The next day we wake up and Tommy's nowhere to be found, but the guy from the Movielife is out front baiting a line on a fishing pole. And he's like, "I'm gonna go fish today." We're like, pretty versatile guy!

CHRISTIAN MCKNIGHT: *Life of a Spectator*, Silent Majority's full-length from 1997, that record's incredible. When you listen to it today, not only has it stood the test of time, but you can listen to it and hear some Taking Back Sunday, New Found Glory, the Movielife, Glassjaw—all these bands that were influenced by Silent Majority.

MIKE DUBIN: "Cross Crowded Rooms" and "Windows Down" were more melodic songs—not screamy, not as shouty. The subject matter was different. They were about girls.

TOMMY CORRIGAN: "Window down" is a graffiti term for when you write on a train below the windows. It's about a graffiti I did on a freight train and seeing it on different train lines on Long Island at different times. It never came out of service, so I'd see it a year later, reflect on it and why I painted it. And there's a little love story mixed in there.

Most of the kids I knew from graffiti in my town were Guidos and club kids. We were in a gang turf war with this other graffiti group from a couple towns over, and they were all skateboarders and punk rock kids. When I finally met them, I'm like, "Oh, I should have been in a crew with these guys!" It's an area thing, you just fall in with the people from your town.

Hardcore was different, because when we got into it we started meeting people from all different high schools. Which was crazy, because if you were out and you ran into kids from another school there would be a fight, you know what I mean? But hardcore gave you a pass to go to different towns like that.

JUSTIN BECK: Ben from Silent Majority and Ariel from Glassjaw came from a town called Sea Cliff. Sea Cliff was this enlightened little town. All the parents were fucking professors or some type of artist. It was just a different pedigree. Nobody had TVs in their bedrooms—it was books and everyone's a vegetarian cooking falafel at age fourteen.

SCOTTIE REDIX: That town was on some hippie shit. They didn't lock doors over there. You could just walk into any of your neighbors' doors because they considered locking doors like being in a prison.

TOMMY CORRIGAN: I remember going to diners in different areas and you got to see all of Long Island.

SCOTTIE REDIX: You would always end the night at a diner. It's all these bands in the same section, or in the parking lot, just doing what we do.

CHRISTIAN MCKNIGHT: There's a lot of Silent Majority songs that reference a place called the Nautilus Diner, which was like, *their* diner.

JUSTIN BECK: The cliché Long Island hardcore night was you'd go to a show and then go to a diner. You'd get a bagel, a seltzer, and lemons—you'd ask for fucking marinara sauce, you'd make a homemade pizza bagel. You'd put sugar and lemon in your seltzer and for like two dollars you got a full meal with a homemade Sprite. And you'd sit there and eat till like 3:00 a.m.

SCOTTIE REDIX: Shit just used to sprout in Long Island. If you were four guys hanging out in a room at the end of the day, you're gonna be a band, there's no way around it. Eddie Reyes was a true Forrest Gump of that scene. He was there for all the important bands.

MIKE DUBIN: He was one of the original members of Mind Over Matter. I think he left or was asked to leave, I'm not sure how that ended. Then he had this band Clockwise that were awesome. They did well locally but didn't really grow outside Long Island. Clockwise ended and then Eddie started Inside. He was in Inside for a while, then his relationship there ended and Inside got a different guitarist. He started the Movielife after that. He did that for a while. He did a band called Runner Up for a minute that didn't really go anywhere.

EDDIE REYES: I always wanted to push myself. I guess it was stubbornness in the back of my brain I was like, "You want to do something else now." I always had a bad habit of either walking away or trying something different. Then I decided to start Taking Back Sunday.

SCOTTIE REDIX: I was like, "Okay, it's good to see Eddie back in the fold." Because I remember him leaving the Movielife was a big deal. He kinda disappeared, then came back with this thing that became Taking Back Sunday.

EDDIE REYES: My vision was a band that didn't give a shit, wanted to have fun, just wanted to be in your face.

CHRISTIAN MCKNIGHT: Our buddy Antonio was the first singer, who named the band. He was the singer shortly.

JOHN NOLAN: Antonio tried me out on guitar . . . Somewhere along the way, we brought in counter-vocals . . . yelling something while somebody else was singing a totally different part.

MIKE DUBIN: When Eddie first started Taking Back Sunday, Jesse Lacey was playing bass. So he was in Brand New and playing bass in Taking Back Sunday. And the Rookie Lot was Brand New before Brand New.

VINNIE CARUANA: The Rookie Lot was Brian, Garrett, and Jesse from Brand New, and Brandon Reilly, who went on to join the Movielife. So it was almost Brand New's lineup.

They were good. They were a heavily-influenced-by-Lifetime kind of young punk band.

ANTHONY RANERI: After the Rookie Lot broke up, I went to Brian Lane's house when we were still in high school, or at least I was. He probably wasn't anymore. He and Garrett had a band called Hometown Hero. And there was this guy Mark, I think, singing and then they needed a guitar player. So I went and I played guitar for like two practices, tried to get it together. And then they were like, you know, we're gonna have Jesse from the Rookie Lot and this guy Vin come in and we're gonna start a new band. And then that became Brand New.

NICK GHANBARIAN: Brand New's first show was at the Garden City bowling alley, opening for Silent Majority.

SCOTTIE REDIX: So Brand New, because those dudes are players, they put in the time and they were always rehearsing, always playing shows. Taking Back Sunday also were players but they didn't always sound good. They didn't sound refined or polished. It was almost like they were putting it together as the shows came, you know what I mean?

VINNIE CARUANA: They weren't very good when they first started. I went to see them play and I thought it was bad. Then I told someone I thought it was bad and Taking Back Sunday heard about it, and Movielife and them were like little kid archrivals for a while.

EDDIE REYES: It was a vibe we got when we first started out, a lot of bands didn't take us seriously.

TOMMY CORRIGAN: It took a couple years for the people that liked us to start bands. Silent Majority really didn't put out a lot of music. We weren't a full-time band, we'd go play a weekend every now and then. We never really went for it, you know what I mean? It wasn't like everybody was quitting their jobs and saying, let's do this. Some of us were going to college at the time. I was working full-time.

NICK GHANBARIAN: It was always like, "How do we get people to hear us?" In the late nineties, there wasn't an internet to support it yet. There would be five hundred to a thousand people at a show—"If this many people on Long Island like us, we're a good band. We're really good. How do we do this in every city in America?" We just couldn't figure it out in time.

We wound up breaking up for very cliché creative differences. Half the band wanted to stick with catchy, hardcore-style stuff. And then the other half of the band went to college, starting smoking weed, and getting into experimental stuff.

CHRISTIAN MCKNIGHT: The last Silent Majority show took place [on January 5, 2001] at a church where there were hardly ever shows. I think Ben from

Silent Majority was a member. The band booked the show themselves. When the flyer came out, there was that feeling that it was the end of an era. But I also think a lot of people were not surprised. As the local hardcore band, they had hit their inevitable end and there really wasn't much to do. I don't think it ever would have made sense for them to sign to a bigger label like Vagrant.

TOMMY CORRIGAN: It was a blizzard. And the protocol back then was if it was going to snow, you'd cancel the show. But we had so much invested into doing the show that we didn't cancel.

EDDIE REYES: It snowed really bad. And I remember being really sad they were breaking up.

TOMMY CORRIGAN: The show was in Manhasset, on the North Shore of Long Island, super hard to get to from Suffolk County, where we lived. People were getting lost and couldn't find it. It was wild, man.

ANTHONY RANERI: It was on Shelter Rock Road somewhere. I used to pass it all the time and never got off it until I went to that last Silent Majority show, like, "Shit, is this the exit?"

TOMMY CORRIGAN: Twists and turns to get there, up on a very hilly part of the North Shore. It was dark and even the driveway to this place was up a big hill.

JUSTIN BECK: It was impossible to get up that hill.

TOMMY CORRIGAN: It was a nightmare.

JUSTIN BECK: It was a weird rich white people church in a nice part of Long Island. I had a Caravan and we'd squeeze all the people and equipment in this piece-of-shit Caravan. All I remember is trying to get up this goddamn hill to unload.

CHRISTIAN MCKNIGHT: This wasn't a regular church you'd picture with the steeple you'd see from the street. It almost looked like a college campus and the show was in the gymnasium. Glassjaw played that show as the surprise guest.

RICH EGAN: Glassjaw was a huge influence, even though they never broke. They were royalty in that scene.

TOMMY CORRIGAN: Daryl from Glassjaw made a fanzine for that show, which had an old interview he did with me and Rich from Silent Majority in it. He handed it out outside.

JUSTIN BECK: We were a generation just behind Silent Majority. They were our elders and we looked up to bands like them. But because we started kind of young, we'd been playing with them forever. So doing their last show, it's like who are the bands that are still around? To be on the, quote, unquote, last Silent Majority show was a good bucket list.

TOMMY CORRIGAN: I wasn't there early setting up or anything like that. I came from work to the show—it was a screen-printing shop in the morning, and then a tattoo shop from like noon to ten at night. I got out of work early to go play the show.

CHRISTIAN MCKNIGHT: The place was packed, sold out, wall-to-wall people. If I were to guess I'd say five or six hundred. It wasn't like booking clubs where it's like, okay, I know I'm allowed to fit two hundred people or whatever. They would allow as many people that fit and hope for the best. Every single scenester, every single person in a band . . . Every single person up front for Glassjaw and Silent Majority was such an integral person in our scene. There wasn't a single person where it was like, "I don't know who that is."

ANTHONY RANERI: All of Brand New would have been there. All of Taking Back Sunday would have been there. I remember specifically hanging out with the Brand New guys. Brandon Reilly and Vinnie Caruana from the Movielife were certainly there.

SCOTTIE REDIX: We got there fairly early. We didn't have to walk far, we got a good spot. Two of my favorite bands playing, I'm camped up on the side of the stage watching what the dudes are doing. I'll do the crowd-surfing thing every so often but I'm watching the players, you know? Silent Majority's last show, Glassjaw reuniting the old lineup.

TOMMY CORRIGAN: They used to be xGlassjawx, then it was the Glassjaw, and then it became just Glassjaw. Even though at the time of the show they were Glassjaw, they dressed up as *the* Glassjaw; that's when they would dress up all in white T-shirts, baggy pants. And they had their early nineties lineup play.

ANTHONY RANERI: Another thing that stands out about that show is Daryl from Glassjaw went on a little rant about hipsters.

JUSTIN BECK: I don't wanna speak for him, but that rings a bell of what was going on at the moment . . . It was like the emergence of the, quote, unquote, hipster and all these kids whose background was being into these hardcore bands, all of a sudden were acting like they were too cool for school. Kids who were total sick Glassjaw fans were like, "Wait, who are you guys?" Like, bro. You know who the fuck we are and we know you like our fucking band, but now you have this awakening with tight pants and fancy belts and snappy fingers and you just discovered the Get Up Kids or some shit and think you're more evolved. It was kind of a nod to that. It was like the precursor to the *Vice* world: you're hypercritical of social shit, you're fucking vegetarian, but you're eating fucking cocaine, like you're a total fucking shithead hypocrite, get the fuck out of my face. You liked VOD six months ago, shut the fuck up, you were probably wearing JNCOs.

CHRISTIAN MCKNIGHT: It's weird when you have hundreds of punks show up at a church because we're pierced, we're tattooed, everyone has dyed hair. The clothing was weird, probably a lot of big pants back then. Definitely a lot of big pants.

ANTHONY RANERI: All these shows you'd have friends of the band standing around the stage, so you'd have this semicircle back around the band but very quickly, they'd run to the front and start doing crowd control, catching crowd-surfers.

EDDIE REYES: I think that was the last time I did a backflip stage dive.

TOMMY CORRIGAN: It was our squad, a lot of the Lindenhurst people we grew up with. Sisters and brothers of people in the band. My mom was back there. There were people we knew from other states. It was the last time a lot of those people were at a show together. A kid showed up from fucking Spain. He bought a ticket and flew. I always considered us a local Long Island band, to have a kid show up from fucking Spain . . . I was like, "What? *Sick*."

CHRISTIAN MCKNIGHT: One thing I remember about Silent Majority's set was there were so many sing-alongs. Given the fact it was their last show, it was the last chance people were going to have to scream these lyrics. So I remember the passion of everyone screaming these songs, especially "Polar Bear Club," which is about the friends you made in the scene. Or "Cross Crowded Rooms," which is about dating somebody you went to shows with, then breaking up with them and having to see them at shows. It was all relevant to our lives, it really hit close to home.

JUSTIN BECK: I just remember good energy. Good energy.

CHRISTIAN MCKNIGHT: Tommy, Irish dude, obsessed with U2. I remember them working "With or Without You" into the beginning of "Cross Crowded Rooms." The end of "Cross Crowded Rooms," "Take this finger, take this thumb, stretch them out to form a gun, point to the left side of my chest, just say bang then it's done." Dude, people lost their fucking minds.

TOMMY CORRIGAN: I definitely was bummed. I didn't want the band to break up.

NICK GHANBARIAN: I was like, "We shouldn't be breaking up right now. We're very good. And people really like us."

ANTHONY RANERI: It continued to snow like crazy as the night went on. And I was driving an eighties Bronco at the time, so I had to drive everybody home 'cause my Bronco did well in the snow.

CHRISTIAN MCKNIGHT: After the show, this is the rumor, the legend of how it went: this kid jumped off the stage, gets hit in the head, walks to the parking lot, and starts looking for his truck. He says to one of his buddies, "Yo, I can't find my truck." And his friends are like, "What are you talking about? Dude, you got rid of your truck three months ago." So there were ten to fifteen scene kids all sitting in the waiting room till six in the morning, taking turns to see the dude that had amnesia who had no idea why he was in the hospital.

TOMMY CORRIGAN: After that show, the younger kids took it over and made the scene their own.

CHRISTIAN MCKNIGHT: That was a changing-of-the-guard moment. Because Silent Majority was really the underground of Long Island. They were never on a big label, they didn't do massive tours, they never went to

Europe. They didn't have the aesthetic of the next wave of Long Island bands, but they had all the credibility in the world. You can name a million bands in the punk scene at that time who all credited Silent Majority as a major influence, but unless you were from Long Island or you were in a touring band and played Long Island, you didn't know who they were.

ANTHONY RANERI: I don't know if anybody else will tell you this from my generation of bands . . . once Bayside, Brand New, and Taking Back Sunday started happening, there was definitely animosity from certain band members of that older guard at how big our bands were getting.

People weren't that psyched. I hate to ever say someone's jealous of me, but it seemed like there was a bit of jealousy. Because a lot of those bands never really made it out of Long Island. There was animosity as the younger kids started getting popular.

JENN PELLY: I have this memory of going to a Hot Topic on Long Island and there were Taking Back Sunday shirts, and it did not occur to me that those shirts were available all over the country. I thought this was like when you go to the record store and there's a local section. I thought that's why there were Taking Back Sunday shirts at Hot Topic. It wasn't until later that I realized that some of these bands were really famous.

EDDIE REYES: There's a big place in my heart that wishes Silent Majority had gotten more of what they deserved. They shoulda been bigger than what they were.

TOMMY CORRIGAN: There's a version of *Life of a Spectator* on vinyl and you know, it goes for like 150 bucks on eBay every now and then. Someone always sends me a link, like, "Oh look what it sold for. . . ." It's cool though.

CHRISTIAN MCKNIGHT: In the past twenty years, the only reason Silent Majority has ever reunited was to benefit friends. One of our friends Rob who was in Iron Chic passed away and they did a benefit show for him. And because there was such a want to see them, there was a lot of money raised.

TOMMY CORRIGAN: Us going out opened it up for the whole early 2000s squad to come around. It put a nail in the nineties. That was it.

CHAPTER 4

"IF PETE WASN'T PLAYING *FOR* US, HE WAS MOSHING *FOR* US"

NEIL RUBENSTEIN: Growing up in hardcore in the nineties, there was no separation between the bands and the audience. Everyone at the shows was in a band. Everyone at the show had a distro, or did a zine, or had a basement that had shows. There was never a separation.

CHRIS GUTIERREZ: The hardcore scene in Chicago in the nineties was very insular. It was maybe fifty people and we all knew each other.

STEPHANIE MARLOW: Chicago does sometimes feel like a small town, but it's a huge city. I mean, we're the third largest city in America.

CHRIS GUTIERREZ: So any new kids coming in were met with a little bit of trepidation, right? Like, "Who is this kid and his little North Shore rich kid friends?"

MANI MOSTOFI: People could get a good sense of the North Shore and where I grew up in Wilmette by watching the John Hughes movies: *Home Alone*, *The Breakfast Club*, and *Ferris Bueller* were all filmed around the North Shore. My elementary school is where they shot *Uncle Buck*.

JIM GRIMES: Wilmette is a northern suburb of Chicago. It's on the shore of Lake Michigan, near Northwestern University. So it's an area that has always had money and a very nice, very prestigious school.

MANI MOSTOFI: You couldn't call Wilmette diverse by any measure—it's a really, really white place—but there [is] a bit more of an immigrant population than you'd have in other North Shore suburbs. My family's from the Middle East. And there were Indians, Koreans, Eastern Europeans, and it was a heavily Jewish suburb. And its location was key. It's on Lake Michigan—a lot of the really nicer houses were close to the lake—and you could get to a show in the city in about fifteen minutes, because it's just two suburbs north of the Chicago border.

JIM GRIMES: Racetraitor was from there. Their whole big pushback was like, "Well fuck you guys, you guys are from Wilmette, what problems do you have?"

MANI MOSTOFI: Racetraitor was our idealized version of what hardcore could be. Confrontational and punk in the way people imagined the Sex Pistols. Politically radical. We were talking about issues that people now talk about all the time: white privilege, systematic, institutional racism versus personal tolerance or intolerance. We were talking about those things at a time when nobody outside maybe one or two other bands were even touching it.

NEIL RUBENSTEIN: People gave a shit about Racetraitor, for sure.

JIM GRIMES: I learned more about politics going to one Racetraitor show than I did in all of my high school history classes.

STEPHANIE MARLOW: Hardcore was still kind of a boys' club not only in Chicago, but probably worldwide, and Racetraitor were one of the first bands talking about these issues, definitely encouraging, like, women up front. Encouraging people to speak up about things that were right or wrong.

GEOFF RICKLY: They were a phenomenon. They were important. And they were brief. In the underground basement scene, Racetraitor was *talked about*. Mostly because their singer Mani had a huge mouth. He would just talk shit, talk shit, talk shit.

CHRIS GUTIERREZ: Even though they were my friends, I was like, "Dude, just turn it off for a minute, man." Everyone hated them. Nobody was ready for it.

HANIF ABDURRAQIB: Being Black and witnessing Racetraitor, it was like, "Oh, they're trying to antagonize a white audience, I already get what's happening here." Racetraitor made a lot of good songs. But the live show was to kind of push around the audience, try to get these largely white audiences to reckon with their complicity in American racism. And this was in like, the late nineties.

CHRIS GUTIERREZ: They wanted to accuse you in front of the stage: "You, right there—you are a fucking racist." And you'd be like, "Dude, what the fuck did I do? I'm just fucking standing here!"

GEOFF RICKLY: Mani would almost be like a comedian talking about stuff that was important. He'd joke about people selling stuff at shows or how vegan somebody is. He would always push buttons.

JIM GRIMES: They were on the cover of *Maximumrocknroll* in 1997 before ever having any music out, which was a huge fucking deal.

MANI MOSTOFI: *Maximumrocknroll* was *the* publication for the underground punk/hardcore scene. The internet wasn't what it is today, so it was one of the things that everybody could get at a record store to read interviews and reviews, learn about new bands. It was like the *Rolling Stone* of punk.

JIM GRIMES: And it was like, Why are they on the cover? Because they're starting shit.

MANI MOSTOFI: We had this show in North Carolina organized by this queer Black kid who was really pissed off at the local scene for being too white. We played pretty early in the day, around two or three. We did our thing, talked about how the punk and hardcore scene thinks it's immune to institutionalized racism, how it thinks it's so enlightened. But it's not enough to not be prejudiced, you have to be active. People would clap for statements we made and we would tell them not to clap because they shouldn't get the catharsis of agreeing with us; they need to go in the streets and fight. We didn't end our set; it just dissolved into everyone yelling at each other about our politics. I was debating like four people at a time for about an hour.

Then this band called Torches to Rome was playing. They were the headliner and everybody was really excited to see them. They had this whole politic that your political behavior and the way you interact with people around you is your core activist element. And our message was the opposite: The way you engage with the system is the core. In retrospect, I think that political analysis came about because the singer of the band—which we didn't know at the time—was a trans woman. At the time they were presenting as a man, so I think that very personalized engagement with the space around you might have been what she was processing. But we didn't know that; we just thought this was a hippie-ish punk band that was just like, "Be kind to each other." Torches to Rome also had this policy where they set up a microphone for anybody in the audience to come up and use it in any way they felt valid.

I was tired and sitting by our merch table, not in the hall where the show was happening. Some kid runs out like, "Mani, Torches to Rome is talking shit on Racetraitor." I ran out into the room and I heard the singer say, "You can talk about systematic racism and class and race repression all you want, but in the end, it's the little things that matter." I raise my hand and say, "Can I ask a question?" The singer points me to the mic and I say, "What did you have for lunch today?" She was kind of like, "Where is this going?" you know? She says, "I had some hummus and pita and carrots," And I was like, "You know how many people didn't eat today? It's the little things that matter."

The room blew up. It was like I took a grenade and threw it in the middle of the room.

JIM GRIMES: I was in a band that played shows with Racetraitor a lot, so we'd almost have to get into altercations with people. It was a bunch of people that did not want to talk it out, but instead use violence. Which at that point in my life, I was okay with. I was like, "I'm down."

MANI MOSTOFI: That North Carolina show built a reputation for us in the scene as political shit-starters. And there were other shows, too. There was an Anti-Racist Action gathering in Columbus, Ohio, and we were asked to play a basement show as the post-gathering entertainment. Anti-Racist Action was this sort of anarchist network across the country of people who went to Klan rallies and tried to fight the Klan out of town. There were many more things to them, but that was the more visual stuff they were known for. The gathering happened because a big Klan rally was supposed to be happening.

Our politics were, "The Ku Klux Klan is not who is in power, it's the

Democrats and the Republicans, these major corporations. These are the major drivers of white power, not the more visual, cartoonish ones." So Anti-Racist Action, the people who were politically closest to us in the entire punk and hardcore scene—*nobody* could have been closer to us politically than these people—we started telling them, "If you wanna cut down a tree, you don't whack at the leaves, you go for the trunk." I remember saying that exact thing during our set. Anti-Racist Action understood the latent danger that groups like the Klan posed better than Racetraitor did because we were so focused on the institutional stuff. But we just told them they were wrong and at one point, a skinbyrd, a female skinhead—and these were anti-racist skinheads—physically attacked our roadie. This was a basement show and the whole basement was lit by one light bulb. The crowd swarmed, the light bulb got smashed, the room went dark, and there was this tussle of bodies. We're in this room with our closest allies, and we got into a fight with them. I had started this whole thing; this time I was the instigator for real.

STEPHANIE MARLOW: You knew Racetraitor was going to be confrontational, something volatile. I think that was a draw for a lot of people.

MANI MOSTOFI: I just remember going behind the bass cabinet and laughing.

PETE WENTZ: It was confrontational, and it was meant to be. When you're a seventeen-, eighteen-year-old kid, it's like doing a line of drugs. You're fired up to change the world. You think you can change it within your community.

In high school I was still trying to fit in, in some ways. I was kind of friends with everyone—I skateboarded, but I also played sports. I went to a really big school and then a very small, private one. But at the same time, I'm not sure that I really let anyone know me. When I discovered punk rock, I felt like I finally got to know people who were like me.

JIM GRIMES: Pete was part of the group that would come to Racetraitor shows. We would call them the North Shore Kids, and Pete came from up in Wilmette. He was this little dude who would wear dog collars, this punk, skater-type dude. Very influenced by the whole vegan straight-edge thing.

MANI MOSTOFI: If Pete wasn't playing for us, he was moshing for us. It was one role or the other.

All these other kids in Pete's group, they could have been in a yachting club, you know? What stuck out about Pete was he wasn't as clean-cut as the rest of them. He was into death metal and he had a gruffer look. Pete was wearing, like, a Deicide shirt down to his knees. He didn't quite have dreads then, but he had this wild . . . it wasn't a 'fro . . . it was like a pre-dread 'fro. But it looked cool. It looked kind of crazy.

PETE WENTZ: Coming from a mixed-race family . . . that's probably a whole other book within itself. My dad's side is German, Irish, something like that. On my mom's side, there's Jamaican, but Jamaica's a melting pot. It's an island, a port nation, where workers and slaves came together. I think there's Jewish-Portuguese; there's a lot of light eyes on my mom's side. It's a bunch of stuff I don't really know, stuff that 23andMe can't really help you with. It's one of those things where only people who experienced it can talk about it.

I grew up in a very white neighborhood, but was super disconnected from that. I think my parents tried to have us be . . . you know, we'd eat at Ethiopian restaurants but you're just the weird family and I'm like, "I just want to eat my fucking McDonald's," you know what I mean?

There's nowhere I felt like I fit in, racially. Like, if I rap with a song, I don't rap the n-word. But at the same time, I'd get called a brown piece of shit. You don't really fit in anywhere. That's one of the things that drew me to hardcore and punk rock. A lot of people who didn't fit in for whatever reason could not fit in together.

MANI MOSTOFI: Pete would do his own pamphleteering. He was the only member of Racetraitor that was Black. So he identified with the Black liberation struggle, he would talk a lot about Frederick Douglass and Malcolm X as important figures to him. And Fred Hampton, who is from Chicago.

CHRIS GUTIERREZ: Pete was an extremely political dude. He was a part of all these rallies for important social justice issues, like Free Mumia Abu-Jamal, the political prisoner. Half the reason I didn't like Pete at first was because he was screaming all the time.

PETE WENTZ: We worked with this group Uhuru, which was run by Fred Hampton's widow and was about the plight of Fred Hampton Jr.

MANI MOSTOFI: We would go to anti-police brutality protests, and Pete would kind of be in the back. He would be there supporting it, but he wouldn't be the guy in the front leading the charge. He believed in it—it wasn't a false conviction—but he would also observe the spectacle of the protest—all these different groups, some who had cool ideologies, some who had crazy ideologies.

PETE WENTZ: People would bring a table to a fest and tell you about Krishna or whatever. It was a little bit like sixties culture, but to the sound of punk rock. The punk rock scene was still overwhelmingly white and male . . . There was an exchange of ideas, and it was the very beginning of the internet, so you'd be on email lists. It was a very interesting time.

MANI MOSTOFI: Pete didn't play with Racetraitor until we started having lineup issues. The original lineup was me, Dan on guitar, Brent on bass, and Karl on drums, then guitar. When Brent and Karl left, that's when Pete started playing with us. And Karl had switched from drums to guitar so Andy Hurley could join.

PETE WENTZ: I first met Andy at Detroit Fest, or whatever it was called, in '96 or '97. He had the craziest vibe—the first time we talked I think he had a snake drawn in marker around his neck. Real feral vibe in the best way. Then I met him again at this show in Milwaukee and he was wearing Wu Wear with an upside-down cross necklace and I knew we were gonna be buddies.

JIM GRIMES: Milwaukee, Wisconsin, is like its own little part of the Midwest that's different than everywhere else. They're Midwest people, but they're just . . . kind of strange. I've never met a normal person from Milwaukee. Or Wisconsin in general.

Andy was very into being vegan, straight edge, and all that. Very political. I think that's why he was pushed to the Racetraitor dudes, because they saw this dedicated dude who was all about being straight edge, all about being vegan.

MANI MOSTOFI: Pete was three or four years younger than the rest of us and

Andy was about five years younger. The rest of the band was in college and they were in high school.

I remember meeting Andy and he was like, the opposite of Pete. Pete from day one was charismatic, right? You laughed at his jokes. He wasn't fully confident when we first met him, but he wasn't a wallflower. Andy barely spoke. He was this kid in a way-oversized hoodie, shaved head, the nerdy glasses. You look at him and you do not think this is the guy you want in your band. But he just got behind the drums and he was a beast. He did stuff that I hadn't heard people do in the hardcore scene at that level yet—his double bass, his blast beats. His playing was so good we threw out almost our entire setlist and rewrote songs around his ability.

JIM GRIMES: Pete didn't really know how to play bass too well. It was more of an entertainment thing with him, where he had good stage presence.

MANI MOSTOFI: Pete would play with us for like three months and then we would get another bass player for three months. There was a period of time around '98 where I would say he was "in" the band, but for a pretty short run. Then after he was "in" the band, he would play on and off, too.

PETE WENTZ: A lot with Racetraitor, for me I was in over my head, over my pay grade.

A lot of times the confrontations would start and I would be like, "What the fuck is happening right now?"

MANI MOSTOFI: The Racetraitor confrontations were just hilarious to him. Cartoonish and funny. But sometimes he'd get pissed.

Pete had cultivated this image for a little while . . . I wouldn't say being thuggy, but being a dude that was a little bit of like . . . how do I put this . . . a dude who's willing to fight. Even though he's from this posh suburb, he had cultivated this image of being a little bit street. He had a sort of second set of friends through graffiti and stuff that were a little more . . . I don't know if there's a better word for it than "street."

Sometimes people would attack Racetraitor, attack me. I remember Pete went up to a member of a prominent band that had made fun of us a lot, and was basically like, "If you ever talk shit on my friends again, I'm gonna kill you." I was far away from this conversation, but I saw them talking and the other guy's face just goes white. Not that Pete ever would have done that. But he had created this image where they took it seriously.

CHRIS GUTIERREZ: Pete and I had a mutual friend in Jim Grimes. Jim was the singer of Extinction and he's also responsible for putting on so many hardcore shows in Chicago over the years. He basically said, "Yo, you need to meet Wentz." And I was like, "I don't fucking like that dude." He's like, "You need to hang out with him because you guys are basically the same dude." I'm like, "What do you mean?" He's like, "You guys are both hoodlums."

JIM GRIMES: We were all straight edge. We didn't drink. Never. Instead of drinking, we would cause trouble all the time. A lot of vandalism. Or you know, just skateboarding. Always out causing trouble.

CHRIS GUTIERREZ: So we had this apartment where everybody would just hang out. It was mayhem: mashed potatoes on the ceiling for years, dried-up puke everywhere. It was vile. But we were a bunch of hardcore kids, right? Everybody would come by at like three in the morning and just rage. One night, Grimes hit me up like, "Hey man, we're gonna be stopping by, a car of us." And I was like, "All right, who's coming?" He's like, "This dude, this dude, this dude . . . and Pete." I was like, "Aw, fuck no, that kid is not coming to my fucking apartment." He's like, "We're almost pulled up, we're here, be cool."

I remember Pete coming in and he sat down. We had this U-shaped couch that could fit like ten, twelve people but he didn't sit on it, he sat up against the wall by the sliding glass door. Grimes goes to Wentz like, "Yo, you should tell Chris about that party you crashed at that frat house at Northwestern where you guys peed on all the coats."

I'm like, "What?! Tell me more!"

MANI MOSTOFI: When Racetraitor broke up, Arma Angelus represented the first time Pete was taking one of his bands seriously and thought he could do something with it. It was Pete's first attempt to do something bigger, and more national.

PETE WENTZ: Arma Angelus was the first band where I was, you know, the tip of the spear or whatever. I was trying to figure out what the band was going to be, what the merch would look like, what shows we could play.

MANI MOSTOFI: Arma Angelus had Pete on vocals. And actually, Andy was in the very first incarnation of Arma Angelus, too—he played bass. Pete had been in other bands and he liked his other bands, but I think there was a level of seriousness to Arma Angelus he didn't have before. It was Pete's first real moment of being a front man. He was writing some of the early music and it was a pretty good band.

SEAN O'KEEFE: A bit after high school, I had a little office-apartment-studio where I produced one of the early Arma Angelus releases. I got a phone call from somebody saying, "We have this band, can you record us?" I didn't know Pete was in the band.

So, Pete, I knew of him in high school. He was in my high school for a little bit and then I think he switched to another school. He was kind of a badass. Generally speaking, I was scared of him. I thought his group of friends would probably want to beat up me and my friends. One of my best friends dated a girl after Pete and I think there was some minor conflict between Pete and my friend over this girl. So if I ever saw Pete, I thought my life was threatened even more.

I opened the door to my studio, and there's Pete Wentz. I had it drilled into my head he wanted to beat me up. I called my friend like, "You'll never believe who's in my studio." And he's like, "Dude, calm down, he doesn't want to beat you up."

CHRIS GUTIERREZ: We were driving around at two in the morning and Wentz was like, "Yo, you gotta listen to this tape." I knew he was in Arma Angelus, but I didn't know what they sounded like, right? He puts the tape in and I'm like, "Holy shit dude, this is like Buried Alive crossed with Damnation A.D., this is fucking amazing. I wanna be in this band!"

PETE WENTZ: I was learning how to be a leader—you can't ask things of people that you're not willing to do yourself. Things that you would learn from working up from the mailroom of an office, you know what I mean? I did that through bands.

JIM GRIMES: Pete always had a hustle going on. He was always a hustler. I'll say that till the day I die about that guy. He always had some kind of scam going on, whether for good or bad.

PETE WENTZ: And I was like, "I don't know what the fuck I'm doing!" But it helped me learn a lot: how to be a tour manager, how to sell merch, how to order merch, how to organize merch . . . Which I kind of knew, but I figured it out better.

CHRIS GUTIERREZ: We were at Arma Angelus practice. And Pete was like, "Dude, I think I can get us signed." I was like, "What do you mean?" He's like, "I'm gonna get us signed to Eulogy." Eulogy at the time was a pretty big label. I was like, "What? How?" And he's like, "Don't worry, I got this, man."

I remember him coming to practice with contracts that his dad had looked over, because I think his dad was an attorney. I was like, "What am I signing?" He's like, "It's our fucking record deal!"

JIM GRIMES: Pete always wanted his own thing to catch on, where he could say, "This is my thing that I built."

HANIF ABDURRAQIB: I often think people misunderstood and misread Pete's musical intensity, where people expected something from him I don't think he was ever that interested in performing. I don't think Pete was popping in Racetraitor just because he fully believed in the mission of Racetraitor, right? I think it was like, a means to an end, a vehicle for him to further himself in the scene. Which I know makes him sound bad, and I don't intend to. I definitely don't think Pete was opposed to the mission of Racetraitor. But I think a part of what he was trying to do was establish himself in the scene. So that he could introduce that scene to something new.

ALL *THE* WAY DOWN I-95

RICH EGAN: There's always that one band that takes everything from the scene and it busts through. Because they make it a little more digestible. A little cuter. A little poppier. And that's the magic sauce for taking it to the masses.

AMY FLEISHER MADDEN: The South Florida scene was still in this stage where it kind of didn't matter if you didn't have a singer that could sing. And not in an experimental sense of like, "Oh, your voice is kind of different." Like, a lot of the bands, the singers were pretty terrible. And it was okay. But when you had somebody that could really sing . . .

CHRIS CARRABBA: I never stopped to consider whether I could sing or couldn't sing, wanted to sing or didn't want to sing. I just knew I was afraid to. Stage fright, I think that's what it was.

Going to high school in Connecticut, you had to take an elective, and I took choir because my mom had taught me how to read some notes. And I'm not kidding you, I don't think I sang a note in front of people from eighth-grade choir through high school choir. My friends in whatever section I was in would maybe sing a little louder when the chorus came by, to cover the fact that I was lip-synching.

But I did sing when I was by myself. I always, always sang.

DAN BONEBRAKE: I grew up in Deerfield Beach and Boca Raton, Florida. Out of high school, I was in the army for three years. When I got out of the army, I met Chris in the winter of '92. He was still in high school. All his skater friends started bringing more of the hardcore stuff.

CHRIS CARRABBA: What brought me to Florida was my mom got a job. My mom was an impressive woman. She raised my brother and me as a single mother, and we were latchkey kids. What I remember most about that was the sense of adventure. We kind of had a curfew but otherwise, it was, "Just kind of stay out of trouble." And have fun.

AARON GILLESPIE: Florida is so big. It's only seventy, eighty miles across in some sections, but it's so long vertically. The first real major city you could play out of Florida was Atlanta. Getting to Atlanta cost money, you know what I mean?

CHRIS CARRABBA: We were in a geographic no-man's-land for touring bands. If you're coming down the East Coast and you get to Georgia, you have to make that call: Are we gonna drive another nine hours to Miami or Fort Lauderdale or start veering west? It just cut us off.

AMY FLEISHER MADDEN: In Miami and Fort Lauderdale, being into punk music and skateboarding and any kind of subculture was not okay. Miami is a very strange town. Sports. Women dress like women. You don't do weird things with your hair and makeup.

DAN BONEBRAKE: Everybody played shows at a place called Club Q in Davie, a really country city in South Florida. They have a huge rodeo there. People ride horses up and down the street. In old westerns, when they get off their horses to go in the saloon, and tie the horse's reins around that pole thing? I'm not a cowboy, so I don't know what you call them, but those are in front of the stores in Davie.

CHRIS CARRABBA: There wasn't a whole lot of culture for young people there. So we forged our own. A sixteen-year-old girl named Amy Fleischer, who had a fan zine called *Fiddler Jones*, came to be known as Amy Fiddler because of it . . .

AMY FLEISHER MADDEN: So the way that I met Chris Carrabba . . . there was a ska band called Jive Step Bunch. I went to see them and their singer had either left or broken his leg, or something weird had happened where it wasn't the regular singer. So I'm sitting there interviewing this guy named

John and he's like, "This isn't even really my band. My band is called the Vacant Andys and we're an emo band." I had never heard the word "emo" before, and I didn't know how to spell it. When I transcribed the interview I was like, "Oh, they're gonna think I'm very not cool when I misspell this word."

So I'm like, I'm gonna go see this guy's other band, the Vacant Andys. And that's when I met Chris.

CHRIS CARRABBA: Vacant Andys had been around for quite a long time, five, ten years before I saw them play. Their guitarist left and I was friends with the singer. So my best friend John and I joined as their guitarists.

DAN BONEBRAKE: We opened for everybody down here: the Specials, Jawbox, the Get Up Kids, Lifetime.

CHRIS CARRABBA: They were really encouraging for me to write songs, and I would teach them to the singer. Dan got really intense and said that I should sing the songs that I'd written. And he was aware I didn't really have a singing voice. I think he was just interested in how I'd improve as a songwriter if I took ownership of the songs. So that's how I became a singer in a band, thanks to Dan Bonebrake.

DAN BONEBRAKE: Chris and I established an honesty early on. And Amy really did drive a scene down there. The internet wasn't like it is today and she kept us in the know with her zine.

AMY FLEISHER MADDEN: I brought my zine to the shows. I gave a copy to the woman who owned the only all-ages venue in Miami, called Cheers. Her name was Gaye Levine—she worked the door, she booked the shows, she owned the venue. She was like, "Do you know who all of these bands are?" Because I was writing about Fat Wreck Chords bands, Epitaph bands, and I think Doghouse bands. And I was like, "Yeah, I love all these bands." So I went to meet with her—she was a jazz cellist and a forty-five-year-old gay woman. She's like, "I know nothing about any of these bands but everybody wants to play here. Can you help me figure out who's big and who's not and how much to charge and all these things?" I was in high school and I needed to have an internship somewhere. And I was like, "So, here's what we're gonna do, you're gonna sign my papers and you don't even have to pay me and I'll come here three days a week and just work for you." So my high school internship was interning at a partially gay bar/partially all-ages punk rock venue, when I was sixteen years old, booking shows.

MIKE MARSH: Almost every day there was a show going on [at Cheers] . . . And then across the street there was this pizza place where you could get a massive slice of pizza, the size of a computer monitor, for like three dollars.

At Cheers was the first time I ever met Chris. I was sitting on the curb, I think the Agency had just played with the Vacant Andys, and we were talking about skateboarding and punk rock bands.

What was Chris like? Chris wore shorts a lot, *hah, hah*, I remember thinking, "This guy's always got shorts on." At the time, he was pretty quiet around people he didn't know well. That first time I met him, he really didn't say a whole lot; I needed to break the ice. Chris was always really well spoken. He seemed like he had a good education. He was smart. And he was a sweet guy, really complimentary. Whether he meant it or not, he just went out of his way to say nice things.

ALEX SUAREZ: The scene was pretty small. Then Fiddler Records popped up, Amy started putting on showcases and all these bands started emerging.

AMY FLEISHER MADDEN: Gaye, despite not needing to pay me, was still giving me 10 percent of door. And I had another part-time job retouching photographs at this art studio in Miami. So I had a couple hundred dollars here and there, and it was like a big deal. I never had cash, you know? And the logical progression was to put out records. My first record was Vacant Andys, in 1996.

DAN BONEBRAKE: The Vacant Andys' first tour was with New Found Glory. They were also on Fiddler Records and it was their first tour, too. I think Amy booked it. We all toured in one Ryder box van together. Four of us rode in the cab and six of us rode in the back of the moving van. It was hot, man. It was summertime. We figured out early on to only drive at night so the six in the back didn't die of heat exhaustion. We played up to Jersey, Pennsylvania, and all the spots in between: VFW halls, basements, we played somebody's backyard pool in Jersey. Chad from New Found Glory couldn't go out on that tour because he was singing for Shai Hulud, who was also out on tour.

GEOFF RICKLY: The way Long Island had a sound and New Jersey had a sound, Florida had a sound. I don't know what to call it . . . like a space-age version of what everybody else was doing? It was smoother and the octaves were cleaner on the guitars. Maybe it was having New Found Glory down there.

CHAD GILBERT: We combined hardcore riffs with pop-punk. Our first show was at Cheers . . .

AMY FLEISHER MADDEN: New Found Glory had this thing where all the members went to different high schools. And their area of Florida, Coral Springs, was more like New Jersey, where it's pockets of suburbs. When you have five cool, attractive-ish dudes in the subculture . . . their first show sold out.

CHAD GILBERT: There were a lot of people for a band's first show, but I don't remember it being packed or sold out . . .

AMY FLEISHER MADDEN: Packed house, 250 kids. And a lot of parents that had driven the kids, it was that vibe. It wasn't scene kids. It was high school kids.

CHRIS CARRABBA: In every band there was a member who was also a member of another band, or several other bands. There just weren't enough players in Florida to not have overlap.

AMY FLEISHER MADDEN: Chad was a little bit of a local legend because he joined Shai Hulud when he was like fourteen. So to have this cool hardcore band that was signed, with this kid singer . . . And he had this voice that people were like, "Who is this child onstage wearing shorts?" He was a big deal. And Chad to have a pop-punk band was way more accessible than a hardcore band.

CHRIS CARRABBA: Chad was in Shai Hulud and they were going on tour and New Found Glory still had shows and they asked me to fill in for Chad on guitar. Standing onstage and seeing the faces of the audience, I thought: "This band's gonna be huge." And I didn't think that about bands, at all.

But seeing those faces looking at Jordan as he sang, I thought, "Wow, this is a band that's going to make it."

AMY FLEISHER MADDEN: So the Vacant Andys broke up for lots of reasons. It's kind of foggy. I was at a party, which I think was at Chris's house, and all of the guys from a band called Strongarm were hanging out with Chris. I think Strongarm had been done for a little bit.

CHRIS CARRABBA: Strongarm were a Christian band . . . I wasn't a Christian and I didn't know there was such a thing as Christian bands. I didn't know that was a thing people did.

AMY FLEISHER MADDEN: And they were like, "We are gonna write arena rock songs, we're gonna go big." I remember Chris coming over to me and saying, "Dude, the guys from Strongarm are here and they want me to sing in their new band!" So he began playing with the Strongarm dudes, and that became Further Seems Forever.

CHAD GILBERT: Chris doesn't give away too much of his personal life publicly.

CHRIS CARRABBA: If you'll forgive me for being a little bit vague here . . . There were two frankly tragic things that happened in my life. And I was dealing with a bad breakup. Breakups are hard and everything, but these tragic things were more life-altering. They were hard to talk about and they're still hard to talk about. But I needed to talk about them, to make sense of them somehow. I really needed to make peace with them.

I wrote "The Sharp Hint of New Tears," "Turpentine Chaser," and "Screaming Infidelities" relatively close together, I don't know which one came first. It was just a matter of days.

AMY FLEISHER MADDEN: Further Seems Forever would hear them and be like, "These are great, man. But these are not our vibe. We just want you to write lyrics and sing." And I think that was really hard for Chris because he was used to writing in the Vacant Andys. He's a songwriter. And he was super discouraged and wasn't sure what to do. At the time he was working at an elementary school in Boca called J. C. Mitchell.

CHRIS CARRABBA: I was a preschool teacher, I worked as a teacher's aide, and I was an assistant administrator for the after-school programs. And I might have had a couple other jobs within the school system. So they gave me this little office space and I kept my guitar in there. In between one job to the next job in the school, I had this two-hour window and I'd sit there and work on my guitar in the air-conditioning.

AMY FLEISCHER MADDEN: He would also play for the kids, which was supercute. And he would call me on a landline and be like, "I just wrote this song, you should hear it." And you know, when someone plays you a song over the phone, it's like *RAAH-AHHH-DADA* and you're like, "Man, that sounds great!" But you can't really hear it.

We were supertight buddies back then, so he would go to my house after work and play me these songs. And I was like, "These are great. You should really show these to Further Seems Forever." And he was like, "No, they don't want them, I don't know what this is. It might be my own thing."

CHRIS CARRABBA: When I wrote "The Sharp Hint of New Tears," the lyrics say, "On the way home, this car hears my confessions." And I wrote "Dashboard Confessional" in the corner. My feeling was, I didn't have a place of my own at that time. I was couch-hopping, spending nights at my mom's apartment, spending nights at Bonebrake's house, just living where I could. My car was really the only place I could go to be alone and work out the shit that was in my head. Often people go for a drive just to think, right?

AMY FLEISHER MADDEN: I remember hearing the songs and thinking, "Whatever this is, it's fantastic and we have to work on it together." It was this feeling of urgency because no one else was doing what he had just done.

CHRIS CARRABBA: I couldn't write them fast enough. One after the next.

JOLIE LINDHOLM: Chris played the songs for me and ended up asking me to sing with him.

CHRIS CARRABBA: Jolie was part of our hub, one of those real friends of mine. She was really interested in singing and would ask me a lot of questions. She would sing with this effortless, airy, pitch-perfect voice.

JOLIE LINDHOLM: I remember walking by the classroom and the kids all watching us. Chris had his guitar and we practiced "Age Six Racer."

AMY FLEISHER MADDEN: No one even did acoustic guitar demos because everything was so punkish. Acoustic guitar was not cool. I remember thinking, this has a Bright Eyes–ish vibe, but it's completely different. It's way more raw punk. It's its own thing. I just knew.

JAMES PAUL WISNER: Because I had produced the Vacant Andys, Chris came to me and said, "I've got this side project." The very first thing we did was a four-song thing. I don't know if it was released. And it just went from there. He'd gotten something done with Fiddler Records, so we did *The Swiss Army Romance*.

CHRIS CARRABBA: I was recording in the guest bedroom closet of James's apartment of a second-story walk-up. It was not like a studio. It was just a closet.

JOLIE LINDHOLM: There was this padded closet made into a vocal booth. I'd go in there and hear James in the headphones telling me what to do.

JAMES PAUL WISNER: He was just really pouring his heart out, these really gritty vocals. The closet was okay for the vocals, but when we had to record Chris with the acoustic guitar, the closet was a little cramped. When he needed to work on something he'd be like, "Hold on, give me a second." Then he'd go out to my patio and come back fifteen minutes later. I'd look at the lyrics and they're incredible, like, "How did you get that?"

CHRIS CARRABBA: We worked through a few nights, maybe two nights . . . I think it was just a weekend. I was done and James gave me a disc to play it to Amy. We went for a drive in her car. She had a good stereo. And she says, "You got it right."

MIKE MARSH: Chris gave me a demo of early Dashboard stuff . . . When I first heard it, I was like, "What is this pussy shit? Where's the Marshalls and the Gibsons and the drums? What's going on here?" I didn't understand it.

DAN BONEBRAKE: When Chris recorded *Swiss Army*, he called me up and picked me up in his truck. I think it was down at the Poorhouse, which was one of our hangouts down in Fort Lauderdale. He was gonna drive me home. So I rode home with him and he played *Swiss Army* before it was released. I was blown away. We're riding in his Ford Ranger, headed north. And just as the last song is the ending—BAM—we get rear-ended on I-95. I think his bumper was done in pretty bad. I don't know whether the other driver was drunk or just falling asleep but he just hit us in the back and then just swerved off and left. We didn't know whether to follow him or whether to get off the road. We thought the safer thing would be to get off the highway, check out the car, wait for Florida Highway Patrol. We weren't hurt. It was just an exclamation point at the end of the record—BAM! If I didn't get a jolt from the songs, I got a literal jolt from the car behind us.

CHAPTER 6

AND OUT *TO THE* GREAT WIDE OPEN

CHRISTIAN MCKNIGHT: I was in southern Florida with Glassjaw in late '99 and I remember hearing some kids, I believe they were in the band Keepsake, talking about this super handsome dude that was going to be this big star.

AMY FLEISHER MADDEN: His first show was in West Palm Beach and there was a line out the door. For shows that weren't national acts, you never really got a line. A line was like, "Whoa, people are excited to be here." It's not just people rolling in at nine o'clock, like, "Let's go see this band, whatever, they're my friend."

Then the weirdest thing happened: people sat down.

CHRIS CARRABBA: From the get-go, it was a challenge for me to stand up there with an acoustic guitar in an environment not accustomed to it.

AMY FLEISHER MADDEN: People stared at him, sitting cross-legged, just tuned-in. You could hear a pin drop. Chris and I thought, "This is bad." Chris had, and probably still has, horrible stage fright. And I was just like, "Oh my god, he's probably so fucking nervous right now."

In the beginning, you got hot or cold. When it was good, it was really good, and when it was bad, it was really bad.

MIKE MARSH: There was this house at the University of Miami that used to host shows, there were probably fifteen or twenty people there. Chris, especially early on, had a lot of stage fright, and it showed. His voice was real shaky and he'd miss chords, forget the words to his songs. It was a really early thing of him trying to figure himself out.

CHRIS CARRABBA: "That's not punk"—I heard that a lot. And my feeling was, it is. It is punk. I just have to stand by my convictions. And that meant I had shit thrown at me a lot. Lots of coins were thrown. Lots. I was doused with drinks. Bottles. And probably worse than that were the verbal slings and arrows.

JOLIE LINDHOLM: A punk rocker girl at Club Q, one of the main places we went for shows, she was like, a skinhead, and I remember her heckling. I can't remember what she said, but she was being pretty rough. I think I told her to get lost or something.

AMY FLEISHER MADDEN: The hardcore community says it's inclusive and all about brotherhood and acceptance, and then you get a guy onstage that's a part of the hardcore community, and they're like, "No, this is not cool." We would always notice the people that would not really approve of his live show—their girlfriends would watch him, and then the girlfriends would go buy merch. Like, the dude you're here holding hands with just threw pennies at my friend but you just spent twenty bucks!

CHRIS CARRABBA: I booked this tour, thinking it would be good life experience to go around and play by myself, it might make me a better player with Further. I was thinking, this'll certainly be hard, I'm terrified of being onstage. Even still, I have a bit of stage fright. So I thought, this will help. But Dashboard wasn't my band; it was my side project. So I was gonna do the one tour, and then I wasn't gonna do it anymore. One record, one tour.

DAN BONEBRAKE: Chris called me and asked if I wanted to hop in the van; he had a tour booked up. I was just there to help drive him around and set up. And I'd play a song or two with him on bass in the early days. We honestly thought we would never do it again, so we took all the back roads. We had one of those big Rand McNally maps. We wanted to see the country because we didn't know if we'd ever get a chance again.

CHRIS CARRABBA: I got to Charlotte and I started playing and the crowd starts singing along immediately. I was so shocked: How could this possibly be going on? They knew every word. I strummed the first chord, they start singing, and then I didn't sing. They kept carrying the song forward. And they didn't stop singing till I played every song I had released. I thought, "Okay, this has already gotten further than my original intention."

I would go to these towns that I had never been to, with Further even, and people I never met would be singing every word of every song. Amy put the record out locally, but she didn't have distribution. I think she pressed a thousand CDs. I'd call home and be like, "They sang along, they knew every word!"

AMY FLEISHER MADDEN: People were coming to the shows and being like, "I downloaded your record off Napster and I love you!" And Chris would be like, "Cool! That's weird . . ."

CHRIS CARRABBA: Without Napster, you had to have some kind of professional foothold, like your label has distribution to get stores to stock your record. Napster was the great equalizer. Anybody had a chance for distribution. Kids taking it upon themselves to make sure people downloaded it, or sent them burned CDs. This genuine peer-to-peer sharing. That gave me a fighting chance. I'd love to know who put it up there first.

AARON GILLESPIE: I thought it was the best music I'd ever heard. Like, literally. I don't know if I ever told him this, but Chris taught me how to sing. I liked Nirvana and Pearl Jam, but I just wanted to play drums like those bands. I had no interest in singing like Kurt Cobain. It's not that I didn't think he was amazing; it was just too brash or something for me. So when Chris came out with that *Swiss Army* record, I literally wore it out in my mom's car, driving to school, learning how to sing.

DAN BONEBRAKE: I remember going to a show and Chris was selling Dashboard CDs out of the back of his truck. He's like, "I paid my rent selling these CDs." To be able to pay your bills making music, it was like there was no bigger feat in the world at the time.

MIKEY WAY: I remember getting the Fiddler Records sampler, hearing Dashboard, and being like, "Man, this guy's gonna go the distance." I knew it.

CHRISTIAN MCKNIGHT: I went to the first Dashboard show on Long Island, at a place called the Long Island Zoo, with New Found Glory and the Movielife. This dude with a pompadour, nice tattoos, and a beautiful grin shows up with his acoustic guitar and I'm realizing, that's the crooner they were talking about!

It was unheard of at that time for a dude with an acoustic guitar to show up at these shows that had such unbridled energy. You know, people were jumping off speakers onstage, and then you've got this guy with an acoustic guitar playing heartbreaking love songs. People ate it up. I mean, just think about the people that grew up in that scene. Everyone thrived off heartbreak.

GEOFF RICKLY: Thursday played the cafeteria of Montclair State University in New Jersey. Alex from Eyeball Records was like, "Here's this acoustic guy, I'm putting him on this show with you and this local hardcore band." I was like, "Are you insane?"

CHRIS CARRABBA: I think it was fall of 2000. It was me playing as Dashboard, just me and an acoustic guitar, opening for Thursday.

MIKEY WAY: I was going to Montclair State at the time; I went to school there briefly. I helped the Thursday guys carry their gear in and I think I made their buttons for the show.

CHRIS CARRABBA: We played on a bunch of tables put together. There was no crowd. It was just Thursday and there were two people in the crowd: the Way brothers. Just Gerard and Mikey. The Way brothers came up and told me about this band they were starting. They started rattling off what their influences were, and I remember thinking, "This is pretty eclectic stuff. This could be special."

GEOFF RICKLY: Chris got up and played right after a tough guy, Hatebreed-style hardcore band. Chris was totally unapologetic. And fucking people were into it.

MIKEY WAY: I was standing there like, "Oh, this is really important. We're going to talk about this show someday."

CHRIS CARRABBA: I had these bands that believed in me before other people believed in me. Before you could say, "Oh he'll sell X amount of tickets."

GABE SAPORTA: Just get your van, follow us, and we'll say, "Hey, this is our friend Chris, he's gonna play fifteen minutes before we go onstage." We didn't ask promoters. People just responded to him really well.

RICKY SAPORTA: Dashboard played in New Jersey—it was a New Found Glory show—with Midtown at the Wayne Firehouse. New Found Glory was like, hey, we have this friend Chris who's doing a solo acoustic thing, he's just gonna play before us for a little bit. And I think I whined and moaned about it, like, "There's no time! We're gonna run out of time!" Ha, ha, ha.

GABE SAPORTA: We had a couple tours under our belts. It started feeling like it was getting to be a national thing. Bands were touring nationally. Bands were getting signed. We signed to Drive-Thru.

STEFANIE REINES: I applied for a credit card and I got a $5,000 credit limit on a MasterCard. And that's how we funded Drive-Thru.

RICHARD REINES: Our office was a garage.

TYLER RANN: The Reines siblings were just big kids. Totally quirky and super weird, and just so LA—in my mind of what LA was about. You know, LA was a place where you never had to grow up and you could always be . . . again, they were older but I don't know how much older they really were. And they lived in a house and had cars and money and jobs. They knew all these people and they never took themselves too seriously. We were going bowling, and they called up their friend Corey Feldman. I beat him and he got super pissed off.

ROB HITT: Richard and Stefanie liked Gabe from the Humble Beginnings days. We're in the mixing room, they call and they're like, "We wanna hear the Midtown music." I hold up the phone to the speaker and they're like, "We want to sign you guys."

GABE SAPORTA: We introduced New Found Glory to Drive-Thru.

STEFANIE REINES: It was after a concert, and we were outside of a diner in New Jersey, it was snowing out and it was freezing. And Gabe Saporta said, "I found this band I wanna play for you." We put the cassette on, and it was New Found Glory, and he was dancing, as Gabe Saporta would, dancing in the headlights as we were blasting the band. They were from Coral Springs, Florida, and we bought plane tickets to go down to meet them.

CHAD GILBERT: We were like, "Well, we're playing a sweet sixteen pool party."

ROB HITT: Drive-Thru flies out for these shows because they love New Found Glory and they're gonna sign them, so they're like, "Fuck, Midtown needs to sign their contracts, we should probably get them the same day." So we walk into Drive-Thru's hotel room and reread the contract. I think we had some dad's friend who was an attorney reread the contract, who probably didn't know anything about entertainment law.

HEATH SARACENO: We disputed something really minor in the contract.

ROB HITT: Back then getting free CDs or free vinyl into your contract was a big deal. So we made Drive-Thru say we got ten free CDs. We sign the contract and as we're leaving the hotel room, New Found Glory is walking in and Chad from New Found Glory says something like, "Well, how many free CDs did Midtown get? We want more." So I think they got fifteen, twenty free CDs. We were all butthurt about it.

By the way, have you ever heard of getting an A&R point or a signing bonus? Gabe got a Sony PlayStation for showing Drive-Thru New Found Glory.

STEFANIE REINES: Did we get Gabe a PlayStation or something? Was it a PlayStation?

HEATH SARACENO: Then I think we went to Olive Garden.

GABE SAPORTA: As a label, Drive-Thru was not really a thing yet. It became a thing after that.

RICHARD REINES: New Found Glory was our first big band. We said to them, "When you go to play a show, if there's five, ten, fifteen people waiting to get in, instead of pulling up to your sound check, stop and talk to them first. They'll remember it forever. Because we remember that shit."

STEFANIE REINES: Who played us Dashboard? Was it Chad who played us Dashboard? We owe Chad a PlayStation.

CHRIS CARRABBA: Chad really pitched it to them.

AMY FLEISHER MADDEN: I sold *The Swiss Army Romance* to Drive-Thru.

CHRIS CARRABBA: They were confident that they were going to be able to sign me, so in the short term, they thought, well, we'll buy this record from Amy. So Drive-Thru expressed interest in signing Dashboard to a deal. And I wanted that. But they weren't the only label at that point.

AMY FLEISHER MADDEN: At the same time, Rich Egan offered me a job at Vagrant.

RICH EGAN: I really liked Amy and her taste and vibe, so we hired her at Vagrant. She was always trying to get me to listen to Dashboard. This was at the height of the Vagrant madness. We'd signed so many bands and so much stuff was going on that I was just like, "I don't want to hear it." If I like it, I'm going to want to sign it.

STEFANIE REINES: We called up Chad and we were like, "You're the one who played us Dashboard, we're in the process of signing him to a record deal. And he's fucking amazing. All the things you said he actually is, blah blah blah. Will you take him on tour?"

So the tour started and labels and people saw him and were like, "Oh wow, this guy's great." A buzz started to build because of that tour. Then he was poached by another label.

RICH EGAN: I finally ended up listening to Dashboard because Matt Pryor from the Get Up Kids had his acoustic side project the New Amsterdams, and they were looking for an acoustic opener on tour. Amy was like, "Here, Dashboard would be good." I flipped out. I put it in the car when I was leaving work and I listened to it all night and then all the next morning. I walked in to work like, "Give me his number." The record was about to be rereleased on Drive-Thru the next week. Amy told me he was close to signing with Drive-Thru but he was having second thoughts. And that he was talking to other labels.

CHRIS CARRABBA: The deal Drive-Thru offered me was a pretty restrictive record deal. It was for a long amount of time and a large commitment of a number of records. And not for a particularly large sum of money. My attorney's advice was, "Don't sign this record deal." He negotiated on my behalf and said, "I can't get them to budge. I advise you to sign somewhere else."

RICH EGAN: So I called Chris that night and we talked for four hours. He had been in LA the week before on tour opening for New Found Glory, so I missed him, but he told me he was playing Club Krome in New Jersey the next night. I got on a plane the next morning, flew in, and drove straight to the show. Chris was opening and the place was packed, but nobody knew who he was. He came out there with just a stool and his bass player. People were kind of talking for the first thirty seconds of the song. Then all of a sudden, the place is dead silent—fifteen hundred kids just mesmerized by him.

MIKEY WAY: You couldn't even move in that room. It was just a heat wave from the bodies being so close.

RICH EGAN: We're talking backstage, it was just Chris and Dan Bonebrake driving around in a van, and Chris was like, "Where are we gonna sleep tonight, Dan?" I said I had a hotel in the city, you guys can come crash on my floor if you want. So they did and the next morning we had breakfast at the Loews hotel in Midtown. It was a two-hour breakfast.

DAN BONEBRAKE: I was there for the breakfast. The contract was there and there were certain things that Chris didn't like and Rich just took a pen and crossed them out.

CHRIS CARRABBA: Vagrant was an artist-first label. They were gonna pay royalties. You were actually gonna get paid if your record sold. That was kind of outlandish at the time for labels to do right by the bands. Some labels were cruelly taking advantage of bands.

RICH EGAN: Chris and I really connected. We have a similar work ethic, almost identical taste in music. And he decided to sign to Vagrant.

STEFANIE REINES: We were at the Drive-Thru office on the last day before Christmas break. This was after we had hosted a massive Thanksgiving at our house. My mom and dad came and New Found Glory and Midtown were there. Chris Carrabba was there and Amy Fiddler was there. Everyone was. New Found Glory's parents were there. And then the last day of work before the holiday, Chris called us to tell us that he wasn't going to sign. And we were devastated.

CHRIS CARRABBA: That was one of the hardest conversations I've ever had to have.

RICH EGAN: Vagrant and Drive-Thru were always on a collision course. It was like the Yankees and Red Sox always competing for the same free agents. Earlier on, they tried to sign the Get Up Kids, and we signed them.

I believe they tried to sign Hot Rod Circuit before we signed them. They assumed they already had Dashboard signed. And we signed him, and they took that as poaching from them, which was not how it was, but I could see how they could see it that way. They were pissed. And they were very vocal about their grievances.

STEFANIE REINES: We took everything really personally. I definitely said things I wish I didn't say.

RICHARD REINES: I mean, we never shit-talked, we loved his music. So it's not like we said anything bad about the music.

STEFANIE REINES: I crossed a different line . . . I can admit that I, not Richard, handled it poorly.

CHRIS CARRABBA: The things they said hurt. It hurt my career, and it hurt my standing with my fans and their fans. It hurt me personally. But it also wasn't lost on me that things hadn't worked out in their favor, and that was hurtful to them.

RICH EGAN: Chris flew out to LA a couple days after he signed. He wanted a new record out immediately because he wasn't happy with the Drive-Thru arrangement.

CHRIS CARRABBA: Drive-Thru shelved *Swiss Army Romance*. So I had nothing to sell that would keep me on tour financially. I couldn't have made gas money or hotel room money without anything to sell. And I wanted to tour more than anything.

RICH EGAN: He wanted the new record out immediately.

JAMES PAUL WISNER: As momentum was building with Dashboard, he quit Further Seems Forever and we did *The Places You Have Come to Fear the Most*.

CHRIS CARRABBA: When I signed with Vagrant, I already had a full-length's worth of music for my next record. And I decided I was gonna rerecord two songs from *Swiss Army* that I really liked to play live: "Again I Go Unnoticed" and "Screaming Infidelities."

RICH EGAN: I think it was like six weeks from when he signed to when *Places* came out, which is insane. He was like, "All right, I got songs. I'm gonna head back to Florida and make the record. I just need to pay off a credit card and if I can store some stuff in your warehouse, I'll go on tour forever." And that's pretty much exactly what he did.

RICKY SAPORTA: These bands, with a huge DIY ethic, are out there driving their vans themselves. They're playing late into the night, loading out, staying with somebody and sleeping on floors. And then they're criss-crossing the country.

CHAD GILBERT: What a time it was when T-shirts were ten bucks, and if you charged any more than ten bucks you were like . . . greedy. On some of my old merch settlement sheets from 1999, it's like, twelve shirts sold for ten dollars apiece. Ten CDs sold for eight dollars apiece. So it was like, $200. That's what would've been a huge night. Like, "Whoa, we sold twelve shirts! We sold almost fifteen CDs?!?!"

AMY FLEISHER MADDEN: It was fucking awesome when I went on tour to New Jersey and New York with New Found Glory. I got to cities that weren't like a weird, secluded area, and there were just so many more people. And there was such a different community, where there wasn't just one single all-ages, laughable venue. There'd be actual clubs. Like, I remember the first time I was in Philly, at the Trocadero, and I was like, "This isn't gonna close next week! No one's getting shut down. It's not in some area forty miles outside of town by the airport. Holy shit, music is real when you leave South Florida."

RICKY SAPORTA: Because they're small bands trying to make their way through the country, it's not like they have these ideal tour schedules where everything lines up neatly. It is not uncommon for a band to play DC, drive up to Boston, and then come down and play New Jersey. When you get out to the Midwest, it gets even crazier. People go from Birmingham to Chicago, down to Nashville, and like, out to Nevada. That's a totally normal tour schedule, because you take the shows you can get. You're driving countless miles, you're burning up gas money, you're not sleeping, you're not eating well. And on top of that, you're driving through the night.

BRYAN NEWMAN: We were on tour with H2O. They had a bus. They were kind of big brothers to us. Ted and I would hang out more with them, and they invited us to sleep on their bus as we traveled from Chicago to Minneapolis. I think we partied until we fell asleep.

EBEN D'AMICO: [The rest of Saves the Day] was driving from Chicago overnight to Minneapolis. This was like, a fancy dad van. There were these two captain's chairs; I think I was sitting in one of them. I wasn't wearing a seat belt. I remember the sensation of being in midair.

BRYAN NEWMAN: I remember being woken up by H2O's tour manager—it was six in the morning, like twenty degrees outside, rural Wisconsin on the highway—and he said, "You guys need to wake up, we just passed your van and there's been a really bad accident." I remember getting out of the bus and the van is on its side and the trailer is behind it. "Everyone's dead," that was the first thought I had.

EBEN D'AMICO: We hit black ice, went off the road, and flipped our van. Poor David's face went into the steering wheel and he lost all his teeth. Chris fractured his collarbone.

BRYAN NEWMAN: The van landed on the passenger-seat side. That was where Ted would always sit, and he never wore a seat belt for some reason. Had he not been in the bus . . .

EBEN D'AMICO: I crawled out of the wreckage and felt my body parts to make sure that they were all still there. And then I called my mom while I was standing at the side of this snowy highway with David spitting blood out of his mouth. I was still young enough that, something bad happens, you call your mom.

PART 2

WILL YOU TELL ALL YOUR FRIENDS...

PART 2

2001–2002

CAST OF CHARACTERS

PART 2

HANIF ABDURRAQIB: author and poet (and Midwest native)
JIM ADKINS: front person, Jimmy Eat World
QUINN ALLMAN: guitarist, the Used
BRIAN ANDERSON: journalist (and Chicago native)
JOANNA ANGEL: adult film star; cofounder, BurningAngel.com; author (and New Jersey native)
JUSTIN BECK: guitarist, Glassjaw; cofounder, Merch Direct
MAX BEMIS: front person, Say Anything
DAN BONEBRAKE: bassist, Dashboard Confessional, Vacant Andys
EDDIE BRECKENRIDGE: drummer, Thrice
AMANDA BRENNAN: meme historian; former head of editorial, Tumblr (and New Jersey native)
LISA BROWNLEE: tour manager, Warped Tour
JOSHUA CAIN: guitarist, Motion City Soundtrack
CHRIS CARRABBA: front person, Dashboard Confessional, Further Seems Forever; vocalist-guitarist, Vacant Andys
SPENCER CHAMBERLAIN: front person, Underoath
IAN COHEN: journalist
TOMMY CORRIGAN: designer, Merch Direct (and previously, front person, Silent Majority)
JONATHAN DANIEL: cofounder, Crush Music; manager, Fall Out Boy, Panic! at the Disco, Cobra Starship, etcetera.
BRIAN DIAZ: guitar tech, Brand New, Fall Out Boy (and formerly, front person, Edna's Goldfish, the Reunion Show)
MIKE DUBIN: photographer, videographer, radio host, tour manager (and Long Island native)
RICH EGAN: cofounder, Vagrant Records; manager, Dashboard Confessional, the Get Up Kids
FRED FELDMAN: founder, Triple Crown Records
JOHN FELDMANN: producer, the Used; front person, Goldfinger
DIA FRAMPTON: front person, Meg & Dia (and later, solo artist and *The Voice* runner-up)
MATT GALLE: booking agent, My Chemical Romance, Taking Back Sunday
GLENN GAMBOA: journalist, *Newsday*
NICK GHANBARIAN: bassist, Bayside (and formerly, Silent Majority)
AARON GILLESPIE: drummer-vocalist, Underoath
MIKE GITTER: A&R, Atlantic Records, Roadrunner Records; journalist, author, and zine maker, *xXx*
MICHAEL GOLDSTONE: A&R, PolyGram, Epic Records, DreamWorks Records, Sire Records

ANDY GREENWALD: author and music journalist
JIM GRIMES: Chicago show promoter; front person, Extinction
CHRIS GUTIERREZ: bassist, Arma Angelus; blogger and author
DE'MAR HAMILTON: drummer, Knockout (and later, Plain White T's)
PAUL HANLY: New Brunswick basement show promoter
TARYN HICKEY: photographer
TOM HIGGENSON: front person, Plain White T's
ROB HITT: drummer, Midtown (and later, manager, Crush Music)
JEPH HOWARD: bassist, the Used
BEN JORGENSEN: front person, Armor for Sleep; drummer, Random Task
DUSTIN KENSRUE: front person, Thrice
MELISSA KUNDRATH: show promoter, the Bergenfield Girls
JOHN LEFLER: guitarist/keyboardist, Dashboard Confessional
SARAH LEWITINN: journalist, blogger DJ (alias, Ultragrrrl), cofounder/A&R, Stolen Transmission Records
ZACH LIND: drummer, Jimmy Eat World
COBY LINDER: drummer, Say Anything
JOLIE LINDHOLM: front person, the Rocking Horse Winner
JASON LINK: graphic designer, Victory Records and others; merch seller, Midtown
KEVIN LYMAN: founder and producer, Warped Tour; cofounder and producer, Taste of Chaos
AMY FLEISHER MADDEN: founder, Fiddler Records; zine maker, *Fiddler Jones*; author; photographer
STEPHANIE MARLOW: publicity, Victory Records
MIKE MARSH: drummer, Dashboard Confessional
BERT MCCRACKEN: front person, the Used
FINN MCKENTY: vlogger, journalist, graphic designer, zine maker
CHRISTIAN MCKNIGHT: talent buyer, Bamboozle, Skate and Surf, This Island Earth festivals (and previously, Long Island show promoter); radio host
ANDREW MCMAHON: front person, Something Corporate, Jack's Mannequin
TIM MCTAGUE: guitarist, Underoath
JOHNNY MINARDI: A&R, Fueled By Ramen
GRETA MORGAN: vocalist-keyboardist, the Hush Sound; zine maker, *Trash Magazine*
MANI MOSTOFI: front person, Racetraitor
TOM MULLEN: marketing, TVT Records, Equal Vision Records (and later, founder/podcaster, *Washed Up Emo*)
JILLIAN NEWMAN: manager, Taking Back Sunday
RANDY NICHOLS: manager, Underoath, Say Anything, the Starting Line
BUDDY NIELSEN: front person, Senses Fail
JOHN NOLAN: guitarist-vocalist, Taking Back Sunday; vocalist-multi-instrumentalist, Straylight Run
SEAN O'KEEFE: producer, Fall Out Boy, Arma Angelus
DENNIS ORTEGA: keyboardist, Madison
JENN PELLY: author and journalist (and Long Island native)
MATT PRYOR: front person, the Get Up Kids, the New Amsterdams
ANTHONY RANERI: front person, Bayside
TYLER RANN: vocalist-guitarist, Midtown
SCOTTIE REDIX: drummer and guitarist, The Stryder
RICHARD REINES: cofounder, Drive-Thru Records

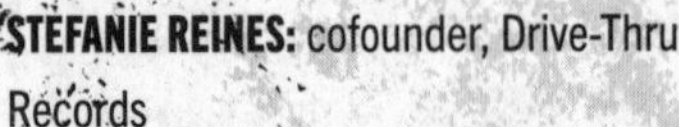

STEFANIE REINES: cofounder, Drive-Thru Records
ERIN RENDON: show promoter, The Bergenfield Girls
EDDIE REYES: guitarist, Taking Back Sunday (and previously, Mind Over Matter, Clockwise, Inside, the Movielife, Runner Up)
GEOFF RICKLY: front person, Thursday; New Brunswick basement show promoter; producer, My Chemical Romance
NEIL RUBENSTEIN: front person, Sons of Abraham, This Year's Model (and later, comedian)
MATTHEW ISMAEL RUIZ: journalist (and New Jersey native)
ALEX SAAVEDRA: cofounder, Eyeball Records
GABE SAPORTA: front person, Cobra Starship, Midtown (previously, bassist, Humble Beginnings)
RICKY SAPORTA: show promoter, Bomb Shelter Productions; photographer
HEATH SARACENO: vocalist-guitarist, Midtown (and later, Senses Fail)
WALTER SCHREIFELS: front person, Quicksand, Rival Schools; guitarist, Gorilla Biscuits, Youth of Today
TOM SCHLATTER: guitarist, You and I
NICK SCIMECA: drummer, 504 Plan (and later, designer, Clandestine Industries)
MARIA SHERMAN: journalist and author
LESLIE SIMON: author and journalist, *Alternative Press*
ADAM SISKA: bassist, The Academy Is . . .
JEFF SOSNOW: A&R, DreamWorks Records, Interscope Records
BRANDEN STEINECKERT: drummer, the Used
PATRICK STUMP: vocalist-guitarist, Fall Out Boy; solo artist; film scorer
JASON TATE: founder/blogger, AbsolutePunk.net
SHANE TOLD: front person, Silverstein
ADAM TURLA: front person, Murder by Death
KENNY VASOLI: front person, the Starting Line
MIKEY WAY: bassist, My Chemical Romance
PETE WENTZ: bassist, Fall Out Boy (and previously, bassist, Racetraitor; front person, Arma Angelus); founder, Decaydance Records, Clandestine Industries
HEATHER WEST: publicity, Victory Records
LUKE WOOD: A&R, DreamWorks Records, Interscope Records

NAPSTER, *THE* MUSIC BIZ & *THE* BIGGEST BAND *TO* COME OUT *OF* MESA, ARIZONA

MIKEY WAY: Saves the Day at Maxwell's in Hoboken for *Stay What You Are* in 2001, that was an important show. Me and my brother were there. Saves the Day were at their apex, absolutely at the top of their game. I remember my brother just being floored. Everybody already knew the album before it dropped. The whole crowd was singing every word, because they had downloaded it two weeks ago on Napster.

IAN COHEN: 2000 was like the last year of the nineties instead of the first year of the 2000s, if that makes any sense. 2001 was something new.

ANDY GREENWALD: It was the last days of the old empire. The people running the music industry were, by and large, the people who had been running it for the last twenty years or longer.

LUKE WOOD: By '98, piracy was starting to become a real conversation. It didn't really hit the P&L—profit and loss—of the labels until the early 2000s. Everyone saw it but they were still selling CDs, so no one wanted to deal with it.

TOM MULLEN: The peak of CD sales was '99 and 2000. After that, it was a precipitous drop.

JEFF SOSNOW: Were we concerned about file sharing in the year 2000? I think labels were still doing well and there was a lot of denial. The music business has a tendency towards denial.

ANDY GREENWALD: The music industry was in a very fraught position. Even if the most powerful people didn't fully grasp what Napster meant or what was around the corner, there was a sense of uncertainty, that something destabilizing was coming. That the things you used to be able to count on couldn't be counted on anymore.

IAN COHEN: There was a sense of "something needs to happen" because rock music seemed a bit stale. It was the tail end of nu metal. Creed was still huge at that time. 2000 was just a sense of trying to figure out what the next thing was going to be and no one really knew.

ANDY GREENWALD: Remember, it had only been about ten years since grunge.

LUKE WOOD: Nirvana was the natural articulation of years of American underground rock, going back to the Velvet Underground in 1967. Finally, it all happened. It landed. A lot of people who grew up with underground music got jobs at major labels. But it ended up being a fad. Like dubstep. By the end of the nineties, you had rap-rock, hip-hop, Eminem, the explosion of NSYNC, Backstreet Boys, Britney Spears—real pop, you know? So as we're trying to figure out what the next thing is, there weren't a lot of people left at major labels to understand what *it* was.

ANDY GREENWALD: We were coming out of this very glossy time of the Backstreet Boys and Britney and rap-rock. And there was the half-step fizzle of "new rock," whatever that was. Like the Strokes and the White Stripes, which was fine, but was really more of a pipe creation of the magazines who desperately wanted people in leather jackets to put on their covers again.

IAN COHEN: The Strokes and White Stripes were around, but Linkin Park and all those rap-metal bands were way more popular.

ANDY GREENWALD: What made people so excited about emo was, *Did we get lucky again?* Did we leave the underground undisturbed long enough for something significant to take root that we could now reap the benefits of? For people who were veterans of magazines and MTV, there was a sense that things move cyclically and there would always be the next new thing to sustain their jobs . . . I guess you could say their interests and passions, but really, it's their jobs. That was the subtext for the emo boom, or almost-boom: Can we squeeze a few more drops out of this rock and roll lemon?

IAN COHEN: As far as emo goes, it had a couple of false starts.

WALTER SCHREIFELS: With nineties Dischord bands going to majors, there were some great ones: Jawbox, Shudder to Think. I think Shudder to Think probably got the most hype, and they got a lot of money to make records.

MICHAEL GOLDSTONE: There was certainly a line in the sand between indie artists and major labels.

LUKE WOOD: What major labels were good for at the time was distribution and radio. Other than that, you didn't need them. There was no point. Right after Nirvana when I was working at DGC Geffen, we signed so many bands like Jawbreaker. I mean, just the pain of watching [Jawbreaker front person] Blake [Schwarzenbach], being in the room with him trying to understand, "What the fuck am I doing with my career? Why am I on this label? Why are these people out here sipping vodka cranberry and wondering what time Aerosmith goes on later?"

MICHAEL GOLDSTONE: When it came to my attention that Shudder to Think was looking to make a step, I spent an inordinate amount of time making sure that was really the case, which it was. I reached out to Ian MacKaye and took a train down to DC and had lunch with him. I remember Ian walking me through the whole world he had created. At one point we had the philosophical conversation. He said, "My responsibility is to get these artists started and if there are aspirational things they want, they should go to a place they think can do that for them. I'm not changing my business model."

WALTER SCHREIFELS: Shudder to Think had a song called "Red House"—that was a fucking pop song, should have been a huge hit. They rerecorded it like three times trying to make it a hit. That would have been the "Smells Like Teen Spirit" of emo. But it just didn't happen.

IAN COHEN: Jawbreaker went to Geffen and broke up. Jimmy Eat World was not getting anywhere on Capitol in the nineties.

ZACH LIND: We were maybe the lowest priority on the entire label.

LUKE WOOD: At the start of the 2000s, I was vice president of A&R at DreamWorks. I was extremely nervous, hyper-reluctant about putting more bands in the major label system that didn't belong there. It was always my weakness. Or strength. Who knows. I heard Capitol was dropping Jimmy Eat World.

ANDY GREENWALD: I had known about them as the band that got signed during the previous emo boom and had crapped out completely. No one understood their ambition or why they had done this and that and everybody knew Christie Front Drive and Mineral were the real stars of that era, blah, blah, blah.

RICKY SAPORTA: Jimmy Eat World was one of those bands where the people who liked them—and this may not have been a large quantity of people—but people who liked them fucking LOVED them. People loved *Clarity*. My wife's AIM screen name was xClarityx.

MIKEY WAY: Within our world, they were one of the largest bands. But our world was still very small and insular.

MELISSA KUNDRATH: Jimmy Eat World was the first band I listened to where the songs were longer than three minutes. We were listening to fast pop-punk when I heard *Clarity* for the first time. It took me till a few years later to really understand what they were doing. Those songs are so gorgeous and beautiful.

TOM MULLEN: *Clarity* came out in 1999 and the fans that were out there loved it. And it made a little bit of a splash with "Lucky Denver Mint."

RICH EGAN: "Lucky Denver Mint" was kind of a hit for a hot minute for them on KROQ but it didn't go all the way. So between making the friggin' masterpiece that was *Clarity* and getting dropped, I don't think anyone saw what was coming next.

JIM ADKINS: How were we feeling about being dropped by Capitol? Oh, we didn't care. We were on tour, man! That stuff doesn't matter, we're on tour!

ANDY GREENWALD: They just rebooted.

CHRIS CARRABBA: Jimmy Eat World became scene heroes for forging ahead, even without a label.

JIM ADKINS: From our perspective, things were getting better and better. We would show up in a town and there'd be a little bit more people or we would get offered a slightly better support slot for a bigger band. And then that kept slowly building and building and building. We knew that wasn't because Capitol's street team had done such a kick-ass job. We were out there building it for ourselves. It was always funny—we'd be selling our records and shit and there'd be some dude with his distro of zines and then we'd plop down our record with a big Capitol logo on it. People were like "What?" But I mean, they see us sleeping on the same floors as them and then we got a pass.

ERIN RENDON: We got to see Jimmy Eat World at a show Ricky put on at the Wayne Firehouse.

RICKY SAPORTA: It was October 2000. Literally a firehouse that had a hall you could rent, tucked away from the neighborhood. It was definitely the largest show I did at the time—eight hundred to a thousand people.

CHRIS CARRABBA: Ricky booked me for that show at the Wayne Firehouse in New Jersey. I was a massive Jimmy Eat World fan. I am still a massive Jimmy Eat World fan. I might be the biggest Jimmy Eat World fan. I had already followed them on tour once, every show they did in Florida and then up to Georgia. I don't remember anything from that show at the Wayne Firehouse other than, "I got to see Jimmy Eat World."

There were about five bands in between us. I got my stuff offstage as fast as I could so I could stake out a place to stand to watch Jimmy Eat World. They played songs off *Static Prevails* and *Clarity*, and some new songs.

JIM ADKINS: We probably played "Sweetness" and "Bleed American." Maybe "A Praise Chorus."

MIKEY WAY: I was there and it was sold out. I remember watching them play like, "Why aren't these guys the biggest band in the world?"

MELISSA KUNDRATH: We were used to seeing a band like At the Drive-In jump up and down and tear shit apart. And Jimmy Eat World just stood there and played their instruments. And you know, they were a little older. And they came from far away.

ZACH LIND: We lived in Mesa, Arizona. It's about twenty, thirty minutes outside of Phoenix. Pretty normal suburb. Not a lot going on. Not a lot of culture happening.

JIM ADKINS: You could just drive and not realize you're in a new municipality unless you're paying attention to what the street signs look like, or you get pulled over. It's just like, "Oh, I guess we're in Tempe now. Oh, I guess we're in Chandler."

TOM MULLEN: We didn't have Google Maps or anything. You just saw the word "Phoenix," or "Mesa," or "Tempe." And you're like, "I don't know what the hell that is or what that means, I just know that's not near me. There's maybe palm trees, and it's hot."

LUKE WOOD: Zach was working at a Mercedes dealership driving shuttles for customers.

JIM ADKINS: I worked at an art supply shop. It was actually really good for me, because I would quit my job there, I would go on tour, and when I came back, they would just hire me again because I had most of the SKU numbers memorized: PM1 is a Prismacolor blender pen. EF1005 is a medium-sized kneaded eraser.

ANDY GREENWALD: They funded their own tour, funded the recording of what would become *Bleed American*.

JIM ADKINS: After producing *Static Prevails* and *Clarity*, Mark Trombino agreed to do the new record basically for free, upfront, and we'd figure it out later. We didn't have the money to pay for the studio time.

We would literally go into the Capitol tower, go to the college radio department, take every single promo copy of our records, and then ship those to Germany to sell 'em over there. So when we got to our first German show, there were four hundred kids there. We felt like putting some of the songs we were working on for *Bleed American* on Napster would be the easiest way for European fans to hear what we were doing.

ZACH LIND: When we were on Capitol, we tracked a version of "Sweetness" we were hoping Capitol would want to put on *Clarity*. They didn't want it.

JIM ADKINS: We'd go to Europe and there would be people who knew all the words to "Sweetness." The only way they could have heard that was through Napster. Like, "Oh, man, this is really gonna be a thing. This internet is really gonna be a thing, you guys!"

JOLIE LINDHOLM: Napster was like a weird musical social media. It felt sneaky—it was a way to get your band's music out.

CHRIS CARRABBA: It happened in our corner of the music scene earlier than most other places. It was an exciting place to be. You felt like you were living in the future and everybody else was living in the past.

ANDY GREENWALD: I remember when those Jimmy Eat World songs hit Napster before the record came out.

JOLIE LINDHOLM: There are very few albums I can listen to front to back without skipping anything, and for me that's *Clarity*. For me, that was the best album they could write. When I heard the *Bleed American* demos, I was kind of disappointed because I wanted it to be a little less . . . pop?

LUKE WOOD: Jim's performance on the new songs was this amazing, poignant rock vocal. Incredible harmonies. He just went to a place where he sounds super polished. He started pointing at that with *Clarity*, but on *Bleed American* he just embraced it. He said, "You know what, I'm not gonna worry about, do I sound like Slint or Rodan or, you know, am I gonna be cool?" He just went and said, "I'm just gonna sing the shit out of the top line of these melodies that I wrote about being in love and not being loved."

JIM ADKINS: I started having panic attacks in '99 when we were on tour for *Clarity*. The way I knew how to deal with it was to write about it. The song "Bleed American" is basically like . . . literal. It's literal! I was trying to figure out what to do with panic attacks while at my parents' house with the TV on, so I didn't feel like I was alone.

ZACH LIND: Aside from me, everyone in the band is naturally very guarded. We have a hard time feeling out permission to be like, "Hey, what's going on here?" Like, you know, clue us in.

JIM ADKINS: How you deal with it now is you do the work and acquire tools to help you deal with it. How you deal with it back then is . . . you drink, ha, ha, ha. Which is totally socially acceptable and almost expected of you.

ZACH LIND: You can enter the music business with a firm center of gravity mentally and not have any issues, but there's elements to this industry that can definitely trigger them.

You're a dude in a band going on tour getting massive amounts of affirmation every day. You know, everything around is just affirming and almost worshipping the person, and then, all of a sudden, the tour is over. And you go home. And you have nothing to do all day. You feel aimless. It's this weird . . . you're reentering a different atmosphere. And you have to take precautions, like, how do you manage that?

JIM ADKINS: I had a little home recording setup in my room. I bought one of Zach's old drum sets and I was trying to teach myself drums, because it's fun. One of the few beats I could play was the Tom Petty "You Wreck Me" beat. It's so simple, but like it has this undeniable YES to it.

Then I started messing around with guitar. I came up with a melody, and wrote most of the lyrics in a day. I remembered that on *Static Prevails*, we thought we were being all future-forward and put an email address in the liner notes. There was a girl who wrote us, explaining how she felt like an outsider at her school because the punk rock kids wouldn't accept her, even though she liked us and a lot of the really obscure bands we toured with. And I just thought, "It's not worth your time to trip on this. Punk rock is and should be inclusive. That's the one thing I know. No matter what your definition of punk is, everyone would say that it's inclusive, it welcomes outsiders. Freak flags welcome. Wave 'em around. These chicks don't get it at all, don't waste your time trying to get their approval." That's where the main idea for the lyrics to "The Middle" came from.

And at that time, I was starting to get into Bruce Springsteen. I had this autographed *Tunnel of Love* promotional flat that an ex-girlfriend gave me hanging above my recording setup. I was stuck with the chorus and I thought of that scene in *High Fidelity*, where John Cusack is like, "What would the Boss do?" And the Boss would say, "Little girl, you're in the middle of the ride, everything will be all right."

LUKE WOOD: I was wishy-washy at the time Jimmy Eat World started recording *Bleed American*. Then I remember I went to Portland working with Elliott Smith and I played a cassette of the final demos, and the songs were so obviously incredible. I wanted to sign them then. But they were hesitant.

RICH EGAN: They had big ambitions for that record. They went straight-up like, "We're making a pop record that's all hits and we're gonna sell it to the highest bidder."

JIM ADKINS: We reached out to the handful of contacts we knew and invited people to come down and hear the new album. Richard and Stefanie from Drive-Thru Records, they came by, we were buddies with them. Drive-Thru was distributed by MCA at the time, and oh man, their main executive contact person at MCA came by to hear stuff. I can't remember the guy's name. He lays out this spiel for us about how MCA works really close with Drive-Thru. He was just there to humor Richard and Stefanie, I think. We played him "Bleed American," "A Praise Chorus," "The Middle," and I think "If You Don't, Don't." He was like, "I'll be back tomorrow." And he brought the president of MCA. He's like, "This is not coming out on Drive-Thru, if this comes to us, this is coming out on MCA." So we had the president of MCA rolling by a couple of times and then the word started getting out.

RICHARD REINES: They didn't sign them. They said it was too much money. That's how dumb MCA was. Typical.

JIM ADKINS: It seemed like almost every other afternoon we had some industry person coming by to hang out or to pitch us and it got to the point where like it's like, "Okay, we really need a manager first because we don't know what the hell we're doing. All these labels want a piece of this and we're not getting the family H&R Block lawyer to do the deal with us this time."

After meeting with a few different managers, we went with John Silva. It's funny, because Gary Gersh was part of his management team at that time, and Gary Gersh was the president of Capitol when we were on Capitol. I think Gary might have felt a little bit of, uh . . . he might have felt some responsibility to get us a really great deal.

LUKE WOOD: What other labels were into them? All.

JIM ADKINS: What's really funny is Capitol was one of them. We were like, "Okay, for us to take a meeting with you, you have to give us back our masters and zero out our balance." They were like, "Nah, we can't do that." Like, okay!

ZACH LIND: We ended up meeting with a bunch of labels in New York: Sire, Atlantic, RCA. We're flying into New York, the sun is setting and dancing off the buildings of downtown Manhattan. I'm thinking, "Man, coming from where we came from, now we're flying into New York City where we're meeting with a bunch of labels, who are basically in a bidding war."

LUKE WOOD: I was fortunate that I spent a fair amount of time with Mark Trombino and the band.

JIM ADKINS: We had a little history with Luke. He was a fan from afar when he was coming up in DGC, and then over at DreamWorks.

LUKE WOOD: I think we closed the deal before mixing was done.

MICHAEL GOLDSTONE: DreamWorks was able to compete financially with anyone.

JEFF SOSNOW: I know the deal was competitive. Maybe more importantly, those guys were probably impressed with the roster DreamWorks was building at the time: Elliott Smith, Eels, Rufus Wainwright.

LUKE WOOD: I think Jimmy Eat World was a seven-figure deal, could have been a little less. I remember it was at least three albums firm. And Jimmy had a lot of cool things built into the contract, because we knew how we wanted to market the record: independent promotion, tour support, guaranteed video budgets.

ZACH LIND: When it was all on us, we delivered.

JIM ADKINS: We had no idea what was possible. I knew we were gonna make some videos. That's about it. I knew we were gonna make some videos and I knew they were going to "work it at radio." Which, I had no idea what that entailed.

LUKE WOOD: "The Middle" wasn't one that really wowed me as a demo. It was cool, but it was like a palm-muted, Bruce Springsteen-y, John Cougar Mellencamp song, you know? Like, "We'll see how this lands!"

JIM ADKINS: The idea of a single breaking out . . . I spent zero time contemplating that. I thought "The Middle" was one of the weaker songs on the record, at the time, because it came together so easily. I think there's a tendency as a creative person to put less value on something that happens easily. It was four hours' time at most.

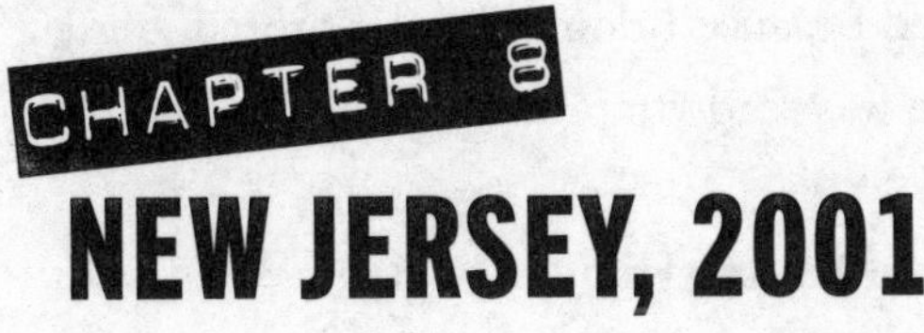

NEW JERSEY, 2001

WARNING: THIS CHAPTER CONTAINS DISCUSSION OF SUICIDE.

MIKE GITTER: New Jersey is a place with a chip on its shoulder. It's Springsteen singing "Jungleland." It's Danzig at the Chiller Theatre Expo [the horror and sci-fi convention], selling 45s. It's that famous scene in *Cop Land* where they're looking out over the river to Manhattan. It's a place of unrequited dreamers. But occasionally there's the ones who get out.

GEOFF RICKLY: Thursday got a chance to tour on [our 1999 record] *Waiting*. We played a kitchen in Atlanta, where a production crew was pulling away because they had just been filming an incident for *COPS*. We were like, "Wait, does this mean that show is real? Was there just a crime?" So we played this black-and-white-tiled kitchen to one person. We walked downstairs and there's a huge card game of like sixteen people who didn't even watch us play.

We played a lot of places that were like a dream to us. We played Wilson Center in DC, which was a Fugazi spot. We got to play down in Gainesville and stay with the Hot Water Music guys.

TARYN HICKEY: Thursday didn't start out like, "We're gonna be huge in the emo world!" That wasn't a thing.

GEOFF RICKLY: Gabe would run into a diner and see me and start singing a Thursday song at the top of his lungs. I'd be like, "Oh my god . . ."

I'd be embarrassed and annoyed because I don't like self-promotion; I don't like being loud. But Gabe was ready to promote us when I didn't want to.

GABE SAPORTA: Eyeball Records put out the Humble Beginnings EP, so I knew Alex Saavedra. I gave him the Thursday cassette and he signed them and released *Waiting*.

ALEX SAAVEDRA: Eyeball Records started in 1995 in New York, on Fourteenth Street and Avenue A, back when that neighborhood was super fucking dangerous. Tourists wouldn't go down there. By the time *Waiting* came out, I was living out of my Chevy Blazer. I didn't have enough room to sleep in it and had all these boxes of CDs so they'd let me keep them in the basement of Generation Records on Thompson Street in Manhattan. Sometimes I would stay in the basement but the thing was, they'd drop the gates and I'd have to get locked in. And I would always get paranoid that the place would catch fire or something and I wouldn't be able to get out of there. So I didn't sleep there too often.

Then we moved the label out of the city to Kearny, New Jersey, in 2000. It was pretty affordable and the landlord was this gazillion-year-old woman who for some reason took a liking to me and never bothered us about anything. Back then, Kearny was such a weird place to be: it's between Jersey City and Newark, these two poverty-stricken, often dangerous areas, and we're right in the middle. But moving to Jersey was an awesome thing for us. It was cheaper. It was still only six miles from Manhattan. We were able to grow a lot easier.

GEOFF RICKLY: Anybody could stay in his huge house. And people could stay for weeks, months. Bands could just live there while they were figuring out who they were.

ALEX SAAVEDRA: It's just funny to think that while releasing *Waiting*, this pivotal first Thursday record, I was like a literal homeless kid putting out the record. I wouldn't say it was rags to riches, but rags to . . . better rags? My parents were Cuban immigrants; I'm first-generation American. I didn't come from money or anything like that.

JOANNA ANGEL: Alex Eyeball didn't live in New Brunswick and it's funny looking back because New Brunswick was so punk rock snobby . . . To me, the bands on Eyeball were . . . I'm not gonna say sellouts, but they were too big, you know what I mean? Ha, ha, ha. To me and my friends growing up it was like, "Oh my god, Alex Eyeball is so rich." Which is so funny, because he was just like, a dude with a job. He had a BMW and I had never seen a BMW before. They were living the high life, ha, ha, ha, ha. I was more in the scene where we went to protests.

GEOFF RICKLY: "Take care of everybody" was always his thing. Alex was like a larger-than-life older brother.

ALEX SAAVEDRA: I knew the feeling of not having anywhere to go, so I just shared it with everyone. So many different people lived there: Tucker from Thursday. Mikey Way. Over twenty-five people must've called that place home at one time or another. We had a room that was basically for anyone to come and go and then for the rest of the house, like, "Find a spot you're comfortable in and you can sleep in it."

ADAM TURLA: He would always show interesting movies when we stayed at his house. He had a huge collection of *Simpsons* action figures.

MIKEY WAY: The Eyeball House was a revolving door of this cast of characters.

PAUL HANLY: It was a madhouse, Alex's version of *Animal House*.

ADAM TURLA: You would walk up a flight of stairs and then you'd be in the hallway; if you went to the left, there was a living room with a table and a TV, his bedroom was to the center, and the kitchen was to the right. And there was an upstairs area that just had his office. So it was a small quarters–type situation.

ALEX SAAVEDRA: When we had parties, there were definitely times you could feel the floor of the house kind of sagging. You'd have to be like, "All right, we need forty people to move outside."

PAUL HANLY: Always a party, always a shitshow, always a shithole, ha, ha, ha. Bands would play different rooms. They utilized every space they had.

GEOFF RICKLY: The parties were crazy. It was hundreds and hundreds of people, from every walk of life. One day, the guy at the keg would be Mike Judge—like, Mike from Judge, straight-edge Judge, at the keg. Like,

"What's going on?" You never knew who was gonna come. Alex is just one of those people that knew everybody.

ADAM TURLA: I remember him hyping up parties: "Oh you gotta go, so-and-so's coming." He used them for networking, as well as frickin' partying. That was a very exciting thing to be a part of, because there was just nothing back in Indiana [where I'm from] that felt like you were part of anything other than kids hanging out, making music. Which is great, but the Eyeball House had this very legitimate veneer of, *There's shit goin' down here*.

ALEX SAAVEDRA: I knew Gerard and Mikey Way for years, since the mid-nineties. I met Gerard first. He went to school at SVA with my friend, and they were both there for comics, for illustration. So that's how I got to know Gerard. And then Mikey was the little brother who became the communal little brother, everyone's little brother.

MIKEY WAY: It was like having a bunch of rad uncles.

GEOFF RICKLY: Mikey Way was my homey, we would hang out all the time there. Mikey was always like, "We're gonna have a band, we're gonna have a band." And I'd just be like, "I've heard this dude talk about being in a band a hundred times. It's clear that he's never going to be in a band."

ALEX SAAVEDRA: Mikey walked around like he was Mr. Burns. He was like, you know, real feeble looking. We'd be like, "Stand up straight! Now, do this! Go talk to that girl, you like her!"

GEOFF RICKLY: Gerard didn't like to come to parties. I'd be like, "Mikey, where's your brother?" He's like, "Probably home drawing comic books in his underwear."

ALEX SAAVEDRA: Gerard dressed like a fucking nerd. You know, nerdy T-shirts and jeans that didn't really fit well. He was a little chubby. He wasn't wearing a leather jacket and fucking motorcycle boots, I'll tell ya that much. A total homebody. He would lock himself in his room, smoke like a thousand packs of cigarettes, and just draw comic books. And even at that time, he had some cool shit going on. He worked at DC for a minute and had a short comic publish through DC. Then he got offered a gig with Marvel for *Spider-Man*. And I'll never forget this, he was so concerned about *Spider-Man* fans not liking his style that he actually walked away from it, because he didn't have the confidence.

MIKEY WAY: A lot of bands in our scene would come to the Eyeball House and stay from out of town. I just watched and studied what they all did. Especially their work ethic, the relentless touring.

GEOFF RICKLY: Alex had a really good ear. He would take big bets on bands, spend literally the whole budget of the label on a record. I'd be like, "You're insane, dude, you're gonna lose this house." And then it would work.

MIKEY WAY: A lot of exciting things were always happening.

ALEX SAAVEDRA: Thursday did the one record on Eyeball. They had a great following locally, and then nationally. I wasn't gonna hold my friends back, so we started approaching other labels.

GEOFF RICKLY: Thursday played with some really strange bands at Wetlands in Manhattan—we opened up for Black Star, which was Talib Kweli and Mos Def. We played so early that there were about three people in the crowd, but we just went fucking bananas as if the place was packed. This A&R guy from Island Records happened to be there: "I don't even know who you were trying to impress but that was amazing, here's my card." We were like, whatever.

ALEX SAAVEDRA: I was friends with this girl Genevieve at Victory Records.

FINN MCKENTY: Victory was the first label to professionalize hardcore, to package it as a product.

MONI MOSTOFI: Victory became the most important hardcore label in the country, around 1993 or 1994 when they put out Earth Crisis, Snapcase, and Strife, the biggest up-and-coming hardcore bands.

I remember seeing really early Thursday shows that were just five people and Tony Brummel. I think he got Thursday because he started hiring people at Victory that had a sense of what was next.

GEOFF RICKLY: "Throw Genevieve a bone and sign this fucking band that probably sucks." That was Victory's attitude when they signed Thursday.

MANI MOSTOFI: Tony was like the dad trying to be cool at the shows. He was kind of a bro, and the scene was much more progressive at that point than he was. It had already surpassed him in terms of politics and vision, and he was out of place.

GEOFF RICKLY: I remember going around to other Victory bands like Grade and BoySetsFire: "Hey, we just signed to Victory, we're gonna be labelmates!" And everyone's like, "Oh, you fucked up. Your life is gonna be hell." And I was like, "They're definitely like . . . hazing us, I guess? This is a hazing thing." They're like, "Nah, man, you're fucked. They treat you like shit." And then Genevieve stopped working there, so we didn't have a champion or anything.

So we recorded *Full Collapse* . . .

TOMMY CORRIGAN: So much of early 2000s emo, it's all music about chicks, 100 percent. Like every song is a relationship song or a love song. Thursday was still on the fringes of being a hardcore band. They had a different message.

GEOFF RICKLY: Writing lyrics for *Full Collapse*, I was like, I need to deal with some shit that really fucked me up. Some things I think I buried when I started listening to angry music and lifting weights, you know?

"How Long Is the Night?" is about my French partner in high school. He had just moved there and his father was the vice principal. He got caught stealing money from the vending machines that he was supposed to collect. There was an assembly and his father screamed at him in front of the whole school, where he was still new and nobody knew him. After that, he laid down on the train tracks behind the high school. There was blood everywhere. It didn't come off for two or three weeks and I'd have to cross those tracks every morning to get to school. I'd hear the train whistle every night and just couldn't sleep thinking about it.

"Understanding in a Car Crash" . . . I was meeting one of my best friends and her best friend, who I was dating. They were in Bergenfield, New Jersey; we were in Dumont. We had open lunches in our high schools and we would drive and meet at the McDonald's in between our schools, as corny as it sounds, you know. And one day, they didn't show up. Later on that day, we found out there was a big accident. People said it was her car. My friend passed away. And the girl I was dating was really horribly injured. There's a lot of stuff about that too in "Cross Out the Eyes," about being in hospitals: the amount of time we spent in hospitals and also like, stealing drugs from people and trying to forget about stuff. Mental health wasn't prioritized the way it is now. So a bit of self-medication was the only real option that I saw for myself. It left a huge imprint on me. *Full Collapse* is really a survey of all the stuff that was banging around in my head.

TOM SCHLATTER: When they started to record *Full Collapse*, they asked if I could come down and do some screams. We're recording at this studio in Jersey City and the first thing they put on was "Autobiography of a Nation." Geoff's like, "All right, Tom, all I need you to do is in the chorus. You scream the emphasis parts. And here's all the words to the song, if you feel inspired to add things, go ahead and try it." The producer Sal Villanueva runs the tape and gives us the go-ahead. Geoff would sing a line and I would scream behind it. The tape stops. And Sal's like, 'This is fucking amazing. I've never heard something like this before. Geoff's melodically singing, and you're screaming behind it. The contrast is awesome."

GEOFF RICKLY: I remember handing in *Full Collapse* to Victory Records. They were like, "'Cross Out the Eyes' isn't bad . . . but the rest of it's pretty bad. And there's definitely no single on the record."

HEATHER WEST: *Full Collapse* was already out about six months when I got to Victory; I was handling a lot of licensing stuff. I know there was already tension between Tony and the band. It wasn't so much that nobody at the label was supporting them. Because everybody was working really hard for them. It was more like financial tension with Tony.

ALEX SAAVEDRA: Tony was all business—no matter who you're offending, no matter whose artistic integrity you're taking away, he was always there for the money.

FINN MCKENTY: I've known people in Victory bands since the mid-nineties. I've never heard a single person say anything good about Tony, ever, in almost thirty years.

GEOFF RICKLY: I think we sold like seven hundred copies of *Full Collapse* when it came out. And everybody's like, "You're basically done."

TOM SCHLATTER: Right after *Full Collapse* came out in 2001, Thursday agreed to play an all-day show I was helping put together at a place called the M&M Hall in Old Bridge, New Jersey. I remember it being on Mother's Day because we had to rent the hall through a woman named Sue who was a mom. So we made a big card for her and we all signed it.

That was the first show I saw a lot of people singing along to them. Like, "Oh wow, people like this new album, this band is probably gonna get really big." I think that was the last show where I didn't go through Thursday's booking agent or management; I just called Geoff and asked, "Do you wanna play the show?" That was like the end of the era. From now on they're not going to fit in a place like this, they're probably going to be playing Club Krome or something.

At the end of the night, after paying for the hall and the PA, I had like four hundred bucks left. I went up to Geoff and said, "There's two touring bands we have to pay, how much do you guys want?" And Geoff was like, "You're not gonna pay us, we live here." "You sure?" "Yeah." That was the mentality.

GEOFF RICKLY: Slowly things started looking up. We were getting bigger tour offers. First, we went out opening for Midtown. Then BoySetsFire asked us out on tour—that was the one where we were actually winning people over every night.

BEN JORGENSEN: I would talk to Geoff about books after shows. I can't imagine a better influence on me at that age. I don't think I'll ever comprehend how much it meant to me. He knew I was extra interested in trying to figure out how he wrote songs.

JASON TATE: I remember the first time sitting down to read the lyrics in the liner notes to *Full Collapse* and thinking, "This is unlike anything I've seen anybody write. Like, where did this dude come from? This is unreal." Going from listening to something like Blink-182 and then hearing *Full Collapse* . . . holy shit.

BUDDY NIELSEN: That album is the perfect mix of hardcore and melody. Like, "I don't really wanna go hang out with people on a Friday night, I think I'm just gonna drive around and listen to *Full Collapse*." It came out my senior year and it just changed my life. I vividly remember not going to a party on a Friday night to just listen to *Full Collapse*, alone. Which is a pretty emo thing to do. Shun social interaction and just listen to music.

JASON LINK: Thursday was the band that everyone was talking about online, in chat rooms, on AOL Instant Messenger. Everyone's putting up their away messages with "Cross Out the Eyes" lyrics, you know? This is pre-MySpace. Blogs were a big thing, like LiveJournal, Xanga. I had my own website where I'd show off my design stuff, but I also had my own little journal to talk about my day, with some "song of the day" or some emo lyric in there. It was called Keyboard Confessionals.

MATTHEW ISMAEL RUIZ: You'd become a fan of a band, right? They have some sort of web presence, but it was web 1.0. It was outward: The band had the site, they put the information on, and then it spread. And maybe there would be a forum that people could talk about stuff. But so much of it was analog.

ANDY GREENWALD: Message board culture was thriving. Songs that only you knew or feelings you didn't feel comfortable sharing with people in your day-to-day life suddenly became accessible to everyone. Now seeing how the internet has turned out, I feel pretty gullible in a way, but at the time, it felt very pure. Very sweet. It felt like maybe the internet would be the great equalizer and bring art to the suburbs and bring subculture to people who needed it. And people who didn't even realize they needed it.

MATTHEW ISMAEL RUIZ: You found VFW hall shows on message boards.

BUDDY NIELSEN: A really important part of all this was this website called NJ Ska. It turned into TheNJScene.com. It was my first experience with what would become social media. People would spread information about local shows, talk about record trading.

DENNIS ORTEGA: This was like a miniature version of Reddit, but specifically for New Jersey punk and hardcore. It was a good year or two before I decided I hated everybody on that message board.

BUDDY NIELSEN: And that is literally where Senses Fail started.

DENNIS ORTEGA: Senses Fail got into more fights than any band I've ever seen. Ninety-five percent of the drama was "this band doesn't like this band" or "this guy called someone's girlfriend a whore." Stuff you'd get called a keyboard warrior for now because you're never gonna meet someone that you talk shit to online. Back then there were repercussions for it, because you would run into that person at Wayne Firehouse or something. And they were probably going to talk shit to you. And Senses Fail were the fucking kings of that. They talked shit to everyone.

A bunch of bands came out of those message boards: Senses Fail, Paulson, Folly, Armor for Sleep.

BEN JORGENSEN: I wrote a song on the first Armor for Sleep album called "My Town," about where I grew up in Teaneck, in Bergen County. It was about a five-minute walk to a bus stop and then a three-dollar bus ride into Port Authority in the city. Teaneck at night is this still-life, this really peaceful place. I remember walking around when everyone was asleep. It's quite beautiful with all the old streets and streetlights, like France in the nineteenth century. It was a big part of my growing up having those images imprinted on my brain. At the same time, it can feel a little suffocating to think you're gonna be there the rest of your life.

MIKEY WAY: I started going to the bar scene and these shows in Manhattan. It was the beginning of Strokes mania.

ROB HITT: New York was still a little dirty, a little scary . . . *If you go on the subway after a certain hour, be careful not to get robbed.* That was the perception people in the suburbs were given, from the news, from parents.

GABE SAPORTA: The Strokes, the Rapture, all this hipster New York dance rock shit was going on at the time . . . Which I love, by the way.

PAUL HANLY: Both Way brothers' interest in music, they were hugely into the Britpop stuff, Bowie for sure . . .

MIKEY WAY: I started seeing kids I saw from Jersey shows at Don Hill's. It was this other happening that was going on across the river.

SARAH LEWITINN: One of the biggest parties in New York we all cut our teeth at was Tiswas.

PAUL HANLY: Tiswas was a dance night at Don Hill's, in the SoHo area.

ROB HITT: After college, before I moved to the city, I moved to Montgomery, New Jersey, in 2001. It was about an hour and a half drive to Tiswas. I remember . . . *ugggh* . . . driving through the woods before you finally get on a highway. Sometimes you'd go to Sarah's house to pre-party. I remember doing one or two or three vodka sodas, having to drink them before eleven thirty because I needed to be sober to drive home when Tiswas shut down at four.

MIKEY WAY: I had seen the Strokes play in Don Hill's, where they did Tiswas. Tiswas was a really important party to me because I was working at a Barnes & Noble in New Jersey and my manager was super into Britpop . . .

SARAH LEWITINN: Brian Molloy was Mikey Way's boss for a while. He was more famously known as Suit Guy. At Tiswas, he was the guy who got onstage at like 10:00 p.m., until 4:00 a.m., miming the lyrics to every song that was DJed. I don't know if he was ever paid or what, but he was a fucking vibe master. He would disarm people and have a good time.

MIKEY WAY: I would ride with Brian to Tiswas. He always had me work Saturday night with him because when our shift was over, I would get in the car with him, and sometimes we would take the PATH.

SARAH LEWITINN: Mikey was like, "See that guy? That's my boss!" And I was like, "No! Shut up! *What's he like???*" I was like, so excited. That was a very, very big celebrity moment.

The stage would start off with just Suit Guy and then more people would go onstage until there's probably more people onstage than on the floor.

PAUL HANLY: Everyone at the time playing the cooler, New York indie stuff was playing at Don Hill's. I saw the Yeah Yeah Yeahs there. I saw Interpol there.

MIKEY WAY: Carlos D. was a regular at Don Hill's. I remember taking note of how well I thought he was dressed. He looked like he just stepped out of London in the mid-eighties. Best-dressed dude in the room, always. I was like, "He's got to be in a band, you know what I mean?" People were like, "He's in Interpol." And I'm like, "Oh! I've seen that name around."

SARAH LEWITINN: They'd have the Strokes, the Realistics, and stuff like that play there. But knowing people like Mikey and Rob, the music they were playing versus the music they were into was so different. I think they all wanted to be in Blur and Oasis and Radiohead, but they were all in, like, Lifetime.

ANTHONY RANERI: Our scene was all honesty and grit and basements and connection. And that scene was, like, drugs, and sort of the revival of glam rock. They were like rock stars. They wore ripped clothes; they were selling what we were doing. But they weren't living it, you know?

That's where "emo" as a dirty word I feel comes from, from hipsters, because it's not as cool as the Strokes. Nothing's as cool as the Strokes, though, you know what I mean? The Strokes are like, the coolest band. They just sell cool. To this day, so many people try to fight off that emo tag. It's because of those early 2000s hipsters thinking it's not cool.

MIKEY WAY: Those shows felt like a party. Everybody dressed well. You know, perfectly tailored suits, leather jackets, and denim jackets. Everyone looks super mod. Whereas the Jersey scene was post-hardcore bands' T-shirts, parks and recreation shirts from the Salvation Army, or vintage rock and roll T-shirts . . . vintage, *ironic* rock and roll T-shirts.

SARAH LEWITINN: At Don Hill's, someone, I can't remember who it was—it might have been Mikey—I just remember being like, "I hope I get to be in a band that plays here one day."

MIKEY WAY: My birthday is September 10. I had been up all night. I had work that day at Barnes & Noble. My good friend Pat called me up like, "Turn on the news." All this is unfolding live on TV. My brother was on his way to [a meeting about an animated TV show he was pitching] that day. The PATH train stopped and let him out because they weren't letting trains go into Manhattan. I remember having to pick him up.

SARAH LEWITINN: I was out partying the night before. There was a Monday night party I would go to at Sway. So I was having a bit of a sluggish start. I turned on the TV, and I was like, "That's weird . . . is it already the anniversary of that van that blew up the World Trade Center in the nineties?" I got into the shower, turned on the radio, and I was like, "Why are they going all-out this year on the World Trade Center bombing from like, five, six years ago?"

BUDDY NIELSEN: We were in high school, my senior year. It was in first period. They came over the loudspeaker: "There's been a floor collapse at the World Trade Center." You're like, "Oh that's weird they're announcing that." We didn't have cell phones, so you don't just look it up. You don't know what's going on. As things start to progress, you can feel the teachers acting like there's this tension, like something was happening that was unspoken. Towards the end of first period they're like, "A plane hit the World Trade Center," and my thought immediately was, "Oh that's crazy that an accident like that would happen." I went to my next period, and you started to realize like, something's going on. Something's not okay. We gathered around a TV and you started to see this attack was happening. It's like, "Are they attacking New York City?" My stepdad was in downtown Manhattan doing a trial. Then the Pentagon thing happened and you're just like, "Yo, we're literally under attack." I was believing it was on a level even bigger than what it wound up being. I got super stressed out, freaked out, and left the school. Everybody was leaving. I got my sister out of her middle school, brought her home. We all got up to the hill in Ridgewood where you could see the city and watched the towers on fire. By the time we got to the top, the first tower fell.

I remember going to a vigil that night. There was a kid in my school whose father worked at the World Trade Center. He left him a message on his answering machine. It was like, "I love you, I'm gonna jump out the window. I love you guys."

JOHN NOLAN: A friend from North Carolina was staying with us and he was gonna fly home on September 11, so I was driving to LaGuardia Airport. We were listening to the radio and Howard Stern was on, and they started talking about the first plane hitting. At first, because it was Howard Stern, we thought it was just a really tasteless bit. We started switching around and hearing it on regular news channels. And as we started getting close to LaGuardia, we could see the skyline and actually see the smoke coming out of the buildings.

ROB HITT: Midtown was in Los Angeles, recording our second album, staying in the Oakwood Apartments.

That morning Gabe's girlfriend keeps calling his cell phone. Gabe's a heavy sleeper, so he wasn't picking up his phone. Finally, he picks it up, we turn on the TV and see one plane had hit the World Trade Center. We're like, this has to be an accident. Second plane hits the tower and we're like, "Holy fuck, what's next?" You try calling your family in New Jersey, lines are full, circuits are shorting. It's all busy signals. It's like, is New York shut down? Are our friends' parents in those buildings? It was such a helpless feeling being out on the West Coast. We didn't know what to do. We had no desire to play music that day. How could you do preproduction when all these people just died? But at the same time, do you just sit in your apartment?

We ended up saying, "Let's just drive to the studio." It was in Hollywood. There was a middle-sized room where the Bangles were rehearsing for a tour, and in the big room, the Red Hot Chili Peppers were doing preproduction for their album *By the Way*, with Rick Rubin. In the middle, there was this courtyard where we sat at this table with an umbrella. Some of the Red Hot Chili Peppers showed up, the drummer Chad and John Frusciante were chain-smoking cigarettes.

HEATH SARACENO: Then Flea came out, he was talking to us as well. They knew we were from New York, New Jersey, so Flea asked, you know, "Everyone okay? How are you? How are we feeling?" Then after another ten minutes we're like, "What the fuck are we doing here? We can't do this today."

PETE WENTZ: Arma Angelus was in Boston recording our album with Adam from Killswitch [Engage]. I was in school at the time, at DePaul University. I told my parents—because I lived with them—that I was house-sitting a friend's apartment in Chicago. I'm pretty sure our drummer was supposed to fly back to Chicago from Boston the day of 9/11, and I think he didn't end up getting on the plane.

CHRIS GUTIERREZ: I flew in to Boston to record the Arma Angelus album the night of September tenth. They picked me up, we went back to our hotel, a tiny little shithole that had two beds with like, five or six dudes staying in it. I woke up in a sleeping bag on the floor, because I never got fucking priority to sleep in a bed. And I remember Dan, our guitar player, was like, "Dude, a fucking plane just hit a building in New York." On TV, all you could see was one of the Twin Towers lightly smoking. Then I came out of the shower, the second plane is hijacked and about to crash, and we started fucking flipping out like, "What are we gonna do? America's under attack."

PETE WENTZ: The parents of one of the band members called my parents like, "The boys are safe. They're in Boston. They're safe." And my parents are like, "What the fuck is happening? These guys were supposed to be in downtown Chicago!"

MIKEY WAY: A day or two later, in one of the local Jersey papers, they used a shot of the Trade Center and you could see the back of my brother's shoulder and his bag. Traumatizing, you know? Traumatizing for years and years after that. It was a big wake-up call for mortality.

BUDDY NIELSEN: 9/11 was a pivotal moment for everybody in that area. I was a senior in high school, and it greatly changed my trajectory. I know it did that for Gerard as well.

MIKEY WAY: From that moment on, we wanted to be a beacon of positivity. We wanted to touch the world in that way. We wanted to give people comfort.

The demos got made shortly after 9/11. I was like, "I need to be in this band," and they were like, "We need a bass player." The first song I heard was "Skylines and Turnstiles." It's a heavy song, you know? I was like, "I want to be a part of this."

CHAPTER 9

"AT *THE* TIME, THEY WERE GEOFF *FROM* THURSDAY'S WEIRD FRIENDS"

PAUL HANLY: Mikey was like, "I'm starting this band My Chemical Romance." I'm like, "Like the Irvine Welsh novel?" He's like, "Come see my band play." I'm like, "Yeah, whatever."

GABE SAPORTA: I was at the Eyeball House and Alex introduced me to Mikey and Gerard. Usually most of the bands that were coming up in the scene, you knew someone from shows or their old band or something. But I didn't know anyone in My Chem at all.

MIKE GITTER: At the time, they were Geoff from Thursday's weird friends.

ALEX SAAVEDRA: Ray Toro was just this killer guitar player. He could play drums and obviously play bass, so he was the fucking talent of that little crew they had together. They were a fucking nerd herd. They would play Dungeons & Dragons and read comic books. And that was their life. And Gerard had this awesome mind to him, just so creative. His imagination was huge. You'd drink a few beers and talk to Gerard for hours about just the most insane ideas for characters, storylines. That made me confident something would come from what they were doing. Between Gerard's mind and Ray's talent for writing, they were gonna get there.

MIKEY WAY: Frank wasn't in the band yet.

ALEX SAAVEDRA: Frank was shy. He was also stoned a lot. He would just sit there sometimes, not say anything and, like, giggling to himself. I'd be so entertained by that, because I knew that he was stoned, and he was just listening to us. There would be times we weren't even saying anything funny and this fucking kid's just laughing like the Joker.

GEOFF RICKLY: Gerard was at a party at the Eyeball House with Mikey and he was like, "Play Geoff the one we wrote!" He had a guitar that was missing strings, trying to play me this song.

ALEX SAAVEDRA: Which is funny, because we definitely had guitars in that house with strings on them.

GEOFF RICKLY: I was like, "These guys are fucking hopeless. Nothing good will ever happen for these guys. Like, I love them, I'd want them to do a comic with me someday, but nothing good is ever gonna come from this band." And Alex was like, "No, they're actually gonna get good."

ALEX SAAVEDRA: It's kind of adorable . . . Geoff being patient and loving and understanding enough to even just sit there and listen to that shit. Considering that, like, Thursday was doing well.

GEOFF RICKLY: The first time we went on tour with Rival Schools, Walter from Quicksand's more Britpoppy band, Walter was like, "This is so crazy, man. Your shows have like, girls and guys." I'm like, "What do you mean?" He's like, "I'm just used to, you know, tough guys. That's who comes to see hardcore shows. We play with you guys and it's people from everywhere. I love it. It's fucking weird, though! They don't want somebody to step on their head!"

WALTER SCHREIFELS: That's when I noticed, "You guys are bringing in girls." Our audience would have been more heads, people that were interested in Quicksand. And yet, there were people there that were ten years younger than us.

MIKEY WAY: I would tag along with Geoff a lot when they would play and I remember going to a lot of *Full Collapse* shows. At Wetlands, they were opening for Movielife, and I remember Geoff swung the mic around the crowd. I remember everyone being like, "What did he just do?" That show was a game-changer. I saw the confidence in Thursday rise.

GEOFF RICKLY: Saves the Day asked us to do a tour, and that was it. That was when Thursday just exploded. We started as one of four on the bill and we were getting encore requests. We ended the tour as three of four on the bill with crowds going bonkers, and partly because while we were on tour, MTV started playing the "Understanding in a Car Crash" video. I don't know why they picked it up—we'd serviced it to them like six months earlier—but they had a Saves the Day video in rotation at the time. Maybe MTV was like, "Here's a band that's on tour with Saves the Day." And "Understanding in a Car Crash" didn't sound like anything else going at the time. You know, we were much more aggressive than Saves the Day. It's like that moment was what the kids had been waiting for.

AMY FLEISHER MADDEN: If you think about it, rap-rock, nu metal, stuff like Limp Bizkit kind of paved the way for Thursday. I would never say they influenced them or anything like that, but shit like "ALL FOR THE NOOKIE!" being screamed kind of made it okay for Geoff Rickly to scream on television. It was like, "Okay, maybe there's a place for us in the mainstream."

GEOFF RICKLY: Victory wouldn't give us money to do a video because they thought the only song that was worth a video was "Standing on the Edge of Summer" and they thought we were blowing it by picking "Understanding in a Car Crash." But we had filmmakers in the band. Our guitarist [Steve Pedulla] went to North Carolina and grew up with David Gordon Green, who wound up doing *Pineapple Express* and stuff like that. Craig Zobel did the "Understanding" video—back then he was a real artsy director, people were saying he was going to be like, the next Terrence Malick. He did it for basically nothing and we pooled about $1,000 of our own money and made that video.

JASON LINK: Yeah . . . that video is not that good.

AMY FLEISHER MADDEN: It was shot on a wing and a prayer. Someone is wearing shorts. In a documentary sense, it was a good representation of what a show felt like. But it wasn't like, art, you know? It was a little bit of like, "Okay, so this is the video that's going to get big? Okay. Cool." I don't want to be an asshole, but the video was not very good.

GEOFF RICKLY: The tour with Saves the Day ended [on December 22, 2001] when I got home for Christmas. My parents left MTV on and that video would play over and over again.

AMY FLEISHER MADDEN: Every band in the genre, tour buddies, everybody was like, "How do we get on MTV? Why are they on MTV? We're bigger than them. Why are they on?" It started this chain reaction. I had grown so used to the music industry being like, Britney Spears. And then all of a sudden, Thursday was on MTV.

JOHN NOLAN: Thursday didn't change their sound to fit into what was happening in popular music. They were just doing what they did.

SHANE TOLD: Nobody thought this scene or this kind of music had any business in any mainstream outlet, especially if there's screaming.

SPENCER CHAMBERLAIN: I'll never forget: the "Understanding in a Car Crash" video came on MTV2 and I looked at my brother and said, "Everything's gonna change." It felt like they were putting one of us on TV. In my opinion, that's where it started, that's where the scene shifted. That started the doors opening. Secret's out! Here goes.

GEOFF RICKLY: Thursday was in a situation where we knew Victory was signing us to another label—either they were selling our contract or they were selling a whole stake in Victory to another label. We had gotten word that the other label was going to be MCA. People called MCA the graveyard of bands' careers: either you're Blink-182, or you're nothing. Even though we were blowing up, we knew we weren't going to be Blink. We figured, "We're gonna end up on a major label one way or another, let's be the masters of our own destiny." So we started talking to major labels.

The president of Warner Bros. flew to Albany to see us. I was like, "Damn, I guess they're sending out the big guns." A private jet to fucking Albany. There was another show in Long Island at a place called the Oasis, or the Mirage or something like that. . . .

EDDIE REYES: The Sahara. We played before Thursday. That's when all the labels were coming out in buses and shit.

GEOFF RICKLY: It had one of those waterfall gardens, like the ones they install in corporate centers. We played in front of that. It was Thursday, From Autumn to Ashes, and Taking Back Sunday, one of those stacked bills. It was packed, oversold by double the amount of people that should have been in there. I remember all the different labels in the back and them all noticing each other. So after we're done, they're all fighting for us, who would get to go to dinner with the band or whatever. People were like, "Yeah, I love that, you know . . . 'Cross Out the Car Crash' song . . ."

EDDIE REYES: Long Island had one of the biggest scenes in America at that point, besides Jersey . . . I like to say the East Coast. A lot of great bands came out of that area that helped the scene to blow up. I guess we're like the Seattle of our genre.

GEOFF RICKLY: Thursday was supposed to be the next Nirvana, that's what everybody said.

ALEX SAAVEDRA: When you're surrounded by people that are not only like-minded but also successful, it creates this air of confidence. The Eyeball House was able to get people out of their shells in that way.

GEOFF RICKLY: Alex dragged me to My Chemical Romance's practice space. I was like, "They sound like NOFX, this sucks."

ALEX SAAVEDRA: It's funny Geoff thought it sounded like NOFX. I definitely wouldn't have put that together. But I also don't think Geoff was a NOFX fan. The majority of us had that punk rock, Fat Wreck Chords phase but I don't think Geoff ever did, and his delving into punk was like, Joy Division. So anything that was fast and a little melodic, he would have been, "All right, that sounds like NOFX!"

GEOFF RICKLY: At that practice, I pulled Gerard aside and I was like, "Dude, your mind is too big for sounding like somebody else. Don't do this, don't go down somebody else's road. Think about your comic books. Think about characters. Draw yourself as a character. Imagine yourself as like a superhero." And then they started writing "Vampires Will Never Hurt You."

ALEX SAAVEDRA: The progression of My Chemical Romance was very, very quick. They recorded some demos in the attic of their drummer's house and then a few weeks later, I had them in the studio recording "Vampires." This was like three months after they formed and it was their first recording studio experience. We worked hard and it came out well. The final version of "Vampires" that's on *I Brought You My Bullets, You Brought Me Your Love* is from that session; we never rerecorded.

MIKEY WAY: Thursday posted "Vampires Will Never Hurt You" on their web page. That was the first flick of the domino for us.

GEOFF RICKLY: My Chemical Romance guys used to tell me all the time that I should produce their record. I'm like, "Why would I do that?" And when I heard "Vampires Will Never Hurt You," I was like, "Oh, okay." There's a little western in it, it's sort of American Gothic . . .

Thursday was going out on tour and I played it maybe fifteen times in our Discman and suddenly was like, "Oh shit. They're gonna be really good." When I got back from that tour I was like, "When are we doing it? Let's do the record."

When we were in the studio, Gerard's wisdom teeth were really hurting him, and he wasn't able to sing, so he went to the dentist to have them out and afterwards they gave him a bunch of painkillers. He didn't sing with the fire or the venom, so Alex took the painkillers away from him. Like, "You gotta sing in pain, fuck you! You gotta feel it!" I was taking the painkillers, watching him sing the record. I remember lying on the floor and coaching him through how to sing "Early Sunsets Over Monroeville," the ballad on the record. I was saying, "You're following the music, make the music follow you. More intense! The music will catch up to you."

MIKEY WAY: They thought I was going to struggle more than I did. And I mean, rightfully so. I'd only started playing bass for the band.

GEOFF RICKLY: Mikey's always had the musicality to do it. He just lacked confidence, because he was a few years behind the rest of the band. And Ray Toro is a monster guitarist. He's like a Brian May, you know what I mean? So I think being in a band with a guy like Ray was very intimidating for somebody like Mikey.

MIKEY WAY: I didn't know what the fuck I was doing. But somehow I did it perfectly. Nailed it. Everyone was pleasantly surprised. They thought it was going to take hours and hours for me to get through it. It was the first one of those moments where I was like, "I can do this."

GEOFF RICKLY: I basically got Frank Iero to join. I had lost my license around that time and Frank was driving me to the studio . . . he was in another Eyeball band.

DENNIS ORTEGA: Frank was semi-known in the Jersey scene from Pencey Prep. Pencey Prep was one of those original NJScene message board bands.

SARAH LEWITINN: I could not remember a single song to save my life, but I remember watching them and being like, "Frankie is supercute."

ALEX SAAVEDRA: Frank was this quiet dude, but with Pencey Prep, he would fucking let loose. He was a great front man. I personally just didn't like what they were playing. But you could tell there was something about him . . . almost like Pencey Prep was holding him back. Which obviously, it was . . .

GEOFF RICKLY: I was like, "Dude, Ray's writing two guitar parts for every song. Seriously, if they don't get another guitar player, they're fucked. And with Gerard, I'm helping him find backups for all these songs; Ray's not gonna sing them all. You should really think about joining this band, man." So it was like . . . it looks like Frank is gonna do this? Is he? I think he is? He's gonna do it!

SARAH LEWITINN: Frankie had this X factor when he ended up joining My Chem. It just felt like, "Yeah, of course." He was always the most enthusiastic person in the crowd at any of their shows.

GEOFF RICKLY: I feel extremely vindicated by that record, because my big things were: You have to fire your drummer, and let's unlock Gerard's potential. They didn't listen to me on the drummer, but they listened to me on Gerard. And later on, the drummer thing became such a huge fuckin' problem for them. I was like, "Do it, get rid of him now! He's not up for it and he does not give a shit. He doesn't care." He thought he was better than them. I was like, "You got to get rid of him now because he'll come back, and he'll be a pain in the ass." And he did. He was such a pain in the ass for them.

I remember saying to Mikey, "Dude, this [album] is really good." I remember turning to Gerard like, "Your band's gonna be fucking massive, dude." He's like, "You think we'll ever be as big as Thursday?" I was like, "No, you guys are gonna be as big as Good Charlotte." That was like, as big as I could imagine. Good Charlotte. Sky's the limit, you guys! If you could unlock Gerard, I knew there was something there. But clearly, I didn't have any idea . . .

GABE SAPORTA: It was the next generation of emo, right? The theatrical, makeup, all-black stuff wasn't a thing until they came around. They had different influences they drew from. To be honest, I didn't get My Chem at the very beginning. And then I got it.

MATTHEW ISMAEL RUIZ: My Chemical Romance, they're forever tied to Thursday for me, because Thursday was probably the band I saw most, growing up in Jersey. I saw Thursday maybe ten times in four years. If there was a Thursday tour, if there was a Thursday one-off show, I was there, and I remember hearing Geoff had produced this band's album. Then listening to the *Bullets* record, I was like, bro, this is raw. This is fucking scary. It's got AFI vibes but less drama and histrionics and more scuzzy punk shit. It's fucking *mean*.

GABE SAPORTA: I know all the words on *Bullets*; I definitely spent a lot of time on that first album. They're like, real Jersey boys. My brother was really close with them.

RICKY SAPORTA: They were always full of energy. They just needed to get it out. In the basement at 120 Hamilton in New Brunswick—there's maybe forty, fifty people there—and they just fucking erupted. I don't even know how they sounded, I can't tell you if they played well or didn't play well. I have no fucking clue. I just remember Gerard was on the floor at one point.

I got arrested at a My Chemical Romance show at a New Brunswick basement, which fucking sucked. The show was over already, and the bands were packing up. The cops were harassing the bands, and I was photographing the cops and telling them to "Stop fucking with everyone." They arrested me for obstruction of justice—they said my camera flash was blinding them and not letting them do their job. So that was fun. I had to go to court for it. It was a fucking bullshit arrest, and the MCR guys were gonna be my witnesses. But they were starting to blow up and kept being like, "We're gonna be on tour!" The charges ended up getting dropped, of course.

MIKEY WAY: Back in that era, we played everything really fast live. Especially a song like "Honey, This Mirror Isn't Big Enough for the Two of Us." I'm riffing, and it was a trial by fire. I got thrown in the ocean and it was like, "Swim." Ray and Frank are two of the greatest guitar players and I had to keep up with them. And that's where that came from—rigorous practice and the relentless need to get better.

EDDIE REYES: My Chem started off the way Taking Back Sunday did, playing VFW halls in front of small crowds. I remember the first show we played with them was the first time I met them—at some VFW hall or some lodge up in upper Jersey. It was a small show, maybe a hundred people. I still remember meeting them: Frank, Gerard, Mikey. And I stayed close with those guys.

MIKEY WAY: Taking Back Sunday hooked us up in the beginning. We became fast friends.

HEATH SARACENO: The first time Midtown saw My Chem, we knew they were gonna be the biggest band in the world. Ray played guitar with this shredder style—no one played guitar like Ray—like an old man who could rip your head off. And Frank would just go crazy. He would leave the stage with bloody hands, a bloody face, there was just blood everywhere around Frank.

SARAH LEWITINN: Their vibe was always bigger than the stage. Right from the jump. They always seemed like they belonged on a much bigger stage.

CHRIS GUTIERREZ: Joe [Trohman] said, "Dude, I got a band I think you'd love, they're called My Chemical Romance. They're like, evil pop-punk." So I went on Kazaa, downloaded like five songs, and was like, "Holy fuck, this is my band." I went to see them at Fireside Bowl in Chicago. There were fifty people max, and maybe ten who were actually into the band. The Fireside stage was maybe a foot and a half tall and I was freaking out. They ended with "Headfirst for Halos," Gerard was singing—and he was fucked up—the finale that goes, "Think happy thoughts, think happy thoughts." I jumped on the edge of the stage, grabbed him by the neck with his collar, and was just screaming, "THINK HAPPY THOUGHTS!" in his face.

AARON GILLESPIE: Underoath took My Chemical Romance and this band called Brazil on tour. My Chem was the first band I knew that would get ready to go onstage every night. We were dirtball kids; those guys put fucking makeup on.

TIM MCTAGUE: They were like, dogshit shows. We're talking a hundred people, max.

AARON GILLESPIE: They weren't bigger than us at all, but it felt like they were because they had outfits and shit. Halfway through the tour, the Brazil guys started dressing like My Chem. I remember that vividly: Gerard being like, "What the fuck, man?" That was when Gerard wore that black thing around his eyes. The guitar player for Brazil started doing it and Gerard got so pissed.

GEOFF RICKLY: Gerard had all these different personalities: Oh, he's Drunk Belushi again. Oh, he's, he's Young Elvis. I love Young Elvis! When he actually started hanging out, we were like, "Yeah, Gerard's a man of many faces. Now he's David Bowie!" And this was before he was famous. This was before he was Gerard from My Chemical Romance.

MIKE GITTER: The first time I saw them . . . not poised. Full of the requisite piss and vinegar. Seriously awkward. But seriously awkward in the best possible way. Not arena gods yet, but with every aspiration of being one.

CHRISTIAN MCKNIGHT: I saw My Chemical Romance at Skate Fest in Massachusetts. Matt Galle, who is a very important person in our scene, booked Skate Fest. Eventually he would go on to be My Chemical Romance's booking agent. Matt's like, "Yo, watch this band with me." I remember thinking to myself, "Matt, I don't get it, I'm not gonna lie." But I met Frank, I met Gerard and Mikey, and we became friends. A month later, they play Long Island, and I saw it that day. The second time I saw them I was like, there's something about Gerard—this Liberace, Freddie Mercury, punk rock rolled into one. The dude fucking writes comic books. He went to school to learn how to make toys. And he took all of that and injected it into this angsty, post-punk apocalypse. It just fucking worked, dude, it fucking worked.

MIKE GITTER: They had this thing . . . sinister in the New Jersey sense, like the Misfits were sinister. Vicious and dreaming. Humongous dreams.

AMANDA BRENNAN: I saw MCR at fucking RexPlex across from the Ikea in Elizabeth, New Jersey, right next to Newark Airport. I was fifteen or sixteen. There were eight people. I remember "Vampires Will Never Hurt You." The music felt so unlike anything I had heard before; so not pop-punk, so far from what I came to the show for. I remember Gerard's long hair, and I want to say he had makeup on, like, incredible eyeliner. This image is burned into my brain of being at this weird skate park watching MCR for the first time and being like, "This is something. I don't know what it is. But this is something." That was what sparked this idea in my brain of, "There is so much more out there than what's happening right here."

THE LONG ISLAND LYRIC POOL

CHRISTIAN MCKNIGHT: Whenever you have a scene as close-knit as Long Island's, it's inevitable there's going to be some kind of drama.

MIKE DUBIN: The Long Island Lyric Pool . . .

EDDIE REYES: No other scene was doing that, really.

BRIAN DIAZ: Someone would write a song, and someone else would pull a reference to it or a lyric from the song.

NEIL RUBENSTEIN: I like to think of art collaboratively. I like to write with people, punch up other people's material or have other people help me punch up my stuff. So back then, if I came up with a line that didn't really fit my band—because I wasn't really doing emo—I'd be like, "This line could fit what you're working on."

JOHN NOLAN: I think "Your best bet, let alone your worst ex" from "Bike Scene" was Neil's line.

NEIL RUBENSTEIN: I came up with "past tense, my best friend" from "Shower Scene" by Brand New. Or vice versa, Jesse would be like, "Hey, I wrote this line, it's not gonna fit for Brand New but I could picture you screaming it."

JOHN NOLAN: Someone would be like, "I had this great line," and then someone would be like, "Can I use that?" And you'd be like, "Yeah, sure." It was that kind of thing with Neil and Jesse from Brand New.

EDDIE REYES: Jesse got in on that. This was back when everybody was cool.

JOHN NOLAN: There was a lot of, "Hey, check this line out." If someone came up with something really good, there was a bit of one-upmanship. You'd go away and come back with something that could top it.

NEIL RUBENSTEIN: We joked that it was like a lyric pool where we would just all write, and then take out of the pool when we needed it, you know?

BRIAN DIAZ: It was a thing people joked about, and I feel publications took very seriously.

A lot of it was on the internet. There was this message board called the Long Island Zoo, hosted by Christian McKnight's promotion company. It was where everyone went to talk shit, post shows, and then talk shit on the shows. It was a joke that went around on the message board.

MIKE DUBIN: When Brand New started to become a real band, Jesse left Taking Back Sunday.

RANDY NICHOLS: Jesse Lacey and John Nolan from Taking Back Sunday both went to like, Christian Bible school together, that's how they met. That's a whole other story. They grew up only knowing Christian music.

MIKE DUBIN: The beef was based on personal stuff that was kind of made semi-public.

BRIAN DIAZ: This was the early days of internet rumors, so people got little bits and pieces of the truth.

SCOTTIE REDIX: The friction between Brand New and Taking Back Sunday was about a girl. That was a big storyline. The girl is a friend of mine so I'm not gonna say her name. Something happened where Jesse or John . . .

BRIAN DIAZ: We were at a party and maybe there was some argument that took place and then two twenty-something dudes went home and wrote songs about it, each from their perspective.

SCOTTIE REDIX: Ten times out of ten it's always over a girl. Like seriously. Back in those days, especially.

JOHN NOLAN: We couldn't hold on to a bass player. People would play with us for a month or two, and then they'd quit, or move on to another band.

MIKE DUBIN: Taking Back Sunday was looking for a bass player. And then that bass player became the singer.

TOMMY CORRIGAN: Let me tell you a story. Eddie was my roommate for a couple years, I knew him from way, way back in the nineties. Silent Majority and Eddie's band played a tiny show in North Carolina around '94, '95. And we met a group of kids we played with and stayed in touch with. Every year we'd go back and play that town in North Carolina and after like the third time we could actually draw a decent amount of people. It was really the only place in America where people actually liked Silent Majority outside of Long Island. We became friends with this whole crew of kids, stayed in their house, played there, whatever. And Adam [Lazzara] was in the younger group of this group of kids.

EDDIE REYES: Adam just had this style, this aura. I played with some great singers, but this kid had something different.

JOHN NOLAN: Even when he played bass for Taking Back Sunday, Adam would throw himself into it very physically. So when he started singing, he had a natural thing for getting up there and losing himself.

EDDIE REYES: I told him to swing that mic and go fucking nuts, and he did. And we became who we are: Taking Back Sunday. We were a crazy live band that went nuts and broke shit. I envisioned the Stooges or At the Drive-In: "I want to be that. That's what I want."

MIKE DUBIN: Not to take away from the first singer Antonio, there wasn't a lot . . . the stuff before Adam was singing was just different. It was still similar, but it just didn't click. And then Adam transitioned from bass and I remember the first show I saw him as the singer, they played a friend's house on New Year's Eve. I was just fucking blown away. The whole vibe changed. It was a different band.

JOHN NOLAN: That was the first time we played in front of people with Adam singing.

CHRISTIAN MCKNIGHT: So what happened was I had a Glassjaw show booked at the Long Island Zoo. Glassjaw has a lyric, "I wish you a broken heart and a happy New Year," so of course we were gonna do a Glassjaw show on New Year's Eve. The New Year's Eve show got canceled because I didn't have insurance or something. So there was this last-minute party at someone's house in East Meadow and Taking Back Sunday played.

Adam was unpredictable. It was like watching fire—you had no idea what direction it was gonna turn, but you couldn't take your eyes off it. And when he starting swinging that fucking mic . . . it was scary. It was like, "Yo, this guy's gonna take out someone's teeth." That's Adam back then.

EDDIE REYES: It was this huge house party. We played in the living room, just jumping off furniture.

CHRISTIAN MCKNIGHT: I remember jumping off a flight of stairs onto people because it's a house, why not crowd-surf?

I was like, this band is the next band. Now, I didn't know what "next" meant at that point, because no band from our scene had been that big.

NEIL RUBENSTEIN: There was another Taking Back Sunday show at Ground Zero in Bellmore, Long Island. You could feel the change in the air.

CHRISTIAN MCKNIGHT: On Long Island, as soon as you saw the kids you didn't recognize singing along to a band and going crazy, you know that shit's going to catch on.

NEIL RUBENSTEIN: Usually there's twenty kids just hanging out in the parking lot, but at the Ground Zero show, the parking lot's empty, everyone's inside, and Fred Feldman's here; he never comes out to shows.

MIKE DUBIN: Fred was gonna sign Taking Back Sunday to Triple Crown. I think that was during one of the beefs between the two bands. And because he had Brand New, he backed off and didn't do it.

FRED FELDMAN: I got a demo from a band called Hometown Hero that I listened to and fell in love with. I called the drummer, Brian Lane, and he's like, "Oh, we broke up, but I have a new band I just started, I'll send you the demos as soon as they're ready." And that was Brand New. I tried to sign them for Triple Crown Records, but Warner had offered them a deal. These were the days of demo deals, where bands would get paid a crazy amount from a major label to go make a demo.

ANTHONY RANERI: They told a story that they had a meeting with Warner Bros. about possibly signing, but Warner said they didn't have a hit, didn't have a single. Jesse went into the next room and wrote "Last Chance to Lose Your Keys," and was like, "Here's the single."

FRED FELDMAN: Warner took some time and passed. I remained friendly with

Brand New. They told me what it would take to close the deal, we tweaked it, and sealed the deal. *Your Favorite Weapon* came out in the fall of 2001.

JONATHAN DANIEL: I had the demo Brand New did for Warner and it was really good. A lot of those songs ended up on the album. I'm trying to think of what song really jumped out . . . "Last Chance to Lose Your Keys." Those titles were great.

ANTHONY RANERI: I had started Bayside already, but we couldn't get booked enough to tour all the time, so whenever Bayside wasn't touring, I would hop in the Brand New van and sell merch for them. I sold the first copy of *Your Favorite Weapon*. I remember opening the first box the night it came out at Brownies in the City. There was a misprint on that first pressing of CDs—"Soco Amaretto Lime" was "Soco Amaretto Lim" before they fixed it.

FRED FELDMAN: It was pretty quick we saw something special was happening. Drive-Thru literally tried to buy the contract the week after *Your Favorite Weapon* came out. Richard and Stefanie loved Brand New; they tried really hard. We had a two-record deal with them. I remember sitting with the band saying, "If we do this right, you are going to be able to pick whatever path you want to go down, whether you want to stay independent or get a crazy major label deal. Let's stay on this road, because you'll benefit from it."

RICH EGAN: I had a chance to sign Taking Back Sunday to Vagrant. And I passed. I blew it. And I still kick myself. They sent me songs from their first record saying they were looking for a label and I was like, "Wow, they're awesome, kind of in the same vein as Saves the Day . . . But I've got a lot of stuff we need to concentrate on. . . ."

AMY FLEISHER MADDEN: I got a demo from Taking Back Sunday. It was either a tape or a CD, I can't remember. And there was one piece of paper that came with it that said, "Sign our band or we will kill you." And it had a phone number. I called them that minute, like, "You guys are fucking great, let's do this." And they're like, "Cool, but we're talking to Victory. Can you match Victory's contract?" Their recording budget was like $10,000 and a van and all of this shit and I was like, "Listen, guys, I work in my bedroom. But I think you're great, call me when you're in LA, let's be friends."

And they signed to Victory, obviously.

CHRISTIAN MCKNIGHT: The TBS/Brand New drama was an inevitability . . . They wrote some lyrics about it, and they wrote some fucking great songs about it. I'm glad it happened.

JENN PELLY: I essentially haven't listened to Brand New in five years so it's hard to remember, but one thing I will say is I think Brand New appealed to people who were . . . more normal? Whereas Taking Back Sunday's music was a little bit darker.

NEIL RUBENSTEIN: When Taking Back Sunday went and recorded *Tell All Your Friends*, they wanted to show their appreciation for helping with lyrics, the stuff I was doing for them. I was a significant fixture, in the Long Island scene, at least: "Oh, guest vocals from Neil, maybe it sells five more albums on Long Island!" They wanted me to make up some lyrics for my screaming part on "There's No 'I' in Team." I remember thinking it was about the Brand New situation, so I was just like, "Oh, it would be funny if I screamed Brand New ['Seventy Times 7'] lyrics back at them."

EDDIE REYES: Neil definitely sang a lot of shit on *Tell All Your Friends* and inspired us. Dubin inspired us, too. I mean, he's the reason the song is called "Cute Without the 'E' (Cut from the Team)." I was like, "I don't know what that means, but it's catchy."

MIKE DUBIN: It was just some shit we would say, in the context of like, you're talking to some girl and she's rude. "Oh, you're cute . . . without the 'e.' You're cut. Get out of here."

EDDIE REYES: I think I told Dubin, "Oh, you're naming songs now?" Because I always made asshole comments to him.

NEIL RUBENSTEIN: Well, I also helped name that song . . . Most of the names off that first record are stuff that you would find on the blue channel, that's what we called the channel that gave you the television guide. So like, "Timberwolves at New Jersey" was a game on channel 9.

EDDIE REYES: There were majors and really awesome indie labels that were interested in us. I had a friend named Michelle who heard our demo. She fucking flipped over it and gave it to a friend of hers named Angel who worked at Victory. He kept coming to hang out, to see us play. He's actually the one who signed us to Victory.

STEPHANIE MARLOW: Tony was like, "Okay, we've got something going on with Thursday, we need to start piggybacking some other stuff to continue the trajectory." Every Thursday album would come with a sampler CD, and every sampler CD would have a Taking Back Sunday song.

HEATHER WEST: Around the week that I started at Victory, they had just gotten signed, and they came to the office in Chicago for the first time to have meetings.

STEPHANIE MARLOW: They were kids. They were so excited.

HEATHER WEST: They were completely new to this. Eddie was the only one who had ever been in a touring band. But you could tell they had it going on.

MIKEY WAY: Victory was really behind Taking Back Sunday. I remember first being like . . . you know, because Thursday was Jersey's band—who's this band? They have a day in the week as well . . .

GLENN GAMBOA: I'd been hearing about Taking Back Sunday while they were playing VFW halls on Long Island or, like, a Middle Eastern restaurant's basement. The first time I checked them out was the release party for *Tell All Your Friends*, at the Knitting Factory in March 2002. When Long Island bands played the City, people would be like, "Oh, you're not as cool as a Lower East Side band." So Taking Back Sunday had something to prove.

By then, the Long Island kids had memorized all the words to an album that hadn't come out yet. You could barely hear the band over the screaming. They felt that Taking Back Sunday had made it—they were headlining and playing the City. I thought, "This band is going to be a big thing." So I made my way backstage and interviewed them upstairs.

FRED FELDMAN: For guys who grew up on Long Island to have a feature in *Newsday*, that's pretty great. That's the big local paper.

GLENN GAMBOA: They were just so happy to talk to a reporter. They were in a great mood. I remember Adam telling me where their influences came from. He was talking about Jade Tree Records, showing me the tattoos he had of lyrics from Jade Tree bands, like Lifetime.

HEATHER WEST: For Taking Back, getting to work with Jillian was also huge. She's one of the best band managers I ever worked with.

JILLIAN NEWMAN: I was at South by Southwest with Midtown and went to see Taking Back Sunday play. They played some barbecue place, nowhere near all the other shows, with like twenty people. I was blown away. Adam was super talented. He was doing all the swinging mic stuff back then. So he was sitting on the floor outside, probably bleeding if I remember correctly. I went up and said, "Hello, it's nice to meet you. I think you're great. You're bleeding, I'm going to talk to you later."

AMY FLEISHER MADDEN: In that era, Adam's stage presence was unparalleled.

JILLIAN NEWMAN: I really wanted to work with them, but they don't know me from anything. So I just started helping them get on shows and just doing things where I could. This was back in 2002, so no one's paying their bills online or anything; Adam's on tour, and his cell phone keeps getting shut off because he's not paying the bill, because he's not home. At that point, one of the videos came out where he had leopard-skin hair. I remember sending a note through his friend like, "Please turn your phone on because I have to call you and make fun of your hair in this video." Eventually they hired me.

NICK GHANBARIAN: The first time I heard Taking Back Sunday I was working at the Urban Outfitters at the Roosevelt Field mall on Long Island. Once the store closed, we had control of the CD player and someone put on *Tell All Your Friends.* A couple of songs in I'm like, "What is this? This sounds like Silent Majority. What the fuck is going on?" They were like, "Yeah, this band's blowing up right now." I was already bitter Silent Majority broke up for not-great reasons, then I was more bitter that a band that sounded like my old band was blowing up.

TOMMY CORRIGAN: I worked at Merch Direct, which Justin from Glassjaw owned, printing all their T-shirts at the time—both Taking Back Sunday and Brand New. I designed the T-shirts when they were battling each other: Brand New put out a shirt that said "Mics Are for Singing Not

Swinging" and then Taking Back Sunday's response was to put out a shirt that said "Proudly Swinging Since 1999."

JASON TATE: The bands didn't like each other, they would throw random snarky comments at each other in interviews. Two bands in Long Island feuding would have felt so minor in like 1970 or whatever, but now the internet exists and all of a sudden, everyone has their own little gossip. Teenagers online could be like, "Oh, did you read these song lyrics? Do you think these are about John? Do you think these are about Jesse? What did Adam say in this interview? I've gotta take sides."

NEIL RUBENSTEIN: I mean, I was better friends with the TBS guys. And then, you know, when push came to shove, Jesse turned out to be a fucking horrible person anyway.

MATTHEW ISMAEL RUIZ: I was always TBS over Brand New. Thematically, the lyrics aren't really that different, but there was something edgier, something that felt a little more dangerous about TBS at that time. And you know, the mic thing stuck out.

LESLIE SIMON: Adam was the undeniable focal point for the band. Not only was he considered to be, how do I say this, very attractive . . . to those interested in kind of not neat and pretty packages. He was a bit untidy and unkempt but charismatic and charming. That's a dangerous combination.

FRED FELDMAN: Brand New's relationship with Taking Back Sunday back then went hot and cold. There were times where everything was great. And there were times when no one was talking to each other. You know, don't forget they did that tour together.

CHRISTIAN MCKNIGHT: Taking Back Sunday and Brand New did that mending of the fences tour [in 2002].

RANDY NICHOLS: In Sacramento, I was going for a walk with Jesse—Brand New was on tour and I was trying to manage them—and he asked me if he thought it was a good idea to do that tour with Taking Back Sunday. There was still some ill will, but not really. I was like, "You absolutely need to do that tour."

FRED FELDMAN: Those shows were insane. You could feel both bands challenging each other.

RANDY NICHOLS: The audience was like, "Holy shit, I feel like these two bands don't like each other—what's gonna happen?"

MATT GALLE: I went to a handful of the dates: LA, San Diego, New York, Boston. All the shows I went to were just packed, perspiration dripping off the walls.

JOHN NOLAN: At the beginning of the tour, we were supporting Brand New. We were getting known across the country, outside of the Northeast. Along the way of that tour, we went from being the support band to the same level Brand New was at.

EDDIE REYES: We went fucking across America and back.

MATTHEW ISMAEL RUIZ: Me and some homies drove down from Gainesville to Orlando. The show was at this bar called the Social. I remember it because it didn't look like a venue; it looked like a bar that might have dueling pianos on frat night or something. The thing we were blown away by was the dueling vocalist vibe of Taking Back Sunday. You could see . . . I wouldn't say tension, but it was like, "Who's the front man of this band?" Lazzara felt like he actually had to really try hard to remind you he was the front man, because you know, the best songs were him and John Nolan singing *at* each other. The thing that stuck in my mind was how he had the microphone duct-taped to the mic cable. I was like, "What the fuck, that looks so ghetto, what is that?" And then he started doing the fuckin' lasso thing. And you know, it was obnoxious and he had all these moves, he would throw the mic out, pull it back in, and like lots of spinning and twirling and like flipping his hair and stuff. And the girls were just *ahhhhhhh* because of the hair, and the pants. Ha, ha, ha. Typical shit. But they crushed it, man, the set was insane. One of the best sets I've ever seen.

EDDIE REYES: Even the one in Utah in Salt Lake, where we were terrified. Back then Salt Lake had a terrible reputation for kids tearing up the shows and starting fights and all this crap. But that show was fucking awesome. It was sold out, too.

I remember driving from Idaho to Oregon. We stopped in the mountains and everyone sat on top of the vans and just looked out, looking at the stars. We had so many moments like that; it was just a bunch of friends traveling, you know? The next city we're going to, people knew who we were. That was exciting. The whole tour was like, Long Island in your face. Everybody realized that Long Island was something to pay attention to.

CHRISTIAN MCKNIGHT: There was no Long Island show on the tour because of This Island Earth Fest. We'd done it the two previous years, named it after a Silent Majority seven-inch. We found this really weird place called County Fair, with a mini-golf course, an arcade, go-karts. They had these massive fields and they were like, "Yeah, do a concert here." We had like four thousand people at that show. Thursday headlined, and we had Midtown, Brand New, Taking Back Sunday, From Autumn to Ashes, the Starting Line, Motion City Soundtrack, the Early November. I remember the amount of money we paid Thursday was by far was the most amount of money I'd ever paid a band. I was in shock when they told us what they wanted, like, holy shit.

GEOFF RICKLY: It was muddy all over the stage, so when we were playing, we're sliding around. I also remember one of the guys from Brand New jumping into the crowd with his guitar and like, breaking this girl's nose. Obviously not on purpose. But I remember thinking like, "Who's this band all these people seem to love that I've never heard of that's gigantic here in the bubble of Long Island?" And then I saw him in the crowd, that girl got hurt, and thinking like, "You've got a lot to learn."

CHRISTIAN MCKNIGHT: That was definitely Vinnie. Vinnie from Brand New jumped off the stage . . . not even off the stage, he fuckin' climbed the lighting truss and jumped off and hit this poor girl on the face with his guitar, and busts her nose. Me, Jesse, Vin, and I think Brian Lane went to the hospital to like make sure this girl was okay.

FRED FELDMAN: The Jersey show on that Brand New/Taking Back Sunday tour was at Birch Hill Nightclub in Old Bridge.

JONATHAN DANIEL: The main thing I remember was everyone singing—a thousand kids singing every word to every band. And if there was anybody from the actual music business there, I didn't see them. That was very striking to me.

CHRISTIAN MCKNIGHT: That show was huge, sold out. I remember watching it from the stage and it just being bananas, people jumping over the barricade for both bands. I was friends with all the security guards at Birch Hill. I remember having a conversation with them ahead of time like, "I want to go over the barricade a bunch," and they were just like, "You better not." And then of course the whole night I was jumping off the stage.

FRED FELDMAN: The heat was stifling. Eddie from Taking Back Sunday literally fell offstage and had to be given oxygen. It was absolute mayhem for both bands.

CHRISTIAN MCKNIGHT: Everybody was coming over the barricade, I couldn't believe the amount of people coming over per second.

FRED FELDMAN: Brand New pretty much played everything off *Your Favorite Weapon.* "Jude Law" was obviously a big one, they'd had modest success with the video for that one. "Logan" was a big, big song in the set. And they didn't play "Mix Tape" a lot, but when they did, people loved it. And "Seventy Times 7" was the one that people just *wanted.* The quieter part with, "Have another drink and drive yourself home, I hope there's ice on all the roads," it's like you're lighting a fuse. And when it hit, people just lost their shit.

CHRISTIAN MCKNIGHT: John Nolan came out and sang that song with Brand New. And that song's like, honestly, about John. Ha, ha, ha.

RANDY NICHOLS: This was before the internet was big, so not everybody saw the first night of tour, the bands getting along. Night after night, the audience was shocked. You just kind of assumed, "Okay, they're doing a tour together, but they're not friends . . ."

EDDIE REYES: We were all friends, that's why we were touring together.

MIKE DUBIN: It got ironed out. And then it got worse again. And then it never got ironed out.

CHAPTER 11

"IF HALF *THE* PEOPLE HATE YOU, *THE* OTHER HALF ARE GOING *TO* DEFEND YOU *TO THE* DEATH"

GEOFF RICKLY: Thursday played a basement show with Arma Angelus. I was talking to Pete because we had had a Racetraitor show in my basement. I was like, "Yo, Pete, this is sick. I'm so stoked we're getting to play together, I loved Racetraitor, how's Mani?" He was like, "Yeah, this is cool. But I've got a band you *gotta* hear. It's more like you guys, it's a little more pop-punk. It's called Fall Out Boy." I said, "Like *The Simpsons* thing?" He's like, "Yeah." I didn't really think anything of it.

CHRIS GUTIERREZ: Arma Angelus had started winding down. We put out a record and a couple EPs, we played important things like CBGB and Hellfest. But Arma just wasn't getting the momentum we thought it would have. To be honest with you—and Wentz would probably agree with me—I think we'd taken it as far as the band could go.

PETE WENTZ: There was a point where the hardcore scene was just preaching to everyone, like no one was good enough: "Oh, you're vegan, but you drive a car!" The reaction to that was like, "Let's just be about moshing." Or the more visceral reaction was to make jokes that weren't PC. It weirded me out.

There's something about the screaming, the relentless chug . . . Like if you worked on an aircraft carrier, the last thing you would want to do is go home and listen to airplanes landing on a pair of headphones, you know? That was the inception of Fall Out Boy. Let's do something that's just fun.

Are we just going to get four hundred people at a show and spin-kick each other's faces off? Let's do something that's the exact opposite of that.

CHRIS GUTIERREZ: We started practicing less and less and the band felt like less of a priority for everyone. We were packing up practice one day in our drummer Tim's basement, Pete was standing to the right of me and he's like, "So, dude, I'm starting this like, weird pop-punk band. We want to sound like Lifetime crossed with New Found Glory." I'm like, "You make fun of me for liking pop-punk!" And he's like, "Yeah, I met these dudes. I think I'm gonna grab Joe and Patrick . . ."

ADAM SISKA: In 2002, I started going to shows at this place called Back to the Office. That was the mecca of the Chicago scene, but it was short-lived. It was this little venue in the suburbs that let these kids rent it out on random nights to put on dollar shows. I went there to see bands like 504 Plan, Knockout, August Premier—those were the heavy hitters in the local scene. After one show ended, everyone was loitering and this maybe eighteen-year-old kid they were calling Patrick Fall Out got on the stage. He did a cover of "What's Going On" by Marvin Gaye. The talent in his vocals next to everyone who was performing then . . . Everyone else kind of had the whiny pop-punk thing going on. Patrick sounded like Elvis Costello. I grew up with pretty good music in my house, so I could tell the difference. Immediately I was like, who is this Fall Out Boy?

PETE WENTZ: I knew he was talented, but I didn't really know how gifted he was. I was like, he's really good at covering Saves the Day songs! But then as I got to know him, I realized, "Oh, this guy is really gifted. At a lot of things and he doesn't even know how gifted he is."

PATRICK STUMP: As a kid, *Saturday Night Live* was the thing I could stay up late and watch, and I would soak up Dana Carvey, Phil Hartman, Mike Myers, and do all their voices. I was always on voices. And then *Animaniacs* came out, *Tiny Toon Adventures*, the *X-Men* cartoon, and I would just do voices. That was just a thing I did. And some characters sing. So I would do Sinatra, and Sting, and Elvis Costello. It was no different to me than doing Mickey Mouse. And I didn't realize that was a thing people couldn't do. I had no concept. I didn't think of myself as a singer.

HANIF ABDURRAQIB: Patrick wasn't a born-and-bred hardcore dude. But he could hang.

BRIAN ANDERSON: Patrick would be rockin' an old busted-out pair of Chuck Taylors and probably wearing the T-shirt of a band you're playing with. I remember seeing him always wearing a 504 Plan trucker hat and glasses like a bit of a dork. And probably a jean jacket with a very tasteful pin.

NICK SCIMECA: Patrick's voice was unlike anything any of us had ever seen. We'd be like, "Hey, play us that idea from last night," and Patrick would sing in this super-deep voice. Then he'd play another song and you'd get this super-high voice.

PATRICK STUMP: I had been in a few bands. Everybody has a band in high school, you know? Drums were the only instrument I'd taken a particular interest in playing. It's so silly—there really is this prejudice that drummers can't write music, that drummers aren't musicians. Just because I don't have a polyphony doesn't mean I don't know how to contribute to it!

PETE WENTZ: Before I knew Patrick, I felt like a painter looking at a wall, trying to finger paint or something. There were things inside I wanted to do, but I didn't have the technical skills to do it.

PATRICK STUMP: Junior year, you're starting to figure yourself out. I said to myself, "Well, I'm gonna try one more band. Maybe I'll try guitar or bass, and then maybe they'll let me write." That was the main thing. All I've ever wanted to do is write music.

Joe and Pete were talking about putting a band together and I auditioned. I didn't know anything about guitar; I just knew some barre chords and I played some stuff I wrote and sang it. They both went, "Hey, you should sing." And I'm like, "Okay, okay, okay . . . How was the song? Did you like the song?"

MANI MOSTOFI: Me and Pete talked about me managing Fall Out Boy really early on. My vision for Fall Out Boy was them being a big underground band in Chicago, like Alkaline Trio, right? Pete was like, "No. Blink-182. Green Day. That's the level I'm shooting for." When Fall Out Boy still had a shitty drummer and they weren't a real band, Pete said to me, word for word, "We're gonna be the next Blink-182."

PETE WENTZ: Everybody's got a dream or whatever. Nobody gives a fuck until you execute it.

MANI MOSTOFI: Their first couple shows, they didn't even have the name Fall Out Boy. I think they said their name was Forget Me Not at their first show. The next show, they were Fall Out Boy.

HANIF ABDURRAQIB: History is revisionist. I think a lot of people will say that Fall Out Boy was beloved in their early moments and everyone knew from the point they heard them that it was going to be a thing. But in my experience, that was not true.

BRIAN ANDERSON: At first, Fall Out Boy was pretty sloppy. And that was kind of the appeal.

MANI MOSTOFI: Patrick didn't even play guitar. There were other guitar players involved.

BEN JORGENSEN: All we knew about this band from Chicago was all they did onstage was spin around in circles with their guitars. I don't think any of my friends had heard a Fall Out Boy song, but they were kind of a joke in the scene: The band that spun in circles really fast and didn't really know how to play their instruments.

BRIAN ANDERSON: When Fall Out Boy first started, they were a five-piece and Patrick just sang. He would put one arm behind his back, doing the front man thing . . .

NICK SCIMECA: Running around, swinging the mic, kind of like Chris Conley.

JOSHUA CAIN: Motion City Soundtrack played with some early version of Fall Out Boy, a basement-type show in Illinois. Patrick was just singing at the time. It was chaos. I remember leaving the show like, "That band is just a mess, but that kid can really fucking sing."

MANI MOSTOFI: The early shows were amateurish but endearing. Patrick actually spoke more then: In between songs he would tell stories, all goofy and charming, and then Pete would come in with a jab. It was this straight man/funny man routine. The live show wasn't quite with it, but they drew the crowd in because they had such a good rapport.

CHRIS GUTIERREZ: Fall Out Boy had just started gaining momentum. They had rabid fans . . . but there were only about thirty of them.

MANI MOSTOFI: They were playing in front of fifteen people in a way that acknowledged, "We're playing in front of fifteen people. But that's still cool, and we're all part of a team." Pete saw the potential. He diverted all his attention and energy to that.

CHRIS GUTIERREZ: Arma Angelus hadn't played in forever. We hadn't practiced in forever. So Jim Grimes said, "Why don't you guys do your last show with me?" Grimes was the singer of Extinction. He was also responsible for putting on almost every hardcore show in Chicago.

JIM GRIMES: It was an all-day show for my thirtieth birthday, a benefit [for a Chicago bully breed dog rescue]. I couldn't do it at a regular venue because they'd tell me to get lost if I said, "I'm going to have this all-day hardcore show, a bunch of people are going to come in and probably ruin your place." So we booked it at an indoor skate park. Pete asked me, "Hey, do you think Fall Out Boy could play?" I couldn't care less. I was like, "Yeah, you're my friend. Arma Angelus is playing their last show. You're more than welcome to take like twenty minutes of that and have the rest of the dudes come on and play a Fall Out Boy set."

CHRIS GUTIERREZ: It was in La Grange, a good half hour outside of Chicago.

JIM GRIMES: The skate park was like, "Can you just keep it to five hundred people because we got fire codes and all that?" But I didn't pay attention. We had seven hundred, eight hundred kids.

CHRIS GUTIERREZ: Jim pulled every card he had, like, "I'm gonna put together a sick-ass lineup of hardcore bands."

JIM GRIMES: I started hitting up all the bands I wanted to have play: "If you're on tour, can you book it around this show?"

STEPHANIE MARLOW: It was from eleven in the morning till ten at night or something, and we stayed and watched every band: Rise Against, Every Time I Die, Unearth, Suicide File, A Death for Every Sin, This Day Forward, Bleeding Through, the Hope Conspiracy, Arma Angelus, Skycamefalling, the Promise, Figure Four, Misery Signals, 25 ta Life, The Killer, Fall Out Boy.

HANIF ABDURRAQIB: The bands would play on one ramp, the fans would sit on another, and in the middle was the pit.

STEPHANIE MARLOW: The sound in a skate park is tough, so it sounded like garbage.

CHRIS GUTIERREZ: We'd practiced for the show up at Trohman's attic only once or twice . . . and then it really showed. By the end of Arma Angelus, almost everybody who was in Fall Out Boy played in Arma: Wentz was singing, Joe Trohman was on guitar, I was playing bass, and we still had our friend Adam, who had been the guitar player for Arma. Andy Hurley had played drums at the end of Arma and he was at the skate park show, but he didn't want to play, so Patrick played drums. He didn't know the drum parts very well. He would stop in certain places and some of the guys were like, "Dude, what the fuck?"

I was more concerned with having fun at the show. And I think Wentz was kind of over Arma Angelus at that point. So we butchered our way through two and a half . . . three and a half songs? Like, fuck it. People had fun.

MANI MOSTOFI: When you play your last show and it's local, people get really invested in making it the craziest show possible.

HANIF ABDURRAQIB: Fall Out Boy played a really small set, like three or four songs. They were the only band that was pop-punky. And they started out getting heckled.

CHRIS GUTIERREZ: You gotta remember, they're playing for hardcore kids. It was 95 percent hardcore kids who were all like, "Okay, we won't throw shit at you because we know that you're all good dudes playing your little project." But then you could see there's a good 5 percent of people who were fucking stoked. Local teenage girls were way into them. It was cool to see these little kids fangirling over this band while I'm like, "Do you know who these dickheads are?"

HANIF ABDURRAQIB: Then something shifted when they played "Dead on Arrival." People got more energetic. The band got a little more comfortable. Joe got theatrical with his guitar playing, as he is wont to do.

It was interesting, because this was a band that people did not take that seriously, at the bottom of a bill, with bands that people took very seriously. And I think they had a really memorable performance.

MANI MOSTOFI: Fall Out Boy was more accessible to this punk rock mall emo scene that was burgeoning in Chicago. None of those people were from the hardcore scene. The Fall Out Boy guys had always been playing really aggressive metal music that only attracted certain people. But now, Fall Out Boy's playing these emo-y and pop-punky shows and getting different people into them.

ADAM SISKA: I was on the football team, but it was very clear I was not part of that kinda thing. And when I wound up going to these shows, Fall Out Boy became my favorite band. They'd be hanging out and even though Pete was nine years older than me, it didn't really seem to be a huge gap. If you were there, you were part of the club. When the show was over, they'd be at the merch table, and when these guys that were just up onstage took the time to talk to you, it felt like you were cool, too. Early on, they had these shirts that said, "FALL OUT BOY IS A GANG." They always wanted to create this community.

As someone who didn't know how to play an instrument, it was the perfect scene because I don't think Pete Wentz knew how to play, either.

STEPHANIE MARLOW: I remember having two friends I'd go to shows with and then before I knew it, there'd be a crew of friends driving in from the suburbs in their parents' station wagon full of people.

ADAM SISKA: The Fall Out Boy guys were straight edge and kind of clean-cut at the time, so I began to look up to this sort of do-good mentality. You know, if somebody falls down, pick them up. I was fifteen and my father had just died of a drug overdose. Discovering Fall Out Boy was a lifesaver. They took me under their wing and showed me this positive attitude, like, "All your dreams can come true if you follow me."

HANIF ABDURRAQIB: I grew up in Columbus, Ohio. The trip to Chicago was about six hours. I grew up with folks who didn't have a lot of money but my friend Tyler had a van and a lot of times, if we got enough gas money to get to Chicago, a lot of people would just go to the shows with no way back. Then we'd just give people rides home and have them cover gas. If someone needed it, we'd drop them in Indiana or we'd drop them in Dayton. Not the safest route, but the scene felt familial for us because a lot of times the people we're giving rides to were the other Black kids at the show. We had this default familial understanding of how to move.

ADAM SISKA: Back to the Office got shut down. I think they were serving liquor to underage kids. That was in summer of '02 and I don't remember going to a lot of shows that summer. Then that fall, the Knights of Columbus in the Chicago suburb Arlington Heights became the centerpiece of what was happening.

GRETA MORGAN: When I saw the movie *Almost Famous*, I had this grand idea that I wanted to be a journalist like the kid in the movie. I had played piano, guitar, cello, had even written songs most of my life, but for some reason at that age I never thought I could really be a musician. So I was like, "I want to be the person interviewing bands." I started going to local shows—the Arlington Heights Knights of Columbus was a popular place for people to play. My friend Jamie Feldmar and I did this print zine called *Trash Magazine* when I was in seventh and eighth grade. We would just look in the liner notes of records we liked and send a handwritten letter to the bands like, "Hey, can we interview you sometime?"

BRIAN ANDERSON: I grew up about a five-minute drive from the Knights of Columbus in Arlington Heights. There was this whole constellation of venues in the Chicago suburban scene at this time, but the Knights of Columbus was the hub in the middle. I'd go see Rise Against, or Fall Out Boy playing to fifty people. The Academy Is . . . wasn't even a band yet, but those dudes were there to see other bands. The usual suspects at the Knights of Columbus were Knockout, 504 Plan, Spitalfield, and August Premier. Every Friday, you could pretty much count on one of those bands playing.

SEAN O'KEEFE: Knockout had gotten signed by a label in California. They were the first of all our friends in Chicago who got a deal, and that held a lot of weight with people.

HANIF ABDURRAQIB: Knockout was good. When I got into them, they had just signed to Fearless Records.

BRIAN ANDERSON: In 2002, when they put out *Searching for Solid Ground*, that was *the* record.

DE'MAR HAMILTON: Everyone in Knockout was a skater. That's where the music came from—fast-paced pop-punk. Us and Fall Out Boy were super close back in the day. We played so many shows together. There was a period where we'd headline and Fall Out Boy would be the second or third band.

SEAN O'KEEFE: Pete was friends with the Knockout guys, so he was hanging around the studio when I was making that Knockout record. He goes, "Hey, I've got this band with Patrick, it's kind of a joke band, we call it Fall Out Boy. Here's a cassette, will you listen to it?" I go, "Okay, Patrick's playing it?" He goes, "Patrick's singing." I go, "Patrick's a singer? I thought Patrick was the drummer." "No, no, he's singing." A couple days went by, Pete would ask me the same question and I still hadn't listened to it. Then the Knockout guys go, "Hey, we're gonna get Patrick to come in and do a background vocal on one of our songs."

DE'MAR HAMILTON: That's how it used to be. We weren't thinking about publishing or writing or anything. Just like, "We're making music over here."

SEAN O'KEEFE: Patrick goes into the booth, and I did not know what a machine that guy was. Not only was he incredibly good at coming up with parts, he was an incredible singer. I said, "That's it, I'm keeping you for the rest of the day. I'm gonna have you sing harmonies on the rest of the record."

I hit up Pete: "All right, I'll check out Fall Out Boy."

ADAM SISKA: I think bands wanted to create their own rivalries—it seemed like a way to entice fan bases. I always suspected that Brand New and TBS were playing off of each other, in a way that was almost friendly. And there absolutely was that in Chicago. The band Spitalfield wrote this song called "Fairweather Friend," which was rumored to be about Pete. The rumor was that T. J. Minich from Spitalfield, who had been the bass player in Knockout, had quit Knockout and was about to join Fall Out Boy on guitar. But Fall Out Boy did a brief tour where Patrick played guitar and I think it became clear to them that Patrick was the best musician in the band, and that they didn't need to be a five-piece anymore. I think that was when they decided Fall Out Boy would be a four-piece. T.J. took it really hard when he was supposed join the band and it was called off.

NICK SCIMECA: When Patrick switched to just guitar, it definitely clicked more.

JOHNNY MINARDI: The first three songs Fall Out Boy recorded with Sean O'Keefe were "Dead on Arrival," "Saturday," and "Homesick at Space Camp."

MANI MOSTOFI: They either kicked out a drummer or had a drummer quit, and it was the best thing that ever happened to them. Patrick was supposed to play drums on those three songs and I was in this kinda garage punk band with Andy Hurley at the time. Andy's like, "Pete's asking me to play on these songs, and I kind of think there's something going on with this band, what do you think?"

At the end of "Saturday," Patrick sings like, "Sat-ur-day—ayyy-AYYY-*ayyyyyy*." I'd never heard anybody in the scene do that before, that kind of vocal run. I remember Andy was like, "This is the reason I want to be in this band."

CHRIS GUTIERREZ: Pete hands me a stack of CD demos and says, "Dude, can you go hand these out to all your friends?" I remember going around and handing them to all my friends at work like, "Yo, check this out. Check this out. Check this out." I even said to Pete, "This shit's legit good." And he's like, "Yo, you think?" I'm like, "I'm not bullshitting. I'm not a dude who blows smoke up people's asses just to fucking blow smoke. This shit's fucking for-real good. When you motherfuckers get to *TRL*, I'm coming with you."

DE'MAR HAMILTON: Fall Out Boy's shows got sort of crazy. They put out that three-song thing and I remember seeing them and it was so rowdy they turned off the PA.

TOM HIGGENSON: Something crazy was happening with that band because back in the day, they didn't sound that good live. It was like At the Drive-In onstage, jumping around, throwing their guitars.

BRIAN ANDERSON: There was a moment where Fall Out Boy became *the* band in Chicago. It had been Knockout, but the hype was building around Fall Out Boy.

ADAM SISKA: There was a show at this place in the suburbs called the Wheaton Grand Theatre, and Fall Out Boy headlined over Knockout for the first time. The whole local scene was in disbelief. And I think Knockout kind of started to implode . . . Just a lot of inner turmoil.

DE'MAR HAMILTON: Fall Out Boy were going up and we were going the opposite way . . . I knew I didn't want to be in Knockout anymore, but I didn't really wanna say anything. One day I called like, "Yo, what's up, are you guys gonna call me for practice?" And I heard someone else playing drums in the background. They're like, "Yeah, man, sorry . . ."

BRIAN ANDERSON: Fall Out Boy just pushed to another level, while Knockout petered out.

CHRIS GUTIERREZ: I don't want to be that person, but it's well documented with all my friends that I knew Fall Out Boy was going to be big from the start because Wentz had nowhere else to go. He couldn't do school. He was a hoodlum outside of this, you know? I think he'd be the first to tell you that if he didn't have Fall Out Boy, he probably would have ended up in jail.

ADAM SISKA: Early on at the Knights of Columbus, I remember Pete telling me how the singer of the Hives would go onstage and basically end shows like, "All the other bands playing today suck, you're free to go home now, we're done." It was so polarizing, and Pete developed this thing that was like, "Infamy is bigger than fame." If half the people hate you, the other half are going to defend you to the death.

CHAPTER 12

"IT WASN'T LIKE WE THOUGHT WE WERE GOING PLACES, BECAUSE THERE WAS NOWHERE *TO* GO *IN* UTAH"

GABE SAPORTA: You had these bands making music that was catchy and universal, but came from places no one gave a shit about.

ANDY GREENWALD: As much as the tastemakers at *Spin* or wherever I was working would look down their noses at these emo bands, they understood conceptually, Long Island or New Jersey, as spaces that might birth this music. So they could cover it, even if they were holding their noses. But Utah? Nobody wanted to be a part of that; it wasn't cool or understandable.

QUINN ALLMAN: In Utah, there was this ceiling we had. And I had no reference, either. I had no idea that New York and New Jersey were even next to each other. I grew up in the mountains, a canyon area. I rode my bike around.

DIA FRAMPTON: I grew up in St. George, Utah. The emo music and punk rock scene exploded for me when I was fifteen, around 2002. I started dating this guy Riley. His family was Mormon, but he didn't believe in the religion. He didn't really follow the rules. He ended up getting kicked out of his house for saying he didn't want to go on a Mormon mission. Growing up in Utah, I'd listened to country music: the Dixie Chicks, Shania Twain, Tanya Tucker. Riley showed me this band called Thursday. With a few of our friends, we were driving in his really shitty car that felt like the doors would fall off if you closed them too hard. We were blasting "Jet Black New Year," jetting down this tiny religious town that felt like walls closing in around you. The song just made you explode and made you feel alive. It also made me feel cool for the first time. I felt like I was part of something, instead of this quiet girl who didn't really know her identity. Sometimes when you like a band, it makes you feel cool. I know that sounds super shallow, but it goes deeper than that . . . Then Riley showed me the Used.

JEPH HOWARD: The Used didn't come from the same scene as other bands. We came from sort of a mess.

BERT MCCRACKEN: I grew up in Utah County, which is the mecca of centralization for Mormonism on the planet. Rock and roll was considered pure evil.

ANDY GREENWALD: New Jersey is normal, right? That's a loose word, but the freaky stuff is rebelling against normalcy, working-class suburbs. Here's the middle, and where they're rebelling is a little bit over here. But in Utah, normal is . . . way over *here*. "Normal" is also totally extreme in its obedience, its religiosity. So the extreme has to be even more fucking extreme.

JEPH HOWARD: Utah is a very extreme place. Growing up in the nineties, I would see people covered in tattoos. I remember going to Salt Lake when I was a kid, seeing people with face tattoos and head tattoos. You can't have a religion shoved down your throat 24/7 without the opposite pushing back.

JOHN FELDMANN: I knew there was this side of hardcore in Utah that was way more extreme than your typical scene. I'd heard stories about people knocking cigarettes out of people's hands and carving the Xs out on their backs for straight edge.

BRANDEN STEINECKERT: I've been sober my entire life but never claimed straight edge because where I lived, I didn't want to put that title on it.

BERT MCCRACKEN: You see a lot of extremes in Utah: the most teenage pregnancies, lots and lots of drug abuse, lots of overdoses for young kids, lots of suicides for homosexuals. The religious oppression creates adverse extremities everywhere you look. I think that's why the straight-edge scene became this nationwide phenomenon.

JEPH HOWARD: "Straight edge" got classified as a gang by the police in Utah.

WALTER SCHREIFELS: It's one of these desert places where meth took off really hard. Straight edge has that appeal to people who are in danger of becoming substance abusers. It's a way to build community before you need a twelve-step program.

BERT MCCRACKEN: I was straight edge for two or three years, but I'd never really done drugs before that. That's the typical story for Salt Lake kids—just jump straight into something.

I was the black sheep of my family, the oldest of five siblings, and I started to have problems with the church really early on. That led to a lot of fighting with my parents. A lot of questioning authority and acting in my own best interest. I used to get kicked out of class all the time for screaming and I'd just tell them I was practicing for my career. Heh, heh, heh.

BRANDEN STEINECKERT: Bert was hardcore straight edge and like, a preachy straight-edger. He would do his own little zine and hand it out at shows.

BERT MCCRACKEN: I dropped out of normal high school and started going to an alternative learning program and there were a few kids there who were really into the hardcore scene. One kid in particular, Blake Donner, gave me a huge box full of CDs. He was a part of the hardcore scene for years, but he was becoming a Krishna devotee, so he was trying to give up all his material possessions. That box of CDs became my whole life: Sunny Day Real Estate, Coalesce, Converge, One King Down, Strife . . . I remember driving around in my mom's minivan listening to music for hours and hours and hours.

JEPH HOWARD: Bert had a metal band called Cobra Kai. We knew he could scream nonstop the whole show, but he also had a good singing voice.

BERT MCCRACKEN: I started smoking pot and the straight-edge band I was in kicked me out. After that, I drifted away from music for a while and drugs became my everyday. Slowly from alcohol, then weed and cocaine to crystal methamphetamines. I got caught up in that world, living with some tweakers in a garage, and on and on and on.

I turned eighteen, and we got busted with meth and I got charged with a felony. My dad had to come bail me out, and I was staying at my parents' house, not knowing what I was going to do with myself. I knew I didn't feel good being on those drugs. My life was seriously suffering.

JEPH HOWARD: I had a band with Quinn Allman on guitar and Branden Steineckert on drums.

BRANDEN STEINECKERT: Jeph's mom was filing for bankruptcy and right before she did, she went to Guitar Center with him and bought him a bass and an amp on some credit she had.

JEPH HOWARD: I went from singer to playing bass because I could scream but couldn't sing. So we were looking for a singer. We wrote a song called "Maybe Memories" and started trying out singers.

BRANDEN STEINECKERT: We were putting up flyers around town, walking around skate shops and whatever, handing a flyer to anybody that looked interesting. And fuck, the people we'd audition . . . It was like, "Fuck, you just made us sound like Disturbed." It was starting to get frustrating: Can we find someone who can sing, but also scream, and be as unique as we're trying to be? And then we remembered Bert.

QUINN ALLMAN: He was really struggling. He was in NA when I met him, for crystal meth, and I think other things. He had dark circles under his eyes.

BERT MCCRACKEN: I was so fresh off of drugs. I was just so out of it. I had no idea how I would ever handle hanging out with three dudes who had never done serious drugs before. Their idea of fun was sneaking into a hot tub at a hotel.

The guys had a really hard time getting me into the studio or getting me to work on a song. I would take a week and a half, two weeks just to write a verse. There was one time they were all like, "Something's gonna have to change. We're gonna have to move on without you." But yeah, I had bad habits, coming from doing nothing but meth all day into a world of pretty inspired guys who all had jobs.

QUINN ALLMAN: He was lost, to be honest. I was patient with him at first. It took some ambition to be like, "Let's do this, dude. You can live at my house, we can share a car, I'll drive you to band practice every day, I'll drive you to Narcotics Anonymous. I'll take care of you."

BERT MCCRACKEN: I immediately moved in with Quinn's mom and dad. The band became our life, right then and there.

JEPH HOWARD: We built a little sound booth in the closet at my mom's house and put a microphone in there. Bert wrote down his lyrics for "Maybe Memories" and went in there and sang it, which is how it went on our demo CD. We were like, "Well this is definitely what we've been looking for."

QUINN ALLMAN: Thursday's *Full Collapse* changed everything for me. When I heard the guitars, that was it. I was like, "I gotta hurry up on this. This is almost close to what we're making: these really driving, bigger moments caught between aggressive punk."

BERT MCCRACKEN: So we recorded a couple songs. And I remember we were at a bowling alley one night, and the guy at the bowling alley played the songs over the loudspeaker and everyone was just freaking out. That was a moment. But it wasn't like we thought we were going places, because there was nowhere to go in Utah.

BRANDEN STEINECKERT: We dreamed and dreamed and dreamed about being able to play music and be a professional band, but everyone would tell us what a pipe dream that was: "Dude, you live in Utah. No one has ever made it out of Utah and had a proper music career, other than Donny and Marie Osmond."

JOHN FELDMANN: Branden and Quinn, and maybe Jeph, drove out to Mojo Records, the label my band Goldfinger was signed to, to see if there was a possibility of me getting them signed.

BRANDEN STEINECKERT: Goldfinger was this rad ska-punk band.

BERT MCCRACKEN: Branden was quite the hustler at the time, sending demos to everyone.

BRANDEN STEINECKERT: I went to every single Goldfinger show, and every time I'd talk to the guys. So we knew each other well enough, but they weren't like, giving me their numbers, you know?

QUINN ALLMAN: When we had our new demo tape with Bert, Goldfinger was playing a festival show. Branden and I went up to the fence screaming for him, like, "John! John! John!" Handing that tape over was the crux of my whole life. It had Branden's number on it, because he had a pager. He ended up calling Branden a little later . . .

BRANDEN STEINECKERT: I was at the airport at 6:00 a.m., waiting for my brother to leave on his mission. There's some weird number that calls; I answer it. "Hey, it's John Feldmann." I was like, "AHHH!" He was in Norway, playing some festival with Deftones. He's like, "Dude, I heard your demo. I fucking love it. I want to bring you guys to LA, I want to produce songs for you guys, and I want to bring you on tour with Goldfinger." And, dude, I was in tears. Instantly, I called Quinn, woke him up, and Bert happened to be there.

BERT MCCRACKEN: I remember Quinn ran into the room while I was sleeping.

JEPH HOWARD: We thought it was a prank.

BERT MCCRACKEN: The guys had been up at Sundance and they met a guy who said he was Dexter from the Offspring. I guess it was just an impostor. A Dexter impersonator. He said he was going to get the band signed and take us on his jet and all sorts of stuff. When they came back from Sundance telling me they met the singer of the Offspring I didn't believe it for one second. So that kind of became the mindset when they were like, "No, the singer of Goldfinger is gonna fly us out to California and record a demo for us." I'm like, "*Goldfinger*, huh? *Sure* he is."

JEPH HOWARD: We were a bunch of poor kids. Some of us were barely even making it. Me and Branden rented a house with a living room and put stuff up on the walls to try to soundproof it so we could jam in there. Bert and Quinn didn't have cars and they lived forty-five minutes from us, so they had to hitchhike most of the time to get to our house. We didn't have a lot of positive stuff going for us; music was all we cared about. Then comes Feldmann, who flies us out to California because he wanted to hear these songs in person. He heard something nobody else did.

JOHN FELDMANN: Some of them had never even been on an airplane before. They weren't high fashion . . . They were skateboard kids—you know, the chain wallets, shorts, Vans, and band T-shirts. Quinn had that super influential white-bleached emo haircut. I think Bert was influenced by Kurt Cobain, the way he dressed and wore his beard.

BERT MCCRACKEN: I'd never experienced any kind of money in my life, any kind of fancy anything. So seeing stuff in LA was a bit of a turnoff. I mean, I remember John Feldmann picking us up in his BMW and I was like, "What the fuck is this? I thought he was in a punk rock band."

JOHN FELDMANN: I had this 3 Series BMW, the first nice car I ever owned. I just remember how wide-eyed they were. This huge city, taking them surfing, seeing the ocean. Six in the morning and we're driving PCH, listening to a burned CD of those three songs turned up to ten, like, "Holy shit. We have something here."

JEPH HOWARD: "Box Full of Sharp Objects"—that was Feldmann's favorite song. He said he'd never heard anything like it, but that there's a few minor tweaks I think you guys should do.

BERT MCCRACKEN: Turns out, every major label that existed wanted to see us and court us. This was still when they were taking bands out to dinners and strip clubs and all sorts of crazy shit that we had never experienced, these regular working-class kids from Utah County. It was immediately this whirlwind of flying from New York to LA and back to New York, playing showcases for major labels.

QUINN ALLMAN: It was the most exciting time of our lives. I had a camcorder the entire time.

BRANDEN STEINECKERT: When we were in New York, we went late after one of the nights of doing showcases for all these labels and had a cab take us as close to Ground Zero as we could. Shit was still smoking. There was still ash in all the gutters. We were all in tears. There were so many highs and lows all at once.

BERT MCCRACKEN: The A&R guys, they were all pretty nervous around the band, nervous about what to say. We were such aggressive youngsters.

One night in New York we were getting courted by Island Def Jam. They sent us out on the full deal, the full New York night out. We went to restaurants, three clubs, a couple strip clubs, and I wasn't even old enough to get into a bar, so they were sneaking me into these places and I got so drunk, so unbelievably hammered, with the people that thought we were for sure gonna sign with Island Def Jam. I remember going to JFK airport the next morning, just throwing up out the limo window the whole way there.

BRANDEN STEINECKERT: Yeah, he liked to drink. He liked to party. We were happy he wasn't doing hard drugs. But it was also like, "Come on, man, are you okay?"

BERT MCCRACKEN: I didn't care about business suits or none of these names, Lyor Cohen, none of these people meant anything to me. I used to throw up a lot during the shows because I would just go so hard. My body couldn't handle it. My natural reaction was just to *BLEHHH,* to spew. I probably threw up on four or five different business suits.

JOHN FELDMANN: Look, I could be wrong. But I remember Barry Weiss. I remember Monte Lipman. Michael . . . Michael from Jive Records. And Craig Aaronson from Warner.

For a guy like Bert, who had so much trauma as a kid, it's like he needed to get out. And he knew this was his only hope for getting out of Orem, Utah. When he's throwing up on these executives it's like he was saying, "Look, I am willing to die for my art."

BERT MCCRACKEN: Warner had this A&R guy named Craig Aaronson, who tragically passed away [in 2014]. He was one of the most enthusiastic, energized individuals you could ever come across. When he first heard "Buried Myself Alive," he was sobbing and jumping up and down screaming.

JOHN FELDMANN: I knew that if we can make Craig Aaronson cry, we can make the world cry.

JEPH HOWARD: Island Def Jam took us out snowboarding. We'd never had any money to go snowboarding, because you have to rent the gear and it was like $300 worth of equipment just to go one time, which was like, a week's paycheck. But Island Def Jam took us snowboarding for the whole bill.

That night, while we're at the hotel for the snowboarding trip, Warner called and made us say who we were gonna go with. We're like, "We can't do it tonight because we're here with Island Def Jam, we don't want to make these guys feel bad because they took us out here, but we are leaning towards you. Can we just say it tomorrow?" But Tom Whalley made us say we were signing with Warner that night. It's pretty funny; I think the Island Def Jam guys knew about it because they were super weird the next day to us.

JOHN FELDMANN: We got them signed. We got them a manager, the lawyer, the label, the whole thing, and then Bert went off to Santa Barbara and was like, "Is this really what I want?"

BRANDEN STEINECKERT: We couldn't get Bert to show up. We couldn't fucking find him.

BERT MCCRACKEN: I wasn't really sure that I was doing the right thing. I didn't want to be in some famous band, sucking ass to all the suits, and just being part of the world that was a nightmare to hear about: Limp Bizkit, payola, paying radio stations to play your jams and all this stuff I thought was so disgusting about music. I felt like I was sitting at that table, which really freaked me out.

JOHN FELDMANN: I'm like fifteen years older than those guys. My role was motivating Bert, who was still doing drugs, drinking, and smoking a lot of weed. And he was dating this girl and he would get unfocused on music and disappear for a week. And I'm like, "Fuck, they're living in my house. I've only got them here for a month to record the album . . ."

BERT MCCRACKEN: I pretty much quit the band during the recording of the first record and disappeared into Santa Barbara for a couple of weeks. I turned my phone off and nobody could find me.

BRANDEN STEINECKERT: *We just did the unheard of, and you can't show up to work now?* That was fucking scary. The more we pushed him, the more he'd push back and disappear on us. *Oh my god, all right, we'll hold our breath . . .*

JOHN FELDMANN: Kurt Cobain was a huge influence on Bert. Some people don't survive the success and some people are arguably more scared of success than they are of failure. And I think because of where Bert came from, the fear of having to go back to that life . . . I think that just outweighed the fear of success, just enough, for him to show back up after that Santa Barbara trip.

BERT MCCRACKEN: Feldmann is a longtime recovering addict . . . I think the fact he understands that whole world has always helped him deal better with me. There's a lot of times he kind of lost his mind that I was taking so long to come around, and dragging the bottom for so long.

JOHN FELDMANN: I know the pain of when you're in that jumping-off place of like, "Do I continue down this path where I know where it's going to end?" You know it's going to end with overdoses or failure, or going back to living at home, death, all those things that can happen down that path of addiction. Or the other end of it, where you don't do drugs, and the future is wide open. Anything is possible if you're allowing the universe to work through.

Bert came back and didn't do drugs for the rest of the record; he stayed sober for a while. And we finished the album.

JEPH HOWARD: On *The Used*, there's a lot of lyrics about trying to escape. "Taste of Ink" is about trying to get out. Saying, I want to leave. I want to be something big. Bigger than me.

BERT MCCRACKEN: I was always really attracted to songs that go to deeper truths about the human existence. Trying to get to the core of something and rip their heart open.

CHAPTER 13

"BETTER GET *A* LITTLE GLOSSIER, *OR* YOU'RE GONNA FALL BEHIND *THE* CROWD"

MAX BEMIS: In general, I had this vision that it was legit on the East Coast.

I didn't have a girlfriend in high school, because all the girls at my school were pretty vapid. I mean, I think that's reductive to some degree. I'm sure they were interesting people if you got to know them, but in terms of how they acted and what they were into, it was all about spending lots of money on clothes. It was like the fucking *Hills* or *The OC*. I just had this vision of some kind of arty girl that I would meet on the East Coast who went to shows and was cool.

The closest thing to a scene was this sort of, like, rich-kids hipster scene that started in LA. The bands closest to my age were Phantom Planet and Rooney, bands like that. Say Anything was tangentially involved in that, but we didn't fit in at all. We were this fast pop-punk band.

COBY LINDER: We stood out, for better or worse, as the pop-punk band, the emo band.

DUSTIN KENSRUE: I had no idea Say Anything was from LA. I thought they were East Coast.

MAX BEMIS: Say Anything would open for bands like the Promise Ring and the Weakerthans when they came through. We opened for Rilo Kiley. We started to get this fan base . . . It was really easy to get a fan base of high school kids because there were no other bands doing this stuff in our age group. So we sort of spread throughout different high schools in

LA. From fifteen on, I was definitely the Guy from Say Anything in my high school.

COBY LINDER: It was awesome playing drums, hard and passionate, versus bands that definitely weren't. You're in LA, and other bands are afraid to be passionate. They're passionate in their own, like, pretentious way.

STEFANIE REINES: In Orange County, the shows were always super fun. The crowds were into it. There'd be dancing. LA is more, you know, stuck-up. It was people standing there nodding their heads.

MARIA SHERMAN: Orange County is just a couple hours' drive from Hollywood. It's funny—you look on a map, and they look so close, but they're so different, in the way people speak and act. Orange County is incredibly suburban.

MAX BEMIS: I grew up in West Hollywood, near the Fairfax District. It's a little bit south of the actual literal Hollywood where the Hollywood sign is and stuff like that. So growing up in West LA was completely entertainment industry. Everyone was a kid of somebody in the entertainment industry, including me. My dad made movie posters.

COBY LINDER: Something Corporate was the first bigger band that let Say Anything open a show outside of LA. It was a college show up in Santa Barbara. I remember driving with my dad and my drums in the car for an hour or however long it was.

MAX BEMIS: Something Corporate was OC.

ANDREW MCMAHON: I grew up watching Billy Joel and Ben Folds Five, you know? My feeling was there are a lot of people who play keyboards, but if I do the work and show up with a piano, the visual's going to be striking enough that people might turn their heads. Instead of just showing up to watch their buddy's band and leaving.

Our bass player, Kevin, who went by Clutch in Something Corporate, had found this piano at his church, and we got it for free. We used to tow the piano on a motorcycle trailer that we strapped down behind my drummer's Ford Explorer. We learned early to hide it under a green tarp, because when you'd see a piano strapped down on an open-air trailer rolling down the highway, people get pretty nervous. It would take all five of us to lift it onto stages. The hands at the stages thought we were absolute assholes.

MAX BEMIS: Their live shows were super energetic. Their crowds were young and into it.

CHRISTIAN MCKNIGHT: California is where the labels were coming out of: Rich from Vagrant, Richard and Stefanie from Drive-Thru. And Chain Reaction in Anaheim was one of the most important all-ages clubs in the country.

DUSTIN KENSRUE: We don't have basements in LA, so you don't have the basement show scene. You can do house shows, but they get shut down a lot quicker.

CHRISTIAN MCKNIGHT: Chain Reaction was a real venue. Bands from all over the place would go and play there.

EDDIE BRECKENRIDGE: It was pretty difficult to get your foot in the door. But once you did, if you brought enough friends, it was a pretty magical venue.

ANDREW MCMAHON: We played this gig at Chain Reaction. The talent buyer Jon Halperin called Richard and Stefanie after seeing us outdraw every band on the bill at this huge gig. They reached out immediately and said they loved the band and wanted to sign us.

RICHARD REINES: We wanted to meet them at their next show. The next show wasn't for a couple months so Andrew goes, "Well, you could come to one of our rehearsals. We rehearse in the garage." So we drove all the way down to Dana Point to see them set up in a garage. They had a few chairs outside . . .

ANDREW MCMAHON: I had no idea who they were. The only reason I knew Drive-Thru was because a girl I dated had taken me to a New Found Glory concert. I remembered really liking New Found Glory, but it wasn't really my style of music. I remember looking at the Drive-Thru roster and I was like, "Oh, I know that one band, New Found Glory."

STEFANIE REINES: They had a couch.

RICHARD REINES: The chairs were for their family, the couch was for us. They said, "We have the executive couch prepared for you guys."

STEFANIE REINES: They thought we were gonna show up in, like, suits and a limo.

RICHARD REINES: They played and we were just fucking blown away. We kept asking them to play another song. Andrew was such a star. Everything about it was so amazing, like, how is this band not discovered? How? We were shocked.

STEFANIE REINES: After they were done playing, we went into the house, sat down at their kitchen table, and offered them a deal. We could tell they had potential, just massive mass appeal. So we took Something Corporate to MCA like, "We found this band and we want to sign them but we're gonna need more money than our usual $35,000 budget, we're gonna have to work them to radio, and we don't have . . ." So MCA signed them directly, through Drive-Thru.

RICHARD REINES: Andrew asked, "Can you make me a giant Drive-Thru sticker for my piano?"

STEFANIE REINES: I remember one of the first Something Corporate club shows we saw . . . Always young, good-looking, well-put-together teenage girls pasted to the front of the stage, screaming. It was pop mania. Which was definitely not a normal crowd for our scene. They also had jocks, a lot of jocks.

ANDREW MCMAHON: By the time we got the 2002 Warped Tour offer, "If U C Jordan" was already on radio and Something Corporate had really started to get some fans. Kevin Lyman offered us a deal, offered to put us on the main stage.

KEVIN LYMAN: Andrew's voice is so easy, I always thought he was going to be a star. I thought he was going to be the second coming of Chris Isaak.

JOHNNY MINARDI: Warped Tour was always the number-one gatekeeper for breaking a band in the scene.

BERT MCCRACKEN: I went to Warped in '95. Deftones were playing and I saw Chino jump off the top speaker stack. I was like, "That's like a hundred feet high!" . . . It's so not a hundred feet, ha, ha, ha. But in that moment, I made that a weird goal, a promise to myself: "We're going to play the

Warped Tour one day and I'm going to jump off the top speaker stack into the crowd."

QUINN ALLMAN: To us, there was no bigger show or scene or festival that we could be a part of. That was a teenage dream come true.

LISA BROWNLEE: Warped Tour was the hardest tour anyone was going to do, by far.

ANTHONY RANERI: That was back when Warped played Montana and Wyoming. I mean, shit, that's not like driving from New York to Philly or Boston. Those are real drives, man. Going from Billings to Cheyenne, Seattle to Boise. Those are real-ass drives.

QUINN ALLMAN: We would park in gas stations in the middle of the night, like an hour outside of town, and we would get to Warped early, like eight or nine.

BRANDEN STEINECKERT: You'd wake up not knowing when you're playing on the schedule: "Oh fuck, we're playing in thirty minutes" or "I gotta sit around for eight hours."

QUINN ALLMAN: It was like a circus, watching the tents go up, the hydraulics go up, the generators kick on. That was the soundtrack to the whole thing: loud humming in the background, and three or four bands playing at the same time.

ANTHONY RANERI: This website called PunkRocks.net had a stage on Warped Tour, and they got Bayside added for two weeks. We grew up attending Warped Tour, so it was fucking surreal. Bayside had only been a band for two years at this point. But the PunkRocks.Net Stage was not a real Warped Tour stage. It was inside Warped Tour, but we were never technically booked by Warped Tour. All the bands playing would have to help build the stage every morning, it was just decks and piping they pulled in a trailer on the back of a van.

Warped Tour would only give the stage enough water for people to drink while they were performing. So we didn't have water to drink throughout the day. But Yoo-hoo was a sponsor that year, so we would just fucking drink Yoo-hoo all day. We didn't get catering, so we didn't get fed by Warped Tour. Sometimes Warped was in the middle of nowhere and it's not like you can just walk to McDonald's, you know? So I would go volunteer at the catering tent, serving food to the real bands. And like, literally wash pots in exchange for food.

But I was fucking nineteen. You could not tell me that it sucked.

BRANDEN STEINECKERT: We'd wander around the crowd and be like, "Hey, wanna hear my band?" and have people put on headphones, and be like, "Yeah, we're playing at three o'clock over at this stage! And we'll be over at our merch tent over there if you wanna say hey!" I mean, even Bert was out doing that, which said a lot.

ANDREW MCMAHON: There were all sorts of things I had no idea about, all sorts of shit on that tour. I broke my ankle jumping onto the piano, missing it, and clobbering my ankle. It blew up, and I was on crutches for half the tour.

There was this monitor guy, an older guy, his name was Timbo. He pulled the whole band aside the first week: "If you guys want to be able to stay out here, you're gonna need to get a lot better, quick. You guys play like shit."

KENNY VASOLI: I remember there was a security guard who had it out for me. Fireworks got set off the first night of tour and this guard just came up to me. I was filming stuff on my camcorder. He was like, "YOU WANNA GO HOME?" And I'm like, ". . . No?" And he's like, "Well, then why are you setting off fireworks?" I'm like, "I'm not setting off fireworks!" I was just filming like, Hot Water Music sound-checking. He's like, "PUT THE CAMERA DOWN." I'm just fucking sixteen, like, what the fuck is going on here?

GEOFF RICKLY: There was this crew that sort of like hazed Thursday and made fun of us, which is fine. And then there were the bands that were like, "Okay, I actually like you guys, you're a cool band, you're not like these other stupid bands." And that was like, Jay from Bad Religion and Circle Jerks. Keith Morris was like, "You guys are one of the few bands I can stand on this tour," which was a huge compliment for kids like us.

ANDREW MCMAHON: Something Corporate would often be playing between two very hard bands whose fans didn't really match ours. Like playing opposite Anti-Flag or something. I remember one day the main stage was indoors, inside an amphitheater, and we played after . . . a much tougher band, let's say that . . . I think it was No Use for a Name . . . Usually, the much tougher band's fans would have left the building, right? Well, this crazy rainstorm started and the amphitheater was the only place to seek shelter, so instead of our fans making their way to the front of the stage, we had to play to a captive audience of people who just hated our band. And in the middle of the set, somebody threw ice . . . not just some ice, but a brick of ice that almost knocked me out cold. I just came back up off the ground like, "Are we okay?"

I think a lot of people see Something Corporate as being part of a scene or something, but we were not—especially in the first month of that tour—we were not some well-loved band everybody was coming out to see and support. I cannot tell you how many times we were playing to a sea of middle fingers of kids who were just disgusted with the kid playing the piano on the stage. That tour more than anything put hair on my chest. I had to learn to just take it and be positive.

GEOFF RICKLY: Thursday started the tour on the side stage and ended it on the main stage. Tents were getting trampled because [of] the crowds we were getting and the vendors complained we didn't belong there, that we were too big for the side stage. I remember hearing we'd sold something like eight thousand T-shirts in one day. Like, how is that possible? We had to hire a second merch guy because the first merch guy was like, "I'm so buried out here, I'm losing sales because I can't go get more boxes of merch, I don't know what to do, there's only one of me."

I called up our booking agent like, "Yeah, it feels like something good is happening." He's like, "You're selling ten thousand records a week." In 2001, we'd spent most of the year just trying to sell our first thousand records.

BERT MCCRACKEN: The Used had done a bunch of random tours before Warped. We went out with Fu Manchu. And we went out with Monster Magnet and went out with Mushroomhead. They just didn't have any idea where to put us until the Warped Tour [in 2002].

GEOFF RICKLY: The Used are one of my "got it wrongs." I remember Bert coming on Thursday's bus on that Warped Tour before their debut album came out. And people were talking about them: "This guy's like Axl Rose." I was like, "Well, I never fuckin' liked Axl Rose . . ." To me, Axl Rose was some bullshit. So, Bert came on our bus, gave us a CD-R advance promo of the record and was like, "Please don't share this with anybody." So I put it on later and I remember being like, "This is nu metal. Nobody's gonna like this. This nu metal shit's already over, man. I don't know what they're thinking."

Then we were walking by their stage one day and the Used played "The Taste of Ink." It wasn't a single yet. I realized, "Oh man, I was totally wrong. They're going to be huge." I hadn't even listened to the CD-R long enough to get to "The Taste of Ink."

LISA BROWNLEE: When the Used came to Warped Tour, they already had this little buzz. So we would put up a "Gone Fishing" sign, close up office, and go see them. I remember thinking, "This is insane. These guys are breaking all the rules." Bert would climb up the scaffolding and go on top of the stage and hang down. I'm like, "I want to be furious of the example they're setting. I want to be pissed about this." But then you see the response from the crowd . . .

LESLIE SIMON: I saw the Used every day on Warped Tour that year. Bert was so captivating. He would climb the scaffolding in a dress and then launch himself into the crowd. I really thought I might see this guy die onstage. But what a way to go.

JEPH HOWARD: The moment I realized, "This isn't just working well, this is doing fucking incredible," was Warped Tour in New Jersey in 2002. We played our whole set up to "The Taste of Ink." And after the first chord of guitar, the power onstage goes completely out.

BERT MCCRACKEN: But the crowd kept the song going, finished the song.

JEPH HOWARD: All those kids sang every word up until the last chorus, when all the power came back on and we came in with the music. It was perfect.

GEOFF RICKLY: With the Used, I also underestimated the power that radio still had. Like, "The song's catchy, but who cares? We're punks, we like zines, this is all about underground and if you're too glossy, you're fucked." I still had a hardcore mindset in some ways and I didn't see how much everything was changing. This was becoming the new MTV craze, you know? You better get a little glossier, or you're gonna fall behind the crowd.

JEPH HOWARD: The first time I heard one of our songs on the radio, the first time I ever heard our song out anywhere, it was in the Times Square Tower Records.

JASON LINK: That was a real turning point for aggressive music in the pop-emo world.

JOHN FELDMANN: The Used opened doors for all these other screamo, post-hardcore bands with big, anthemic, melodic choruses and screaming verses.

MIKEY WAY: They took off and started exploding on a mainstream level. They were from a different scene. They were from Utah. But they took a liking to us.

BRANDEN STEINECKERT: I don't remember the first introduction, like, "This is Gerard. This is Mikey . . ." I just remember instantly feeling like we were friends.

BERT MCCRACKEN: When I first saw My Chemical Romance I just loved their kinda funky vibe.

Gerard, so trashy with his leather jacket that was way too small for him and his smell, you could smell him from almost the back of the venue because he was so stinky. And *Bullets*, their first punk rock record. Pretty cool stuff. We became friends quickly.

"IT DIDN'T MATTER THAT 99% *OF* MAINSTREAM AMERICA DIDN'T KNOW WHO HE WAS"

ANDY GREENWALD: The front of *Spin* magazine was a section called Noise where they covered up-and-coming bands and things. The editor Tracey Pepper would often, generously, give me opportunities to cover bands other people weren't interested in, or she herself didn't fully understand or appreciate. I was given the opportunity to write about Dashboard Confessional at CBGB. I went to the show a little skeptical, having listened to Chris's records and not personally connecting with them. Emo hadn't been my scene at all.

That night, the clientele was almost entirely suburban high schoolers, wearing like, pleated khakis and Gamecocks hats. Chris was up there singing songs that had felt kind of mono on record, but they were exploding into this outrageously intense stereo because the audience was singing along, singing everything back to him. It was something I'd never seen before.

MIKE MARSH: Chris really went out of his way to condone it. He would step off the mic, step to the front of the stage, and sing with them. It became like a church thing, where you're trying to get the people to sing the word of God back to you.

IAN COHEN: If you didn't know all the words to the songs, you were gonna feel out of place.

CHRIS CARRABBA: This is when things really started to snowball for Dashboard. When people started to have a real sense of community.

RICH EGAN: When *Places You Have Come to Fear the Most* came out in March 2001, we had no setup for it, just because we had to rush it out. We sold 2,500 records the first week. Most records in their second week drop off 70 percent. This went up. It got to about 2,550. And it just stayed there for a year. I remember that was right around a year later when the record hit the 100,000 mark. The kids loved him. It wasn't a press-created thing. The press was reacting to the cultural shift. He was unlike anything before him in our scene.

CHRIS CARRABBA: That album cycle took us from playing VFW halls to headlining our own shows at big clubs.

I would end up talking to the kids at the merch table—forgive me when I say "kids," you know what I mean—the people attending the show. They would tell me why the songs were important to them or what was special about the night. And then they would tell me about other bands they were excited about or books they read or things that were going on in their lives. And I thought, this doesn't feel that different than being back in Florida.

MIKE MARSH: When Chris finally signed to Vagrant and [booking agent] Andrew Ellis, I think there was a lot of talk about, "You need to get a band. We're not gonna do the guy-sitting-on-a-chair, Bob Dylan shit. We need a band. It's going to be more powerful, it'll sell more tickets, the records will be cooler."

RICH EGAN: Interscope really wanted to get into the Dashboard Confessional business. So they bought part of the label to get into that business.

JEFF SOSNOW: Jimmy Iovine bought half of Vagrant Records to get Dashboard Confessional—that's all you need to know. He went to the end of the earth for Chris Carrabba.

RICH EGAN: We sold 49 percent of Vagrant to Interscope around October/November of 2001.

ANDY GREENWALD: There was a lot invested in the idea that Chris Carrabba was the next big thing.

RICH EGAN: Bill Carroll, Vagrant's head of radio, and our publicist Brian Bumbery had really sold MTV on Dashboard. So they got all of MTV down to Irving Plaza to watch Chris. That was the tipping point.

CHRIS CARRABBA: A couple of folks came backstage after the show and said they found it really exciting: the volume, the ceaselessness of the sing-along. And one of the guys said, "I'd always wanted that to happen on my show, and it never did." I said, "What's your show?" He said, "*MTV Unplugged*." That was Alex Coletti, the one and only.

ANDY GREENWALD: Alex Coletti was a major voice and tastemaker at MTV. Alex saw Chris live, understood it, and was the person inside MTV championing him.

RICH EGAN: Alex was sitting in the balcony during Dashboard's set and he called Van Toffler and the heads of MTV saying something like, "I'm gonna bring *MTV Unplugged* back and start it with this kid. You wouldn't believe it, the crowd is just singing every word at the top of their lungs. Not just the choruses!" Alex was like, "This will play REALLY well on TV."

JIM ADKINS: Chris also looks like a model. So when he's on TV, people want to watch more of that. Seriously, Chris is hot, man!

CHRIS CARRABBA: I was like, "This can't be real." But then the next week, Alex was emailing me about dates and logistics.

DAN BONEBRAKE: At that time, I'd watched almost every *MTV Unplugged* and I was like, man, they do it well.

CHRIS CARRABBA: I liked the idea of songs you'd come to know one way being delivered in a fully different way. The ones that stood out to me most were obviously Nirvana's and Pearl Jam's, which they did pretty early on in their career.

MIKE MARSH: I remember feeling like, "Are we ready to do *MTV Unplugged*?" For me, that was like, Eric Clapton, Nirvana, Alice in Chains, Jay-Z . . . We were a band [as a trio] for about a year and a half. We hadn't done shit yet. We were still trying to figure out our sound. And it was exciting, but it was horrifying. With that type of notoriety comes fame . . .

ANDY GREENWALD: For MTV, I think being able to be back in the authenticity business mattered. They'd feel better about their jobs if they were putting a guy like Chris on TV, with his fan base who adored him, than they would by putting Fred Durst up there, you know? They were hoping to fill the same role that they had filled ten years before.

RICH EGAN: MTV needed to kind of justify why they were doing an *Unplugged* with this kid, so they started playing the "Screaming Infidelities" video *a lot*.

JOHN LEFLER: The first show of note we did as a four-piece was the *Unplugged*. I played guitar and keys.

RICH EGAN: *Unplugged* was recorded for MTV, and released as an album with a DVD of the session. We filmed at MTV Studios. The windows look down onto Times Square. We got there in the morning.

CHRIS CARRABBA: I remember walking by the line for the show and thinking, "That's a long fucking line." The nerves really set in when I saw that line. It's in Times Square, in the theater district. So when you walk through there and see a line it's like, "They're here to see something excellent." And I really wanted it to be excellent.

RICH EGAN: They put out a call saying "first come, first serve" and way too many kids showed up than that studio could handle. Not even a hundred kids could fit in there.

CHRIS CARRABBA: Walking onto the set I was like, "We better rise to the occasion because this is very real now." This is what I'd seen on my TV so many times, what I'd been moved by so many times: these thick, hanging, red velvet drapes with beams of blue light cascading through. There's this mix of grandeur and intimacy without being gaudy. What made our *Unplugged* different than other bands' was they had the audience wrap behind us and even onto the stage with us. You can see the audience's faces more than any *Unplugged* at that point.

I remember saying, "Hey, listen, they've told me it's okay if you guys sing along." That was a wash of relief: Okay, we get to be ourselves. You can conduct yourselves like you would at any Dashboard show.

MIKE MARSH: I don't particularly care for how campy it was, if I'm honest. I didn't like it at the time; I don't like it now. They put a lot of emphasis on something that happens at every show.

JOHN LEFLER: I don't feel that way. It's Dashboard Confessional. Chris being genuine, the lack of irony in his music and performances I think works well with something like that . . . Yes, people sing at shows. But Dashboard, in those years especially, was a different-level thing.

RICH EGAN: There's that blonde girl with the glasses. I remember her and her boyfriend distinctly in every shot. They were directly behind Chris.

ANDY GREENWALD: The kids who filled the studio at 1515 Broadway that day were essentially the same kids who'd been at CBGB. His people came with him.

RICH EGAN: Man, it was exhausting. I can't imagine what Chris and all the kids were going through. We had to do every song multiple times: a string would break, a bad camera angle, or maybe a camera would fall over. And Chris is a perfectionist; if he didn't feel the song was right, he'd say we need to do it again.

JOHN LEFLER: From what other people have said, we played "Screaming Infidelities" like seven times. I don't remember that. It was a very unusual situation to be in, when two weeks prior you're a waiter who's never heard any of these songs before.

MIKE MARSH: Even as a drummer, it wasn't as physically exhausting as the mindfuck of having to do things over: because the lighting's gotta be right, or you gotta make sure this person's being seen. It wasn't like telling Eric Clapton and his band to redo it, where it would be the same exact take. We'd just done these great takes and we weren't gonna synch together like that again because we weren't that good of a band yet.

CHRIS CARRABBA: Sometimes there'd be ten minutes in between songs.

RICH EGAN: You'd expect him to go back to the green room but Chris would just start talking to the kids and working his way through the audience.

MIKE MARSH: I remember the audience being really tired. I'd turn around and there'd be people leaning their head on their hand. They knew they were gonna miss the last train home. But as soon as "PLACES EVERYBODY!" they were back singing along again.

CHRIS CARRABBA: There was all this intensity. And then it was over: "Okay, everybody turn in their badges. Nice having you today." We had to pack up the euphoria. And holster it for a minute. I'm used to finishing my work in a bar or a club, then spilling out into an alley, then hopping in a bus and turning the music really loud. I remember thinking, "What do I do with all this energy?"

RICH EGAN: It was 5:00 a.m. the next morning when we finally wrapped. It was about a twenty-four-hour shoot.

CHRIS CARRABBA: I got out into the street and saw the people who'd been in the audience, hanging out, waiting for us. I viewed them as my bandmates for the night. Finally, without feeling self-conscious or anything, I was high-fiving them like, "Wasn't that fucking amazing!"

MIKE MARSH: We went to Jimmy Iovine's house [months later] to view *MTV Unplugged* in his massive theater room. I remember some of his comments: "You guys are gonna be the next big band, you guys are gonna be the next Nirvana!"

JIM ADKINS: A lot of people saw *Unplugged* and said, "Hey, that looks like me! I want in on this party!"

RICH EGAN: *Unplugged* went platinum. *Places You Have Come to Fear the Most* eventually went gold.

CHRIS CARRABBA: Dashboard Confessional's popularity was growing because people were burning CDs for friends and bringing their friends to shows. It wasn't really based on, "I heard the song on the radio." That's not how it happened for us. I guess there is a certain elegance about . . . you just have this song. It's a single. It serves as an invitation.

IAN COHEN: I was a junior in college, working at the radio station, 91.9 WNRN in Charlottesville, Virginia. We were able to play songs that weren't necessarily singles. On Jimmy Eat World *Bleed American*, I think pretty much everything besides "My Sundown" and one other song were cleared for us to play, which was unheard of. Like, aside from greatest hits albums, you don't clear nine out of eleven songs for airplay.

LUKE WOOD: Jimmy Eat World's single "Bleed American" had been starting to move up rock radio rotations . . . twelve, to maybe nine, and we start to think, "Oh fuck, it could be a hit." After 9/11, it died immediately. But we were all very mature about realizing, "We're gonna work this album for a long time, how do we move past this conversation?"

There was a desire to prove the album. We didn't want to lose it because of a tragedy that wasn't related to anything the band did. We had to decide what single to go with next. It was between "If You Don't, Don't," "Sweetness," and "The Middle." Their manager Gary Gersh told me how perfect the lyrics to "The Middle" were.

IAN COHEN: One of Jimmy Eat World's best qualities is the ability to sing about people who are like, five to ten years younger than they are.

LUKE WOOD: You feel isolated and alone, you're stuck in the middle, and it takes some time to find your place. Everybody feels like that at some point when they're a kid.

ANDY GREENWALD: "The Middle" is a perfect pop song. But it's also a perfect pop song that encapsulates that yearning that's endemic to Jimmy Eat World, as a project. It's like, "Imagine if 'Goodbye Sky Harbor' was three minutes long, and you could sing along to it."

LUKE WOOD: DreamWorks had just had "Last Resort" with Papa Roach. We had "Hanging by a Moment" with Lifehouse. We had Alien Ant Farm with the "Smooth Criminal" cover. And Nelly Furtado's "I'm Like a Bird." We had a lot of hits. A lot of things were happening. Nobody was looking at Jimmy Eat World to be *the* hit. The band was gonna go tour, play to their core audience, make sure people saw the band they loved.

JIM ADKINS: We played at Tom DeLonge's wedding reception. It was a surprise for Tom. He seemed stoked! We played "Episode IV" from *Static Prevails*, "Call It in the Air," "If You Don't, Don't" from the new record, and probably "Sweetness."

IAN COHEN: That Jimmy Eat World album got the lead review in *Rolling Stone*. One of the main talking points was that they played Tom DeLonge's wedding. Like, that's their peg? Okay! This was before "The Middle" was big, this was the first thing that made me aware Jimmy Eat World could be a big deal.

LUKE WOOD: *Bleed American* was clearly a little different than *Clarity*. I just wanted them to play to as many people as possible and get over the baggage of having been dropped by a different major label recently.

JIM ADKINS: It was a frog-boiling-in-water situation. We didn't realize how big it was getting until much later.

LUKE WOOD: At first, "The Middle" was driven by major market modern rock radio stations, where it climbed the charts relatively quickly. By that time, it wasn't uncommon for rock records to cross over into pop. There was a track record of this. But not for bands from the underground of third-wave emo.

RICH EGAN: "The Middle" is one of the catchiest songs ever written.

LUKE WOOD: At that point, after a decade of working at major labels, and working with MTV, I knew what we needed: How do we get them on *TRL*? I knew we needed a video to drive the story.

JIM ADKINS: We hadn't done many videos up to that point, and we certainly had never done anything with a narrative behind it.

LUKE WOOD: We all felt like it had to be some crappy high school party. Okay, well, what makes you not belong? Not wanting to be in my underwear at this party!

JIM ADKINS: No approachable, normal people were cast at first.

LUKE WOOD: It was all LA music video casting kids. I remember someone bringing out Polaroids and they all looked like video girls, for lack of a better word. I was like, "We don't want to see some Keanu Reeves–looking lead guy! This is Jimmy Eat World!"

JIM ADKINS: Luke was like, "We want an actual dream sequence of showing up alone at a party in your clothes and everyone's in their underwear. It wouldn't all be models, there'd be all types of people there."

LUKE WOOD: There was a scramble seventy-two hours before the shoot. We ended up recruiting everybody from Arizona State University. There was no Screen Actors Guild, just kids.

ZACH LIND: A bunch of our friends wound up being in the video. We basically said, "Anybody who wants to come down and be in a video and be in their underwear, come on down."

LUKE WOOD: I'm not gonna say we still didn't cast really good-looking people . . .

IAN COHEN: This was back when MTV still mattered. It was one of the primary conveyances for interacting with popular music. And you would just see that video all the time. For obvious reasons. It's very photogenic.

JIM ADKINS: "The Middle" went to number one [on] alternative radio. On the Hot 100, it went top five.

LUKE WOOD: Dashboard was a cultural moment. But in terms of radio, "Screaming Infidelities" did not get that kind of airplay.

JIM ADKINS: When "The Middle" was headed to number one, we got asked to play *SNL*.

LUKE WOOD: In New York City for *SNL*, we went to a sneaker store and they're playing "The Middle" on the radio. At Starbucks an hour later, "The Middle" was on the radio. Then like four times the next hour Jim got recognized: "Are you that guy? Are you 'The Middle'?"

JIM ADKINS: Will Ferrell, Jimmy Fallon, and Amy Poehler were on the *SNL* cast then. There was like a four-foot hallway between our dressing room and the host's. Cameron Diaz was running in and out of there all the time for costume changes. It's a tight situation, you meet everybody.

I was doing a dummy check of everything before I left the dressing room, there was no one else around, and I bumped into Philip Seymour Hoffman. He was like, "Hey, I've never heard you guys before, it's good stuff!" I'm thinking, "Famous people are hearing our stuff now?" The best I could think to say was, "All of us are big fans of your work!"

CHRIS CARRABBA: I remember thinking, "We made it! Our scene! We made it! We're on *Saturday Night Live*."

JIM ADKINS: That was the most nervous I'd ever been. I grew up watching *SNL*. I would set the timer to record it so I could watch the musical guests in the morning. Then all of a sudden, you're there. We'd played "The Middle" so many times by that point. And we were on tour. Once we started playing it's like, "Oh yeah, we got this." But up until that point? Hooooooly shit. Insane.

ZACH LIND: *SNL* was such a blur.

LUKE WOOD: Then it got to, "What's the next single?"

JIM ADKINS: "Sweetness" was the next big *Bleed American* song.

LUKE WOOD: It had a massive hook, but it also had this silent conversation with their core audience—the whole call and response, "sing it back" thing. Those of us who came from the scene knew what that was.

Trying to pick our fourth single, we went with "A Praise Chorus." In hindsight, I would have gone with "Hear You Me" one thousand times. It was probably the biggest A&R mistake I ever made. The band was worried, "How do we be a rock band on tour and suddenly have a power ballad?" But it's one of those records you don't worry about, like Green Day's "Time of Your Life." We should have gone with "Hear You Me." It would have been a number-one song. It would have changed their entire career.

JIM ADKINS: It was a matter of how much are we going to push this album? Versus, maybe we should switch gears and just work on a new album. Traditionally, our fans thought of us as more of a rock band. We didn't want to be blowing up as the acoustic ballad band, when for a lot of people, that would have been their only experience with us.

MATT PRYOR: I remember playing a festival in Germany and seeing Jim and Zach. Jim had to go do like, six interviews. He got pulled away and goes, "I gotta go explain to people what emo is . . ."

JIM ADKINS: For a while, every interview we did was, "What's with this emo thing? Where'd you get your band name?" And, "So you played Tom DeLonge's wedding . . ." Those three questions. Every single interview.

ZACH LIND: We treated the word "emo" like a dog you're training not to jump up on you. The best way to train that dog is just to ignore the dog.

IAN COHEN: Jimmy Eat World's what really cracked it open: "Well, fuck, man, whatever is going on in this genre of music, I want all of it."

TOM MULLEN: I was so amazed that people were paying attention. Because emo was largely ignored for so much of my life.

JOLIE LINDHOLM: Rocking Horse Winner did a *Seventeen* magazine photo shoot about the emo scene at the time. It's so funny to me now . . . I think it was shot in New York City—we were in there with Jimmy Eat World and Dashboard in the same section.

IAN COHEN: I was reading *Pitchfork* at the time, and they just hated all that shit.

AMY FLEISHER MADDEN: Things like *Pitchfork* came for us and used really negative words to describe what we were doing. We didn't even use the word "emo" back then. That made it worse. "Emo" was a derogatory term. We didn't say, "This is gonna be the biggest emo band of all time," because that was like saying, "This is the worst thing you're ever going to hear." Emo didn't really become cool until much later. And it's still surprising to me.

RICH EGAN: Vagrant bands, we never used the word. Not because "emo" was a like four-letter word or forbidden, but because it was . . . kinda lame. To us, it was punk rock, it was indie rock. The mainstream didn't really start labeling it "emo" until Dashboard was taking off. Then they started to drop that word all over the place.

CHRIS CARRABBA: I didn't have a clear picture of how big our band was going to get.

MATT PRYOR: Dashboard is its own thing. It's a unicorn. Chris's trajectory doesn't follow any norms you read about in music autobiographies. It's just a phenomenon.

CHRIS CARRABBA: We were supposed to have a run of shows in the UK and we got nominated for the VMA. I felt really guilty canceling those shows. I remember that morning in New York City, getting coffee and feeling conflicted. It felt like skipping school.

RICH EGAN: The morning of the VMAs, I remember thinking we had no shot of winning. It was Dashboard, the Strokes, the Hives, and Norah Jones all nominated in the same category, for the MTV2 award.

CHRIS CARRABBA: "Hopefully, I'll get to meet some people I see on TV, like Jimmy Fallon. Wouldn't that be amazing. If I get to meet Jack White, wouldn't that be cool." It was at Radio City Music Hall. These are the things I was thinking about. I was not thinking, "What if we win?" I thought it was nice to get nominated. I wasn't gonna write a speech. That seemed weird.

FINN MCKENTY: This is the peak of MTV's relevance. A lot of people forget or pretend that MTV fell off in the nineties. MTV was at the peak of its relevance in the 2000s. *TRL* alone! *TRL* started in the late nineties, but it was mainly the 2000s. *Jackass*, *Viva La Bam* . . .

TOM MULLEN: Someone who was part of our scene was on the VMAs. That's crazy! I was definitely watching that award show.

RICH EGAN: We were going over in a limo and you know, you gotta stop at the red carpet, get out and do all that stuff. We felt like freshmen crashing the seniors' party. We had no business being there.

CHRIS CARRABBA: I was from a scene I was proud of. I didn't want to get disowned by that scene, for visiting another one. And that moment of being on the red carpet, I really felt like, "Oh shit . . ."

RICH EGAN: The press didn't know who Dashboard was. There's all these pop stars around him and I could hear people: "Who is it? Who is it? All right, pose for a picture!" Then Chris got interviewed by Triumph the Insult Comic Dog. That was awesome.

CHRIS CARRABBA: Actually seeing Robert Smigel there face-to-face with the puppet dog . . . I'm thinking to myself, "I'm about to get dunked on so hard, and it's going to be the best."

RICH EGAN: The dog was like, "And who are you?" And Chris was like, "Dashboard Confessional." He's like, "What are you gonna confess to, sucking?"

CHRIS CARRABBA: That was pretty disarming.

Then I remember somebody saying, "Hey, what if you won and you got up there and forgot to thank somebody important?" So I wrote a list.

RICH EGAN: We had gotten tipped off from the MTV people like, "Hey, you may want to prepare a few words." The category Chris was nominated in was fan-voted. So it didn't matter that 99 percent of mainstream America didn't know who he was.

JOHN LEFLER: Whoever's fans were the most internet savvy in 2002 probably had the best shot at winning.

CHRIS CARRABBA: At award shows, they stage a camera near you. I was really aware of the camera. I felt uncomfortable in my own skin. I remember them announcing the names of the nominees, which included the Strokes and Norah Jones. Norah was sitting not far from me, and I could see the camera on her. The Strokes were a couple rows behind me.

MIKE MARSH: I remember I couldn't get my armpits to stop dripping. I couldn't get my legs to stop moving. Chris was the same.

RICH EGAN: I was thinking either the Hives or the Strokes were going to win it. Brittany Murphy and Anthony Kiedis announced the winner.

CHRIS CARRABBA: I don't remember this, but my name was announced.

RICH EGAN: She didn't even pronounce Dashboard Confessional correctly. She's like, "And the winner is, Dashboard Confessions . . . 'Screaming Infidelities!'"

CHRIS CARRABBA: "They just said me. Wait, I think we won this." Avril was sitting right in front of me. I remember her turning around to clap when they announced my name, which I thought was nice.

MIKE MARSH: I remember walking down the aisle to get up onstage and seeing Gwen Stefani looking at us . . . "How did I get here, man?" Eminem and all these massive artists. "I don't know how we got here so fast."

CHRIS CARRABBA: And then I was on the stairs. And I was reaching in my pocket. And I'm thinking, "I'm glad they suggested I write thank-you notes." I remember thinking, "Just speak clearly."

JOHN LEFLER: When the Strokes didn't win, they bailed right away. I was disappointed because I wanted to hang out with them.

RICH EGAN: Afterwards, we went to the Interscope after-party and Eminem performed. A hundred people in this little bar up in the balcony. Then like an hour in, he comes up to the railing, the music drops, he starts freestyling. We're like, "What kind of life are we living?"

We had a shoot for *GQ* the next morning. And I had a *Newsweek* interview at 9:00 a.m.

MIKE MARSH: Axl Rose sat down next to me at that after-party and leaned back on the couch; he was exhausted. He looked over at me and I looked at him. He says, "Hey, I'm Axl." I said, "Yeah, I know." He said, "Who are you?" I said, "I'm Mike, I play in a band called Dashboard Confessional." Eminem and 50 Cent were upstairs blaring rap music and Axl Rose leaned into me and said, "I fuckin' hate rap."

CHRIS CARRABBA: I remember getting an attaboy from Eminem about winning the award. And he started asking me how many songs I had for my next record, what I was most excited about . . . I was surprised how much he knew about my music. I remember him rattling off song titles of mine. Also, what he did that was really nice . . . I wasn't really looking for an autograph myself, and he said, "Do you have a sister? What's her name?" And he signed something on a cloth napkin for her. He signed it, "Marshall." I remember wondering if he always does that.

RICH EGAN: The next morning, I completely slept through my *Newsweek* interview. I woke up at 11:30, checked my voicemail, the writer was totally cool and ended up meeting us at the *GQ* shoot. DMX walked in with two pit bulls, in a huge fur coat.

CHRIS CARRABBA: I could see someone having an animated conversation with DMX. And DMX seemed to be a willing audience. This kind of piqued my curiosity because I was only a few feet away. I heard them say "Napster" a few times.

RICH EGAN: This was right when Jimmy Iovine started on his thing of suing Napster. They were going to go after users, go after kids. So these Universal Music executives were trying to get all these artists to speak out against downloading. That was their big initiative. So a couple suits from the legal department corner us. They had this big chart.

CHRIS CARRABBA: They said, "You're exactly who we came to talk to."

RICH EGAN: "You're the number one most illegally downloaded artist in all of Universal."

CHRIS CARRABBA: My response was, "That's amazing."

RICH EGAN: "Oh, that's killer!"

CHRIS CARRABBA: And the guy said, "Right?! What are we gonna do about it?" And I said, "I guess . . . hope more people download it?" They started yelling at me instantly.

RICH EGAN: They're like, "We need you to do a PSA and speak out against downloading!"

Chris was really pissed. He goes, "Those are the kids that come to my shows. The fact that you're selling less because of it is not my problem."

CHRIS CARRABBA: They went red-faced.

RICH EGAN: We played grown-up, dress-up for the night. We went to the

MTV awards and had a *GQ* photo shoot. It was all foreign to us. This was not our punk rock world. *We're not in Kansas anymore.*

There was no turning back. It was almost like an ending when we won that VMA.

ANDY GREENWALD: It felt like a rubber band: How far could you stretch this music, which was predicated on a very intimate connection between performer and audience? Could you stretch it around the whole country? Could you stretch it around the whole world without something essential snapping? What happens when subculture goes mainstream?

RICH EGAN: I didn't want to be in the mainstream. With Vagrant, with Chris—everything we did was based on a DIY aesthetic. We bought in wholesale to Ian MacKaye and Dischord, that whole thing. It was almost like betraying it. I just remember feeling like, "Well, that was a good ride. It's over now. Being the underdog is over."

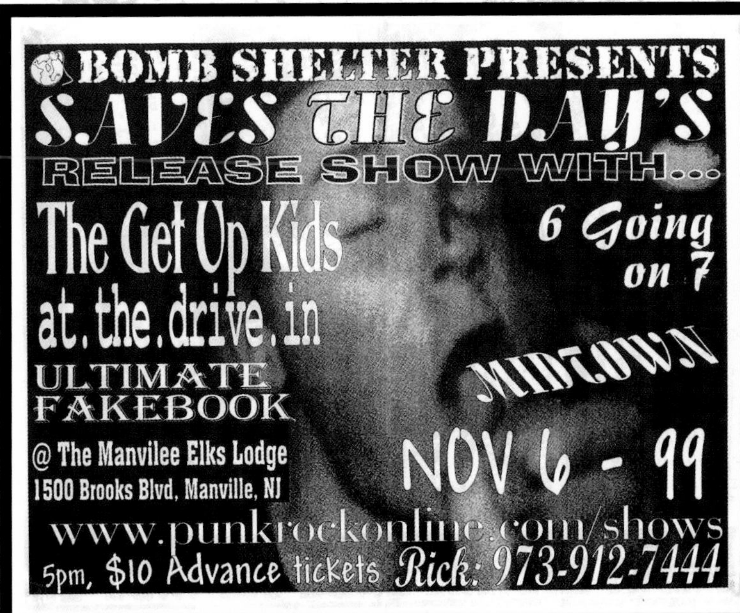

Flyer from Saves the Day's *Through Being Cool* release show at New Jersey's Manville Elks Lodge. *(Flyer designed by Ricardo Saporta)*

Taking Back Sunday takes on Manhattan: bassist Shaun Cooper, vocalist Adam Lazzara, and guitarist Eddie Reyes perform at Brownies in 2001. *(Michael Dubin)*

Three of our heroes: Gabe Saporta, Chris Carrabba, and Geoff Rickly backstage in 2002 at New York's Irving Plaza. *(Ricardo Saporta)*

Jimmy Eat World pose for a *Bleed American* press photo (left to right: Rick Burch, Zach Lind, Jim Adkins, Tom Linton). *(Christopher Wray-McCann)*

SATURDAY.... NOVEMBER 16TH
THE JIM GRIMES XXX BIRTHDAY SHOW

BENEFIT FOR THE CHICAGO BULLY BREED RESCUE

RISE AGAINST (FAT WRECK CHORDS)
EVERY TIME I DIE (FERRET RECORDS)
UNEARTH (EULOGY RECORDS)
SUICIDE FILE (INDECISION RECORDS)
A DEATH FOR EVERY SIN (ALVERAN RECORDS)
THIS DAY FORWARD (EULOGY RECORDS)
BLEEDING THROUGH (INDECISION RECORDS)
THE HOPE CONSPIRACY (EQUAL VISION)
ARMA ANGELUS (EULOGY RECORDS0
THE PROMISE (EX~EARTH CRISIS/ANOTHER VICTIM)
FIGURE FOUR
MISERY SIGNALS (EX-7 ANGELS 7 PLAGUES)
SKYCAMEFALLING (FERRET RECORDS)
25 TA LIFE
THE KILLER
FALL OUT BOY

14 DOLLARS/DOORS 12PM/SHOW 12:30
LA GRANGE SKATE PARK
31 EAST OGDEN AVE. IN LA GRANGE,IL

MORE INFO: HDEVILBOOKING@AOL.COM

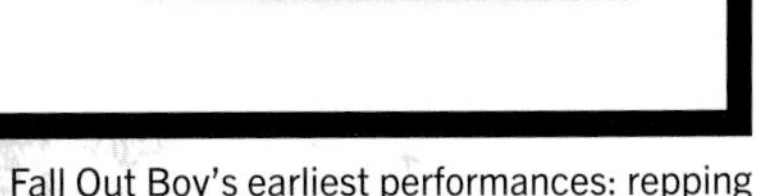

Flyer from one of Fall Out Boy's earliest performances: repping Chicago softcore, November 16, 2002. *(Flyer designed by Jim Grimes)*

Gerard Way salutes the crowd at the Downtown in Farmingdale, New York, July 25, 2003. *(Drew Guarini)*

A rare shot of My Chemical Romance's basement days: Frank Iero, Mikey Way, Gerard, and Ray Toro rock out at Midtown's former New Brunswick residence in 2003. *(Ricardo Saporta)*

The Used hit *TRL* in early 2003 (left to right: Quinn Allman, Jeph Howard, Branden Steineckert, Bert McCracken). *(Scott Gries, Getty Images)*

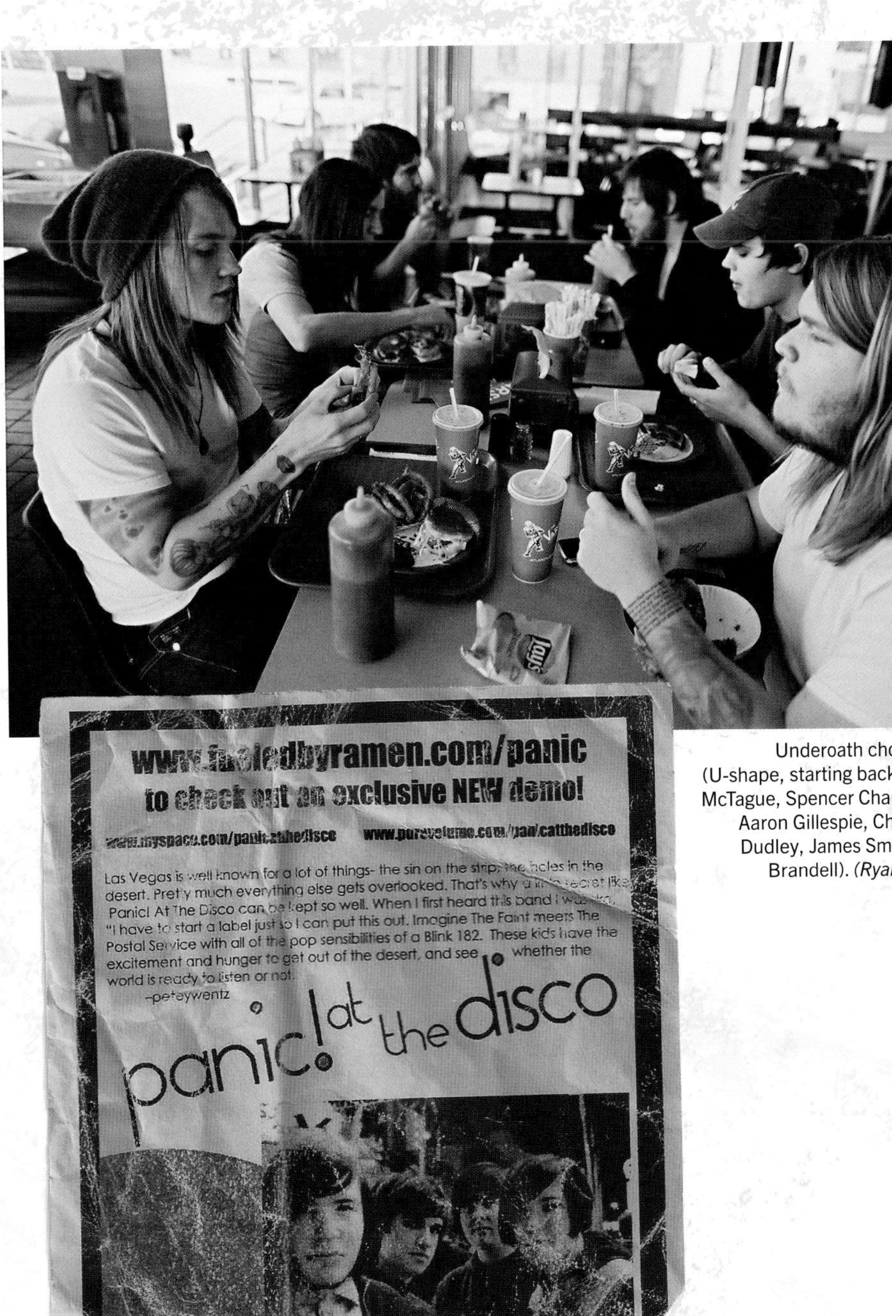

to check out an exclusive NEW demo!
Las Vegas is well known for a lot of things- the sin on the strip, the holes in the desert. Pretty much everything else gets overlooked. That's why a ... secret like Panic! At The Disco can be kept so well. When I first heard this band I was like "I have to start a label just so I can put this out. Imagine The Faint meets The Postal Service with all of the pop sensibilities of a Blink 182. These kids have the excitement and hunger to get out of the desert, and see whether the world is ready to listen or not.
-peteywentz
panic! at the disco
out in Fall `05
Ramen

Underoath chows down (U-shape, starting back left: Tim McTague, Spencer Chamberlain, Aaron Gillespie, Christopher Dudley, James Smith, Grant Brandell). *(Ryan Russell)*

Early Panic! at the Disco flyer, handed out at Bamboozle 2005, four months ahead of *A Fever You Can't Sweat Out*. *(From the collection of the author)*

Warped Tour ticket stub, 2005. *(From the collection of the author)*

Hayley Williams performs at South Hackensack, New Jersey's School of Rock in 2006. *(Dana Kandić)*

Motion City Soundtrack laminate from Fall Out Boy's 2005 Nintendo Fusion Tour. *(Brian Diaz)*

Leslie Simon and Pete Wentz at Misshapes in New York City (Geoff Rickly photobombing). *(Leslie Simon)*

A reunited Lifetime returns to New Brunswick basements (pictured: guitarist Dan Yemin, vocalist Ari Katz). *(Ricardo Saporta)*

Mikey Way congratulates Patrick Stump after Fall Out Boy's surprise win over My Chemical Romance at the 2005 VMAs, as members of both bands (and Usher) take in the moment. *(Kevin Kane, Getty Images)*

Cobra Starship at New York's Highline Ballroom, 2008. *(Dana Kandić)*

Tour laminate from Fall Out Boy's ill-fated attempt to play Antarctica. *(Brian Diaz)*

PART 3

THE MATCH YOU STRIKE TO INCINERATE

2003–2004

CAST OF CHARACTERS

PART 3

HANIF ABDURRAQIB: author and poet (and Midwest native)
QUINN ALLMAN: guitarist, the Used
BRIAN ANDERSON: journalist (and Chicago native)
VICTORIA ASHER: keytarist, Cobra Starship
JONAH BAYER: journalist, *Alternative Press*; writer, *Steven's Untitled Rock Show*
MAX BEMIS: front person, Say Anything
EDDIE BRECKENRIDGE: drummer, Thrice
AMANDA BRENNAN: meme historian; former head of editorial, Tumblr (and New Jersey native)
CHRIS CARRABBA: front person, Dashboard Confessional, Further Seems Forever; vocalist-guitarist, Vacant Andys
PARKER CASE: multi-instrumentalist, JamisonParker (and later, Say Anything)
SPENCER CHAMBERLAIN: front person, Underoath
IAN COHEN: journalist
JAMIE COLETTA: founder, No Earbuds PR
TOMMY CORRIGAN: designer, Merch Direct (and previously, front person, Silent Majority)
EBEN D'AMICO: bassist, Saves the Day
JONATHAN DANIEL: cofounder, Crush Music; manager, Fall Out Boy, Panic! at the Disco, Cobra Starship, etcetera.
ALEX DELEON: front person, The Cab
BRIAN DIAZ: guitar tech, Brand New, Motion City Soundtrack, Fall Out Boy (and formerly, front person, Edna's Goldfish, the Reunion Show)
MIKE DUBIN: photographer, videographer, radio host, tour manager (and Long Island native)
RICH EGAN: cofounder, Vagrant Records; manager, Dashboard Confessional, the Get Up Kids
MARIANNE ELOISE: author and journalist
HANNAH EWENS: author and journalist
FRED FELDMAN: founder, Triple Crown Records
JOHN FELDMANN: producer, the Used; front person, Goldfinger
DIA FRAMPTON: front person, Meg & Dia (and later, solo artist and *The Voice* runner-up)
MATT GALLE: booking agent, My Chemical Romance, Taking Back Sunday
GLENN GAMBOA: journalist, *Newsday*
CHAD GILBERT: guitarist, New Found Glory; (and previously, front person, Shai Hulud)
AARON GILLESPIE: drummer-vocalist, Underoath
MIKE GITTER: A&R, Atlantic Records, Roadrunner Records; journalist, author, and zine maker, *xXx*
ANTHONY GREEN: front person, Circa Survive, Saosin

ANDY GREENWALD: author and music journalist
CHRIS GUTIERREZ: bassist, Arma Angelus; blogger and author
TOM HIGGENSON: front person, Plain White T's
ROB HITT: drummer, Midtown (and later, manager, Crush Music)
JEPH HOWARD: bassist, the Used
DUSTIN KENSRUE: front person, Thrice
ELLIE KOVACH: blogger and journalist
SARAH LEWITINN: journalist, blogger DJ (alias, Ultragrrrl), cofounder/A&R, Stolen Transmission Records
LIGHTS: musician and comic book artist
COBY LINDER: drummer, Say Anything
KEVIN LYMAN: founder and producer, Warped Tour; cofounder and producer, Taste of Chaos
FRED MASCHERINO: guitarist-vocalist, Taking Back Sunday; front person, Breaking Pangea
TRAVIE MCCOY: front person, Gym Class Heroes
BERT MCCRACKEN: front person, the Used
CHRISTIAN MCKNIGHT: talent buyer, Bamboozle, Skate and Surf, This Island Earth festivals (and previously, Long Island show promoter); radio host
JOHNNY MINARDI: A&R, Fueled By Ramen
GRETA MORGAN: vocalist-keyboardist, The Hush Sound; zine maker, *Trash Magazine*
MANI MOSTOFI: front person, Racetraitor
TOM MULLEN: marketing, TVT Records, Equal Vision Records (and later, founder/podcaster, *Washed Up Emo*)
BRYAN NEWMAN: drummer, Saves the Day
JILLIAN NEWMAN: manager, Taking Back Sunday
RANDY NICHOLS: manager, Underoath, Say Anything, The Starting Line
BUDDY NIELSEN: front person, Senses Fail
JOHN NOLAN: guitarist-vocalist, Taking Back Sunday; vocalist-multi-instrumentalist, Straylight Run
SEAN O'KEEFE: producer, Fall Out Boy, Arma Angelus
JENN PELLY: author and journalist (and Long Island native)
WILL PUGH: front person, Cartel
ANTHONY RANERI: front person, Bayside
TYLER RANN: vocalist-guitarist, Midtown
EDDIE REYES: guitarist, Taking Back Sunday (and previously, Mind Over Matter, Clockwise, Inside, the Movielife, Runner Up)
GEOFF RICKLY: front person, Thursday; New Brunswick basement show promoter; producer, My Chemical Romance
MATT RUBANO: bassist, Taking Back Sunday
NEIL RUBENSTEIN: front person, Sons of Abraham, This Year's Model (and later, comedian)
MATTHEW ISMAEL RUIZ: journalist (and New Jersey native)
ALEX SAAVEDRA: cofounder, Eyeball Records
ADAM SAMILJAN: marketing, Fueled By Ramen (and later, day-to-day manager, Paramore)
GABE SAPORTA: front person, Cobra Starship, Midtown (previously, bassist, Humble Beginnings)
HEATH SARACENO: vocalist-guitarist, Midtown (and later, Senses Fail)
ALEX SARTI: merch manager/seller, Clandestine Industries (and later, manager, Crush Music)
NICK SCIMECA: drummer, 504 Plan (and later, designer, Clandestine Industries)
MARIA SHERMAN: journalist and author
LESLIE SIMON: author and journalist, *Alternative Press*

ADAM SISKA: bassist, The Academy Is . . .
SPENCER SMITH: drummer, Panic! at the Disco
JEFF SOSNOW: A&R, DreamWorks Records, Interscope Records
BRANDEN STEINECKERT: drummer, the Used
PATRICK STUMP: vocalist-guitarist, Fall Out Boy; solo artist; film scorer
ALEX SUAREZ: bassist, Cobra Starship; multi-instrumentalist-vocalist, Kite Flying Society (and Florida native)
JASON TATE: founder/blogger, Absolute Punk.net
SHANE TOLD: front person, Silverstein
ADAM TURLA: front person, Murder by Death
BRENDON URIE: front person, Panic! at the Disco
MIKEY WAY: bassist, My Chemical Romance
PETE WENTZ: bassist, Fall Out Boy (and previously, bassist, Racetraitor; front person, Arma Angelus); founder, Decaydance Records, Clandestine Industries
NICK WHEELER: guitarist, the All-American Rejects
JOSH WILLS: drummer, Story of the Year
LUKE WOOD: A&R, DreamWorks Records, Interscope Records

CHAPTER 15

PRIVATE JETS & MAGAZINE COVERS

BRIAN DIAZ: August 2003: Brand New went on tour opening for Dashboard Confessional. Dashboard was cruising off "Screaming Infidelities" and "Hands Down." And they were doing fucking big places, man. As a guitar tech, that tour had been my first arena show and there were big theaters, some House of Blues shows. The crowds were so passionate. I remember this girl . . . At one of the shows early on, this girl's got her arms on the barricade, Brand New is playing, and here comes this crowd-surfer over the top of the crowd. Kicks her in the nose, she's spraying blood everywhere and I'm like, "UHH?!?!" I don't know what to do. Security guys are pulling her out, she's holding her face. She's in the little medical triage corner backstage. They're telling her she needs to go to the hospital, she's got a broken nose, blood pouring out, and she's just like, "BUT I HAVEN'T SEEN DASHBOARD YET!"

I'm thinking, "This is big rock show time now. We're not doing VFW hall shows anymore." And I think about that all the time. I hope her nose is all right.

BRANDEN STEINECKERT: Something was happening that we weren't necessarily aware of. These bands were starting to really find their family. It was unbeknownst to us, because we're all just out, touring our asses off.

ADAM TURLA: We did a tour with Thursday in July of 2003, every show was absolutely packed, but in three-hundred-capacity all-ages spaces that had like, an $800 PA system. Punk was still DIY, basically. You would never see a band that's blowing up doing a tour like that today. You'd be playing much nicer venues, you wouldn't be working with punk promoters.

TOMMY CORRIGAN: There was a show in 2003 at this place on Long Island called Sports Plus that we delivered merchandise to. The Used, Thrice, My Chemical Romance, and Story of the Year. It was a gigantic show.

MIKEY WAY: I was talking to Christian McKnight . . . He was like, "Dude, remember that Sports Plus show?" I was like, "Dude, I was drinking a lot back then. Maybe that was one of those shows where after our set I was blitzed."

CHRISTIAN MCKNIGHT: I was the promoter. Sports Plus was one of these huge complexes that has a skating rink, arcade, bowling, all this shit, and a banquet space they let me do shows in. It was a two-thousand-cap venue. The day of the show I started getting these calls: "Hey, it's noon, and there's already three hundred kids outside waiting and a lot of them are drunk." Then my production manager calls and tells me the venue started giving out bracelets to ticket holders because they figured they could get people in quicker. They didn't tell us they were doing this. I said, "Uhh, I don't love it. But I guess I don't have a choice."

The evening goes on and I'm getting even more texts from my crew: "This is a shit show, everyone's drunk, a lot more people are coming in the venue than we expected."

JOSH WILLS: It felt like we were at a mall . . . I remember feeling weird because there was this patterned carpet on the floor. You guys are gonna do a show here?

BRANDEN STEINECKERT: Dude, it was going on. What a fucking show. Thrice killed it.

ED BRECKENRIDGE: We were the main support for the Used. Story of the Year was opening, and after them was My Chem.

CHRISTIAN MCKNIGHT: The room is jam-packed, you can't move. People started calling the cops because with the underage drinking, a couple young kids got wasted.

I had it in writing that I sold two thousand tickets but the cop was like, "Well, there's at least three thousand people in here." I'm like, "How?"

TOMMY CORRIGAN: The show was on a busy road, and it just caused chaos. They closed the road and the whole show got shut down.

BRANDEN STEINECKERT: We didn't get to play, right? We had to walk out onstage and fuckin' tell everybody.

ED BRECKENRIDGE: You could tell something was going down by the time the Used were about to play.

BRANDEN STEINECKERT: We were playing last, about to go on. The fire marshal came and shut us down during the set change. They were threatening that we would all be arrested and charges would be pressed against us if we incited any kind of riot.

So, they wouldn't let just anybody go onstage and announce the show had to end. We had to fucking do it. They thought that would keep the crowd calm, but it did the fucking opposite. Like, the crowd sees the headlining band walk onstage, they're fired up! Now we have to fucking tell them we can't play because there's too many of them. Bert started talking, and we're all just standing there feeling bummed and sorry. We were getting booed and stuff was getting thrown at us. They're gonna arrest us if this goes south. We got the fuck out of there.

CHRISTIAN MCKNIGHT: I found out the next day that the people from Sports Plus bought the bracelets from Party City across the street. Anybody could have went to Party City and bought those bracelets. Somebody showed up and was selling bracelets for five bucks to anyone that didn't have one. I called Party City the next day: "Hey, do you have those light blue admittance bracelets?" And they're like, "You know, it's crazy, we actually sold four boxes of them yesterday!" I'm like, how many does each box hold? "About fifteen hundred."

ED BRECKENRIDGE: A scene that was a couple people at your high school all of a sudden had a lot more people involved. All of a sudden, it wasn't music just for the kids that wore all black, you know? 2002 was the year I started seeing the shift. And 2003 was when a lot of those bands started getting signed to those major labels.

RICH EGAN: This was the height of the Saves the Day madness.

LUKE WOOD: I had gone and seen Saves the Day in New York behind *Through Being Cool*. I loved that it reminded me of early eighties hardcore, but poppier. I was talking about signing them from Equal Vision to DreamWorks back then, but we were just kind of waiting for the moment. I was thinking, "Is the major label system the right path?" Then before I knew it, Rich signed them to Vagrant for *Stay What You Are*, the album with "At Your Funeral." I didn't even know there was an opportunity to get them.

EBEN D'AMICO: Rich was double-dipping as our manager and our label, while we were still with Vagrant. He was kind enough that he didn't take a managerial cut.

At this point, our stock was incredibly, incredibly hot. While we were mixing *In Reverie*, we were courted by pretty much every major label head.

LUKE WOOD: I was friends with Rich Egan and Rob Schnapf, who produced *In Reverie*. I knew Rob because of all his years of working with Elliott Smith. I remember going down to Sunset Sound in Hollywood, where they were making the record. I just thought the music was phenomenal. What they were writing was so sophisticated.

EBEN D'AMICO: I remember Chris saying, "I want to be as big as the Beatles," to a lot of A&Rs and CEOs. I don't want to pin it all on him, though. We were all sort of like, "Yes, it's time for us to do this. We've outgrown Vagrant."

We went to Jimmy Iovine's house. He had a German attack dog that understood German and had a kill word. And we also went to David Geffen's house; I remember that very vividly. We drove down this grand driveway and he's standing there underneath an arched entryway with pillars and walks us into his house and sits us down in his dining room at this gigantic stone table and says, "You're sitting around a thousand-year-old piece of alabaster. I'm going to have my assistant Chang get you a beverage of your choice." The point of these label heads being trotted out was to impress the kids enough to sign with their label. But at that point, we were principled and we weren't really impressed. We were like, "Yeah, it's cool to go to David Geffen's house and see he has a Pollock on every single wall and he tells us that's the one that was on his easel when he died." We sat there and listened to Jimmy Iovine tell stories about John Lennon in the studio or whatever and we're like, "Okay, cool, but what about your label?"

RICH EGAN: Vagrant had that deal with Interscope and one of the fringe benefits was getting to fly on Jimmy Iovine's plane with him. I used to book my trips to New York just based on when Jimmy was going, so I could jump on his plane. He'd be like, "I'm going to New York next Thursday," and I'm like, "Oh, no way, me too!"

Jimmy Iovine was the musical director of the 2003 Super Bowl [Raiders–Buccaneers] in San Diego. No Doubt was playing. A couple of the executives from Interscope were renting a jet to go down there: Iovine, Steve Berman, David Cohen. I got invited and was like, "Hey, can I bring a couple people?" So I invited Chris. It was bizarre, totally bizarre. What I remember most about that night was when the game was over, Berman got a text saying the new 50 Cent album *Get Rich or Die Tryin'* had leaked. Someone was releasing tracks like hostages every fifteen minutes. Berman was flipping out that he was gonna lose cell service when we took off on the plane. They were in full panic mode trying to shut down the leak. Chris and I were like, "Where are we?"

EBEN D'AMICO: It was Luke Wood who brought us to DreamWorks.

LUKE WOOD: At DreamWorks, I was having a lot of success with Jimmy Eat World and AFI. So we had a lot of momentum.

EBEN D'AMICO: He pulled the whole, "I was in a punk band, I'm just like you," and started showing up at gigs, [sidling] backstage like, "Hey, what's up?"

LUKE WOOD: The Saves the Day deal was seven figures.

EBEN D'AMICO: I was in Luke Wood's office and he was talking about promo photos for the new album. I remember him saying, "I don't want you sitting at a restaurant eating a bunch of dim sum. That's over! We're not doing that anymore! I want you to look like you just had a really satisfying meal." That was the first time where I was thinking, "What did we just get ourselves into?"

MATT RUBANO: At the end of the day, it comes down to who was willing to spend what and who was really committed to your band. But there was this big changing of the guard in rock where all of a sudden it was like, "Okay guys, nu metal fucking sucks, emo is cool now."

BUDDY NIELSEN: Kenny Mayne on *SportsCenter* was calling highlights and goes, "Mics are for swinging, not singing!" in reference to the feud between Taking Back Sunday and Brand New. Like, "What the fuck? People are referencing this shit on *SportsCenter*?" That's when I knew shit got weird.

JASON TATE: Taking Back Sunday . . . there was so much drama with that band.

JILLIAN NEWMAN: Taking Back Sunday did the Takeover Tour in 2003, at the end of when John and Shaun were in the band. Taking Back Sunday was headlining, selling like 2,500 tickets a night, playing on a lineup with From Autumn to Ashes, Recover, My Chemical Romance, and Breaking Pangea on some of the dates.

FRED MASCHERINO: Eddie told me, "Yeah, we're about to hit one hundred thousand CDs sold." So the idea that anyone would leave that band was ridiculous.

CHRISTIAN MCKNIGHT: I tour-managed From Autumn to Ashes on the Takeover Tour, where they were direct support for Taking Back Sunday. And I honestly didn't know there was any friction or any trouble with Taking Back Sunday. I was with them every day. I had no idea. And then three days later, I heard about the split.

JOHN NOLAN: Shaun and I had some things in common with what we were unhappy about. I think we were both overwhelmed with what was happening with Taking Back Sunday. In addition to other things, we were looking to pump the brakes a bit, and the rest of the band was not at all.

EDDIE REYES: It was getting weird. There were some personal issues inside of the band that I'm not going to discuss, but they just, you know . . . people want to go do their own shit. And that's how it goes.

FRED MASCHERINO: Breaking Pangea was on the tour, but we left when it headed west and this band Count the Stars was opening. Their drummer Dave Shapiro told me what happened with TBS. He's like, "John and Shaun, they just quit. They had a huge fight the last night of the tour. It was real ugly and then they just went home and that was it." I heard Eddie was gonna keep going with Mark and Adam but I was like, "How are they going to keep going without those guys? That's a lot of the meat of the band."

NEIL RUBENSTEIN: John and Shaun left the band, and Mark was on the fence.

RANDY NICHOLS: Straylight Run had formed with John and Shaun. And Mark was the original drummer for that.

FRED MASCHERINO: Mark was playing both sides of the fence: He was practicing with John and Shaun on some new Straylight Run songs they had written, including "Existentialism on Prom Night." But he was keeping his foot in the door with TBS, like, whichever one continues, I'll do.

CHRISTIAN MCKNIGHT: Randy Nichols, who manages the Starting Line, lived in a house in Rockville Center [Long Island]. John's sister Michelle Nolan lived there. And eventually John lived there. That was where everybody hung out.

RANDY NICHOLS: I don't think we all lived there for even a year, but this house had everyone. Everyone was there on a regular basis. Jesse Lacey and John were friends at that point, so Jesse was there all the time.

I had an office at the top of the stairs. While I was sitting up at my desk doing my management work for Starting Line and Underoath, John used to sit at the bottom of the stairs and I'd just hear him playing piano and singing and writing for what would become Straylight Run's first album.

JOHN NOLAN: Will Noon ended up being the permanent drummer and we brought my sister Michelle in to sing and play on some demos.

GLENN GAMBOA: Michelle and John, because they're brother and sister, their harmonies are cool.

JOHN NOLAN: Shaun and I left Taking Back Sunday in April or May, and we were playing Straylight Run shows by September 2003. We'd recorded five or six demos. Our first show was at the Downtown in Farmingdale, Long Island.

JENN PELLY: I went to Straylight Run's first show, and they quickly became me and my friends' favorite band. Our friend Lauren got in a skateboarding accident before the show, so she couldn't go, and we asked everyone in Straylight Run to sign a card for her, and they did.

JOHN NOLAN: At the beginning of the band, it was looked at almost like a novelty that we had a woman in the band, like, "Oh, that's interesting, you play music with a woman." Or people talked to Michelle like, "What's it like being a girl in a band?" I remember a lot of that. And I remember a lot of the crowd response being inappropriate catcalls from guys.

JENN PELLY: They were pretty much the only Long Island band I had seen at that point with a woman member. I don't know if that was consciously why they became my favorite band, but I have to imagine it was a part of it. I also think they were writing music that was a bit more thoughtful than some of the other bands coming out of that community.

JOHN NOLAN: Immediately, we were not doing anything that sounded like Taking Back Sunday.

GLENN GAMBOA: Straylight Run had a strong sense of melody, focused around John's piano. It was more atmospheric, whereas Taking Back Sunday kind of grabbed you by the collar.

EDDIE REYES: At that point, Taking Back Sunday was pretty much breaking up. But I refused to let that happen.

JILLIAN NEWMAN: I'm not a voting member, per se, on who's in or out of the band. I'm not in the band—that's up to them. They tell me what they want to do. When John and Shaun left, that was devastating. There was a period where we didn't know what was gonna happen. I spent a lot of time with Adam, and he was very down. It was hard. The main message I told him was, "Those guys did what's best for them, but they don't dictate what's best for you. So if what's best for you is to keep this band going . . ."

EDDIE REYES: I got Fred Mascherino, from Breaking Pangea, to join the band on guitar and vocals. I got Mark to come back. And then Mark had a friend he grew up with named Matt Rubano, a sick bass player.

FRED MASCHERINO: Before I joined Taking Back Sunday, the next tour I had booked with Breaking Pangea was opening for Brand New. When I joined, I didn't know about the feud. So I said, "Look, I can join your band. But we have to go do this two-week tour with Brand New. It's really big for us, I just want to finish that out and have some closure, and then I'll join Taking Back Sunday." Eddie was like, "No, if you do that tour, you're not going to be in our band." And I was like, "What? It's just two weeks." And he's like, "No, no. You have to come to Long Island right now if you want to be in the band." He didn't want me to go and be friends with those guys. So we canceled the tour, I went to Long Island, and we didn't practice for two weeks.

MATT RUBANO: A month or two after John and Shaun left the band, they announced they were returning. And when they announced Fred and me, I remember the response being not too stoked. Those guys came out with Straylight Run, so there was this, "Oooh, which half of TBS is the real half?"

MIKE DUBIN: Taking Back Sunday shot the video for "You're So Last Summer" in Brooklyn Bridge Park in Dumbo. They set up a stage and people came and hung out for a party and they kind of played a show. They had Flava Flav lip-synching John's parts.

FRED MASCHERINO: I think we had to overnight him a CD of the song and we typed up the lyrics. He wants us to pick him up in a limo, so we drive him over to Brooklyn Bridge Park. He's like, "You guys are going to get the full Flava experience, get ready, because you're about to see a whirlwind up on that stage!" And then we come to realize, he doesn't know the name of our band. He didn't bother listening to the song. He doesn't know the lyrics, and the whole idea was he was going to lip-synch John's parts. We're trying to teach him the song: *All right, say, "And she says don't . . ."* We had to do like twenty takes.

We were like, "Wow, this guy's a celebrity." We weren't used to dealing with people like that. It was very surreal.

CHRISTIAN MCKNIGHT: I got a phone call from Jillian, Taking Back Sunday's manager: "Because the band technically broke up, they canceled Warped Tour, but they're gonna do the last three dates, can you go with them?"

FRED MASCHERINO: Kevin Lyman said, "If you can get a replacement lineup together, I'd love you to play the end of the tour."

CHRISTIAN MCKNIGHT: Those last three dates—Philly, New York, and Jersey—were their first shows with Matt Rubano and Fred.

MATT RUBANO: We got to Warped Tour, we got off the bus, and they were like, "See you at showtime!"

I was walking around with somebody—it might have been Christian McKnight—who was being nice to me by way of association and we ran into the Brand New guys. I wouldn't have known them if they were standing next to me. Jesse was on crutches because he was injured or something. Someone introduced us: "Oh, this is Matt, he just joined Taking Back Sunday." I put my hand out and Jesse refused to shake my hand. I was like, "What the fuck is going on here? How does everybody hate me? No one knows me!"

FRED MASCHERINO: Matt didn't come from our scene . . .

MATT RUBANO: I had been living in Williamsburg and playing mostly jazz and shoegaze-y indie rock.

FRED MASCHERINO: He would have been completely caught off guard like, "Why are we mad at them?"

CHRISTIAN MCKNIGHT: Fred I knew from Breaking Pangea but seeing him with Taking Back Sunday was like, "Ooooh shit, this is the real thing." Rubano was so technically gifted on bass and Fred is such a charismatic performer. I mean, obviously there's a real energy with the five OG Taking Back Sunday dudes. But those first shows with the new lineup on Warped Tour, playing in front of thousands and thousands of people . . . It was seamless.

FRED MASCHERINO: They let us go on last of the night, just as it's getting dark. We hit the stage and there's thousands of people singing every word.

MATT RUBANO: I didn't know how big the Warped Tour shows were going to be, and I definitely didn't have any sense for how fucking rabid the audience was to see the band after they announced that they were still doing it. I was still trying to make sense of the John and Shaun drama, the Brand New drama, the internal drama, the Victory Records drama. It was really like, as *TBS* as it could be, from the get-go. And it never let up from there.

FRED MASCHERINO: We did those Warped dates, then we went out in the fall on a really long tour opening for Saves the Day. They were sort of the godfathers and we were honored to go out with them. But we were blowing up to the point where our fans were grabbing up the tickets before the Saves the Day fans could even get them.

EBEN D'AMICO: Taking Back Sunday was becoming as big as Saves the Day or maybe even overtaking us. And at the time, I was the big mouth of the band. I remember being really competitive like, "We have to show up this band that is opening for us!" I sort of bullied my band into taking extra production on tour, like a lighting rig and shit like that. I think my band hated my guts for it later on, because I was obnoxious at that point. Bands are all bitchy to each other.

FRED MASCHERINO: It's weird—when Taking Back Sunday and Brand New were supposedly fighting, it really was all about Jesse. Vinnie, the guitarist from Brand New, if we played in town, he would come and stand onstage while we played. He was cool as hell. So as much as it seemed like, "This band and this band," it was really, "This guy and this guy."

A lot of times when you're in a band, you're on the lead singer's ride. And if you don't like it, you get off. And it sucks if you're not that guy.

GLENN GAMBOA: Brand New felt like I had taken TBS's side, so they really didn't want to talk to me for *Newsday* after that. It had to have been someone from their management or publicity team. They were like, "Is there someone else? Because they really don't feel like talking with you." At some point, they felt you had to choose sides.

MAX BEMIS: We found it funny in my group of friends, because there were people who really took it seriously and really felt the need to be like, "I'm a Brand New person! I'm totally with Jesse on this one!" It's like "No. These are people, they're all complicated." That whole thing was just a load of shit, but it was also really entertaining.

GEOFF RICKLY: My impression of Brand New was that they're just this pop-punk band, until I heard *Deja Entendu* before it came out. Thursday's management had a college radio promotion arm that did promotions for that record. I was like, "Who the fuck is this? This is fucking awesome." Graham, the college radio guy, was like, "It's Brand New, you played with them." And I remember saying, "This isn't the band we played with. That band sounded like a pop-punk band." I was like, "Graham, I know you're already working this and you probably believe this, but this is huge. HUGE!" He was like, "I'm glad you're not deaf."

FRED FELDMAN: The bigger press things started coming when *Deja* came out: *Rolling Stone*'s "hot band" issue. I remember getting a phone call that MTV was gonna put their video in rotation.

JASON TATE: Brand New, *Your Favorite Weapon* . . . whatever, pop-punk album. When they put out *Deja*, it was a completely scene-altering album at the time: what people were listening to, what was being made. It felt like such a shift in style. It was so good that literally overnight, bands were ripping it off and needed to make the next version of it.

BUDDY NIELSEN: Senses Fail played the fucking *Deja* release show at Irving Plaza, their hometown New York show. Brand New had already built a fan base with *Your Favorite Weapon* and they were starting to get bigger in other parts of the country. Later on, Senses Fail opened their B-market *Deja* tour, which was fucking insane. Every single venue was sold out beyond capacity.

TOMMY CORRIGAN: For one of the first big Brand New tours, I worked like thirty-six hours in a row printing sweatshirts that they had to get done before they left. I couldn't believe how many zip-up sweatshirts we printed . . .

Later on, I did a Brand New shirt that had a BMX bike on it. It was a photo I stole off the internet. And the guy who took the photo happened to be in Hot Topic with his kid, looked up and saw his BMX bike on the Brand New shirt, and tried to sue us. I got a phone call from the beach—I took the day off because I'd been working so much—like, "Yo! We're getting sued, where'd you get that picture of the bicycle from?" I'm like, "Oh, I can't remember . . ."

I think we settled for $1,000 or something like that. Little did he know that it was like the best-selling Hot Topic shirt all summer. That thing was a number one Hot Topic banger for months.

LESLIE SIMON: For many, many young people in Middle America, Hot Topic was the center of culture. This was the only place you could connect with other outsiders—at a store, at a mall. And that's not a great slice of diversity. It's not a big one, it's not a very layered slice, but it's better than none at all.

MARIA SHERMAN: I remember my first time walking past Hot Topic. I was curious because it was so loud. Then, I got rid of my mom and had the bravery to run in. They were blasting Underoath. I remember the store being very dark, and wanting to feel less intimidated, but I was also really excited to be in there.

TOMMY CORRIGAN: Hot Topic would take twenty thousand T-shirts at a clip. These kids in these bands were making so much money. When you came up with a Hot Topic banger at Merch Direct, you'd be like, "Yeah, in your face, I just did thirty thousand at Hot Topic!" I wouldn't see any of that money, but I would be proud of it for some reason.

FRED FELDMAN: The scene started out mainly male. And there's a point where girls start coming and it sort of changed things, you know?

JILLIAN NEWMAN: For all the stats we kept on Taking Back Sunday throughout the years, one thing we loved was that their fan base was kind of fifty-fifty, men and women.

TOMMY CORRIGAN: Speaking of women in the scene, that's when you knew things were changing. From a T-shirt perspective, all of a sudden you're printing youth medium T-shirts. That was a classic early 2000s girl size. Back in the nineties everything was extra-large, double extra-large. All of a sudden there's hundreds of youth mediums getting added to every order. That was a signifier of who was actually going to the shows. It was moving from the macho, stomp-in-your-face crowd to being accessible to more women. More women could go to these shows and not get the crap kicked out of them.

AMANDA BRENNAN: There was this understood girl code. You watched out for other girls. And like, if a girl showed up in heels, you might make fun of her: "God, that girl doesn't know what she's getting into." But there was this understanding of, "Oh, that girl's crowd-surfing, I'm going to keep an eye out." It's not anything I was really taught to do. When I went to shows,

I usually went with a big group of girls, and we would keep an eye out. Because, you know, girl code.

Everyone always talks about drunk girls in the bathroom complimenting each other, but at punk shows, that's usually amplified, and you don't need to be drunk to do it. You're just running into someone like, "Oh my god, they have good hair," or, "I love that shirt," or maybe they did something DIY that they're wearing and you want to talk to them about it.

JENN PELLY: By the time I got to middle school, I was excited to listen to music that wasn't mainstream. The late nineties and early 2000s could feel like a damaging time for girls in pop culture. When you think about the biggest pop stars, whether it was Britney Spears or Christina Aguilera or whoever else, they were these pristine, perfect people making pristine, perfect music, and I think that level of perfection could set a damaging aesthetic standard. I was looking for something different, and discovering non-mainstream music felt like an alternative. But once I got involved and could see below the surface, I started to realize there were ways in which it was also damaging.

GEOFF RICKLY: Why was our era so big? Why did it explode? I think because it brought everybody into the tent.

TOMMY CORRIGAN: In the supermarket the checkout kid's wearing a Thursday shirt. It used to be you'd recognize every hardcore kid. But these weren't hardcore kids; these were this newer generation into different shit, you know what I mean? I was only like twenty-five, and I remember starting to feel out of touch. It was blowing up into a different universe.

GEOFF RICKLY: When Island Def Jam signed Thursday, their vision for us was, "Be the band you want to be. Have a career. We have some of the best people in the world in marketing and sales. Tell them exactly what you want and they will tell you what's gonna work and what's not."

And Island Def Jam was fucking bangin' at the time. They had hit after hit and Kanye was about to happen. Jay-Z was in the offices a lot. I remember having a conversation with Lyor Cohen, Julie Greenwald, and maybe Jay-Z about what the next *College Dropout* single should be. They were like, "Should we do 'Get Em High' or 'Jesus Walks'?"

ANDY GREENWALD: Geoff really had a sense of the narratives that appealed to me as a writer. You know, having the Island logo on his record, he could talk about his parents having U2's *War* on vinyl and the Island logo being on the spine of that and what that meant to him as a childhood music fan, and also for his family. He tried to weave his band into the larger consciousness.

JONAH BAYER: I wrote the *Alternative Press* cover story for Thursday's *War All the Time*.

JOHNNY MINARDI: *Alt Press* was the MTV of our scene. The holy grail was the fucking *Alt Press* cover story.

GEOFF RICKLY: *War All the Time* was like a test: can you deal with a record that's much less commercial than the last one?

ADAM TURLA: We got to go to Big Blue Meenie studios, and it was wild. I had never seen what was basically a record that was going to be huge get made. I remember seeing Geoff in the vocal booth just doing take after take. And they sounded good, but they were looking for that perfect one, trying to get two or three words to sound just right.

GEOFF RICKLY: We handed in a version of the record that was so dark and claustrophobic that I remember our A&R guy saying, "I'm not telling you you can't give us this record. We'll put it out. But like, it's really dark. And we're in a pretty dark time—have you noticed the world?" You know, at that time it felt like that's as bad as it gets. He was like, "I just want to get you out of that studio in New Jersey. We're gonna book you three weeks in this beautiful studio up in Massachusetts that the Rolling Stones rehearsed in. It's a beautiful, old house, there's a cook on staff twenty-four hours a day, she'll bake cakes and shit. Just ask her and she'll make the meal."

While we were out there, we wrote "Signals Over the Air," "Division St.," and "This Song Brought to You by a Falling Bomb." And that changed the record. We weren't trying to write radio hits, but we were like, "Let's try and write something a little less claustrophobic and see what comes out." And those are maybe three of the four best songs on *War All the Time*.

MIKEY WAY: Alex would be like, "Hey, come over, I got the new whatever," and we would listen to it front to back at the Eyeball House. We did that for *War All the Time*. I loved the line where Geoff's like, "All those nights in the basement, the kids are still screaming." He was talking about basement shows and this was an album on Island Def Jam, you know what I mean?

JONAH BAYER: For the cover story, I remember people trying to figure out if it was going to sell a hundred thousand records its first week, and it sold about seventy-five thousand. It's so crazy to think about.

GEOFF RICKLY: Jay-Z thought Tucker was a drum machine. He heard the first song on *War All the Time* ["For the Workforce, Drowning"] and he's like, "This is a drum machine." And we're like, "Nah, man, that's a person." He's like, "Wow, that guy's good." I was like, "Well, Tucker's gonna be thrilled forever."

Although sometimes I would be like, "Uhhh . . . is Jay-Z mixing us up with another band?" Like, he'd see us in the hallway at Island Def Jam and be like, "Hey guys, it's good to see you, that new video's amazing!" And we're like, "What's he talking about? We haven't done a new video. Do you think he thinks we're Thrice or Hoobastank?"

JONAH BAYER: Thrice had a big record coming out on Island around the same time as Thursday's, so *Alternative Press* made it a Thrice/Thursday split cover.

DUSTIN KENSRUE: It felt like a milestone moment.

ED BRECKENRIDGE: The thing I remember most about the *AP* cover was the photo shoot. There was hair and makeup and it was just super uncomfortable.

DUSTIN KENSRUE: That whole period was chaotic and exciting and a bit overwhelming.

TYLER RANN: *Rolling Stone* was still a little too mainstream for this scene. And *Alternative Press*, Midtown definitely wanted to be on the cover, for sure. That never happened.

RICH EGAN: *Alternative Press* was huge. I mean, shit, Dashboard was probably on the cover of *AP* three times. Saves the Day was on there. Alkaline

Trio was on there. *AP* played a huge part, even if it and Vagrant didn't always have the friendliest relationships with *AP*. They were a huge part of moving the needle, to the point where they were kind of the main driver of press for that scene.

JONAH BAYER: I'd interned at *Alternative Press* in 1999 or 2000, when I was in college. At that point, the covers were like Coal Chamber, Limp Bizkit, Insane Clown Posse. Creed was on the cover of the magazine. They were just covering what was popular at the time. I came back in '02, and soon after that they did this Dashboard Confessional cover.

GLENN GAMBOA: Once Warped Tour got twenty thousand people to show up across the country all summer long, advertisers started to realize, "Okay, this is a group we want to target." That version of *Alternative Press* was healthy enough to support bigger things.

JONAH BAYER: Then the covers would be like: nu metal band, New Found Glory, nu metal band, Good Charlotte. And then around 2003, it totally transitioned from nu metal to the Warped Tour scene. There was a group of us there who were all young, like Trevor Kelley and Leslie Simon.

LESLIE SIMON: As a female, I had to work actively and consistently hard to prove my worth and that I wasn't a groupie and a frivolous fangirl. Those are things that male reporters don't have to deal with.

Your Jonah Bayers, Andy Greenwalds, James Montgomerys, they were the ones the male band members wanted to hang out with because they were a good time. So not only could they get the job done, they could have a good time doing it. And if you were a girl in the same position, there were lines you'd have to establish early, otherwise you could fall into oh, "She's a starfucker," which I wasn't, or "Oh, she's a narc," which I sort of was, because I was reporting on what was happening. But coming from me versus a man . . . it's like I was tattletale-ing on debauchery versus partaking in debauchery. I still have some hard feelings about it because there was a lot of work no one ever saw. You read the story, but you didn't know how hard it was to *get* the story.

Brand New disliked my 2003 cover story so much that they refused to do press with *AP* a while after. And the reason they didn't like the story was I had seen them do things . . . If you're hanging out, unless you say "off the record," it's on the record. And the first night I was with them on tour, there was this after-party. Not one of them talked to me, not one of them acknowledged my presence. So I sat on the balcony of this bar and just watched them do stuff all night, which included getting wasted, pulling girls into photo booths and making out, and some of that made it into the story. And they were pissed. They were just douchebags. The whole band. Except Brian. Brian was really nice. Everybody else was a fucking asshole. Jesse thought he could manipulate the story and try to flirt with me. He turned to me randomly and was like, *Has anyone ever told you that you look like . . .* And he'd say some weird, dark-haired female celebrity who I don't look like. And I said, *No, no one's ever said that before.* He's like, *Yes, you're very striking*. And I'm thinking, *Okay, that's not going in the story, get out of here.*

"I REMEMBER PLAYING HOLLISTER. IT *WAS A* RIOT *AT THE* MALL, BASICALLY"

PETE WENTZ: You're dudes in your twenties—or you know, I was in my twenties, Patrick was eighteen or nineteen—and you're figuring out how to be creative together, but then you're also living on top of each other. So there was a lot of button-pushing. I pushed Patrick's buttons way more than he pushed mine.

CHRIS GUTIERREZ: Wentz, Patrick, Joe, and our other friend all lived together in this apartment in Chicago, in Roscoe Village.

PETE WENTZ: Listen, we were in the era of *CKY* and then *Jackass*. We would prank each other all the time.

The maddest Patrick ever got . . . For some reason, I had a picture of Ayatollah Khomeini. I think the guys in Racetraitor had randomly given it to me. One day, Patrick drove me home and I switched out his license with the Ayatollah Khomeini picture. Patrick's a by-the-book kind of guy. He would never want to drive without his license. He got halfway where he was going, came back, and I remember him pulling up to the house and just stomping out of his van. Dude was fucking *pissed*.

TOMMY CORRIGAN: It was late on a Friday and we wanted to go home. Fall Out Boy needed shirts printed that night. I remember turning to my friend and I go, "Fuck these guys. They're never going to be anything, anyway. They suck."

We lost the account because we didn't print the shirts on time. Whoops.

PETE WENTZ: Whatever everyone else was doing, Fall Out Boy was like, "Let's do what's counterintuitive." At the time, everybody was trying to get people to go to MP3.com and this and that online. So we started climbing things with a bucket of glue and wheat-pasting Fall Out Boy posters everywhere, like, "This is what Mötley Crüe did." We tried to have every show be an event.

ADAM SISKA: When Fall Out Boy was getting to the point where they would sell out shows locally, they played a secret show under the name Saved Latin. If you were a core fan, you knew what that was, and you would be there, because that [*Rushmore*] reference had been on their merch: "Fall Out Boy Saved Latin, What Did You Ever Do?"

GRETA MORGAN: I would see kids wearing these white sweatshirts that had half of a broken heart on each side. I don't think they even said Fall Out Boy's name; it was like a secret society thing. I would start seeing those all around town before I even knew who they were or how they sounded.

CHRIS GUTIERREZ: They wanted to do a secret, invite-only apartment show. The only way you could get in was if you wrote an email, telling us why you want to go. And Wentz was like, "Dude I don't want to read all these fucking emails. Can you read them?" I still remember some girl was like, "Hey, I'll fly down from Alaska to go to this." I was like, "You're definitely in." And then I remember all these people in the emails asking things like, "Do you know who so-and-so is dating? Can you tell me about Joe, what does he like to eat?" Like, why are you asking me these goddamn questions?!

JASON TATE: Fall Out Boy first came on my radar when I was either a freshman or sophomore in college, a couple years after I started AbsolutePunk.net. Pete Wentz sent me a burned CD-R that said something like, "I think you'll like this," and then in parentheses, "Two to ride, three to die for," some weird Pete Wentz thing.

It was the first five songs they recorded for *Take This to Your Grave*.

SEAN O'KEEFE: After the three-song demo, labels asked for two more: it was "Grand Theft Autumn/Where Is Your Boy" and a song called "Hey Chris," which people now know as "Grenade Jumper."

JASON TATE: My first impression was, "Holy shit, this singer can sing." We don't have anything like this right now in the scene.

MIKEY WAY: When My Chemical Romance was on tour with Piebald, we played the Fireside Bowl. Joe, Pete, and Chris came out to see us play; they had heard about us somehow. After the show, Pete came up to me and gave me their demo, with his email address written on the CD-R.

MANI MOSTOFI: Pete circulated that demo and they knew they had something.

NICK SCIMECA: Once those songs hit the internet, it was a matter of weeks before labels were involved. And Crush Management.

ADAM SISKA: Crush, at the time, was a really small management company.

ALEX SARTI: Bob McLynn and Jonathan Daniel were the owners.

JONATHAN DANIEL: The first meeting with Pete was on the phone. Right away, he's supersmart. And I remember him talking about Patrick: "My singer is wild, he doesn't like new music, he only listens to Tom Waits and Prince." I was like, "I think I love this kid."

ADAM SISKA: There were rumors Fall Out Boy was about to sign to Drive-Thru, or the Militia Group.

MANI MOSTOFI: They were definitely thinking about Drive-Thru. Definitely thinking about Victory.

JONATHAN DANIEL: Victory made an offer, and Drive-Thru didn't make an offer, but they had a subsidiary label called Rushmore Records which made an offer, and Militia Group made an offer. I wanted to do it with Militia Group because I knew them, but they wouldn't step off from a contract for a lot of records.

So I went to Rob Stevenson at Island. I had just done a deal with the Bronx, this amazing punk band, which was a hybrid deal: their first record with an indie, and then you can have the option on the second record with Island. So I said, "What if we do the same thing with Fall Out Boy?" Rob said, "Talk to Fueled By Ramen, I like that label."

ADAM SISKA: When they chose Fueled By Ramen, everyone was kind of like, "Huh, that's weird." Fueled By Ramen had put out a Jimmy Eat World EP, but it wasn't one of the band's big releases.

RICH EGAN: Fueled By Ramen started in the late nineties. It was Vinnie from Less Than Jake and John Janick.

ADAM SISKA: They put out Less Than Jake records because Vinnie was involved. So that made sense, but Fueled By Ramen didn't really have a winning track record. You'd think they would have signed to one of the heavy hitters.

MANI MOSTOFI: Pete came from the underground scene, so he knew the credibility that came from doing an indie label first instead of putting your first record out on a major.

SEAN O'KEEFE: We got the budget from Fueled By Ramen and went into the studio to record the other seven songs on *Take This to Your Grave*. I didn't even end up remixing those five songs from the demo.

Smart Studios, in Madison, Wisconsin—they'd always stock the fridge with soda. And bowls of candy were there. We're talking the early 2000s, before anybody was really thinking about health, so it was just this atrocious diet. They would routinely ask bands, "What kind of soda do you want in the fridge, and what kind of candy do you like?" I remember Fall Out Boy said, instead of soda and candy, can we get ramen noodles? It literally had nothing to do with being on Fueled By Ramen. So they got a bunch of ramen noodles and peanut butter and shit. The band was living off that.

MANI MOSTOFI: Even though Patrick was writing the songs, Pete was dictating the direction.

PETE WENTZ: I wouldn't say we were like oil and water, but we were like oil and vinegar. On its own, it's not great, but together . . .

PATRICK STUMP: By the time we did "Where Is Your Boy," Pete was like, "I can't stomach some of these words, you gotta change this, this, and this." By the time we got signed, Pete was like, "I got the steering wheel now." And I was fine with that. I just wanted to write music. It takes me longer to write words, anyway.

SEAN O'KEEFE: They were butting heads. There was one song that had like nine drafts of lyrics because they couldn't make it work. The issue would be Pete had a lyric and Patrick couldn't logistically take those words and fit them into a melody. At a certain point, Patrick would be like, "I can't do it. Give me new words." And Pete would say, "Give me a new melody!"

PATRICK STUMP: Pete was like, "I don't give a fuck what it sounds like. I want it to say *this*."

SEAN O'KEEFE: Those guys were straight edge at the time. I was twenty-two and I would smoke pot once every couple months with my friends. I told them in the studio about smoking pot once and it became this ongoing joke that I was a huge stoner. They had all these stoner names for me. When they submitted the thank-yous for the album artwork, they submitted like ten different stoner names: "Thank you, Dimebag Darrell O'Keefe. Thank you, Gotta Munch Before You Punch O'Keefe. Thank you, Hot Box the Camaro O'Keefe." The label came back like, "Everything is cool with the artwork, except the ten stoner names is excessive. We'll let you pick three."

MANI MOSTOFI: I'm not objective, but I think they were clearly head-and-shoulders above the bands that were similar at the time. Patrick's a much better singer, Andy's a much better drummer. Pete writes more interesting lyrics. Pete, Andy, Joe, and Patrick are all smarter than the average person in the hardcore scene. There was a level of chess playing going on with those kids that wasn't happening with others. I remember Patrick listening to the Starting Line, one of the big Drive-Thru bands at the time. He was listening to those bands to study them, to understand what people liked about them. He was thinking, "Okay, how can I do this better?"

SEAN O'KEEFE: When the record was done and mixed, I played it for them. The one critique Pete had was, "The screams aren't loud enough." I couldn't go back into the mix and change anything at that point in time. So Pete went back to my studio with me. We had the master recordings in Pro Tools, and he added new screams to that.

MANI MOSTOFI: They had the energy and delivery of a hardcore band, right? But they weren't playing hardcore. The key to *Take This to Your Grave* was it sounded like Hot Topic, but it felt like CBGB.

PETE WENTZ: We played at the mall. Hollister used to do these shows . . .

ADAM SISKA: They played the Woodfield Mall Hollister in Schaumburg,

Illinois. It might have been the first time the people there were looking at Fall Out Boy as rock stars.

PETE WENTZ: You'd play these in-stores in other places and they'd be like, "Don't touch this." So you're not really playing a show. Hollister was super dope because they were just like, "Do whatever you want." So I remember playing Hollister. It was a riot at the mall, basically. I look over and see our merch guy [Jordan], he's wearing board shorts, takes a surfboard off the wall and is literally surfing on the crowd.

BRIAN ANDERSON: They played the *Take This to Your Grave* release show at the Metro in Chicago. My friend Leslie—she took some of the very early Fall Out Boy promo photos in the art room of our high school—she's a year older than me, and Patrick asked me to the prom on her behalf. There was some banter in between songs and all of a sudden Patrick was like, "Hey B.A., Leslie wants to know if you'll go to the prom with her!" And then they launched into the next song.

PETE WENTZ: That was the era where the fire marshal came into every show and always pulled the plug. Back then it felt like, "Were fucked, we're so fucked right now, we're so fucked because we can't finish the set."

BRIAN ANDERSON: Fall Out Boy playing the Arlington Heights Knights of Columbus on Halloween 2003—a pretty legendary show. They had just finished their first national tour. They were starting to blow up and they came back to play that show. It was just madness.

HANIF ABDURRAQIB: I know a lot of people in Chicago probably feel . . . it's not a very good venue. Knights of Columbus was thrown together, kind of haphazardly arranged. It never felt very safe, or it never felt very safe to me.

BRIAN ANDERSON: Fall Out Boy played on this little riser that me and my buddy built.

HANIF ABDURRAQIB: The band had begun to get some real traction and the venue wasn't prepared for the amount of people. I think they were still thinking, "This is a little band." By that time, "Saturday" was big and a lot of those other *Take This to Your Grave* songs were big, at least in the scene. And by that time, some of the skepticism of the hardcore scene had faded. So people were very into them. It was fucking packed.

BRIAN ANDERSON: There were so many people there, it was packed to the ceiling, like I can't even describe it. There was literally no room to move. It was Halloween, so everyone was wearing their goofiest shit. Fall Out Boy all dressed up as priests, and Joe also had some corpse paint thing going on.

PATRICK STUMP: I'm actually quite short, I'm a very short adult man—that would be the thing of note about me if I wasn't in a successful band—and when people would crowd-surf they'd go over me. So many people bled into the stage that I moved my microphone back behind Andy. I was diligent about trying to keep the music going. The show must go on . . .

BRIAN ANDERSON: I was jumping out into the front of the crowd to do crowd control, just wave after wave of people smashing into all the gear and the dudes in the band. Just using all my strength to try and hold people back. Peak Fall Out Boy at the Knights of Columbus. Just bodies everywhere.

HANIF ABDURRAQIB: Towards the end, I think during "Saturday," the stage couldn't handle the weight of all the people and just kind of collapsed. They had to stop and try to figure out what to do. I remember that night feeling like, "Okay, this is a different thing. This band is gonna be a different thing."

PATRICK STUMP: We realized, "We can't do this anymore. It's just too crazy. You're putting people at risk when there's this many people in this tight a space."

BRIAN ANDERSON: They played the Knights one more time after that. Right on the floor. If I remember correctly, it was kind of a secret show, but of course, word got out, and the place was mobbed. Every song they would have to stop because their shit would get unplugged.

You know how a guitar player will do that lean and fall backwards into the crowd? Joe was wearing corduroy pants and—I don't think he did this purposely—but when he went into the crowd, he put his ass directly into my face and I got like, a rug burn from his corduroys. Which was a nice little parting memory from that end of an era at the Knights.

PETE WENTZ: There was a show we headlined at the Metro and our parents came. We had these giant inflatable penises, like six or eight feet tall. It was like, "What production can we add to the show?" We couldn't add anything, so we would blow up inflatable things, throw out CDs, whatever. I remember throwing one of the giant dicks into the VIP section and it hit my mom and she kind of stomped it out. It was after that show that my parents were like, "I think it's cool if you take a year off." To me, that was like, "Oh, someone's looking at this not as a dumb little thing you do, it's worthy of a sabbatical." That was a moment.

ADAM SAMILJAN: Looking back on some of the big moments for that era of Fall Out Boy, there was the 2003 Skate and Surf Festival in Asbury Park.

PETE WENTZ: It's weird to think of Jersey as a promised land, right? But for that kind of music, it definitely was.

SHANE TOLD: New Jersey felt like the sacred land of emo.

ALEX SAAVEDRA: I would get calls and emails from bands from all over the place, asking for advice on where to move to in New Jersey. So many times. I would be like, "Dude, you don't have to move your whole band over. Just come play here."

ADAM SISKA: We idolized Jersey. In high school with my friends it was really like, "We're gonna quit school and we're gonna drive to New Jersey and we're gonna be at Skate and Surf Festival. If only our parents would let us go . . ."

MATTHEW ISMAEL RUIZ: Those Skate and Surf Festivals felt like a turning point for Asbury, in particular. I don't know if you remember what Asbury Park looked like in, say 2001, but shit was not cute. I would go to the rare Stone Pony or Convention Hall show and it was like, "If you go at night, don't park too far away from the venue because the walk is dicey." The boardwalk had fucking *Weird New Jersey* haunted fucking vibes and you know, the creepy mural of the clown with the fucking mouth and all the paint peeling. Everything's closed. You see rats scurrying across the boardwalk. Shit was dicey, bro.

PETE WENTZ: Starting Line was playing and right before their set started, these two flags dropped on both sides of the stage that said "I HEART

NJ" or something like that. And maybe there was a Bon Jovi song playing? It was like some big Jersey moment.

CHRISTIAN MCKNIGHT: Skate and Surf weekends were so important for the evolution of this scene, because so many people met and a lot of people saw these bands for the first time. And for a lot of these bands, this was the first time they played to a really large crowd.

JEFF SOSNOW: That year, Brand New played to thousands of kids inside Convention Hall. Michael Goldstone and I saw Brand New and we're like, "That's gonna be the biggest band in the world."

ADAM SISKA: I have a very distinct memory—and I know this hasn't aged well with Brand New—but when *Deja Entendu* came out, Pete was like, "This is the future of music, Fall Out Boy is gonna aim towards this." When *Deja* came out, nothing was the same. Every band was starting to aim for this intelligent poetic lyricism, this sort of East Coast poetry, with long song titles.

FRED FELDMAN: Triple Crown tried to re-sign them after *Deja* came out, but I knew it was a long, long, long shot. They were coming out of a two-album deal. Every label was trying to sign them, A&R guys were flying out left and right.

LUKE WOOD: How it works within the same label is, whoever spots them first, they're in. I remember seeing Sosnow at the show and then talking to Goldie, and he's like, "Yeah, I'm talking to Brand New." Like, "Fuck. Okay."

GEOFF RICKLY: I'd consider Skate and Surf 2003 the biggest thing Thursday ever did. There were thousands of people inside the main stage at Convention Hall and Taking Back Sunday played before us. And they blew the doors off it. We didn't know how we could go on after them. I hear the crowd singing and I see Adam hanging from the light fixtures doing things that I would never do in a million years.

When we went on, we opened with "Autobiography of a Nation." I remember every person all the way back in the bleachers standing on their seats and singing that first line: "WRITE THESE WORDS BACK DOWN . . ." It was so much better than I ever thought it was gonna be.

This was the crest of *Full Collapse* into the first few weeks of *War All the Time*. That was the height of the band's popularity. Taking Back Sunday were right on our heels. They were about to get so much bigger than us. It felt like everything was exploding, right then.

JOHNNY MINARDI: In Chicago, Fall Out Boy was crazy. They were selling two thousand tickets each show. We get to Asbury Park, I'm walking around with the guys. At this point, there's not a lot of photos or music videos out. But we're walking around and they're getting stopped. They're stopped by thirty, forty people, to the point of where we actually had to go somewhere else and wait for the set because Patrick couldn't warm up, and they still had to figure out the set list.

CHRISTIAN MCKNIGHT: Inside Convention Hall, there's the main room and this middle part we called the Arcade; basically, the other areas of the hall would empty into it. We would put bands on the stage in the Arcade that weren't that big.

While MxPx was playing the main room, somebody set off the fire alarm . . .

PATRICK STUMP: Somebody was goofing around backstage and they sprayed someone with a fire extinguisher. That set off the fire alarm . . .

CHRISTIAN MCKNIGHT: So maybe five thousand people emptied out into the Arcade area, which should hold a thousand. I was like, "Holy fuck, but I'm okay, they'll all go away." Fall Out Boy was on next. Much to my dismay, Fall Out Boy was a much bigger band than I thought. Those five thousand people I thought would go back to the main room did not.

PATRICK STUMP: The label showed up to that show; it was a close enough train from New York. L.A. Reid was there and he said something like, "You better impress me."

JOHNNY MINARDI: I went back down to where Fall Out Boy was getting ready. They're standing there with their guitars, and I'm like, "Guys, have you seen the room? It's full capacity, leaking onto the boardwalk."

PETE WENTZ: The fire marshal was there.

JOHNNY MINARDI: Skate and Surf at the time was super known for shutting down for hours because of fire marshals. I remember feeling this energy in that room like, "Guys, this is crazy, I can't even watch from here." I grabbed John Janick and watched from upstairs. The band came out, did their high-fives . . .

PATRICK STUMP: I turned around and I could actually see everyone I was playing to. We've played to bigger audiences since, but none of them looked like that many people. And there was this weird energy because they were all confused: "What happened? Is there a fire? Is Fall Out Boy really gonna play?" And the stage manager's like, "Go! Go!"

JOHNNY MINARDI: They get the feedback going, they lean into the crowd. And right when they start "Tell That Mick," the barricades just fucking collapse. Security is just holding kids up. Patrick sings "Light that smoke . . ." and you can't even hear him, but it's full volume. And the whole room . . . I just got a chill thinking about it. In between every song, they're like, "You have to back up, security's telling us we cannot continue . . ." I don't even think they got through the full set.

CHRISTIAN MCKNIGHT: This is the crazy bassist I had seen seven years ago playing in a hardcore band! And he's totally acclimated to playing in front of that many people! This just works.

PETE WENTZ: This feels like a real thing . . .

JOHNNY MINARDI: I remember looking at John Janick and saying, "It's over. This is what it's gonna be forever. This is New Jersey. This has nothing to do with the crowd we've been building for two years in Chicago. This is it."

CHAPTER 17

"IF YOU DON'T SIGN *THIS* BAND, YOU'RE GONNA REGRET IT *FOR THE* REST *OF* YOUR LIFE"

JOHN FELDMANN: The Used had just played 2003 Skate and Surf in New Jersey—My Chemical Romance was one of the bands on a smaller stage.

MIKEY WAY: We weren't on someone's show; it was a festival. We had a lot of people in that room there to see us: "Oh, we want to check out this band that we're hearing about . . ."

My Chem, at the time, you never knew what was gonna happen. Frank, and Gerard, and Ray would pinball around. I was kind of the tentpole in the middle. Frank was a tornado, throwing mic stands, throwing his guitar in the air. None of it was rehearsed: Frank would break his gear . . . the things anyone would say into the microphone, everything was just gold.

MATT GALLE: Gerard's boots were all ripped and duct-taped together. The drummer at the time, Otter, had some crazy, weird drum set connected by rods, with all these hi-hats and cymbals that a normal hardcore punk band wouldn't have. Frank was just going off onstage, rolling on the floor and falling into the crowd, screaming into the mic and spitting in the air. It was chaos, but it was awesome.

JOHN FELDMANN: My Chemical Romance at Skate and Surf, I just didn't get it. I was like, "This kid is just out of shape. He's drunk." I just didn't see in Gerard what I saw in Bert.

QUINN ALLMAN: I never thought they were gonna be the next humongous band in the world; they were a vampire biker band to me. I loved it.

BRANDEN STEINECKERT: They had so much piss and fire in them.

BERT MCCRACKEN: We started touring with My Chem as much as possible, it was such a great combo.

CHRIS CARRABBA: When I finally saw My Chemical Romance play, they were opening for the Used and Taking Back Sunday. I remember looking around at Gerard and Bert—"These guys have long hair! Are we allowed to have long hair now?"

My Chemical Romance brought the house to a state of frenzy I've rarely seen. I remember Gerard coming offstage, looking at me, and I went, "That was amazing." He looks at me and smiles ear to ear: "IT WAS AMAZING, RIGHT?" And then he just full-speed runs away . . .

JOSH WILLS: For lack of a better term, I refer to that era of My Chemical Romance as, "Very dirty and not showering." Leather jackets and torn-up black pants. That's my image of them from back then. And then drinking all the alcohol.

QUINN ALLMAN: Hanging out in hotel lobbies, hanging out in the van with My Chem . . . Everybody getting Sidekicks for the first time. Listening to random bands, Ray showing me awesome, crazy world music.

Mikey and I would get drunk . . . just kind of happy drunk, so we'd be fearless and go up to people. I remember in Vegas at the Hard Rock, they were having a big convention. Everyone's sitting on their computers, watching a corporate lecture onstage and we're just walking up drunk to people like, "You're doing a good job!" "*Really?* What are you working on?"

BERT MCCRACKEN: I became drinking buddies with Gerard and we would have the most debauch. They were such a great live, entertaining band. I would watch them every day. We took them on their first European run.

MIKEY WAY: The Used brought us to the UK for the first time, which is where MCR kind of caught on first.

ALEX SAAVEDRA: I went with My Chemical Romance the first tour through Europe because they were still on Eyeball. Touring with Bert at that time was very difficult.

ANDY GREENWALD: Gerard and Bert, when they were touring together, it was like the Spider-Man pointing at a Spider-Man meme. And they just went for it.

BERT MCCRACKEN: We would definitely feed off each other. With anything in life, I tend to push it to the limits.

QUINN ALLMAN: My Chemical Romance was motivated. And it used to kind of bug me because I'd watch Gerard and those guys, and they were pushing it every night. I could see a bit of that had gone to Bert's head and he was kind of giving it 5 percent less, 5 percent less. Like, "I'm kind of the king" shit.

LESLIE SIMON: Bert had become friendly with Gerard. They were close. And Bert had a lot of like . . . gossip baggage from dating Kelly Osbourne.

BERT MCCRACKEN: I met Kelly when the Used was on Ozzfest. One of her friends came up to me like, "Kelly wants to hang out." I didn't know Ozzy had any kids. I was never really an Ozzy fan, so I was never blown away or starstruck.

JOHN FELDMANN: I don't know if Bert being on *The Osbournes* on MTV helped their career in any way, but it certainly didn't hurt. I remember Bert with his Good Charlotte shirt on, waiting to get picked up in front of the Osbournes' house . . . I think the episode was called "Beauty and the Bert."

BERT MCCRACKEN: Ohhhh, that one. . . .

JEPH HOWARD: They made Bert look so dirty on that episode. He was just a normal kid from Utah. At the time, there were dirtier people in our band, I'll say that.

BERT MCCRACKEN: I'm not sure I ever watched the episode, but I know that they slandered me pretty good, saying I had some STD that I didn't have.

Sharon never really liked me.

JEPH HOWARD: And Bert kind of rolled with it, because it was funny.

BERT MCCRACKEN: The show was fully scripted and they would have to perform their little reality TV show parts. I was heavily sedated during that whole moment, so I barely remember what it was like. I got to hang with Ozzy a bunch of times, cool guy. I got to hang with him and Marilyn Manson at the renewal of his vows, where Ozzy was supposed to not be drinking but I was getting wasted. Ozzy was never supposed to be doing anything, it seemed. But he was always doing something.

I don't think I ever saw the shows. But I think our breakup was pretty nasty. I was in a pretty bad place. And I think I broke up with Kelly tragically, like on Valentine's Day and from just a phone call. I was probably a pretty big dick about it.

JEPH HOWARD: It put us in the limelight, in a good and bad way.

JOHN FELDMANN: A lot of people saw Bert . . .

BERT MCCRACKEN: Yeah, I hated it at the time. I hated reality TV before it was a thing. Except for *Survivor*. And *The Amazing Race*. I love a good reality TV game show. But any type of reality celebrity eye-fuck-fest is a bad thing for the world. I hated getting asked about it. There would be heads-up in all of my interviews beforehand: "Don't mention Kelly, don't mention *The Osbournes*."

ANDY GREENWALD: That show immediately made him famous. Which was a huge deal—being famous is different than being in a popular band. It also helped because the industry—and when I say industry, I don't mean the labels, I mean the magazines and MTV—they were desperate for a star. So when you have someone like Bert who looks and acts the way he does in front of their cameras on *The Osbournes*, that was a no-brainer. And you know, I don't know how much cynicism was baked into any of this, but it was a similar thing with My Chemical Romance. My Chemical Romance, on their own terms, was willing to deliver on the access and the visuals, the videos and stories.

MATT GALLE: My Chemical Romance was going to LA and everybody wanted to sign them. People are flying out to their shows to wine and dine them.

ALEX SAAVEDRA: DreamWorks was the first major label that was on top of them.

LUKE WOOD: I remember meeting with Gerard in New York in the DreamWorks offices. I think I was the first major label A&R he ever met. He came up, I think with Mikey, into the conference room. I loved the Smashing Pumpkins, and there's a piece of what My Chem were doing that reminded me of the Smashing Pumpkins. The grandeur of it. I also love the Cure and I was deeply schooled in darkwave because I was working with AFI. With My Chem, I thought you could take the goth and put it in emo-pop, with a little bit of metal on top. That's what they could do. I remember me and Gerard, both of us just being like, "Who the fuck knows? Should you be on a major label? I don't know!" He was really into art, and we talked a lot about bands. At the time I had had success with Jimmy Eat World so he was interested in, "Oh, you've obviously had success with emo bands."

BERT MCCRACKEN: I was talking to Craig Aaronson about signing My Chemical Romance to Warner: "If you don't sign this band, you're gonna regret it for the rest of your life."

JEPH HOWARD: Craig Aaronson didn't really want to sign them.

MIKE GITTER: I saw My Chemical Romance open for the Used in 2003. Great show. Roadrunner certainly wasn't the only label looking at the band at the time. I fell in love with the band.

ALEX SAAVEDRA: Roadrunner just wasn't a good fit. I think Roadrunner would have just treated them as like, you know, a heavy band. And that's where they would have stayed.

LUKE WOOD: I think I was the first person to offer Gerard a major label record deal. We had pretty much fully negotiated a record deal. It was down to us and Warner.

QUINN ALLMAN: I remember sitting in a Land Rover across from the Troubadour in LA with Craig Aaronson, the A&R for Warner. He's got *Bullets* in there, he took it out of the CD player, he looks at me: "Tell me honestly, do you really think this band is really that good? Because we're thinking of signing them." And I'm like, "Dude, don't even question it."

MIKE GITTER: Warner just went for it.

LUKE WOOD: I remember having a meeting over breakfast with the band in LA, and it was really bittersweet, because it just didn't feel like the best fit with DreamWorks. You know, after a year and a half of hanging out with them.

MATT GALLE: They vibed the most with Craig Aaronson and Tom Whalley, the chairman at Warner.

MIKE GITTER: Craig Aaronson, god rest his soul, made absolutely the right record with them.

JEPH HOWARD: My Chem signed to Warner Bros., which was awesome. We had a brother band on the label.

JOHN FELDMANN: I did this big animal rights event in Orange County, that My Chemical Romance played with the Used, Good Charlotte, and Goldfinger. I hung out with Gerard and he was in his David Bowie–kinda phase with makeup and all that. I remember Gerard open-mouth kissing Bert. They were just fucking around and being idiots. Gerard and Bert were wasted. They were like the toxic twins.

ANDY GREENWALD: I wrote a story for *Spin*—it was in Chicago, and My Chem was opening for the Used, before *Three Cheers for Sweet Revenge* came out. I had one night in a room at the Hard Rock Hotel in Chicago with Bert and Gerard. Gerard wrote "You Know What They Do to Guys Like Us in Prison" about that night.

BERT MCCRACKEN: At the time, Gerard and I had such a close friendship that we weren't afraid to hold hands or, you know, kiss for fun. It was never anything truly intimate, or actually sexual. It was a fun little show we were putting on. So I associate "You Know What They Do to Guys Like Us in Prison" with that kind of carefree sexual freedom.

ANDY GREENWALD: They kept getting up to go to the bathroom. They were doing a lot more than drinking, but they didn't do that in front of me. And it was fun. But a little concerning. They were methodically emptying the hotel room minibar, like, to the point where . . . minibars used to have disposable cameras and Bert unwrapped the camera and took twenty-six photos of me. I never got those developed . . . The next day, the Used was due at someone's house who had won a radio contest, so we had to drive like an hour outside of Chicago, which is like driving to the moon, to be in someone's suburban home to take pictures and Bert bailed on it because he was so fucked up from the night before.

MIKE GITTER: Howard Benson produced *Three Cheers*, put together a record of My Chem's best attributes.

BERT MCCRACKEN: My Chemical Romance was recording *Three Cheers* in LA and I think we were in LA working on our new record as well. Gerard said he wanted me to be on this song, "You Know What They Do to Guys Like Us in Prison." They were working with Howard Benson at the time and it was really late. I got really, really drunk. Howard claimed that I broke his expensive mic by screaming into it too hard.

MIKE GITTER: Howard Benson found what made My Chemical Romance special. Gerard's vocals aren't always note perfect, but they're fucking resonant as hell. They figured out who they were in a very short amount of time.

ANDY GREENWALD: It felt more dangerous. I think the emo bands I covered previously had their own struggles and demons, but either they weren't articulated in the music or they were able to hide them from the press. And that wasn't what My Chemical Romance was doing.

Gerard was an avenging angel from some comic book galaxy here to tear down the world.

GEOFF RICKLY: Mikey first played *Three Cheers* for me . . . Well, he didn't play the record, he only played "I'm Not Okay." And I was not psyched. I thought it was a real dumbing down of what they were doing. I felt they were trying to be what everybody else wanted them to be. But also, I was really projecting what I wanted on them. They wanted to write a song from a really great John Hughes movie soundtrack, you know? They love that shit. I was such an asshole about it. I was like, "Mikey, this fucking sucks. I'm really disappointed in you guys."

I saw Alex later and he was like, "Pretty fucking good, huh?"

ALEX SAAVEDRA: I knew that they were going to do well.

GEOFF RICKLY: "Dude, it sucks. I don't know what you're talking about. Nobody's gonna like this. This sucks." And he's like, "I don't know, man. I got the whole record right here. You want to listen to it?" He put it on, and the first song is "Helena." That song just blew my mind. That's what I wanted them to do. I wanted that sense of drama—I wanted all that shit—but I also wanted it to be campy. But also, totally dead serious.

I was almost a little depressed because I was like, "Yeah, this is so good, I could never write an album this amazing."

FRED MASCHERINO: Taking Back Sunday had finished *Where You Want to Be* and we were so proud of it. My Chemical Romance were our friends and we let them hear it. They're like, "Oh my god, your record's so good, wanna hear our new record?" They played us "Helena" and I'm like, "FUCK!" And then they played us "I'm Not Okay." After hearing those two songs I wanted to go back and rerecord our shit.

ANTHONY RANERI: When I heard *Three Cheers* I thought, "This is probably the best band in our scene."

MIKE GITTER: MCR figured it out without skipping any steps: they played the basements, the opening slots, the sweaty festivals.

Three Cheers for Sweet Revenge is like Nirvana's *Nevermind*, when all the brashness, frayed ends, and sharp, jagged edges got smoothed out enough to connect with everybody. Yet still be totally subversive in its own way.

JASON TATE: AbsolutePunk.net, we were the ones that "leaked"—working with the label—the first song off *Three Cheers*. It was "I'm Not Okay." Warner basically let us post the MP3 as a hidden link in a news post. I remember the comments would go one of two ways. There was a group of people who were like, "This is poppy garbage, what happened to the cool band I was listening to?" And then the people who had either not heard them before, or were just starting to hear them, who thought it was awesome.

MIKEY WAY: The *Three Cheers for Sweet Revenge* record release show at Starland Ballroom in New Jersey sticks out to me. Just walking out and seeing an ocean of people. At the time, your depth perception is different. To someone who's never played a room like that, playing Starland looked like twenty thousand people.

BUDDY NIELSEN: Seeing the rise of My Chem was superspecial. Senses Fail were good friends with them because we'd shared a bus and we'd been on small tours together. Shows where fucking no one was there, like some place on campus at the University of Delaware. I'd known Gerard and Mikey and all those guys forever. We'd toured with them when Otter was still their drummer.

AARON GILLESPIE: I never thought Otter was great . . . They seemed a little disjointed because of Otter. He didn't fit in. Mikey and Gerard are brothers, they had a thing. They all looked like they went together except for him. I don't think it was really a musical ability thing, even though he wasn't the best musician.

GEOFF RICKLY: If he didn't have the talent, but he had the heart, fine. He'll catch up, he'll find a way to learn, that's what always happens. But if he doesn't give a shit about the band . . .

JEPH HOWARD: So My Chemical Romance needed a new drummer.

GEOFF RICKLY: Bob Bryar was the Used's front-of-house guy [their sound guy]. He was also a great drummer. When we met him with the Used, he showed me that he could play all of Converge's *Jane Doe*. Ben Koller's one of the best drummers in the world; if you can play that album, you're good.

BRANDEN STEINECKERT: I remember Bob pulling me aside one day and letting us know that My Chem had kicked out their drummer, and they asked him to join the band. And I was like, "Fuck yeah, dude!" I was so excited.

BERT MCCRACKEN: Bob and I had a brief argument about something in the back lounge of our bus. He was playing video games and I wanted to bring people back there, and he kind of used that little argument to say, "I can't be around Bert anymore, I'm quitting. I quit doing sound for you guys." We were like, "Whaaat?" He's like, "Yeah, I just quit." And then the very next day, we find out he's the brand-new drummer for My Chemical Romance.

BRANDEN STEINECKERT: Bob was one of Bert's party buddies, and I think Bert was kind of bummed that he left us to join My Chem. I remember there being *little* bits of friction there.

BERT MCCRACKEN: The same thing happened with our tour manager. Our tour manager at the time was Brian Schechter and he was like, "I'm sorry guys, I gotta quit." Didn't tell us why and the next day we find out he's My Chemical Romance's manager. We're like, "What just happened? It's like they stole all our crew!"

LESLIE SIMON: In between *Bullets* and *Three Cheers*, Gerard started wearing suits onstage and that's what he ended up wearing for the "I'm Not Okay" video.

MIKEY WAY: Bob had just joined the band a couple of weeks prior.

ADAM SAMILJAN: Craig Aaronson had sent us an early version of the "I'm Not Okay" music video. He was just curious: "Hey, this is the new My Chem single, what does the Fueled By Ramen office think of this?" I remember watching it and thinking, Is this a music video or a trailer for a movie?

MIKEY WAY: We had a lot of classic moments in that video, like the one where Frank looks like he's gonna make out with the girl, but he takes something off her eyelashes. He looked like an actor, you know what I mean? His timing was perfect.

ROB HITT: I saw "I'm Not Okay" on TV, and once Gerard comes into focus, up close to the camera in that music video, it was game on.

CHAD GILBERT: Shooting New Found Glory's "I Don't Wanna Know" video, I remember our video lady pulling up a computer and playing the "I'm Not Okay" video. She's like, *This video's amazing, it's gonna be huge!* And we're at our video shoot.

BUDDY NIELSEN: You could see things snowballing after *Three Cheers* came out in June '04. At the start of Warped Tour that summer, Senses Fail were a significantly bigger band. Then we came home and did a tour with them and we're like, "Oh shit, there's a lot of kids waiting. And they all look like Gerard."

ANDY GREENWALD: I got to know Gerard and that band a lot better during those days with the Used, which helped my relationship with them going forward. But that was also Gerard at his lowest personally. A story for *Spin*, they did a photo shoot in Red Hook, Brooklyn, and it was a really hot day and Gerard wouldn't take off his leather jacket, which was just ripe. And he was miserable. And then we went to some shitty Brooklyn café on Smith Street afterwards but he was still dressed like he was in the *Phantom of the Paradise*.

GEOFF RICKLY: Adjusting to the fame of My Chem was not great for them on a personal level. That's when I think drugs and alcohol were becoming a more serious part of their lives.

LESLIE SIMON: On 2004 Warped Tour, I saw Gerard throwing up off of the side of the stage because he was wasted and in like five layers of clothing in crazy heat.

ALEX SAAVEDRA: I wasn't touring with them anymore, so I wasn't aware of how bad it was. Until the falling-down-and-not-being-able-to-get-up-type stuff. I tried reaching out to Gerard but couldn't get him. Which, knowing Gerard all those years, was not surprising. There were times when he was hard to get in touch with when he lived the next town over. But I did talk to Mikey a lot. I was concerned. I didn't want them to die.

LESLIE SIMON: On Warped Tour '04—and I'm quoting from my *AP* cover story—Gerard says, "I worked out a system . . . If we played at noon, I was basically just hungover, still drunk probably from the night before. If we were playing at one or two, I was already drunk. If I wasn't fully drunk, then I was trying to get drunk at any signings we had to do."

GEOFF RICKLY: In 2004, Warped Tour had a show canceled, and instead a local promoter put on a show with a few of the bands: us, Glassjaw, My Chem.

What I remember most of that show was watching My Chem play, and Gerard walking around onstage drunk, saying weird shit in between songs. Daryl from Glassjaw was saying like, "This is your boy, what's up with him?" And I was like, "I don't know." At some point he crawled under the stage—it was like a box truck stage—and he was singing from under there. Like peering out at the crowd, below where the barricade was, but no one could see him. I think Mikey or Ray was like, "Come back? Please come back?" He was down there being a drunk weirdo.

Stuff like that was my most vivid memory of that summer, where I was like, "Oh shit. This is a lot of change." Being on tour all the time, people giving a shit about your music and asking for autographs is a huge change.

"LOVE *IN THE* FACE *OF THE* APOCALYPSE"

WARNING: THIS CHAPTER CONTAINS DISCUSSION OF SUICIDE.

CHRIS CARRABBA: I was part of the red-carpet premiere for *Spider-Man 2*. Dashboard saw some people we kinda knew—Maroon 5 comes to mind. Adam was like, "You're the single!"

"Vindicated" comes in as the last scene fades into it, and I remember, all the guys in Maroon 5, their hands were around my shoulders like I'd made the game-winning shot.

EBEN D'AMICO: When you spend your late teens and early twenties in a band that's on a constant upward trajectory, it's like every door in the world will instantly open for you. To get that kind of attention, it's like the best candy you've ever tasted. "Ooh, people know who I am? This is delicious." For an insecure kid from the suburbs, that's exciting. But there's also a part of you that's like, "I'm not comfortable with this. I don't want it to change who I am."

RICH EGAN: Saves the Day went to DreamWorks Records and made *In Reverie*, which people did not like.

ADAM SISKA: When you hear *Stay What You Are* and you're like, "I want more!" *In Reverie* wasn't the more that you wanted.

RICH EGAN: Saves the Day discovered smoking weed. They were getting much more into the Beatles and growing their hair out.

BRYAN NEWMAN: Chris came to visit me in North Carolina [after I left Saves the Day] and loaned me a CD of rough mixes of *In Reverie* . . . It didn't match up with what Chris was saying. He was saying, "People are saying this is going to be the next *Ziggy Stardust*." Like, "Nah, dude, this is not." Then I went into the self-doubt of, "What if he's right?" Jimmy Iovine's telling him that. He knows more than I do. But it wasn't great. It was a good album that sort of made no sense in their catalog.

EBEN D'AMICO: Every Saves the Day record made people angry for different reasons. Until *In Reverie*, it was the stodgy, old head hardcore dudes who were like, "That's not punk, fuck you!" *In Reverie* made our fans angry—the people you *don't* want to be angry.

MATTHEW ISMAEL RUIZ: *Stay What You Are* is Saves the Day's big blow-up moment . . . Even though it's a little polished, it's still got the lyrical sharpness and wit. And then they sign to a major label, Chris Conley becomes obsessed with John Lennon and wants to write Beatles songs . . . and they're garbage. There might be people to this day who think *In Reverie* is important, but to me it was important in understanding the way music fandom works. I felt like they had a responsibility to not be awful because they were my favorite band, they were some of my friends' favorite band. Like, I can't even go to your show, because you'll play most of this new record, and I'll get maybe three or four songs that I actually like. *This sucks.*

But the more distance you put from that, you realize, how can you expect a band to stay the same way they were when they were fifteen, sixteen? Or twenty? Or twenty-three, twenty-five?

EBEN D'AMICO: We had several bad breaks: we made the wrong record and then our label folded.

LUKE WOOD: DreamWorks got sold to Interscope and Saves the Day got stuck in this transition zone. I remember flying to St. Louis and having the awkward conversation with the band and Rich: "Universal's buying DreamWorks and, within Universal, we're going to Interscope . . ." There was a lot of turnover at the label. It was obviously a mess.

Michael Goldstone, who'd been the A&R pursuing Brand New for DreamWorks, was going to Sire Records. He called me and said, "Listen,

I'm gonna leave, but you shouldn't lose the band. I know you love them. You should go sign them." So I just got on a plane to London. Brand New was playing a small club in Camden. That was the beginning of a really difficult process, trying to get them to sign to Interscope. For about six months, every label was trying to sign the band, chasing them all over the world. It was brutal. So competitive.

GEOFF RICKLY: Lyor Cohen called me personally and was like, "Hey, could you do me a favor? We're trying to sign Brand New to Island. Could you talk to Jesse and tell him how great of a time you're having on Island?" And I was like, "Fuck yeah. I love this label." Thursday was riding high, *War All the Time* had just come out, we were in the top ten of *Billboard*.

I called Jesse and was like, "Dude, I heard you might sign to Island, that's great news. We all fucking love your record." And he's like, "Yeah, but I heard it's fucked." I'm like, "What's fucked?" He's like, "'Cause Island made you write those singles, they sent you back into the studio because they didn't like your record. We don't want that shit happening to us." And I'm like, "What? No, they didn't send us back into the studio, they just gave us time to . . ."

And I'm thinking, maybe they did send us back, you know what I mean? He planted the seed.

RICH EGAN: I tried incredibly hard to sign Brand New to Vagrant after *Deja Entendu*. It came down to us against DreamWorks. Vagrant had the money to match if we wanted to bet the whole company on 'em. I tried everything, but I eventually just couldn't compete.

Brand New got paid an insane amount of money. I don't know the exact figures, but I know the terms of it. I believe it was more than the Saves the Day deal. The offers our bands were getting to leave Vagrant were around $6 million guaranteed for a three-album deal, a lot of creative control, things like that.

LUKE WOOD: Brand New really wanted creative control. They were embarrassed by the success of *Deja*, they genuinely didn't expect that. They started off as a pop-punk band, listened to a lot of Blink, but they evolved really fast. They felt emo was becoming commodified, like a Hot Topic

T-shirt wall. Jesse, in particular, was interested in Pinback, Archers of Loaf, Neutral Milk Hotel, he had very broad musical tastes. I think he worried, "Am I gonna be in this genre forever?"

EBEN D'AMICO: There was a certain disdain between the *Pitchfork* music—the cool guy, college kid rock—and the music the bands in our scene were making, which was more earnest, heart-on-its-sleeve stuff. It felt like they were on opposite sides of a gymnasium, looking at each other like, "We don't like you." "Well, we don't like *you*."

ADAM SISKA: We were definitely not the Strokes. We didn't come from any culture. I think that was kinda part of the appeal of emo. It was a DIY thing where the band and the audience were equals. We were a bunch of dorks.

NICK WHEELER: The All-American Rejects are from Oklahoma. So name any domestic beer, we were probably drinking the light version of that. That's what we thought drinking was. When all these labels started taking us out, that's when I started drinking wine. I would always want to go to Benihana. That's what we thought was fancy.

ADAM SISKA: The record labels must have been laughing at how easy it was to please us. We were so happy just to be in the room. I remember The Academy Is . . . going to Atlantic and they opened up their closet and we got to take all the free CDs we wanted. We went to Capitol in LA and left with this Beach Boys box set. It was like in *Home Alone* when he breaks into the toy store.

NICK WHEELER: I started going on these trips to New York with an extra suitcase or duffel bag so I could come home with more free CDs.

ADAM SISKA: We definitely went with Atlantic one time to Applebee's in Secaucus, New Jersey. We had no clue. One time they wanted to take us to dinner and we pretty much could have gone to Sardi's or any of the legendary steakhouses of New York City. And we picked the Olive Garden in Times Square.

RANDY NICHOLS: Brand New did their record release party for *Deja Entendu* at the Chili's [in Westbury] on Long Island. Or it could have been *Your Favorite Weapon*. Chili's in the Long Island music scene was a very important piece of the puzzle. That's where everybody would go after shows.

CHRISTIAN MCKNIGHT: Kids who were not necessarily friends would just show up because they knew all the cool band dudes would be there.

RANDY NICHOLS: The go-to order was the bottomless chips with cheese melted on top, which they weren't supposed to do. But if you found someone on staff that liked everyone, they would melt cheese on top of the chips. I took Aaron from Underoath to the Chili's in Cherry Hill, New Jersey, after a show because I was part of this obsession. He was like, "Nah, man, they won't do these chips." I was like, "Nah, man, you can get them if you ask."

JOSH WILLS: Someone at our label [Madonna's Maverick Records], told us that if *Page Avenue* went gold, we would get to meet Madonna. We didn't meet Madonna. And our record went gold, ha, ha, ha. We were pissed! I don't know which label person was out with us on tour when the record went gold, but we went to McDonald's.

IAN COHEN: At the time, emo was often seen as not serious. *Pitchfork* just hated it. I think a lot of the people who were writing for them at the time were punk people who were in their twenty-three-, twenty-four-year-old phase of, "This is what we are against, it's not even real punk, it's basically major label pop-punk." That's what they saw emo as. It was seen as a sign that punk rock had gotten corrupted.

BUDDY NIELSEN: The guys in bands wearing girl jeans was always a constant topic in the early days: "Oh, these fucking emo bands wearing fucking girl jeans, painting their fucking nails." Bunch of Generation X confused-ass old people who were mad that a bunch of young people came along and got bigger than them.

NICK SCIMECA: When I was a sophomore or a junior in high school, I wanted tighter pants. I would see photos of bands playing—I specifically remember a photo of Midtown, with Gabe jumping with his bass—and I was like, "Where do I get pants like that?" I didn't know Gabe at the time, but I emailed him and he was like, "They're women's jeans and I get them from these places . . ." So eventually all the dudes at shows were wearing women's jeans from Abercrombie or Hollister or Levi's.

BUDDY NIELSEN: I'm pretty sure the girl jeans started in Long Island with bands like From Autumn to Ashes and also Eighteen Visions, they're from Orange County. They started wearing designer girl jeans and then they made these shirts called "fashioncore." They were branding themselves as hardcore bands that were fashionable. Senses Fail didn't wear girl jeans until we toured with A Static Lullaby; they were real into wearing girl jeans and flat-ironing their hair and shit. And they would make fun of us, like, "You look like shit, you need to put on some fucking jeans." We're like, "All right man, this is our first tour, you guys are from California, you guys are cool." So then we all started wearing girl jeans.

ANTHONY GREEN: On the East Coast, people had great style, but there wasn't this emphasis on fashion like there was in California. People were really into straightening their hair, wearing their hair in that emo style, guys getting ready to go out to the show, ironing your jeans. Like holy shit, some of the jeans were so expensive. Like you'd get looked at funny if you didn't have a $200, $300 pair of Diesel jeans on.

SPENCER CHAMBERLAIN: We'd buy girls' jeans back in the day because they didn't sell skinny jeans. We'd go to the Gap and go to the women's section. In Florida, we've got tight pants, long hair, people called you the word that starts with an "f" that you should never say. We'd get called that all the time from cars driving by.

NICK SCIMECA: Guys painted their nails. That was a supernormal thing. When I was sixteen, seventeen, I had white nails in high school. People were like, "What's up with that?" Outside of our crew it was not normal.

BUDDY NIELSEN: The fashion was to dress a little more androgynous, or feminine . . . while also writing lyrics about killing girls. Kind of a weird juxtaposition.

The scene seemed like the only place for anybody who was kind of alternative to go, if you were young and questioning anything. Obviously, there's some critiques to it. But it wasn't like there was somewhere else to be that was more inclusive, you know? Maybe some of the indie scene, but you can't go and be a part of the indie scene when you're fucking seventeen. They're gonna look at you like you're a little idiot.

RANDY NICHOLS: Managing the Starting Line, I remember them being furious some indie band played above them on a radio show, like, "We're so much bigger than them, but the industry perceives them to be the bigger one." Who was the band that had the song "Bandages"? . . . Hot Hot Heat? I think that was the indie band. I remember saying, "They won't be around three years from now. You have to be happy in that you'll have a long career."

IAN COHEN: Bands like Fall Out Boy, My Chem, Say Anything—this era of emo is almost like *The Real World*, where people on *The Real World* are influenced by people who were on previous seasons of *The Real World*. They're acting out the ground rules that had been established by people who didn't quite know what they were doing. It's a lot more meta—emo bands who *know* they're being emo, reckoning with the reputation of it. Whereas, Jimmy Eat World and the Promise Ring didn't really comment on their genre.

MAX BEMIS: I had a view of the whole emo scene that maybe people sensed, but no one was writing about in the music. It was more sociological, in terms of how the scene fit into the world at large: Why are people writing music about this? Why is this happening right now? What is the point of this scene? So I really wanted to write an album about that—dissecting the meaning of being an emo band.

IAN COHEN: Max is a smart fucking guy.

EBEN D'AMICO: He's the first person who wrote meta music, about emo.

COBY LINDER: Say Anything's . . . *Is a Real Boy* is a concept record. We wanted it to be big. But also *real*.

MAX BEMIS: So growing up in LA, if you've ever been to Silver Lake . . . that's what high school was like for me. Say Anything was this scrappy pop-punk band and there were people who were getting signed to major labels for sounding like the Strokes, you know what I mean? So I grew up around that, and I always resisted it. These were the popular kids. Most people think of popular kids as jocks beating them up; for me, it was a kid who was artsy, but a bully about it.

COBY LINDER: Just like me, he just couldn't wait to get out of LA, and be around more people that felt the same as him.

MAX BEMIS: I was living in Brooklyn; I had just dropped out of Sarah Lawrence.

At Sarah Lawrence, a lot of people are gay, dudes and women. I was sort of successful with girls at the time because I was an artsy kid, and a straight guy—or whatever I was, ha! Seemingly straight . . . And so at that point I was getting more hate for being the, quote, unquote, popular, successful guy than I was for being too weird or artsy. So that all came out on "Admit It!!!"

If you went back ten years in the scene, there's people just getting picked on by horrible, homophobic jocks. But once punk started to become more popular generationally, there were people in my generation who were getting picked on for being norms. You'd have the most pretentious people picking on you for not being artsy or weird enough. Even though I wrote it about hipsters—Silver Lake and Brooklyn assholes—it started to resonate with kids who went to our shows, because of scene politics. Kids obsessed with maintaining some detailed haircut who looked down on you if you didn't have it, like a fucking popularity contest at a Thursday show.

IAN COHEN: A song like "Every Man Has a Molly" . . . if you approach it from a certain perspective, you're like, "Oh, this is everything wrong with emo."

MAX BEMIS: Emo was always exaggerated: "I'm gonna fucking dieeeee if you don't go out with me. . . ."

I was like, "What if I took this even further, and intentionally?"

IAN COHEN: Max knows exactly what he's doing. He's not condoning being that kind of person, you know? That's what I hope people understand.

ELLIE KOVACH: You don't have to be Jewish to love Say Anything. But it really does help.

MAX BEMIS: Jewish comedians were always a big influence on my sense of humor; making fun of yourself or making fun of the world, but for a serious reason. There's a reason those comedians exist—Jewish people were marginalized, literally picked apart for years.

COBY LINDER: When I first heard "Alive with the Glory of Love," I had to look up what Treblinka was. I had only heard of Auschwitz.

MAX BEMIS: My grandparents didn't speak to me or my family because my mom married a non-Jewish guy, an Irish-Catholic dude. It wasn't necessarily my grandparents' fault; that's how they were raised. Having gone through the Holocaust, it was this logical conclusion—and I know this sounds bad—but that I was like what Hitler intended. That's what my grandmother would throw on my mom, that she was just perpetuating the extinction of our race. It's so fucked up, but it's what she thought.

When I wrote "Alive with the Glory of Love," I had just seen *The Pianist* or some Holocaust movie. It immediately made me think of my grandparents. What was it like to be in love during that time? The Holocaust was deeply ingrained in me from a young age. My first serious fear was people coming to my house and taking my family away. It was this apocalyptic thing I knew personally, because my grandparents had been through it. I wanted to do some *Moulin Rouge* kind of song about that. "Alive with the Glory of Love" is about love in the face of the apocalypse. Let's take this as far as it can go.

COBY LINDER: I thought I had to put everything into it. Recording the drums, the producer stopped me like, "Coby, you don't have to hit that hard." And I was like, "I do. I definitely do."

PARKER CASE: With Say Anything, there was this sense of anxiety and danger. That things could go bad at any moment.

MAX BEMIS: I'd been wanting to make an album for literally five years. I held off making singles or an EP or touring because I needed to make a perfect album. When I finally got the opportunity to go into the studio, there was this hype in our world.

JASON TATE: When I first heard those demos, I heard a step into the next generation of our scene.

PARKER CASE: Say Anything was on an indie, Doghouse Records, but that didn't mean anything back then because all these big bands like Fall Out Boy were on indies, on incubator deals.

MAX BEMIS: Doghouse had just had a big success with the All-American Rejects. There were already major label people working with Say Anything. I felt an immense amount of creative pressure. I love music so much. I analyze music so much. I'm so aware of every part of every one of my favorite records.

I just knew I was complicated. I dealt with emotional issues.

COBY LINDER: That's when I was most concerned about Max—during the making of . . . *Is a Real Boy*.

MAX BEMIS: I had two or three episodes around the making of the album.

COBY LINDER: Max is running around New York and I'm on the phone with his mom like, "What the hell's going on?" And then the record gets put on hold for like three months.

MAX BEMIS: I ended up in the hospital and they're like, "You're bipolar."

For most bipolar people, you have a manic episode, and it's so foreign to reality that later on, you can just chalk it up to, "Oh, I thought I was Jesus. Oh, I thought I was gonna be the next Kurt Cobain." But at the time, people *were* telling me I was the next Kurt Cobain. That made it very difficult to deal with.

COBY LINDER: Mental health wasn't being talked about as openly then. I'm sure other bands experienced stuff like this, but it wasn't getting out to the public.

MAX BEMIS: You can't divide someone's art from their illness as much as people want to be able to say you can. Genetically, you have the ability as a bipolar person to be able to keep rolling and rolling with those larger-than-life visions of things most people don't think about until they're on shrooms or something. Even when you're on meds, you have the ability to, A) have more energy, and B) let your mind go to those larger-than-life places. For me, the problems were compounded by how much weed I was smoking.

COBY LINDER: There were times when I thought, "This is not gonna work."

MAX BEMIS: I went to the hospital, in Brooklyn, for about a month. I was in there with a bunch of people suffering from mental health issues. There were also crackheads and prostitutes. That's cool, they need help, too. But at the same time, being more of a normal kid thrown into it, you're like, "Fuck, this is serious." I had no friends. I had no one to talk to. I just sat around reading comics and the Bible.

There was this prostitute. She was really cool and sweet and definitely had issues beyond what I was dealing with, probably some kind of learning disabilities. It was a shock to my system. Like, Jesus Christ, her life must be nuts and the fact she's mentally ill on top of it, it really put into perspective what I was going through, because I was lucky to have this cushion.

COBY LINDER: It felt like there was too much on the line for it to not work. And the album was too good for it to not work.

MAX BEMIS: I remember my mom bringing me the record and playing it for me when I was in the hospital. When I left the hospital, thankfully, the album was almost done.

ANTHONY GREEN: Circa Survive was supposed to do a full US tour supporting Say Anything, with Emanuel also opening. We had our very first show in Arizona at Hotel Congress. It's a cool venue and they have hotel rooms upstairs where the bands can stay. Everybody had all of the drugs they were compiling to bring on tour with them. We partied so hard that first night. This was before weed was everywhere and practically legal in most places. I remember having edibles for the first time that night, taking lots of pills, Xanax, all this shit. We all just got fucking shitfaced. The next day, Max had suffered an episode, I think because of getting so fucked up. He had to cancel the tour and go to treatment.

MAX BEMIS: That was our first headlining tour . . . And that was the first time we canceled a tour because I had to go to the hospital.

ANTHONY GREEN: I couldn't get in touch with Max. He was away, he was in the hospital. Circa ended up headlining that tour and it was a really good thing for us. And it sucked for Max and Say Anything, but I honestly feel like part of the mystique . . . people were always wondering, "Is he okay? Is he going to show up?" And then he'd show up and just murder it.

RANDY NICHOLS: I found out Max was going through a manager change and I was like, "I have to work with this act." I was completely obsessed, like everyone was in that moment when Say Anything started blowing up. There's this group of ex–Say Anything managers who all remained friends and were never upset that they were fired when the next person came in.

Working with Max in that era was just a whirlwind, he required so much attention. But we all did it because we loved it. So when the next person came along, it was like, "Okay, here's everything I know, here's how you can do this job . . ."

He played CMJ in New York, and it was this moment where anything could happen at any moment. It was the last show with some of a former lineup; he kind of hated the band at that point. You didn't know if he was gonna get in a fistfight with the band or walk off the stage. He spent the entire set just looking at one person in the audience. It felt like everyone in the scene was watching this incredible show.

We did a photo shoot for the reissue of *. . . Is a Real Boy* and there's a song on the record called "Belt." Max had this belt that he was trying to strangle himself with, to make a statement, while the shoot was going on. But he wasn't just holding the belt on his neck and making a weird look. He was terrifying everyone in the shoot and eventually that night, they tried to take him to the hospital, and got him to the hospital, and he ran away.

ROB HITT: I was living in Williamsburg, Brooklyn, off the Graham Avenue stop with Max. Say Anything needed a guitar player.

ALEX SUAREZ: I lived right above Rob and Max. Rob was like, "Hey, my friend's got this band, he's about to put out this CD, they're gonna start touring. It's gonna be this big tour with Saves the Day and he needs a guitar player."

This was an interesting time for Max. At this point, I think he decided to stop taking his medication. While Max was slowly defusing . . . or fusing . . . Rob was out of town, so it was just Max and I. He's like, "I'm gonna teach you these songs. We're so excited for this tour. It's with my favorite band of all time, Saves the Day." He told me the reason he named his band Say Anything was so it would be next to Saves the Day on his iPod. He started telling me about his condition: "You know, I'm supposed to be taking this medication, I'm not gonna take it anymore. I just want to feel free . . ." And of course, I'm gonna be supportive of that. I had no idea what was going on and I didn't know anything about him.

We were practicing all the songs on . . . *Is a Real Boy*. He was really particular about everything and had the skill to pull it off. It was intense. He fired me like three times. I'm on the phone with his manager like, "Max said I'm not going on this tour anymore. He got really mad at me because he asked me if I loved Saves the Day and I was like, 'Gotta be honest, man, I was never a fan.' Max was like, 'You're fired!'"

MAX BEMIS: We were supposed to go out with Saves the Day and we had to cancel. It felt terrible. But I wasn't completely bummed.

COBY LINDER: He had to get himself right. Or right enough.

MAX BEMIS: After I had been to the actual hospital in Brooklyn for about a month, I went away [to the Menninger Clinic in Houston] for about six weeks. It was pretty torturous and intense. And isolating and lonely. What it did for me, in a good way, was mostly just give me space from the music industry and trying to succeed and all that stuff. It gave me space to concentrate on getting better. But to some degree, all I really needed was to stop smoking pot, realize I had to take my meds, and that was it.

We were such good friends with Saves the Day, we knew it was gonna happen eventually, so I wasn't completely bummed: Oh of course, this tour is gonna happen like fifteen times, ha, ha, ha.

COBY LINDER: It's the ultimate pursuit of the dream. There's a part of you that thinks this still can work.

JASON TATE: There is a magic to those . . . *Is a Real Boy* songs. You read those lyrics and it's like, "What the fuck are you saying? How were you even able to fit that into the music?"

RICH EGAN: Max is one of those kids, man. He's a savant.

EBEN D'AMICO: I remember hearing . . . *Is a Real Boy* and being shocked by how intense it was. Guys like Max bleeding all over the paper . . . that's important. We need people like that. If you can do it effectively, it's going to connect with people.

RANDY NICHOLS: Max's mom told me his grandmother, who was a Holocaust survivor, was in the hospital . . . Then I went back and read the lyrics . . .

MAX BEMIS: I didn't meet my grandma until "Alive with the Glory of Love" came out. I played it for her on her deathbed.

It was a huge compliment for her to recognize me as . . . not a mistake? I know that's so dark, but it's true. I saw she appreciated me and appreciated the music.

She loved it. She cried. She said I was beautiful.

NEW FRIEND REQUEST

TOM MULLEN: A few years into the 2000s, you started to see the difference between bands that understood the internet and the bands that were stuck with, "Oh, we have an email address, it's fine."

ROB HITT: Heath from Midtown was all over AOL Instant Messenger and he was good on the Yahoo! boards and everything like that, talking directly to people about the band. And I was the one building our websites and making profiles for whatever platform you'd put a band on. There was Friendster and I was like, "Oh, we need a Midtown account." And then there was MySpace . . .

GABE SAPORTA: I remember creating Midtown's MySpace profile while we were in [the] Ruby Red studio in Atlanta recording our third album. We were one of the first bands on MySpace, this brand-new thing.

ROB HITT: Midtown had fallen into major label purgatory. Our label, MCA Records, all of a sudden was no more, which was not uncommon with major labels back then. So the other labels under the Universal umbrella had to come see if they wanted to sign these MCA bands. None of them wanted Midtown. Eventually we were able to get out of our deal, so we were free agents.

GABE SAPORTA: We booked two shows—one at the Knitting Factory in New York, one at the Troubadour in LA—and a week before the New York show, we used MySpace to leak new songs from our unreleased album.

ROB HITT: The kids at the show knew we were unsigned, and knew what the shows were about, so they kind of went extra. These major labels came out . . .

GABE SAPORTA: And they're like, "How the fuck do these kids know the words to these songs?"

ROB HITT: We looked like the biggest band in the world, ha, ha, ha.

GABE SAPORTA: The labels freak out, and there's this bidding war for Midtown.

HEATH SARACENO: That Knitting Factory show pretty much got us signed to Columbia.

JASON TATE: MySpace was a validation of a lot of the things that I believed in with the internet. We have the capability to stream music online, let's put these songs on our profiles. Let's find new music, let's have some sort of community. MySpace allowed that on a much larger scale—for people and their own friends, but also for more personal interaction with bands.

SHANE TOLD: Friendster came out before MySpace. Not a lot of people remember Friendster . . .

ANTHONY RANERI: Friendster kind of sucked, but it was pretty . . . eh, it was terrible. If you were a band, you'd make a page, but it wasn't a band page; it was a person page. It was like any other page, except you'd call it "Bayside," or whatever your band was. You couldn't put music or tour dates up. You'd just use it to find people, message them, and say, "Hey, listen to my band." That was the extent of it.

VICTORIA ASHER: My friends and I had all been on Friendster, and Friendster started to get whack. So I was like, "Next move!"

WILL PUGH: MySpace killed Friendster.

VICTORIA ASHER: I joined MySpace when it first started. Before you could edit your top eight friends display, it used to fill it with people who joined MySpace first. So it was always Tom, the creator of MySpace, first on everyone's list.

LUKE WOOD: Music lived on MySpace because of Tom's passion. He had this twelve-year-old's excitement about music. He was fearless. Not very cunning. And not meaning he wasn't smart—he was smart—but it wasn't like he was a calculated business person. MySpace wasn't a calculation of how to get rich. MySpace was this idea of, "How do I connect all these people? Friendster's doing it a certain way, but they're missing music."

ADAM SAMILJAN: This was before streaming had taken off. MySpace profiles had music players, where artists could post a couple songs.

ROB HITT: People realized they could customize their MySpace page: a massive header at the top, additional audio or mailing list sign-ups, all sorts of things, just by embedding HTML, CSS, and JavaScript into the page. I think there's a whole generation of damn good developers today that started because they were social people who liked music and wanted to customize their MySpace pages.

TOM MULLEN: MySpace was this little beast that few people realized in the beginning. But then slowly, everyone was like, "Crap. We need to get really proficient in this."

LESLIE SIMON: If you were of a certain age, you couldn't exist without having a MySpace page. And our scene really percolated and brewed and bloomed on the pages of MySpace.

MARIA SHERMAN: So many people associate that time in their lives with music, because MySpace was much more music-forward than any social media we have now.

HANNAH EWENS: Music discovery and how you presented yourself were so intrinsically linked.

MARIANNE ELOISE: Everyone had a profile song, on auto play.

JAMIE COLETTA: I changed mine every week or so. Your song mattered.

HANNAH EWENS: You're taking bits of other people's personas, adopting other people's music tastes so fast. You're all feeding into each other and reflecting each other.

TOM MULLEN: Things got faster very quickly.

LIGHTS: Fans learned, for better or worse, that artists need to be accessible. That remains to this day. I don't think that existed before MySpace.

DIA FRAMPTON: MySpace was the first way to really connect with people directly. It was so easy to maneuver. You had your music, your photos, you had ways to message people and comment. I still remember we put our

CDs up for sale and the first person who bought our CD sent us this really long email about how much he loved our music.

ANTHONY GREEN: We played a secret MySpace show in Baltimore. It was a free show for kids and it was so fun. They ended up paying us in gift cards for Chili's, like $500 in Chili's gift cards. Just getting asked to play a MySpace show was like, "Aw, sick! FOR SURE."

TOM HIGGENSON: Plain White T's did a poll on MySpace: What song should be the next single off our album? We put "Revenge," "All That We Needed," "My Only One," "Breakdown," and "Hey There Delilah." It was like 96 percent for "Hey There Delilah."

SHANE TOLD: Silverstein had so many friends on MySpace and we'd be able to send them bulletins, like, "Hey, we're going on tour . . ." Nowadays, you might have a million followers on Instagram or Facebook, but you can't send that kind of message out to every single one of them. It doesn't work like that. But on MySpace, it did. And everyone was checking their bulletins all day.

SARAH LEWITINN: It was all chronological; the bulletins had no algorithm to them. If I posted something the night before saying, "I'm going to be DJing tomorrow," it wasn't going to be reshuffled. So there was a bit more democracy to it.

LESLIE SIMON: As a way to connect, research, and discover new things, MySpace was unprecedented. That's really where influencers came from.

JASON TATE: Pete Wentz understood the identity aspect of music better than basically anybody. He understood that people were willing to invest their identity in a band.

Fall Out Boy would do stuff like limited edition T-shirts that you had to know to ask for at the merch table at their shows. They'd send a bulletin to their MySpace friends: "Ask about this special shirt that we only printed four hundred of."

MANI MOSTOFI: They came from the hardcore scene, where there was no division between who's onstage and who's on the floor, at least ideologically. They were very transparent about who they were.

ADAM SAMILJAN: Pete was the one who always had the ideas, always networking, always trying to grow the band. He had the big vision for growing the empire.

ADAM SISKA: Post-Napster the music business was scratching its head saying, "How the fuck do we stay alive?" And then Pete Wentz showed up. The labels were like, "Wait a second, you already have thousands of fans? You're selling *how* much merch every night? And wait . . . you know like five other bands that are doing this, too?"

ADAM SAMILJAN: Fall Out Boy opened the door to introducing fans to something different with Gym Class Heroes. I remember how exciting it was to take on an artist that, sonically, did not make sense right away.

ANTHONY RANERI: Emo-rap is fully a thing now . . . But at the time I was like, "Holy shit, Gym Class Heroes . . . it's emo *and* rap." I'd never seen anything like it.

TRAVIE MCCOY: Nick Scimeca reached out asking if Gym Class Heroes needed merch designs and we're like, "Hell yeah." And he played our shit for Pete and then Pete reached out like, "Yo, this shit is dope."

NICK SCIMECA: I would hit up any band that sounded good to me and email them: "Hey, here are five shirts I've designed, if your band needs shirts, hit me up." That's how I met The Academy Is . . . and Gym Class Heroes. Once you were in Pete's inner circle, you were on a rocket ship.

TRAVIE MCCOY: It was crazy that Pete was reaching out to us. He's like, "Yo, we've got a show in Buffalo, come out." And we're like, "Fuck, that's an hour and a half away from us, we'll be there." So we went out and hung out with those guys in Buffalo. That was my first time seeing a crowd of kids singing every single fucking word to every song. I was like, "This is what I want." We're hanging out after the show and Pete goes, "Oh bro, I see you got tats." I was like, "Yeah, bro, Black people have tattoos too, heh, heh."

MANI MOSTOFI: When Pete was in the hardcore scene, there wasn't a clear place for a kid like him back then, for Black kids and mixed-race kids, and he was trying to carve out his own space. Fall Out Boy's gravitation towards hip-hop culture was partly because of that.

ANDY GREENWALD: There was no question that the dominant pop music in America was rap. And these other emo bands had absolutely nothing to say about it and no interaction with it, except maybe, ironic distance or posing.

MANI MOSTOFI: Pete had all these influences feeding into Fall Out Boy you didn't see in other bands of that era, where everything about them was really white. It also helps that Patrick's obsessed with soul.

TRAVIE MCCOY: The Buffalo show was the day Ray Charles died. My first time meeting Pete and Patrick in the dressing room, Patrick was crying. I was like, "Whoa, dude's a real one," you know what I mean?

ANTHONY RANERI: Then Gym Class Heroes drove from upstate New York to Iowa to play one show so they could showcase for Pete. Pete was starting his label [Decaydance] with Fueled By Ramen, so he was looking to sign bands. They drove halfway across the country. And it paid off.

TRAVIE MCCOY: Fuck it, a chance to open for Fall Out Boy? We hopped in the van and fucking bounced to Davenport, Iowa. We opened for them, Bayside, and Armor for Sleep. We got there hella early, like ten in the morning, nobody was there. So we're chilling in Davenport, Iowa, and I'm sticking out like a sore thumb: six foot six, big-ass Afro, tattoos, and shit. And we crushed that show, man. In my mind, these kids are accepting of what we do because of this song . . .

ANTHONY RANERI: The song where he names all the bands . . .

TRAVIE MCCOY: When we put "Taxi Driver" up on PureVolume, that's when motherfuckers started bugging. Like, "Yo, what is this shit? How does this kid know about all these bands? How did he tie this shit together?"

PATRICK STUMP: He mentioned us!

ADAM SISKA: "Taxi Driver" references all these pillar bands in the scene: Dashboard Confessional, Jimmy Eat World, My Chemical Romance, the Get Up Kids, At the Drive-In. For white suburban dudes, it validated us in a sense that this graffiti artist from upstate New York thought we were cool.

TRAVIE MCCOY: I got really good at making everybody feel like they were included, making eye contact, making them feel like they were part of our shows. I mean, we played with death metal bands. We'd play with feminist slam poets. We'd play with bands like Every Time I Die. Like, what the hell are we doing here? But after our set, everybody felt like, "Whoa, this is something new," but they didn't feel isolated, you know what I'm saying? If anybody felt isolated, that motherfucker was me.

Our first time we ever played in the UK, we played in Manchester. The show was amazing, but there was this one kid that kept talking shit. I stopped the show, like, "Where's he at?" The whole crowd split like I was Moses out in this bitch. They pointed him out, he thought I was gonna punch him. I grabbed him and I kissed him on the lips.

SPENCER SMITH: Going to shows at the time, you could sense something was happening. It was palpable. You were part of this scene and everybody knew the words to the songs, everybody knew everything about the bands. And outside of that room of eight hundred or a thousand people, nobody knew who any of those people were. But in that room, it felt like you were part of something big.

ANTHONY RANERI: On that same tour with Fall Out Boy, we were in a dressing room and Pete pulled up MP3.com and he said, "Listen, I'm gonna sign this band." First of all, I was like, "What do you mean you're gonna sign them?" He was like, "Well, I got a label."

I don't remember being particularly blown away, but I remember they were already doing the whimsical show tune–y thing.

BRENDON URIE: In Las Vegas, every band sounded basically the same—this post-hardcore, nu metal stuff. The walls were really thin in our practice space, and on each side of us it was those kinds of bands. We were trying to compete with that.

SPENCER SMITH: Growing up in Vegas, it's not as exciting as it seems from its reputation. It's difficult to do anything if you're not over twenty-one. Outside the Strip, it's suburban—sprawling, preplanned communities with all these clones of the same five house designs throughout the whole neighborhood. There's Cheesecake Factory and Chili's. There's slot machines inside the 7-Eleven.

ELLIE KOVACH: I would describe suburban Vegas around that time as a place where kids acted way too much like grown-ups and grown-ups acted way too much like kids.

SPENCER SMITH: We would just sit in our practice space after school, doing the best imitations of bands we liked. I was a junior, Ryan was a senior, and right around that time we met Brendon. Ryan went to a private Catholic high school and that's where he met Brent, our bassist. Then Brent got kicked out of that school for smoking weed and had to go to the public school, which is where he met Brendon. Brent was like, "Yo, there's this kid in my guitar class who's pretty good, we should have him come to practice." I remember hearing his voice for the first time when he did a silly impression of the dude from Journey, or something. I was like, "Shit, this guy's got an amazing voice."

BRENDON URIE: Ryan and Spencer had laptops, so we were able to mess around on GarageBand.

SPENCER SMITH: GarageBand was new. We would write songs, but we couldn't record them the way we envisioned with live instruments and all of that stuff, so we would sort of create MIDI versions of them with GarageBand. The electronic drums and keyboards we used were partially out of necessity because we couldn't really record everything the way we wanted.

BRENDON URIE: I broke Ryan's laptop one time and we had all our demos on it. We were like, "Holy shit, we don't have a laptop and we don't have a backup?" I thought I completely screwed us, but luckily he was able to play the files off the laptop I broke. My parents had a desktop and I was starting to learn to record and produce. A lot of the stuff was Spencer and I recording beats, writing the song, and putting the song over it.

SPENCER SMITH: Early on, Panic! at the Disco perpetually never had more than three or four songs because once we'd write a new song, we didn't think the others were good anymore, or didn't reflect the new sound we had. We had like three songs and we put them on PureVolume and we would just put links in bands' LiveJournals, hoping somebody would actually listen. We started with Fall Out Boy, because they were our favorite band.

PETE WENTZ: One of them—I think Ryan—was commenting on my Live-

Journal along the lines of, "I do this band, check us out." I was thinking I'd check out his band and tell him how bad it is.

SPENCER SMITH: Pete listened and reached out to Ryan on AOL Instant Messenger.

PETE WENTZ: I think the song was "Time to Dance," and I thought I wanted to sign them, or do something.

SPENCER SMITH: Pete was like, "I'd love to meet you guys."

PETE WENTZ: I drove to Vegas with my friend.

SPENCER SMITH: We were really, really nervous. I remember telling my parents, "You'll never fucking believe this: Pete Wentz from Fall Out Boy listened to our song, he's coming here, it's all happening." And my parents were like, "I don't know what Fall Out Boy is, I don't know who Pete is, this stuff doesn't mean anything."

BRENDON URIE: We met Wentz in a casino. It's now Planet Hollywood, but it was called the Aladdin back then. We met him at the hotel. He was there with some hot girl, just chilling and looking awesome. We went out to our practice space . . .

PETE WENTZ: Their practice space was like a thousand degrees, basically a hallway. They were like, "We don't really know how to play the songs because we've never performed them."

BRENDON URIE: We weren't old enough to play shows. If we attended, we'd be kicked out by 9:00 p.m. because you couldn't be on the Strip past 10:00 p.m. if you were under eighteen. It was a struggle finding venues to play in and bands to play with. It was kind of pointless, so we just spent most of our time writing songs. We explained that to Pete and he said, "Yeah, that's awesome. That's exactly what you need to be doing—writing songs and trying to perfect the craft, instead of playing shows to get people to notice."

SPENCER SMITH: We'd kind of figured out how to play a version of the songs we could do while Pete was there.

BRENDON URIE: We didn't have the instruments to play the demos, so we just played acoustically, for him and this girl.

SPENCER SMITH: We'd have to stop, mid-song, and be like, "Just imagine there'll be this crazy electronic part right there!" These were stripped-down versions of the three songs we had, with Brendon on a MIDI keyboard. But Brendon's an incredible vocalist.

BRENDON URIE: He was like, "Cool, that was good." That was all he said. We went down to Del Taco, and over a meal he explained that he wanted to sign us.

SPENCER SMITH: He bought us burritos and was like, "I want to sign you guys. I'm starting an imprint at Fueled By." That was the extent of our interaction with labels at that point. We hadn't talked to any. We didn't know anything about anything. But it was the dude from our favorite band, who's on the label we think is the perfect label, saying he'd love to sign us. Of course. Everything was happening exactly as we'd dreamed.

JASON TATE: John Janick from Fueled By Ramen sent me a crappy demo—I believe it was "Time to Dance"—and said, "What do you think of this band?" I wrote back something like, "Is that Patrick Stump on vocals? What is this?"

ADAM SAMILJAN: The Fall Out Boy LiveJournal community was buzzing about these two demos from a band called Panic! at the Disco. There were rumors that it was a Fall Out Boy side project, that it was Patrick singing these electronic songs.

ADAM SISKA: The Academy Is . . . was playing this club called Jillian's in Vegas, which was like an arcade that put on concerts. Scott from Crush Management came into the dressing room and said there was this new Vegas band that was huge fans of ours and wanted to meet us. So Panic! at the Disco was introduced to us for the first time. I was three years younger than everyone else in The Academy Is . . . , so I was still very much a baby-faced kid. And Panic! was all like, my age. But even at that point, I felt like I looked at them like little brothers because they were so . . . honestly, I can't even exaggerate how green they were coming into that room. Brendon wore these glasses. They looked like little kids. Just like us going to the Olive Garden, you could tell these kids were just like that.

ALEX DELEON: I was a big Fall Out Boy fan, as everyone was. I remember Pete posted on his blog about a band called Panic! at the Disco. At the time, they only had two demos—"Time to Dance" and I don't remember what the second song was. I remember being like, "Oh shit, these guys are from Vegas. Pete Wentz is talking about a band that's from Vegas!" I was in high school and I had a band, so I was blown away that there was a band from Vegas I hadn't heard of. I listened to those two songs over and over again. Then out of nowhere, they're playing their first show ever. It was at this place called the Alley, and it was tiny. It couldn't have held more than two hundred people.

TRAVIE MCCOY: "Time to Dance." That song was so ill. Pete was like, "Hey, I want you to come check out these kids in Vegas with me." I was like, "Cool, let's go." They had never played a show before. Ever. They had just made these demos. So I go to the show and I'm like, "Pete, son, what the fuck is going on? This shit don't sound like what we were listening to!"

PART 4

"THE PINNACLE OF HYPE"

2005

CAST OF CHARACTERS

PART 4

HANIF ABDURRAQIB: author and poet (and Midwest native)
QUINN ALLMAN: guitarist, the Used
NEAL AVRON: producer, Fall Out Boy
AL BARR: vocalist, Dropkick Murphys
JONAH BAYER: journalist, *Alternative Press*; writer, *Steven's Untitled Rock Show*
JUSTIN BECK: guitarist, Glassjaw; cofounder, Merch Direct
LISA BROWNLEE: tour manager, Warped Tour, Taste of Chaos
JOSHUA CAIN: guitarist, Motion City Soundtrack
SPENCER CHAMBERLAIN: front person, Underoath
JAMIE COLETTA: founder, No Earbuds PR
BRIAN DIAZ: guitar tech, Brand New, Motion City Soundtrack, Fall Out Boy (and formerly, front person, Edna's Goldfish, the Reunion Show)
JOHN FELDMANN: producer, the Used; front person, Goldfinger
MATT GALLE: booking agent, My Chemical Romance, Taking Back Sunday
NICK GHANBARIAN: bassist, Bayside (and formerly, Silent Majority)
AARON GILLESPIE: drummer-vocalist, Underoath
MICHAEL GOLDSTONE: A&R, PolyGram Records, Epic Records, DreamWorks Records, Sire Records
ANTHONY GREEN: front person, Circa Survive, Saosin
MIKE GREEN: producer, Paramore
ANDY GREENWALD: author and music journalist
ROB H!TT: drummer, Midtown (and later, manager, Crush Music)
JEPH HOWARD: bassist, the Used
MIKE KENNERTY: guitarist, the All-American Rejects
ELLIE KOVACH: blogger and journalist
JASON LINK: graphic designer, Victory Records and others
KEVIN LYMAN: founder and producer, Warped Tour; cofounder and producer, Taste of Chaos
STEPHANIE MARLOW: publicity, Victory Records
FRED MASCHERINO: guitarist-vocalist, Taking Back Sunday; front person, Breaking Pangea
TRAVIE MCCOY: front person, Gym Class Heroes
BERT MCCRACKEN: front person, the Used
CHRISTIAN MCKNIGHT: talent buyer, Bamboozle, Skate and Surf, This Island Earth festivals (and previously, Long Island show promoter); radio host
BOB MCLYNN: cofounder, Crush Music; manager, Fall Out Boy
ANDREW MCMAHON: front person, Something Corporate, Jack's Mannequin

TIM MCTAGUE: guitarist, Underoath
JOHNNY MINARDI: A&R, Fueled By Ramen
JAMES MONTGOMERY: author and music journalist, *Spin*, *MTV News*
MANI MOSTOFI: front person, Racetraitor
SCOTT NAGELBERG: manager, Panic! at the Disco
RANDY NICHOLS: manager, Underoath, Say Anything, the Starting Line
BUDDY NIELSEN: front person, Senses Fail
JUSTIN COURTNEY PIERRE: front person, Motion City Soundtrack
ANTHONY RANERI: front person, Bayside
TYLER RANN: vocalist-guitarist, Midtown
EDDIE REYES: guitarist, Taking Back Sunday (and previously, Mind Over Matter, Clockwise, Inside, the Movielife, Runner Up)
GEOFF RICKLY: front person, Thursday; New Brunswick basement show promoter; producer, My Chemical Romance
TYSON RITTER: front person, the All-American Rejects
ALEX SAAVEDRA: cofounder, Eyeball Records
ADAM SAMILJAN: marketing, Fueled By Ramen (and later, day-to-day manager, Paramore)
GABE SAPORTA: front person, Cobra Starship, Midtown (previously, bassist, Humble Beginnings)
HEATH SARACENO: vocalist-guitarist, Midtown (and later, Senses Fail)
ALEX SARTI: merch manager/seller, Clandestine Industries (and later, manager, Crush Music)
MARIA SHERMAN: journalist and author
LESLIE SIMON: author and journalist, *Alternative Press*
ADAM SISKA: bassist, The Academy Is. . . .
SPENCER SMITH: drummer, Panic! at the Disco
STEVEN SMITH: host, *Steven's Untitled Rock Show*
JEFF SOSNOW: A&R, DreamWorks Records, Interscope Records
MATT SQUIRE: producer, Panic! at the Disco
BRANDEN STEINECKERT: drummer, the Used
PATRICK STUMP: vocalist-guitarist, Fall Out Boy; solo artist; film scorer
JASON TATE: founder/blogger, AbsolutePunk.net
SHANE TOLD: front person, Silverstein
KATE TRUSCOTT: merch manager/seller, My Chemical Romance
BRENDON URIE: front person, Panic! at the Disco
KENNY VASOLI: front person, the Starting Line
MIKEY WAY: bassist, My Chemical Romance
PETE WENTZ: bassist, Fall Out Boy (and previously, bassist, Racetraitor; front person, Arma Angelus); founder, Decaydance Records, Clandestine Industries
HEATHER WEST: publicity, Victory Records
NICK WHEELER: guitarist, the All-American Rejects
HAYLEY WILLIAMS: front person, Paramore; founder, Good Dye Young
JAMES PAUL WISNER: producer, Paramore, Underoath, Dashboard Confessional, The Academy Is . . .
J. T. WOODRUFF: front person, Hawthorne Heights
SHIRA YEVIN: front person, Shiragirl; organizer, Shiragirl Stage

TASTE *OF* CHAOS, 2005

ROB HITT: Music goes in phases. Sometimes it's a big change—you can almost put your finger on it.

ALEX SAAVEDRA: Local kids would find out where the Eyeball House was. If there was a van or a bus near the house, kids would just happen to be across the street, skateboarding for six hours. They'd be like, "Who's here?" I would either make up a band, or if the band was cool and didn't care, I'd tell them. I knew it was getting weird when kids from really far away were showing up and just sitting on the curb across the street. It's a residential neighborhood; it's not a hangout area . . . There'd be Gerard-looking kids outside, after My Chem was already breaking, and hadn't even been in the house for a year. There'd still be kids doing this pilgrimage.

KATE TRUSCOTT: In 2005, it was just like, "This is mainstream now."

BUDDY NIELSEN: Taste of Chaos 2005 and 2005 Warped Tour were the pinnacle of hype around this scene.

MATT GALLE: My Chem and the Used did Taste of Chaos tour in 2005. That's when My Chem really started to take off.

AARON GILLESPIE: [In] '05 is when it really started to become commercial. We were playing in front of ten thousand people a day. "Holy shit, this could be it." And it was.

SHANE TOLD: Taste of Chaos was so pivotal to growing the scene.

KEVIN LYMAN: We thought it was time to do a Warped Tour spin-off, an indoors Warped Tour. 2005 was the year of the hockey strike. We had very favorable deals with the arenas because they were looking for business. So we just went out in the middle of January and February. No one went out in January and February then. We booked the Used, My Chemical Romance, Killswitch Engage, Senses Fail, Underoath . . .

BERT MCCRACKEN: Taste of Chaos was an unbelievable experience. Massive arena shows every night.

KEVIN LYMAN: You'd see the kids lined up like for Warped Tour, but wearing long coats and winter gear. Then they walk in, drop their stuff at coat check, and it became this indoor Warped vibe. We were the only people going to Saskatoon and Calgary and Winnipeg. It was the only youth rock show coming that whole winter, so they were going to absorb every minute of it.

SHANE TOLD: The doors for Taste of Chaos would open super early, at like 4:00 p.m. It was an after-school kinda thing.

KEVIN LYMAN: We were doing crazy things with that tour because the bands were young. Like, "Oh man, we're playing facing forward, we can't sell the arena seats behind us." And I'd go, "Hey, guys, we thought of an idea to sell the seats behind us. Let's call it the Chaos Zone and aim some speakers backwards and charge kids twelve or fifteen bucks to come to an arena show." And those sold out immediately. We were catching this wave. The wave was growing.

LISA BROWNLEE: You got to see Warped Tour bands, but in full-on theatrical mode in the arenas, with production and lighting. And they didn't have to play for just a half hour.

QUINN ALLMAN: Our second records had both come out around the same time—*In Love and Death* and *Three Cheers*.

KEVIN LYMAN: When we booked My Chem and the Used for that tour in August or September of 2004, the Used was the bigger band.

MATT GALLE: The tour was owned by Kevin Lyman and John Reese. Kevin owns Warped Tour and John Reese managed the Used. So he put them on to play last and made them look like the headliner.

BERT MCCRACKEN: It was the first time we tried to make our show a huge deal. We had Kabuki drops—a huge sheet in front of us when we started—and backlit to make it look like we were fifty feet tall. We were still young enough to be able to drink all day every day and pull it off without being too hurt to keep going the next day.

BUDDY NIELSEN: I mean, the Used was the biggest band, or had been the biggest for the longest. My Chem was in the middle of their meteoric rise.

I could tell they felt that they had to step it up. I'd been around them before, and they wanted to be the biggest band in the world. They were just executing their plan. These were the things they were talking about on the bus we shared with them on Warped Tour in 2004. It was coming to fruition.

STEVEN SMITH: That band knew who they were immediately because they would open with "I'm Not Okay," and that was the only video they had out there.

SHANE TOLD: That's a big move—opening with your hit.

STEVEN SMITH: Open with it, and then just play on. And Gerard and Bert were friends then, so that was fun . . .

AARON GILLESPIE: It was young, it was youthful, and . . . angsty, angsty. The show closed every night with Bert and Gerard singing "Under Pressure" during the Used's set.

BERT MCCRACKEN: I remember talking to Gerard about doing our "Under Pressure" cover on tour. And how cool it would be to live in those voices, to be Freddie Mercury and David Bowie.

BRANDEN STEINECKERT: We'd go offstage and our encore would be to come back out with My Chem.

KEVIN LYMAN: That wasn't put together by the tour. That was put together by them.

LISA BROWNLEE: Every night, I would order low-budget pizza, hundreds of pizzas for everybody on the tour. You could see whoever was bringing the pizzas walking through the venue. Every night they changed the lyrics—"people on streets"—and made it "pizza on streets."

AARON GILLESPIE: Everyone hung out back then. It wasn't like it is now. The only social media was MySpace. People weren't too big for their britches, you know?

BERT MCCRACKEN: I'm very sociable on tour. Whoever wants to come should come to the party . . .

STEVEN SMITH: *Steven's Untitled Rock Show* was there filming for Fuse opening day through the first three weeks.

JOHNNY MINARDI: For gatekeepers in the scene, *Steven's Untitled* was a monster one, because we couldn't get MTV for 90 percent of our stuff, but we could always count on Steven.

BERT MCCRACKEN: I remember being so wasted on his show so many times, there's probably so much embarrassing footage of me.

STEVEN SMITH: I was riding on My Chem's tour bus so I could get to know 'em. I'm a big comic book nerd and I remember geeking out with Gerard because he'd worked for Vertigo Comics. He was like, hey, "Check out this thing I'm working on—it's a comic book about kid superheroes called *The Umbrella Brigade*." He showed me a notebook of drawings before it became *The Umbrella Academy*.

JONAH BAYER: There was no oversight, except when Steven would want to like, get a tattoo on set and they were like, "No, you need a special license to do this." I think he did something with putting on Gerard's makeup . . .

STEVEN SMITH: Gerard and me painted our faces, the band walked me through how they did their makeup. And . . . I'm such a dick . . . Gerard shows how he does his face paint to me and I'm like, "Did you go to clown school to learn this?" He goes, "Art school." I went, "Same thing."

AARON GILLESPIE: On that tour, you started to see kids coming looking like Gerard, with the black across both eyes. It still felt homemade.

STEVEN SMITH: Then Bruce, the producer of *Steven's Untitled Rock Show*, had this idea to have Bert and Gerard read fan mail together. They both wore sunglasses and sat in the back of the bus. The fan question I remember most was like, "Are you two dating?" and then Bert kissed Gerard.

SPENCER CHAMBERLAIN: If you put a bunch of kids in a bus and tour around the world, they're gonna start to experience life. You become your own man.

BUDDY NIELSEN: I always knew about Christian bands. We always toured with Christian bands, even on our smaller tours. Just like hardcore kids who were straight edge, you'd run into bands and they're just Christian.

Underoath was interesting, because some of them were super devout, and some of them weren't.

SPENCER CHAMBERLAIN: In my mind, a Christian band was singing about Jesus all the time and we never did that. We were singing about life: the ups and downs and struggles we were going through.

ELLIE KOVACH: I feel like people always thought of Christian music as a pale imitation of the genre it was aiming to be at; Underoath was a band where you cared about the music first and whatever religion the band was second.

LESLIE SIMON: There were a lot of bands that were very open about the fact their songs were not about girlfriends and boyfriends—they were about G-O-D, and his son, Jesus. And there were also a lot of people who may have been religious but didn't want to be misconstrued as a "Christian rock band." That's different than being just a rock band with people who are Christian.

AARON GILLESPIE: The phrase at the time was, "We're Christians in a band, but not a Christian band." That was a thing.

BUDDY NIELSEN: We spent a lot of time with Underoath. I remember having discussions with them about sexuality and they're kind of like, "Well, you know, we don't hate gay people. We just don't approve of their lifestyle." Ha, ha, ha, dude, such cop-out bullshit.

TIM MCTAGUE: [In] 2005, 2006, I would say we were all more conservative than we are now.

JAMES PAUL WISNER: Producing Underoath, I remember hearing that blood-curdling screaming, and then to find out it was Christian hardcore . . . that they were screaming for the Lord . . .

AARON GILLESPIE: Dashboard taught me how to be a singer and weave melodies in and out of songs. We made it heavy.

RANDY NICHOLS: I learned a lot about religion managing Underoath. I'm a Jewish kid from Long Island, what do I know about Jesus? One time I said to Chad Johnson, their A&R at Tooth & Nail Records, "I'm surprised you don't have a problem that I'm Jewish and managing them." And he's like, "Well, you're one of the chosen people. You should be leading us."

I think he was joking . . . *a little*? But not really.

AARON GILLESPIE: Taste of Chaos was a really eye-opening time for us. 2005 was the year I realized, at twenty-two, this is my life now. The fuck? I feel so lucky. It's so fun to feel lucky.

SPENCER CHAMBERLAIN: Our first big album, *They're Only Chasing Safety*, had come out in 2004, a week apart from *Three Cheers for Sweet Revenge*.

AARON GILLESPIE: Underoath had taken My Chem on tour before, so we knew them well. By Taste of Chaos, you just knew they were going to be the biggest band.

BUDDY NIELSEN: It's fun to be on a tour that is so undeniably the biggest, best thing that's happening in the entire world. Like, I've been on plenty of big tours that underperformed, and the vibe is BAD. But when you're just cruising, the vibe is wild. Everybody is excited.

LISA BROWNLEE: Bert was always getting in trouble.

TIM MCTAGUE: Touring with Bert, to me, was probably the closest thing to sex, drugs, and rock and roll, that idea everyone has about the Rolling Stones or Guns N' Roses. That feeling of, *I'm literally in a movie right now* . . .

AARON GILLESPIE: Oh dude, Bert was on one at the Canadian border crossing. Band guys know, Canada's the hardest border to travel through as a musician.

BUDDY NIELSEN: All these buses about to cross the border, they're going to have a fucking field day ripping them apart. So we'd do the Weed Olympics, everybody brings all their weed and you gotta smoke it all because you can't bring it, you gotta get rid of your bowls and any paraphernalia.

AARON GILLESPIE: Bert took a bunch of pills because he didn't want to throw them out.

BUDDY NIELSEN: Our guitar tech was a complete psycho at that point, a crust punk that wouldn't shower. He got a staph infection in his hand because he poked himself with guitar strings by accident and then it got infected.

He's got this massive pus buildup and Bert is just obsessed with it. That night, Bert was like, "I'm going to pop this." It was one of the grossest things I'd ever seen.

AARON GILLESPIE: Bert cut it open at the border while we were waiting to get searched. Pus and blood all over and all of us thinking we were going to prison. It was a disaster. John Reese, the Used's manager at the time who was also running Taste of Chaos, managed to get us through.

TIM MCTAGUE: Bert rolled in *bananas*, and they just said, "You sit here," and this other guy goes up. There's a conversation, something's exchanged, and it's just sorted.

KEVIN LYMAN: Where Gerard was just a consummate young gentleman, Bert wouldn't wear his pass, so he's constantly fighting the security, doing something that distracted from the big picture of the tour.

SHANE TOLD: I love the Used, but it was getting to the point where My Chemical Romance probably should have been headlining because they had so much hype at that moment. I was at the LA show and some people were walking out before the Used played. It was clear there was a new king, you know?

The record cycle before *Three Cheers*, My Chem opened *every tour*. I don't know how many times I saw them, but I wasn't really into it. I didn't get it. They were just this vampire rock band. And when I saw them play that Taste of Chaos show, I got it. Right away.

BRANDEN STEINECKERT: My Chem would kill it every night. Which was great, because that would force us to really step it up, because we were the headliner.

QUINN ALLMAN: People weren't leaving after My Chem; they were still there for us.

BUDDY NIELSEN: The reason why the tour was crushing was because My Chem was getting so big right in that moment. Everybody knew it.

MATT GALLE: My Chem was smoking the Used every night onstage, getting massive crowds, and people were leaving in big groups after they played. We felt My Chem was slighted a little bit because the Used made the majority of the revenue and they got the billing, but the tour was selling a lot more tickets than expected and venues were being upgraded and My Chem wasn't really getting a bonus or getting paid any more.

BRANDEN STEINECKERT: The "Under Pressure" cover was one of the first sources of drama I heard about.

KATE TRUSCOTT: There was a beef going on because the Used did the rerecording of "Under Pressure" for tsunami relief. They were like, "We'll do it this one time, that's it."

BRANDEN STEINECKERT: Both of us were going to rerelease our albums with that song added.

KATE TRUSCOTT: And then the Used's manager was like, "We're gonna rerelease our record with 'Under Pressure' as a bonus track." That was never part of the deal with My Chem. That started some pretty not-awesome beef for a while.

BRANDEN STEINECKERT: My Chemical Romance didn't want to blow up for playing a cover song, which I completely get. So many bands were doing that in the nineties and 2000s and it's like, this is way too good of a band for people's first impression of them to be a cover song.

And Gerard and Bert had really partied together. I think Gerard's sobering up ended that dynamic.

BERT MCCRACKEN: It was toward the end of Taste of Chaos that Gerard had a change of heart. I think he quit drinking for a little bit on that tour. I remember him being like, "Dude, you've got to slow down," which is just not anything that I was ever willing to hear, especially from, quote, unquote, friends. So I took it very personally. You know, kid stuff. Like, "You don't know what you're talking about, I'm gonna drink till I die!" Heh, heh, heh.

BRANDEN STEINECKERT: I think that feels threatening; you feel like you're being judged because they're better than you now that they're sober. Gerard was certainly not behaving in that way, but I can only imagine the demons Bert would struggle with, as a person with addictive tendencies.

JOHN FELDMANN: It was challenging for Bert, because Bert was still in the midst of it all. It couldn't have been easy to watch My Chemical Romance blow up and become the band that they became with Bert being, sort of, the founder of the movement.

BERT MCCRACKEN: Around that time the band was like, "Oh no, Bert's uncontrollable, he's out of his mind." That was the beginning of a long road of dragging the band and myself along the bottom to see what happened.

It's not easy to change lifestyles overnight. Gerard made it out alive. For me, that took another six or seven years before I finally hit bottom hard enough to be like, "Well, I gotta do something different. Or I'm never gonna make it out."

BUDDY NIELSEN: *Three Cheers* was just gaining traction; My Chem didn't need to figure out a follow-up yet. They didn't need to figure out anything. They could really just coast. After Taste of Chaos, they went nonstop—constantly touring, constantly writing, constantly practicing. That tour was the last time I saw them being exactly who I grew up with.

KEVIN LYMAN: I'll never forget the last show of the tour, in California at Long Beach Arena, there were three thousand people that wanted guest list. We bamboozled the fire marshal and I kind of swept them in through the back door. People from management companies, record labels, press—everyone just wanted to witness what was going on with this thing. It got so crazy that I ended up closing the production office and telling everyone, "It's a free-for-all, just make sure your stuff doesn't get stolen." And I'm laughing all the way through the night, just reveling in it.

KATE TRUSCOTT: I think there were about 19,000 people there. I remember selling upwards of $20,000 worth of merch for My Chemical Romance.

KEVIN LYMAN: The last show was just rabid for everyone. People were hanging over the back railings of the arena and high-fiving the bands. That's how close the back of the stage was to the arena.

We made it. It was April when the tour ended and My Chem and a lot of the same bands were going out again in a few months for Warped Tour. We knew that summer was going to be huge.

ANDY GREENWALD: Gerard was the engine. I remember spending time with the band for their first *Spin* cover story, in 2005. And I don't mean to belittle anyone else in the band, but Mikey, especially then, was extremely, paralyzingly shy and just really excited about his Nintendo DS. And Ray's just kind of a music guy. And Frank is a fantastic guy, but he knows who he is—he's a Jersey punk lifer. Gerard was the Wizard of Oz. That's not to say he wasn't kind and equitable to his bandmates, but he was the star. He sucked up the oxygen and set the tone.

You know, one of my favorite memories of those bus rides was when the bus stopped in the middle of the night to get gas. We were somewhere in the Northeast, in the middle of nowhere. It was freezing and some of us were awake. Gerard was wearing his onesie skeleton pajamas, the ones now popularized by Phoebe Bridgers. He hopped out into the slush and was just standing there next to the bus in his skeleton pajamas. I was just like, "This seems right." It was a very different vibe from just a year before.

CHAPTER 21

GOING DOWN SWINGING

WARNING: THIS CHAPTER CONTAINS DISCUSSION OF SUICIDE

JAMIE COLETTA: Something Corporate played this business college in a small town near Boston, in this neighborhood with a noise ordinance policy. Ten p.m., you had to be done. The show's in this huge gymnasium, the stage was at one end and we were sitting up in the bleachers. Something Corporate starts playing and two or three songs in, you can see there's commotion. There's cops on the side of the stage. They cut the power to the instruments one by one and Andrew McMahon was like, "We're gonna keep going!" It got to the point where it was just Andrew and the piano. He started doing "Konstantine," and they pulled the sound completely. The crowd of this packed gymnasium finished the song, all screaming, while Andrew jumped off into the crowd. Cops were chasing him and the crowd parted like the fucking Red Sea; everyone tried to prevent the cops from catching him. He made it all the way to the other side of the gymnasium and was standing on the merch tables singing. You couldn't hear him but the crowd was still singing "Konstantine," this fucking ten-minute song.

ANDREW MCMAHON: I was catching a layover flight to Ohio and I couldn't make it from one gate to the next without having to put my bags down and catch my breath. That was the first time I noticed it.

ADAM SISKA: He was sick with leukemia.

ANDREW MCMAHON: It came in dribs and drabs.

My doctor left a message and said, "I don't know where you are, but if you are outside and near people, you need to get someplace where there are none because the wind could blow and you could catch a virus and it could kill you. Call me, I have a hospital bed waiting for you across town."

The kind of leukemia I had is much more common in young children and older adults. It took doctors nearly a week to get me an actual diagnosis. That first night, there were a handful of breakdowns. Then there was a moment of peace and clarity. I'd just gotten to finish recording and mastering the first Jack's Mannequin record [my new project after Something Corporate]. And I think I knew I had gotten out of control a little bit. I was partying really hard. I have addiction in my family and there were a lot of signs to me that I was heading in that direction. When I found out I was gonna have to fight some other fight, there was a bit of relief.

ADAM SISKA: My ex-girlfriend at the time worked at the UCLA Medical Center, where they sent Andrew. When I was off the road with The Academy Is . . . , I would go sit at his bedside and just talk shop with him about music. We'd hate on new bands coming up or whatever. A lot of people forgot about him or were too unsure of what to say to him while he was sick. I really looked up to him, so you couldn't keep me away. I visited him somewhere between five and ten times while he was in the hospital. One time I got there around his birthday, he might have been turning twenty-five, or twenty-four, even. He had shingles all over and he had no hair. He looked very frail. I said goodbye to him, in a strange way, because I didn't think he was gonna make it.

BUDDY NIELSEN: My grandma died while I was on tour in 2004 and I went into a real phase of shutdown. But people were kind of like, "Well, you got to go on tour!" I remember the label manager was going to have one of the people at the label drop off Xanax for me so I could start to deal with my anxiety and do the European tour Senses Fail was supposed to do. I'm like, "I'm not fucking taking Xanax. I don't even know what that is."

There is this idea that emo is inappropriately angsty . . . I don't think the people making the music were putting it on. It wasn't made-up.

PETE WENTZ: Mental health wasn't spoken about publicly the way it is now.

BUDDY NIELSEN: Mental health wasn't really a thing. I don't think a lot of people understood it. Now that I look back on it, everybody involved knew there was this bubble, this big business of our music scene that was gonna last a couple years, and everything's gotta be squeezed out. I didn't have that perspective or understanding. I was just along for the ride. People were trying to get theirs.

ANTHONY GREEN: The mentality of: *Get them out there, get them on tour, get it done*. In our scene, there's all these artists writing songs about suicide, self-harm, depression. There's all these songs about it, but no one's talking about it.

A lot of artists have mental illness—difficulties and challenges they deal with. And a lot of times, it's one of the things that makes their art so good. I can say for myself, I don't know if I would be able to write as deeply about what's going on with me if I didn't feel things the way I feel them, being bipolar. I don't think there was any dialogue back then about mental health care.

TRAVIE MCCOY: My friend died from a heroin overdose, and the night I went home for the funeral we ended up going to this party. I'm like, "No, that place is like a frat house, we don't belong there, it's water and oil." I grew up with these gutter punk kids, these skate kids, like straight savages. It was like a record scratch when we walked in. I went upstairs started talking to some girl, ten minutes later I just hear all hell breaking loose. I go downstairs and a dude punched my friend dead in her face, so I busted through the whole living room, grabbed the cue ball off the pool table, and smacked this motherfucker. When I hit him, I fucking slipped because there was beer on the floor and I tore my ACL, MCL, and meniscus. Long story short, they pulled me out of there and they put me on OxyContin until I could have the surgeries. And that's the start of the whole fucking opioid shit. I had no idea. I'm like, "Dad, I don't know what's going on, I can't sleep, my stomach hurts, blah blah." I had never done hard drugs before but once I ran out of those fucking OxyContins, I was sick as fuck. I went to the doctor and they were like, "You've been going through withdrawals, we gotta give you more," and I was like, "Nah, you're not giving me nothing." So I went cold turkey for thirty days straight and kicked it.

About four months later, OxyContins started coming around my hometown as a recreational drug. I was like, "Oh I know these, I'll take a couple." The first time I snorted it, it was like I was back in the womb. It's like the devil. It makes you feel everything you want to feel. If you want to disassociate and feel warm and nurtured, that's what opioids do. It fucked me up.

From that point on, it went to pills, pills, pills, and then pills started getting more expensive, and I was like, "Oh, I can just get a bundle of heroin for a hundred bucks." I'd never shot up in my life. But I had a friend in Chicago who was a nurse and she was like, "I don't want you to be sick, I know how to administer, I can hook you up." She shot me up with an IV needle and like, bro, I'm not trying to sensationalize or condone it, but I've never felt more beautiful or safe in my life. It's such a fucking joke. I spent four or five years of my life chasing that same feeling.

BUDDY NIELSEN: In early 2005, I was dealing with a lot of things I was coming to terms with: all the success we'd had and all the personal things that happened to me, mostly my grandma dying while I was on tour in 2004, which I didn't get a chance to deal with. I was just having a complete mental breakdown: I wasn't eating, I wasn't sleeping. I had so much anxiety that I couldn't really leave the house.

Senses Fail was supposed to play *Conan*. There was a lot of pressure to perform. People don't realize how important those late-night shows were for our music scene. This was before the internet was ubiquitous, this was a moment everybody in the country could see who you are.

MIKEY WAY: You look out at that brightly lit studio and you're like, "This is beaming across the world right now." For bands like us who played VFW halls, it was like a Martian landscape.

BUDDY NIELSEN: Senses Fail had already done *Jimmy Kimmel*, so there was a part of me that knew, "I can do this." But on *Conan*, mentally, I was in such a fight-or-flight freeze mode that I got overwhelmed as soon as we went on set. If anybody's ever frozen in a situation, that's exactly what happened. I didn't forget the lyrics as much as accepting how big the moment was just made me freeze. And my body kept on like, "Oh, I've got to make the noises." And I made the noises and recovered it. The performance ended up being, you know, whatever. But coming back into the dressing room, I was mortified. I'm not quite sure everyone knew what just happened, but I was distraught. That sent me down an even larger spiral that I don't think I really recovered from until, man . . . it wasn't until the last couple years I could accept what happened and not hate myself for it. And I never should have been put in that situation. Any of my people around—publicist, management, label—should have been like, "Hey man, he freaked out, he forgot the lyrics. Can we shoot again?" Those shows aren't live. I mean, ultimately, did it derail our career? No. But it definitely destroyed who I was as a person.

MIKEY WAY: Buddy didn't come back from that for a long time, I remember.

ANTHONY GREEN: I think if you started talking about that stuff, people would be like, "Oh boo-hoo, get your shit together. You're doing what you love; deal with it." There still is this hardcore mentality of like, "If you're an artist, you have to starve, you have to suffer."

BUDDY NIELSEN: I was very, very depressed. I wasn't singing well. I was on antidepressants, but I don't think I was on *enough*. My therapist was real shitty. And I wasn't speaking with my mom or my family at the time.

During the writing of *Still Searching*, I spent thousands of dollars seeing all sorts of different sex workers. I was drinking a lot and in a really bad place because I was repressing my sexuality, because I didn't feel comfortable being out, at all. I didn't want people to find out I was seeing girls and guys, people who were transgender. I didn't feel like I could have an open relationship with anybody that wasn't a woman, or else it would hurt my career, and my family, and everybody.

ELLIE KOVACH: People would have been like, "Shut up and play the songs."

BUDDY NIELSEN: Senses Fail got big enough where we had normal fucking fans: "Yo, man, I was just over in Iraq driving a tank." You know? I don't know if that guy would be stoked.

MIKEY WAY: It was important, preaching individuality and anti-bullying themes, it being okay to not be okay. The whole sentiment of "I'm Not Okay" is you're not always gonna be happy, but that's fine. There's sometimes a stigma in society that you have to be happy all the time, and I don't think that's realistic.

NEAL AVRON: Pete was going through some stuff during the making of *From Under the Cork Tree*. I feel he internalized the pressure the most out of the band.

PETE WENTZ: Patrick and I used to live in Los Angeles in the Oakwoods, which is a pretty sad place: transients, people trying to be stars, some don't make it. I became obsessed with mortality. I would lie under a blanket, just lie there for hours, and be like, "This is going to be what it's like when you're dead. Except you won't even be able to think this is what it's going to be like." Patrick was freaked out. Like, why does this guy lie under a blanket all day on the floor?

PATRICK STUMP: I was the youngest of three, so I was used to, "Stay out of my room!" I kind of just took it that way: He doesn't want anybody around, I'll just give him his space. I was also pretty naive. I didn't realize you could have substance abuse; it was a thing I saw on PSAs.

PETE WENTZ: I had so many different things going on, so it wasn't like pure depression. There was anxiety, because maybe you're on the precipice of a thing, maybe you're not. And then that generalized and I couldn't fly and I couldn't get in elevators. I'd be at our management's office and I would walk up six floors. To me, I hate going too deep with anything like this because I feel like there's the possibility that you romanticize it. And there's nothing really romantic about it.

ADAM SISKA: We were close friends at that time period and I actually had plans to meet up with Pete at a Denny's restaurant in Schaumburg, Illinois. And he was a no-show. He wasn't answering his phone, and this was the night . . . I don't know how true it was that he took Ativan or something, like maybe it was a call for help that some people were calling a suicide attempt. I don't know, I never really pressed him on it.

PETE WENTZ: I think on that day, I needed to fly to Europe or get ready to fly to Europe the next day; I can't totally remember. But it all kind of came on a little too much. And I think I just wanted to shut my brain off, you know, what I mean?

It wasn't about, "Oh, you know, like, I want to kill myself." It was more like, "I just want this feeling to stop."

JAMES MONTGOMERY: I did a phone call with Pete for a *Spin* "band to watch" interview. He was like, "Oh, sorry I'm running late, I'm in my car, I just went to my therapist." Right off the bat, I was struck by just how open and upfront he was. And there's a song title on *From Under the Cork Tree* that mentions Ativan.

LESLIE SIMON: Fall Out Boy was on my radar for an *Alternative Press* cover story and they were passing through Cleveland to play a matinee show. I was joking around with Pete, saying I was really torn about seeing Fall Out Boy because I already had tickets for a Kelly Clarkson concert. He joked back, "Well, I would go to Kelly Clarkson." I said, "Well, I have an extra ticket and you're playing in the afternoon, do you wanna go?"

We had really good seats. Pete was just a face in the crowd; no one knew who he was. We had just come from a real mushy, active, teen hormone situation at the Fall Out Boy show to Kelly, which was in a theater with families, and I just saw Pete's jaw drop. He liked all the punk, metal, and screamo, but he also had this huge sweet tooth for pop.

We got along like a house on fire. During this extended hang sesh, he was revealing small things about the next record, and things he was processing and going through. I said if he would let me deliver that story to his fans, I would do it with the utmost care: because the story we were telling was him in the parking lot and attempting, or thinking of, you know, ending his life, and it was moving and intense and emotional. When it became time to do that cover story, it unfolded exactly as we had hoped.

JAMES MONTGOMERY: That kind of honesty resonated with a lot of their fans who were going though similar things, taking the same medications. It was another bond they shared with their audience.

NEAL AVRON: Pete came to me and said, "Hey, what do you think about Brendon Urie singing on a song on *Cork Tree*?" Pete had just signed Panic! to his label and Brendon came out from Vegas. So we put him in the studio to sing "7 Minutes in Heaven (Atavan Halen)." Patrick had already sung the whole song, so I just muted the parts we were going to have Brendon resing. Or maybe I muted those parts entirely and they sang it together. One thing I can tell you for sure is I was dismayed at how much Brendon sounded like Patrick. I switched mics several times but no matter what I did, there was still a pretty good similarity. I ended up panning them to different places in the mix so people could tell who was who.

ANTHONY RANERI: Bayside was on tour with Fall Out Boy when they had just been upstreamed from Fueled By Ramen to Island. I remember sitting in each other's vans and Patrick playing demos of "Sugar, We're Goin Down" and "Dance, Dance" and thinking, Oh my god, you guys are gonna be so fucking big.

NEAL AVRON: Island's first choice for a lead single was "Sugar, We're Goin Down." When we were making "Sugar," Pete suggested Patrick should sing each chorus on a different day. He thought this chorus was so important. It had to be amazing. Patrick couldn't be tired by the third chorus. It was a great idea.

ANDY GREENWALD: Patrick can really sing. And not in a cute, "I was in a punk band because I had nothing else to do and didn't like sports" way. Patrick can belt. That raw ability coupled with Pete's marketing savvy was about to explode them.

MANI MOSTOFI: Once Fall Out Boy got on Island Records, these super serious A&R people started showing up to the shows. They saw our little group of hardcore kids like, "You guys are a liability, you guys are gonna get this band sued." The band was attracting these suburban fourteen-year-olds in Chicago and we were these hardcore dudes in our twenties stage diving on their heads. These kids didn't quite know what was going on. And it was probably inappropriate. I remember they played at this venue in Chicago. We, for the first time, had this real stage to dive off of, and I remember the A&R people being like, "You guys need to chill."

GEOFF RICKLY: When Thursday was on Island—jeez, being on Island was so weird—I think I was with Jay-Z and Bon Jovi and they were like, "Yeah, you gotta come out to this Fall Out Boy show and welcome them to the label." And I was like, "Fall Out Boy? Is that the kid from Racetraitor?" And they're like, "What?" I'm like, "Pete Wentz! Isn't that Pete Wentz's band?" They're like, "Oh . . . yeah, Pete's in the band."

We went out to see them somewhere in New York, I think it was Irving Plaza. They played "Grand Theft Autumn" and I was like, "Fuck, Patrick can sing. This guy's got a voice." I didn't see them becoming the biggest band out of the scene, but I thought they were good, you know? And man, did they fucking explode.

JOHNNY MINARDI: With "Sugar, We're Goin Down" and *Cork Tree*, Island was doing a lot of the grunt work, but Fueled By Ramen was still very much involved.

ADAM SAMILJAN: The name of the label meant something. Obviously, the label was nothing without the artists, but the label had a fan base, as well.

TRAVIE MCCOY: The Fueled By Ramen & Friends Tour was one of the illest I've ever been on in my life.

GABE SAPORTA: Midtown was the main support on the first half of that tour for Fall Out Boy.

SHANE TOLD: Fall Out Boy had a bus. That surprised me. I thought they would still be in a van.

GABE SAPORTA: This still mostly felt like a punk rock tour. We were still playing skate parks, VFWs. It wasn't all real venues, but it was the kind of energy that every show was packed to the brim, eight hundred kids or whatever. You felt the energy, you felt like this was the last tour you're ever going to do like this. And Fall Out Boy was like four years younger than me, right? Four years is like a generation in music. These kids were where I was at four years prior—just starting, just getting excited. I'm with the Midtown guys, and we're all twenty-three, we all live in the city and have girlfriends . . .

HEATH SARACENO: We had recently put out an album that we were excited about. And it did not connect. All we wanted to do was play the new songs on that tour, and no one wanted to hear 'em.

TYLER RANN: After you've seen so many of your peer bands get really successful and surpass you, it definitely takes a toll. My Chemical Romance, New Found Glory, Dashboard, Taking Back Sunday—essentially any band from that era that has a gold record opened for Midtown at some point.

HEATH SARACENO: That Fall Out Boy tour got dark, and it got depressing.

GABE SAPORTA: Misery loves company.

TYLER RANN: Fall Out Boy was having all this success, we shared a manager with them, and all of a sudden, the attention was no longer on us. That made it difficult. The version of Midtown that was excited to play with the Get Up Kids and At the Drive-In at Manville Elks in 1999 was not this band. We lost the focus of what made us want to record a CD before we ever played a show. It started being about jealousy and growing up.

ADAM SISKA: Because the Fueled By Ramen thing was blowing up, we were surpassing bands left and right. The Academy Is. . . . was second of four on that Fueled By Ramen & Friends Tour and we were smoking Midtown. As far as Fueled By Ramen bands go—this was before Panic!'s first album—we were the second biggest band on the label.

MIKEY WAY: On a day off from My Chemical Romance's tour with Green Day, I went to a Fall Out Boy show at the House of Blues. *Cork Tree* wasn't out yet, but Patrick played me some of the songs.

SHANE TOLD: Fall Out Boy was performing "Sugar, We're Goin Down" and it wasn't released yet, but the place just exploded when they played this song no one knew.

During the tour, I remember they got back the first cut of the video for "Sugar." And I'll be honest—they probably don't care at this point—they fucking hated the video.

ADAM SISKA: They thought the boy with the antlers turned out cheesy. They had this idea . . . there was something in *Jay and Silent Bob Strike Back* where they got the IP address of anyone who talked shit on message boards about them and they went around the country and kicked their ass. I remember Fall Out Boy conceptualizing this video where the antler boy video came out, it was so bad people talked shit on it, and the video was them going around kicking people's asses.

SHANE TOLD: But it was already too late, and they had to roll with it. And then it blew up on MTV.

TYLER RANN: By the time Fall Out Boy released "Sugar, We're Goin Down" as a single, people were coming to the shows that were different than the people who normally came to these sorts of shows. They were coming just to hear that song, you know what I mean?

SHANE TOLD: Pete was so business-minded. He was always on the computer doing stuff. He was the first guy I ever saw on tour spending that much time on the computer working the band. I was playing poker with Andy Hurley and Billy Beckett from The Academy Is. . . . every day. And smoking weed with Joe from Fall Out Boy.

HEATH SARACENO: Gym Class Heroes were a new band, they were up-and-coming and hitting their stride on that tour. Travie was totally cool. Great guy. He would come out with us and sing on Midtown songs.

TRAVIE MCCOY: Those formative Fueled By Ramen tours, man. It was a bunch of boys in bands running around recklessly just fucking being bastards, man, just debauchery.

ADAM SISKA: Fall Out Boy was always into pranks. I think it was that straight-edge mentality—"We don't get drunk, so we're just gonna shit in your dressing room!"

ANTHONY RANERI: Bayside had toured with Fall Out Boy the previous year and there were some good pranks. I wanna say there were Roman candles involved at one point. I think that was the most dangerous, like shooting somebody with Roman candles. Trailer dodgeball was another one—you'd get in the trailer and play dodgeball in the pitch black. We filled their water bottles, their stage bottles, with vinegar. So they played one song, grabbed their water bottles, and shook them into the crowd, but it's all fucking vinegar, and the front row of the crowd is covered in vinegar. And one time our bass player had just gotten a new phone and his old phone was the same exact one Pete had. So at one point while Fall Out Boy was playing, we waved the bass player's old phone in front of Pete and threw it into the crowd.

GABE SAPORTA: I'm like, dude, this is sick, this is why I got into music in the first place. All I have to do is reconnect with this.

HEATH SARACENO: Gabe got along really well with Pete.

PETE WENTZ: We didn't know where Midtown was at, we didn't know what the vibe was. So it's the last day of tour, and on the last day of tour, bands always pranked each other . . .

GABE SAPORTA: OH MY GOD I REMEMBER THIS SO CLEARLY! This is the perfect example of what would happen . . .

ADAM SISKA: As an end-of-tour prank, we decided—this was Pete's idea—that we were going to *antique* Midtown onstage. I didn't even know what that meant. Pete explained antiquing someone to me—it's when you take a bag of flour and just hit them with it.

GABE SAPORTA: During our last song . . .

ADAM SISKA: We ran onstage and hit them with bags of flour. Then we jumped on their backs. We were really having fun with it.

ROB HITT: If you're onstage playing, you're gonna be sweaty. So imagine pouring all this flour onto a sweaty body . . .

GABE SAPORTA: I thought it was fucking hilarious. And Heath and Tyler were so fucking pissed.

HEATH SARACENO: They didn't really read the room on it, you know what I mean? Not everyone was having a good time on that tour. I was wearing contact lenses, so when you get that much flour in your eyes, your eyes are like glued shut from fucking flour. And I couldn't breathe and it was all inside the cavities of my guitar. And my clothes . . . I gotta fucking get in a car and drive for hours home now feeling like . . . I wasn't amused at all.

PETE WENTZ: When they came offstage we were like . . . "I think we just broke up Midtown."

ADAM SISKA: After the show, Midtown got in a blowout fight that involved Heath saying that he quit the band, saying that he no longer wants to play music for little kids.

HEATH SARACENO: I don't remember what I said. I know that I tried to find people and hurt them. But I'm glad that I didn't find anyone, ha, ha.

GABE SAPORTA: It showed me the difference of getting older versus still staying young and dumb. I wanted to still think things like that were funny. I didn't want to turn into an adult that doesn't know how to have fun. Once you start getting to twenty-three, twenty-four, twenty-five, you're fighting that calcification, the death of your humor. Twenty-five is kind of late to start a new band. But my next band was my attempt to fight that . . . I'm gonna be young until I die, baby.

CHAPTER 22

THE EYE *OF THE* STORM

LESLIE SIMON: There were so few women in the scene, especially on the stages. I could maybe count them on two hands. The women were not often seen as more than muses for jilted males. They were the inspiration for the songs, not singing the songs. So when you have somebody with the pipes and the look and the approachability . . .

ANDY GREENWALD: Paramore was the band we were all hoping would exist, you know? There needed to be a band with a woman fronting it that has something to say about all of this.

HAYLEY WILLIAMS: There was a bidding thing going on. It was the early 2000s. Avril Lavigne was fucking massive. Kelly Clarkson was on her heels trying to do guitar pop. Ashlee Simpson had signed with Geffen and is pop punk. Suddenly I was this prospect for a label.

MIKE GREEN: You had No Doubt and Evanescence, but you never really had a prominent band in the scene with a female presence.

HAYLEY WILLIAMS: I'm fifteen at the time, in 2004. I wonder what words I used because I didn't have the perspective I do now. We had all these songs the label liked more than the songs I'd written by myself, but the label wanted me to put them out as Hayley. I didn't want to do that. I told [the then-president of Atlantic] Julie Greenwald I didn't want to put out a song or do interviews under my name. There was a heated conversation with a team of people in which I said I would be just as happy to play these songs in Taylor's basement for the rest of my life. It was a very empowered moment. My voice was shaking. I was crying.

MIKE GREEN: The band was the two Farro brothers—Josh and Zac—Jeremy Davis, and Jason Bynum. Josh and Hayley always worked on the writing together, even when the project was just Hayley. It was very much a band, like any other band. It wasn't some kind of industry plant.

HAYLEY WILLIAMS: Fueled By Ramen was working with Atlantic, and we wanted to be on a label like that.

JASON TATE: At the time, Fueled By Ramen had that cachet in the scene—*someone has signed off on this band, this is probably pretty good.*

HAYLEY WILLIAMS: My dad and my mom wanted me to be smart. They didn't want me to pass this up. I'd have that talk with them, then go to the guys and be like, "I don't know!" I didn't want to do this as Hayley. I was like, "You're the only label that's entertained the thought of the band, so let's figure out how to make this work." During that time, we found our manager, Mark [Mercado]. I really thought a contract didn't matter. In a lot of ways it doesn't. I was so ashamed of myself for being the only name on the contract. Later, Mark was like, "Here are all the bands where only one person is signed." I'm not gonna list them. I'm not gonna be a rat. But it's not that big a deal. My thing was, "Mark, just make sure everyone's safe." I don't want to know about contracts. It never mattered to me. I was so ashamed of myself for being the only name on the contract. I've never talked about this. I still don't know how to articulate it. I feel like the part of me that speaks on it is still fifteen.

JAMES MONTGOMERY: Fueled By Ramen had a deal with Atlantic Records behind the scenes. So there was always a weird level of suspicion with that band, because some people knew what the situation was: Atlantic signed Hayley Williams to a deal, she's Paramore Incorporated, and everyone else in the band is sort of a hired gun.

MIKE GREEN: Tom Storms from Atlantic Records called me and said they signed this girl Hayley and they wanted to make a record, but it's not going to be just Hayley, it's going to be called Paramore.

HAYLEY WILLIAMS: I didn't wanna put out an album of songs I wrote with my bandmates and recorded alone.

ADAM SAMILJAN: Around a year before *All We Know Is Falling* came out [in July 2005], we started hearing the name Paramore around Fueled By Ramen. Paramore was a bit different. It wasn't the same situation where Pete was shepherding in bands like Gym Class Heroes and The Academy Is . . . They were all Crush Management. Paramore was a different management group and they were a lot younger than everybody. I remember meeting them, and Zac was so young, fourteen or fifteen at the time. They were tour managed by Hayley's father. They were very protected as they were getting started.

JOHNNY MINARDI: My first memory of Paramore is sitting on John Janick's couch in the Fueled By Ramen office super early one day, and he was listening to a demo of this song, "Hallelujah." I was like, "What the fuck is this?" He's like, "Listen to her voice." I was blown away. Everyone knows that song now, because it came out on their second album.

MIKE GREEN: Paramore had recorded with these two guys in Nashville, but it wasn't the right look. "Hallelujah" was one of those songs.

JOHNNY MINARDI: I was like, "John, this song's incredible. But if you lead with it, the religious undertones of the song—the hook is 'hallelujah'—don't connect to the mainstream. Unless you want it to go that religious way."

MIKE GREEN: They were never a Christian band, but they were Christians. Especially Josh.

JAMES PAUL WISNER: A big part of why they wanted to work with me was because I'd produced Underoath's *They're Only Chasing Safety*. I did three songs on Paramore's debut album: "All We Know," "Never Let This Go," and "My Heart." It was really because my schedule was so busy at the time, I didn't do the whole album. But that ended up being a good thing, because Mike Green does such great work.

MIKE GREEN: *All We Know Is Falling* is a time capsule of where they were at the time.

They were very distraught that Jeremy, their bass player, left the band right before we started working on my portion of the record in Orlando. He wrote this big thing on the door of their practice space, like, "I love you guys, I just have to leave!" I don't remember the specifics of it, but it was this long, artistic thing.

Over about a month in the studio, we did "Pressure," "Emergency," "Franklin," "Brighter," "Whoa," "Conspiracy," and this other song that didn't make the album called "O Star."

HAYLEY WILLIAMS: The guys and I didn't listen to pop punk before writing "Pressure." We listened to heavier stuff like Deftones. We wanted to be darker. Suddenly, we wrote "Pressure," and that was it—we were gonna write emo bops! Sick!

MIKE GREEN: Hayley loved heavier bands. Hayley loved Underoath. A lot of the issues of the Nashville Hayley material was that it dulled down the edge. It was too Nashville, for lack of a better term.

You could tell the Farro brothers and Hayley were the core of it. They brought on a bass player to play on the record named Lucio. But they kind of had their own thing going. Josh and Hayley were together at the time.

On that song "Emergency," Josh wanted to scream on the verses, because they loved bands like Underoath and Norma Jean. I was like, "Yeah . . . I don't think that's the right move. I don't think that's going to age well." And they were like, "No, noooo, we wanna do that!"

It's crazy to think Zac was fifteen when we did that record. I distinctly remember him crying because they thought they were going to be able to go home to Tennessee, but then they had to go play Bamboozle Festival in Asbury Park.

CHRISTIAN MCKNIGHT: 2004 was the last year we did Skate and Surf; in 2005, we transitioned to Bamboozle. Bamboozle had been a hippie festival in Asbury Park. In 2005, my boss John D'Esposito called me and said, "Hey, we're leaving Skate and Surf, we're taking Bamboozle, we're going to book it." [The year] 2005 was the first Bamboozle with the emo, punk, hardcore bands.

That was one of the first times anybody had seen Paramore—end of April 2005.

MIKE GREEN: There were like ten people that watched their set.

ADAM SAMILJAN: Hayley's voice and charisma was immediately apparent to anybody who watched them. I was stuck in the merch booth for the Paramore Bamboozle performance. I drew the short straw on that one, and everyone else there from Fueled By Ramen got to see them.

JAMES PAUL WISNER: Up till 2004, it was more of an indie scene with the emerging of emo and then around the beginning of Paramore, that was when things started to change.

CHRISTIAN MCKNIGHT: Bamboozle 2005 was one of the hardest weekends of my life.

Fall Out Boy and My Chemical Romance played, and they were big-ass fucking bands at that point. People that didn't even have tickets for Bamboozle were literally showing up to Asbury Park just to hang out because it was such a gathering. I remember how many tickets we sold and there were way more people than that in Asbury. We were making up schedules as we went along because the town and the fire marshal kept shutting us down: "No, no, no, it's gonna be too crazy to do this show inside the Stone Pony . . . It's gonna be too crazy to do this show inside Convention Hall . . ."

JUSTIN BECK: These kids rented out the hotel next door, and these savages destroyed the fuckin' place. I remember my wife was back at the hotel while I was doing work for Merch Direct. She called me like, "What the fuck is this? These kids are destroying the place, there's girls blackout drunk." It wasn't cool. It was just such a foreign thing to the genesis of our world. It was more like a Jersey Shore experience, literally and figuratively.

CHRISTIAN MCKNIGHT: At that point, we realized how big it was and how big all the bands that were loyal to the festival were. The festival got too large. We needed to find a bigger space. It was John D'Esposito's vision to move the festival to Giants Stadium at the Meadowlands eventually, and that's where we went the next year.

SHANE TOLD: And then of course Warped Tour that summer . . .

MATT GALLE: My Chemical Romance and Fall Out Boy played Warped Tour, and it was massive.

PETE WENTZ: That summer it went totally supersonic. One minute we weren't famous and the next minute, we're famous.

SHANE TOLD: Fall Out Boy was probably booked for '05 Warped in like, October of '04, so the band wasn't that big yet.

KEVIN LYMAN: In 2004, My Chemical Romance and Fall Out Boy came out for part of the Warped Tour, and I really saw the transition to this music. I went to Fall Out Boy and My Chemical Romance and offered them $2,500 a show for the following summer. I never booked that early, but I thought maybe I could get a good buy, because I saw the energy coming. They both confirmed for the next year. In 2004, I think I was paying them $500 a show. So giving them a 500 percent raise going into the next year was a pretty big jump for the economics of Warped Tour.

KATE TRUSCOTT: Kevin always says that 2005 was the year Warped was almost crushed under its own weight. That's the only year that Warped has ever made money on tickets alone.

KEVIN LYMAN: When we turned a profit, it was typically off sponsorships and merchandise.

In 2005, we sold about 740,000 tickets, our biggest number ever. Throughout the years, Warped Tour averaged around 500,000 kids. So a quarter of a million extra kids came out this summer to hear those hits.

KATE TRUSCOTT: It was largely because *TRL* was the biggest thing in the world and those emo bands were starting to get airplay. My Chem and Fall Out Boy were in the top ten countdown that summer.

MIKEY WAY: To us, that was something reserved for boy bands. Blink-182 had invaded *TRL*, which was cool, but it didn't seem possible that somehow both us and Fall Out Boy did it. *And* we were on the same tour, you know what I mean?

PETE WENTZ: When "Sugar, We're Goin Down" went to number one on *TRL*, we went to a water park in New Mexico. That was the celebration. There was this big dichotomy . . . our bus didn't even have air-conditioning.

KEVIN LYMAN: The audience coming to Warped Tour transformed from that hardcore person who was out skating or going to the beach to a crowd that was watching TV all summer. We managed to get them off their couches for one day! But they weren't ready to be in the sun for nine hours. They would stand in front of the stages all day long waiting for those hit songs. It wasn't like you could just come, watch those bands and leave; you were there the whole day. By the time the band went onstage, these people hadn't eaten, hadn't drank water, hadn't put sunscreen on, so many of them just collapsed. Our medical tents were full.

BUDDY NIELSEN: You had the new bands and the old Warped Tour bands, like the Dropkick Murphys, the Offspring . . .

KEVIN LYMAN: Dropkick Murphys were probably the highest-paid band on that year's tour. Them and the Offspring were probably both making $15,000 to $17,000 per show.

JONAH BAYER: Fall Out Boy and My Chemical Romance were kindred spirits, in a way. But I also think that now we have the advantage of hindsight, knowing those bands stood the test of time. Back then, you didn't know how things were going to shake out. There were so many hyped bands where you could say, "*This* is going to be the band . . ."

BUDDY NIELSEN: Senses Fail was really big into our career. Underoath played the side stage. You throw in Thrice, the All-American Rejects . . .

JONAH BAYER: The All-American Rejects were another band that had a lot of mainstream success.

NICK WHEELER: Our second album, *Move Along*, came out in July of 2005, so we were on Warped Tour when it got released. "Dirty Little Secret" hadn't taken off yet.

MIKE KENNERTY: We were playing "Dirty Little Secret," "Move Along," and the big songs from the first record, like "Swing, Swing." We were really proud of "Move Along" and thought it should be the first single. And Jimmy Iovine was insistent on "Dirty Little Secret."

JEFF SOSNOW: I thought "Move Along" should be the first single. I sat and talked to Jimmy Iovine about it and he said, "Sosnow, do you want to have a good summer?" And I said sure. And he said, "Well, 'Dirty Little Secret' is the first single." You don't really argue with that guy.

MIKE KENNERTY: Sosnow told us there were these meetings where Jimmy was yelling at their radio people about "Dirty Little Secret," going, "THIS IS A FUCKING HIT, MAKE IT A FUCKING HIT."

BUDDY NIELSEN: Hawthorne Heights were also fucking massive at that point.

J. T. WOODRUFF: We were on a rocket, trying not to fall off. That's the only way I can describe it. Within a year and a half, we signed to Victory, released our first album, and were on the main stage of Warped Tour. We'd never played any Warped Tour show before 2005. Not even a local stage. It was the first time we'd ever had our own tour bus.

The tour started in Columbus, Ohio—one hour from our house. So the tour bus picks us up, and we're not hanging out in the front lounge or the back lounge, we're laying in our bunks to drive an hour. It was hilarious. And while we're laying there, I get a call from the label: "Hey, your album just went gold."

PETE WENTZ: One day you get off the bus to brush your teeth and you're a normal person. And then the next day . . .

J. T. WOODRUFF: It's like when you tell your parents, "Hey, I'm going to go try and do this band," and they're like, "What a dumbass. Dude, please go to college and maybe do the band for fun." This is the moment where you could actually look them in the eyes and say, "I was right. You were wrong."

HAYLEY WILLIAMS: The first time we got offered Warped Tour [in 2005], I'd been waiting. Never attended, was too young, wasn't allowed.

SHIRA YEVIN: I was on the tour in 2003, working for the Truth campaign as an emcee. I noticed there were very few, if any, females onstage. I didn't understand why. I lived in Brooklyn at the time, and was friends with all sorts of all-girl punk and hardcore bands. My band approached Kevin in 2004. He said, "Okay, great idea, maybe next year. It's the tour's tenth anniversary, we got a lot going on." I said, "Next year?!"

KEVIN LYMAN: Shira's from New Jersey, so you know how progressive people from New Jersey won't take no for an answer.

SHIRA YEVIN: We ended up crashing the tour. I drove in with my pink RV and just set up—super scrappy punk rock. Kevin walked by and loved it: "Shira, this is great. So are you on for the whole tour now?" 2005 was the year we made it legit. His team helped us get sponsorships for the stage. MySpace was our media partner. We hand-painted their logo on our truck. We did the whole application process for the Shiragirl Stage through MySpace. In the 2005 music scene, MySpace was a big platform for how new artists came up. The Dollyrots played that year and were amazing. L7's bassist Jennifer Finch had this side project called the Shocker—it was really cool to have them on Shiragirl. They repped old-school Warped.

LESLIE SIMON: I remember seeing Paramore on Warped Tour that year. They played the Shiragirl Stage.

HAYLEY WILLIAMS: I did not know how toxic that world could be. The pop-punk and emo scene in the early 2000s. It was brutally misogynistic. A lot of internalized sexism, and even when you were lucky enough to meet other bands who were kind and respectful, there was other shit that wasn't. And I was really feisty. We got offered Warped tour, and there was a caveat: "It's a stage called the Shiragirl Stage. It's all female." I was pissed! I wanted to qualify for a real stage. When I've been offered female opportunities, it feels like a backhanded compliment. But people sometimes think that's anti-feminist, that I don't wanna be grouped in with the girls. As a sixteen-year-old who had dreams of playing with the big boys, it felt like we were being slighted.

JAMIE COLETTA: The Shiragirl Stage was this tiny, little stage on a truck. I remember it being super far away, off in a corner, the farthest back you could possibly be. Nobody was going to accidently walk by this stage. There wasn't even a crowd, dude. Their record *All We Know Is Falling* came out a couple weeks before and I knew all the words. I wish I had footage of that; I was going nuts in a crowd of nobody. That was my jam, I knew it from that moment. After they played, I went up and I got my record signed by the band.

HAYLEY WILLIAMS: The stage was a truck that had a flatbed on it. It was so flimsy it would shake and fall apart. There might have been one other female in a band [on tour], and people were gawking. I don't think in a pervy way. They were confused, like, *What's in this for me? What's she singing about? I'm a guy—how do I relate?*

MARIA SHERMAN: She was subjected to this environment that was not very welcoming to women . . . It's interesting to watch how she performs bodily, even early on. You would see her do the thing where one leg is bent up on a monitor and the other one is stretched out; it's like, manspreading onstage, right? Which is something Warped guys would do when they're headbanging or whatever. It's not a conventionally feminine way to perform. As this tiny, powerful woman, she was sort of mimicking what dudes were doing, occupying space that way.

SPENCER CHAMBERLAIN: Zac was playing the drums so hard that he broke the drum riser.

LESLIE SIMON: You're on asphalt with the sun reflecting onto you . . . One of the times I saw Paramore that summer, the drummer Zac Farro passed out from heat exhaustion. Just dipped out one day and fell over. He was like a wilted piece of lettuce.

HANIF ABDURRAQIB: In Cleveland, Paramore played through a storm. I mean, it really stormed—tents were blowing all over the place. Paramore was the only band that kept playing through it.

Early Paramore was like a whirlwind. They were a mess. An entertaining and very good mess—"Pressure" is a phenomenal song and *All We Know Is Falling* is a fun album to listen to—but seeing Paramore live off that album? They were a mess. But they were so fun to watch. They gave off this vibe of, "If they can do it, we can do it."

SHIRA YEVIN: Hayley was just one of the guys. That was sort of her thing. She wore the same T-shirt every day, the red and blue striped shirt she wears in the "All We Know" video. She was very sweet, polite, very reserved. No makeup. Just came on, did her set, went back in the van, read her book. It was a little bit of a culture shock for us. We were these radical feminist punk rock riot grrrls. They were a very reserved band. They prayed before they went onstage. They kinda kept to themselves, but they killed it onstage.

LESLIE SIMON: I don't have a huge memory of Paramore being around. They were all very young. Hayley's dad was around, helping manage them. So they were insulated. Josh and Zac, at the time, were very religious. They were straight arrows.

JONAH BAYER: Their mom or dad was there and they had Wi-Fi in their van, because they were all finishing school on the road. And at that point having Wi-Fi in a van was pretty unheard of.

SPENCER CHAMBERLAIN: [The year] '05 was the first Warped Tour with From First to Last. Underoath had taken them on their first tour with Sonny Moore, so we were already buddies.

MIKE KENNERTY: Sonny was so fucking tiny. He was seventeen. He was like a fucking troll doll. He hung out with us a bunch. Very talkative, super-nice kid.

BUDDY NIELSEN: This was when Wes Borland was in From First to Last. That blew my mind. Why the hell is a guy from Limp Bizkit here? I remember hanging out with Sonny and giving him a hard time, as a joke.

SPENCER CHAMBERLAIN: They used to come to our tour bus to play *Halo*. Sonny Moore's *Halo* name was Skrillex.

AARON GILLESPIE: He was having trouble with his voice back then.

MIKE KENNERTY: He put himself through torture with his voice for that band, having to deal with surgeries.

SPENCER CHAMBERLAIN: He was such a sweetheart, and he had a lil' personality on him, too. He would ask me, "How do you guys sing every night?"

BUDDY NIELSEN: Warped '05 was two months long. I mean, we fucking played Quebec City. There were *three* Eastern Canada shows. There was a real sense of, "Yo, we're goin' big." Every day was a show . . . Between July 28 and August 15, there were no days off. Nineteen days with no day off.

SPENCER CHAMBERLAIN: A band—who we won't name—needed money. We let them borrow money and they all came back with new clothes and tattoos.

AARON GILLESPIE: Oh my god, that's right! They were struggling on the tour . . .

SPENCER CHAMBERLAIN: They were struggling with something else. But we can't say, because people might know. They went to the Christian band, knowing we'd be giving.

AARON GILLESPIE: Did we give them a bunch of money or a little bit?

SPENCER CHAMBERLAIN: A bunch.

BUDDY NIELSEN: I made some political statements about the Marines recruiting at Warped Tour. Especially given the nature of the Iraq War, I thought it was not tasteful. And I remember hearing noise that one of the dudes from Dropkicks wanted to fight me because I said the Marines should not be at Warped Tour. I think he had just had a conversation with a fan who was injured in Iraq, so he felt what I said was an insult to the people who were serving. And I was like, "No, I just don't think they should be here recruiting young impressionable kids at a punk show." I went and explained myself and that was it. And then someone from a band like Anti-Flag would come over and be like, "Hey, man, you're doing the right thing." So I definitely had older bands molding my ideas, but also trying to keep me in check.

SHANE TOLD: The success of My Chem, Fall Out Boy, and the other young bands put a bit of a . . . what's the word . . . It split up the vibe. The punk rockers thought, "What is this kind of music even doing on Warped Tour?"

KATE TRUSCOTT: We had to call a doctor because Frankie thought his sinuses were bleeding. He'd do those red Xs over his eyes. The doctor looked at it and was like, "You don't happen to wear makeup onstage, do you?"

AARON GILLESPIE: I remember My Chem complaining about how hot they were because they were wearing all that shit. In Phoenix it was like 110 degrees and they were wearing all that makeup. But people loved it. Kids were dressed up in that stuff at Warped, just makeup melting everywhere, all summer.

KATE TRUSCOTT: I did my best to air out My Chem's show clothes, but that level of smell doesn't really come out. And you can't wash a bulletproof vest. I remember hanging them all up on a fence and Febrezing them until my hands cramped. We couldn't hang the costumes everywhere because then kids would know that that was their bus and then they wouldn't leave us alone. Like, I got a lot of hate for working for them. Girls would stand on top of those concourses when they were getting on and off the bus and I got yelled at because they assumed I was someone's girlfriend.

I'd be working in the venue and then someone would come up to me like, "Whose girlfriend are you? I fuckin' hate you," and they lift up their shirt and show me the tattoos of the lyrics they had like, under their boobs. And I was just like, "What am I doing here?!"

KEVIN LYMAN: A lot of merchandise was being sold.

KATE TRUSCOTT: I was selling so many different things for My Chem: five black T-shirts, one red T-shirt, one white T-shirt. And then like three hoodies. Belts and ties . . . Frankie used to wear the gloves with bones on them and he would cut the fingers off, so we sold those gloves. I used to carry scissors around on my belt and cut the fingers off the gloves so that the kids would buy them. Kids would buy one of everything.

J. T. WOODRUFF: Hawthorne Heights had an "Ohio Is for Lovers" shirt. That was by far our biggest seller that year. We could not keep them in stock.

BUDDY NIELSEN: Everyone's paying in cash. We didn't have machines to take credit cards. Kids didn't have credit cards. The amounts of cash the bands would have to deal with after a show . . . For Senses Fail we're talking $20,000. And multiply that times two or three for the bigger bands.

J. T. WOODRUFF: Our record that year was $40,000, at a massive show in Detroit. And we did thirty-five grand at a show in Denver.

KATE TRUSCOTT: My Chemical Romance's highest day was $60,000, which to my knowledge, is a record that's yet to be beaten by any band on Warped. It was in Detroit, a thirty-thousand-person show at the Silverdome.

BUDDY NIELSEN: Some of the stories I heard about My Chem and the amount of cash they had on their tour bus . . .

KATE TRUSCOTT: I would have these gallon ziplock bags with names of cities written on them in Sharpie: "Scranton," "Dallas," "New York," whatever. If you've ever seen gallon bags with bricks of weed, it was just like that, only with cash. We figured out that we could lift up the cushion of the U-shaped couch in our back lounge, and we'd just fill it with the cash.

J. T. WOODRUFF: You had to get rid of the cash. People would think we were drug dealers. We're like, "Nah, we're an emo band, sorry. The moment's really firing now, we gotta do our emo cash drops."

BUDDY NIELSEN: I don't think people who haven't toured understand what it's like to carry that kind of money. You'd have to go to the bank with thousands of dollars in cash and just deposit it. And some of these Warped Tours were in amphitheaters, like thirty miles from the nearest bank.

KATE TRUSCOTT: Nineteen days in a row with no days off . . .

BUDDY NIELSEN: If you don't drop it off for a few days, you're gonna have hundreds of thousands of dollars.

JOSHUA CAIN: I had to walk through New York City with something like $120,000 in a backpack.

KATE TRUSCOTT: Occasionally, I would go on the bus, take over the back lounge, and organize money. And what I didn't know was that the boys used to watch porn—this was mostly the crew—the boys used to watch porn during the day on the bus. The way that it worked was whatever you wanted to watch in your bunk you had to put on in the back lounge. And then you could watch it in your bunk on the little TVs. So I go in the bus, and there's porn happening in the background, but I don't have time to care. I don't know how to change the channel, so I just leave it. At some point, one of the guys opened the door and was like, "You're sitting in the back lounge, covered in money, watching porn."

J. T. WOODRUFF: It seemed like there weren't enough stages for how big every band was getting. Underoath was on the second stage when Underoath easily could have been a main stage band.

JOSHUA CAIN: Motion City Soundtrack was playing a side stage, called the Maurice Stage, every day. Then at one point, Maurice—this weird, sun-baked man who managed the stage—would look at the crowd and hold us back from going on. Calmly in this soft voice he'd be like, "No, no, no. We need more security."

KATE TRUSCOTT: I was selling merch out of a ten-foot-by-ten-foot tent. The crowd would push into it, start crushing into us. I had to get up on the table a couple times and say nobody was getting anything until everybody calmed down. There was a day in Camden, New Jersey—the site was too small for the crowd there—I had to stand on my table and wave down security because kids were moshing and throwing themselves inside our tent.

LESLIE SIMON: Fan clubs were really active at this point. Fall Out Boy was Overcast Kids and My Chemical Romance had the MCRmy.

JONAH BAYER: We'd do signings at the *Alternative Press* booth: Fall Out Boy one day, My Chem the next day. Both of those bands got huge amounts of kids and we'd have to cut off the line. Fall Out Boy had this membership card for their fan club. I remember this kid coming up to me after we cut off the line like, "I'm an Overcast Kid!" I was like, "Oh . . . are you okay? You're feeling overcast?" I thought they were going through some kind of problem.

KATE TRUSCOTT: The My Chem superfan wanted to like, be in the band; they wanted to be close to it and share those feelings. The Fall Out Boy superfans, to me, wanted to sleep with someone in the band. It was a much more sexually charged thing. If My Chem fans wanted to be the band, Fall Out Boy fans wanted to fuck the band.

MANI MOSTOFI: I remember girls just screaming at Pete as he walked by. We were on the edges of Warped Tour; there's a fence, which is like the de facto backstage. These girls—and I mean girls, these people were not eighteen yet—were trying to reach through the chain-link fences to touch him. I just remember thinking, "This whole thing is hilarious." It wasn't entirely surprising, because he was always appreciated by women. Like, Pete never had trouble with women, like ever, ever, ever, ever, ever. It didn't matter if he was this nobody kid wearing a death metal shirt or the reigning prince of mall emo. I'm not surprised he became this teen sex symbol, because in some ways, he kind of already was, on a very local level. But it was funny to watch at that scale. I know to him, it was funny.

BUDDY NIELSEN: This was the first year I saw people walking around with bodyguards. When this scene blew up, all the straight-edge dudes that were in hardcore bands became bodyguards for these guys, because they were all big and jacked. It wasn't like you're worrying you're going to get shot, it was because they would get mobbed. It was like, "We have to get Pete to the stage, how do we get through the crowd?" My Chem would never make it to the stage if Gerard had to walk through the crowd.

AL BARR: Fall Out Turds and My Chemical Shit Pants—that's what we called them—were both blowing up, and I kept going around Warped Tour the whole day going, "Jesus Christ, this singer must be so tired because he sings for every band!" Because it all sounded the same to an old-timer like me. But that's when I realized I sound like my dad! Those bands? Not my cup of tea at all. But they were working their asses off, just like we did, and nothing was handed to them. They worked for everything they got.

BUDDY NIELSEN: I always thought that was interesting—how do people deal with the fame?

MIKE KENNERTY: I can think of one dude on 2005 Warped whose MO all day was to try to find chicks. Like, "Who's next?" It seemed like, for most people, if there were tour hookups, it was normal, post-show hanging out with some girl for a while and then they hook up. Nothing that seemed predatory or out of the ordinary. I feel like it was the next generation of Warped Tour bands after us, where there was more of trying to revive this *real rock star* attitude. But one drummer of one specific band . . . Man, that dude. I saw him one time get off the bus, kiss a chick goodbye, and then he pulled out his Sidekick and just looked at everyone and goes, "Next?" And then started texting somebody else.

BUDDY NIELSEN: I think people on Warped through the social media years later on might've thought their fame was bigger than it was. Whereas back in '05, it's like, "Your video's on MTV or Fuse? Cool, everybody's is. Fuse is here interviewing everyone." Yes, there were bands that were bigger and doing better, but it wasn't just two bands that were doing well. It was, like, twenty bands.

JAMIE COLETTA: I'm sure I watched almost all of the big bands, but that Paramore set was the most pivotal thing that year for me.

LESLIE SIMON: Hayley had buzz, Paramore had buzz . . .

HANIF ABDURRAQIB: Paramore was one of those things where if you were plugged into the rumor mill, you were excited to see them. People were talking.

LESLIE SIMON: You could be on your way to get a lemonade and a fifteen-dollar pretzel . . . Hayley starts singing and you stop, turn, and go right towards the voice. So they gained a lot of momentum through . . . not even word of mouth . . . *word of ears*. You couldn't listen to her and not be struck by how this powerful voice was coming out of this teeny, tiny person. They earned their stripes on the Shiragirl Stage. That stage was not for the faint of heart. Afternoon times going up against big bands is tough. But they dominated. They moved up [to the Hurley and Volcom Stages] the next year.

MIKEY WAY: I remember Pete telling me on Warped Tour: "Yo, I found this band. They're gonna be huge."

I met Panic! at the Vegas Warped Tour date. They were young. Super sweet. Pete was like, "Hey, can you meet these guys, they love you, you're one of their favorite bands."

BUDDY NIELSEN: There'd be twenty thousand people at each show and afterwards, two or three thousand would wind up getting backstage. You weren't as worried about five thousand people partying at the end of the night—epic bonfire parties with every band and also people that found a way to stay. If you stayed long enough, security left, so . . .

JOSHUA CAIN: I remember hanging out with Leslie Simon and Mike Kennerty a lot, walking around at the barbecues, just gossiping about what boys people like and don't like, just everything, ha, ha. 'Cause Leslie worked for *AP* and interviewed all these big bands and she would come out on Warped Tour for the *AP* tent and hang out all summer.

LESLIE SIMON: You're waiting in line for the shower or catering, or you're at a bonfire. There's so many opportunities to meet people you never would have met. That's where a lot of relationships between bands started and evolved: "Hey, do you wanna come up during my set?"

PETE WENTZ: Joe had to leave Warped Tour for a show and Ray from My Chem filled in on guitar. We didn't practice or anything, Ray was just supersmart and musically gifted.

MIKEY WAY: I would play a song with Fall Out Boy almost every day. At the end of their set, during "Saturday," Pete would throw the bass to me and he would jump in the crowd with the microphone.

PETE WENTZ: Mikey's who I knew the best from My Chem. I got to know Gerard later, but I've always been really close with Mikey. We had similar taste in eighties nostalgia. I remember we were talking and he referenced Fruit Brute, which is one of the Count Chocula characters no one really knew.

MIKEY WAY: While either of us played, we had to stop like ten times in the middle of the set because of crowd avalanches. We would have to stop our songs like, "Hey, everyone pick each other up." And then we'd have to go, "All right, we're gonna start on the second chorus," and have the drummer count in. It happened every day.

J. T. WOODRUFF: We're all supposed to be on the same playing field, but Patrick Stump's basically a pop singer and My Chem's really theatrical with these wonderful outfits. I'm just this hack from Ohio, trying to keep up.

MIKEY WAY: Us and Fall Out Boy had gotten really close because we had an understanding of what was happening to the other, you know what I mean?

KEVIN LYMAN: They were working on *The Black Parade* on their bus.

KATE TRUSCOTT: I remember being in my top bunk, right up against the wall to their studio, and they were doing vocals for "I Don't Love You." I heard Gerard singing, "I don't love you like I did yesterday." I opened the door and said, "That's fucking brutal."

JUSTIN COURTNEY PIERRE: Gerard and I were both sober. We were both excited about Coke Zero, which was this new thing: "It's better than Diet Coke, but you gotta drink it fast because it loses its fizz faster!" That's what I remember about Gerard that summer, Coke Zero and him drawing comics.

BRANDEN STEINECKERT: Gerard sobering up was one of the most empowering things he could have done. The moment he did that, the creativity of the band really kicked into gear.

KATE TRUSCOTT: Gerard used to get into his own head about stuff, but like, that's just how he was. And he wasn't a shithead about it . . . You don't come up with the things he's come up with by being supernormal all the time, you know?

TYSON RITTER: You'd stroll this alley of buses and see Gerard doing a sketch in front of the headlights on the ground in front of his bus. He was too shy to talk to the group, but he could still sit out in front of his bus drawing a piece of art, which I thought was so fun. He would get in front of the headlights and show off his talent.

KATE TRUSCOTT: Gerard was writing *The Umbrella Academy* back then. So now to see that come to life is so cool. I remember seeing him doing those drawings and talking about the butler monkey and being like, "I don't understand what you're saying, but that's okay!"

KEVIN LYMAN: He'd go sit under a tree, or on one of those cement parking curves with his sketchbook out. There's always a party on Warped Tour. There's always a barbecue, there's always drinking. Maybe that's why he seemed to be reflecting into himself.

JOHN FELDMANN: When Gerard got sober, he probably separated himself from people that were in the party zone.

BERT MCCRACKEN: We kind of had a falling-out.

STEVEN SMITH: It got all weird at a House of Blues Warped event in LA.

QUINN ALLMAN: Bert's alcoholism was peaking. My Chem's career was starting to take off and everyone around them was like, "No, we have to protect them. Bert's not going to get in here and take away Gerard's sobriety."

JEPH HOWARD: I was there when it happened. I was going backstage to say hi to everybody and then My Chem's manager just pushed me out and closed the door.

QUINN ALLMAN: Schechter was like, "Nah, dude, you can't be back here."

BERT MCCRACKEN: Different paths, different times . . .

QUINN ALLMAN: Very shortly after that, Bert was carrying that grudge. Like, disgustingly holding that against Gerard. I think he went on Warped Tour and had a megaphone saying like, "Don't watch these guys," while My Chem was playing. When he drinks, he's a fucking monster. And no one knows that monster better than me. *No one.*

LESLIE SIMON: My Chem and Fall Out Boy ended up being the frontrunners of this marathon.

MIKE KENNERTY: One specific thing I can picture from that summer—I can't remember what city it was—but My Chem and Fall Out Boy were playing the main stage, back-to-back. I'd seen a million shows, but this was really fucking something: the crowd-surfing, the energy. It was the biggest crowd I'd ever seen on Warped Tour.

LESLIE SIMON: They had these parallel rises to fame. But they had such different aesthetics. There were still people who were either Team Fall Out Boy or Team My Chem: Do you like pop with a side of screamo, or do you like pop with a side of goth?

MATT GALLE: I know they knew each other and were friendly but I don't think they had a big, strong relationship. I don't think there was any dislike between the two bands, but they just weren't as close. They were on the Warped Tour together, but there's so many bands on the Warped Tour.

LESLIE SIMON: Were they friendly during touring? A hundred percent. They didn't go out of their way to not be around each other. I just don't recall deep ties for Gerard and Pete. Yes, Mikey and Pete were close. Joe and Mikey were close. Andy kind of did his own thing. At this time, Andy was sober and Pete was sober-ish. And Gerard was sober, but My Chem was not, so there were just different interests. Like, pick your poison. For some it was drugs and alcohol and for some it was girls. It depended on the day, and on the band.

PETE WENTZ: That VMA award came up [and] it really did feel like it was between us and My Chem. They had done fan voting on this award [the MTV2 Award].

PATRICK STUMP: We were nominated for a fan-voted award . . . We weren't nominated in any other category. So we were like, "It's neat that we're here."

MIKEY WAY: That night was important. That 2005 VMAs, that was kind of the beginning of it all. Us and Fall Out Boy, we had just done Warped Tour prior to that.

PETE WENTZ: We'd only seen the VMAs on TV before this. The VMAs were massive at the time.

PATRICK STUMP: That was the day before Hurricane Katrina. It was one of the first times they'd done the VMAs in Miami. It was starting to rain. We were opening the preshow outdoor stage; it was us and Rihanna, before she really popped off. It poured all day, every day for the rehearsals and we thought they might cancel our performance, but then, in true MTV fashion, the minute they go live, it's dry and we play.

JAMES MONTGOMERY: They did "Sugar, We're Goin Down" right after Rihanna [performed "Pon de Replay"].

PATRICK STUMP: And then we went to our seats inside and watched the whole show. I think we sat in front of the Black Eyed Peas. The whole thing felt very nineties Disney movie, where some random kid gets plucked from obscurity.

PETE WENTZ: They performed "Helena" in the main show and had a pretty crazy performance, with a dancer.

MIKEY WAY: Puff Daddy announced us, and Kelly Clarkson had just done her performance where she had rain coming down . . . it's starting to come back to me now . . .

PATRICK STUMP: MTV was like, "Okay My Chem's gonna win this." There is just one cameraman, and they're on My Chem. We weren't on. When they're reading off the nominees, we're not on camera. They announced us as the winner. The cameraman's like, "Oh no!" He comes running over and we're all surprised. No one wrote a speech.

ALEX SARTI: When Fall Out Boy won the VMA, the first ones they thanked in their speech were My Chem. It was almost like they both won, because they were the two scene bands nominated.

MIKEY WAY: We were both rooting for each other. We had just been in the trenches on Warped Tour.

PETE WENTZ: When we won that VMA, it was one of those moments . . . It was one of those documented moments where I really felt in it with My Chem, you know? When I see pictures of us hugging and stuff, I think that's pretty fucking cool.

ANDY GREENWALD: I think they genuinely liked each other. And they felt very connected because of their ride on this roller coaster. This was a time when their agendas lined up.

MATT GALLE: My Chem were nominated for five VMAs that night. And they didn't win any of them. Billie Joe Armstrong said to My Chem, "Don't worry guys, we were nominated a lot our first year and we didn't win, either."

ANDY GREENWALD: The Fall Out Boy/My Chem thing is so interesting because they knew each other very well. But they always looked at each other a little bit sideways, because they thought of each other as competition. And I think they both . . . they would *never* say it—never say it on the record in any real way—but I think they were both deeply skeptical of the other. They were supportive but I think they were watching each other as competitors. And as benchmarks.

"PANIC! *AT THE* DISCO *WAS* LIKE POURING GASOLINE *ON THE* FIRE"

SPENCER SMITH: "Sugar, We're Goin Down" was big on MTV and radio. Fall Out Boy had broken, and so had My Chem. But it was still this magic in-between time where it felt like summer camp.

ROB HITT: Fall Out Boy came in and said, "It's going in this direction now, you're gonna follow us." They started something new. And they kept it going with Panic! at the Disco.

MATT SQUIRE: Fall Out Boy was really hoping for another successful artist to launch.

ADAM SAMILJAN: I remember emails going around Fueled By Ramen with Pete, John Janick, Johnny Minardi—everyone talking about these Panic! at the Disco songs . . .

MATT SQUIRE: "Time to Dance," "Nails for Breakfast," and "Relax, Relapse."

JASON TATE: The original chatter about Panic! on AbsolutePunk.net was that they were a Fall Out Boy rip-off. Like, of course, "Pete Wentz is signing another band that sounds exactly like his lead singer." And nobody wanted to engage on anything besides that.

MATT SQUIRE: The guys in Panic! were conscious about just being Fall Out Boy–lite. They didn't want to be looked at like that. But at the same time, Fall Out Boy was their favorite band.

SPENCER SMITH: *A Fever You Can't Sweat Out* was all about timing. Pete met us, the release date was set, and we knew we were going to record a couple weeks after graduating high school. We had been listening to bands like Fall Out Boy and Taking Back Sunday, but in the middle of that writing process, we started listening to stuff outside that world.

BOB MCLYNN: Brendon was seventeen when we started managing them. We had to get his parents to sign off on the contract. I think he was eighteen by the time the album came out. They were all teenagers.

JASON TATE: With a lot of help from their producer Matt Squire, they sounded polished and radio-ready immediately. That was such a rarity.

MATT SQUIRE: I had just produced a record called *Between the Heart and the Synapse* by a band called the Receiving End of Sirens. Its impact was smaller, but it was a record that bands really dug. It was an incredible learning experience for me with wrapping my head around programming [electronics and computer software]. Panic! reached out to me, but they had concerns I wouldn't know how to program. So I put Panic! on the phone with the Receiving End of Sirens, and they convinced them to record with me. All of this was so small, none of us knew what it was like to sell records. We were just having fun and trying to get our names on AbsolutePunk.net.

SCOTT NAGELBERG: They finished their last high school final. They didn't go to graduation; they got in a van and drove from Vegas to College Park, Maryland, where they made the record with Matt Squire on a very generous budget of $10,000—$11,000, if you include mixing.

MATT SQUIRE: It was like, "If you don't master by this date, then the Panic! guys can't go on the Nintendo Fusion Tour with Fall Out Boy in the fall." This was dictated to me every single day by Crush and Fueled By Ramen. We only had three and a half weeks to make the record.

SPENCER SMITH: Matt's studio was in Maryland, so we drove out from Vegas. We probably bought some of our gear at Guitar Center on the way out of town.

MATT SQUIRE: I told them to go set up in my live room, and I got on the phone, chilling, as producers do. I'm looking out into the live room, and they'd kind of set up some stuff, but they were all stuck. They kind of set up the drums, but no cymbals. They're all mystified, standing around one of those rack tuners they had on top of the bass amp, trying to figure out how to get the rack tuner patched into the amp. I'm watching this whole thing thinking, "Dude, it's a rack tuner. You plug the one cord here, the one cord out there, come on." It was a brand-new rack tuner they'd just taken out of the box. Like, "Why don't they have gear? What is this?" I remember hanging up my one call, calling up Scott Nagelberg, and being like, "Dude, I forgot to ask you, have these guys ever played a show before?" And he says, "No, why?" I was like, "Never mind!"

SPENCER SMITH: We had no frame of reference. We were just doing it. Whatever seemed right.

JOHNNY MINARDI: They would talk about how heavily influenced they were lyrically by Third Eye Blind. In 2005, it was not cool to like Third Eye Blind. Scene bands were referencing Taking Back Sunday. They were not referencing Third Eye Blind. Panic! always marched to the beat of their own drum.

MATT SQUIRE: Ryan Ross and Brendon Urie were like Lennon and McCartney. Ryan wasn't the most proficient player, but he's a *writer*. If he got an idea he really believed in, he beat the fuck out of it, looked at every angle, until he was like, "Okay, I've got this one idea. I can't even play it, but this one idea will be huge." And Brendon is the kind of dude who can play anything. An oboe, a violin—put an instrument in this dude's hand and he'll just get it. He could interpret Ryan like *that*.

SPENCER SMITH: Ryan would write the lyrics first, which is a bit unusual. It's also why some of those lyrics are so unorthodox. We wrote vocal melodies around the lyrics. We weren't necessarily writing to have the syllables match up to the music.

MARIA SHERMAN: Brendon Urie can enunciate a three-dollar word with the best of them.

MATT SQUIRE: Pete collaborated with the guys on some lyrics. I don't know if any of that actually made it to the record, but there was definitely a dialogue between the band and Pete during the making of the album.

BRENDON URIE: Pete is such a smart lyricist, so he was always there to help out with a line here, a line there. We'd ask his opinion and he would tell us. That really helped.

ELLIE KOVACH: Ryan Ross was clearly mining a similar Chuck Palahniuk-influenced vein of lyricism—that wry, literate, darkly comedic take on things. I do think, in retrospect, Ryan Ross sounds a lot more theater kid than Pete Wentz, who sounds much more like he's trying to emulate gutter poetry on those early Fall Out Boy releases.

MATT SQUIRE: Ryan wrote those lyrics from the heart. His mom left while he was young and his dad was a Vegas card dealer who struggled with substance abuse real bad.

SPENCER SMITH: His dad drank a lot. I was probably over at Ryan's house just as much as my own growing up. Ryan was on a traveling hockey team, and his dad wanted him to go to college. When it was apparent that wasn't what Ryan was interested in, that did not go over well. It was a fractured, hostile relationship.

MATT SQUIRE: I think the hospital scene in "Nails For Breakfast, Tacks For Snacks" describes a real event where his dad was in the hospital.

BRENDON URIE: "London Beckoned for Songs About Money Written by Machines" came after we met with Pete and our management. They were explaining, "If this does take off, you will need to deal with webzines and interviews." It kind of irritated us, just to the point we wanted to relay, "If we're gonna do that, guess what—we're going to be your fucking wet dream."

MATT SQUIRE: They were making the long song titles and I was like, "That's the stuff that's gonna get you called out for being like Fall Out Boy . . ."

BRENDON URIE: We saw that Fall Out Boy had a couple song titles that were really long. We were like, "Oh, that's fun." We started doing it. Bands like Name Taken and a lot of the bands in the scene were doing cool stuff like that, so we took it a step further. Nobody had song titles that were as long as ours. A lot of it was just inside jokes. The song "I Constantly Thank God for Esteban" was from an infomercial for these guitars. It's such a shitty infomercial—a lady on there has one of the guitars and she's like, "I constantly thank god for Esteban!" So we wrote this song with Latin flavor, like, "Fuck yeah, we're using that."

MATT SQUIRE: "I Write Sins Not Tragedies" started off being called "Flam Chorus."

SPENCER SMITH: A flam on a drum is two notes right after each other. It was like, do-KAH, do-KAH-do, do-KAH—I do that in the bridge of the song, but that part started out in the first and second chorus.

MATT SQUIRE: I don't have all of Ryan's background on the lyrics, but I know that the "closing a goddamn door" line was about his parents or somebody fighting—like, "Yo, I can hear you!" That was a real moment. If I remember correctly, the wedding was a bit of storytelling.

I remember being against Brendon talking the verses, but being outvoted. Like, "Groom's bride is a . . ." I was like, "Dude, you sound goofy, man."

SPENCER SMITH: We needed to find a cello player to do the intro to "I Write Sins." The MIDI cellos don't sound very good.

MATT SQUIRE: Ryan was playing the intro on guitar. He's like, "Dude, it's way too metal. There's no way, right?" I was like, "What if we put it on another instrument?"

SPENCER SMITH: We needed the cello and a trumpet player, for another song. I think we asked John Janick for $500 and he said, "No, it's not in the budget." Matt either put ads on Craigslist or . . . knew somebody who knew high school band kids in Maryland? This girl showed up and played the "bump-bump-bump . . . bump-bump" for the "I Write Sins" intro.

MATT SQUIRE: The vaudeville stuff was kind of all they wanted to do.

SPENCER SMITH: If we had recorded three months earlier, *Fever* would have been a pop-punk record. And if it was recorded three months later, it would have just been musical theater.

MATT SQUIRE: They thought the hooks to their songs sounded too much like Fall Out Boy. So they would come in on an almost daily basis like, "We rewrote the chorus to 'Relax, Relapse.'" I'd be thinking they refined the hook or something like that, but it'd be something bizarre. Like, "Brendon's gonna go 'ba-duh, duh-da!' and then there's gonna be a clarinet!"

I would call the label like, "They wanna take the chorus out of that song," and they'd be like, "Dude, we need that song! We already have promo lined up on that song!" About forty-five minutes at the beginning of every session was me being like, "Yo, I have bands that would give a pinkie to be able to write a hook like that, you can't change it." So I said, "Why don't we do a theme to the record? The poppier tracks will be up front and the second half will be more where you're headed on record two."

SPENCER SMITH: We were just like, "This has to be a masterpiece."

MATT SQUIRE: Brendon sang all his low vocals, but he couldn't hit his high notes because his shit was fucked up. I was like, "Yo, we blew this kid's voice out in preproduction." Four days to deadline, I got on the phone with Crush and Fueled By Ramen: "Dude, it's not gonna happen. We don't have any high vocals and I have to mix the record. There's no time. I'm calling it, your deadline's fucked."

Then that day, Brendon came in, and somehow, he had his high register. It was around noon. I put him on a mic and said, "You're not leaving the booth until we're done with this album." He sang all the high vocals for the album in that one session, and I'm emailing Crush and Fueled By Ramen like, "Don't even breathe. I think we're gonna get it."

BRENDON URIE: Every song that we wrote for the first album made it. We didn't think about writing a bunch of songs and picking the best ones. We had to just make the best songs we ever wrote.

MATT SQUIRE: They weren't arranging their tunes and going, "Oh, that won't work. I could never sing that live. I can't play synth and bass and guitar at the same time." Panic! had no rules. It was like, "Yo, this song has sixty-four tracks. There's beats and I'm gonna play live drums and let's do some guitars. And some synths! And the vocal lines are going to overlap so it's humanly impossible to sing." That ignorance turned out to be really cool. They wouldn't have written that record if they'd been touring for two years.

PATRICK STUMP: I always wanted to do synthesizer stuff—on the cover of *Take This to Your Grave*, you can't see it, but I'm wearing a Faint shirt—

but synth stuff wasn't really acceptable at the time. I was also too scared to take risks, but Panic! just came out and did it.

MATT SQUIRE: Every day working on *Fever*, I'd be like, "Dude, you guys gotta play me those original demos Pete heard." Brendon and Ryan wouldn't play them for me. I was like, "I have to hear them." On the last day, they finally played me those GarageBand demos and they are . . . *Dude*. It's a mess. It's hilarious. It's beats all over the place and the vocals are super Auto-Tuned. I don't know how Pete heard through it. I just don't know.

PETE WENTZ: The first time they got onstage on the Nintendo Fusion Tour, their mics weren't working. I was like, "This is the greenest band ever."

ADAM SAMILJAN: Nintendo Fusion Tour was Panic! at the Disco, Boys Night Out, Motion City Soundtrack, the Starting Line, and Fall Out Boy. You look back at that bill now and it's pretty unbelievable. Especially how small Panic!'s name is at the bottom.

JOSHUA CAIN: They were some opening act we'd never heard of.

SPENCER SMITH: When we started to meet these other bands, it felt like when you're in high school and you see kids in college. They might only be two, three years older, and it feels like ten years.

ALEX SARTI: Panic! was only playing twenty, twenty-five minutes at the beginning of each show. *Fever* came out October 27, the day before the tour began. So kids only knew one or two songs from the internet at the start. And you know, the band wasn't very good.

HANIF ABDURRAQIB: They sounded like a band who spent a lot of time thinking of how the performance was going to look but not how the performance was going to sound.

PETE WENTZ: Before the Nintendo Fusion Tour, they were in basketball shorts and hats. Then they showed up the first day of the tour in these paisley suits.

BRENDON URIE: The first show we ever played was at my church. My mom said we could play because there was this youth dance. I grew up Mormon, and there's a dress code—you have to wear nice clothing. So I told the guys, "It'll be really fun, a lot of cute girls, and a lot of people our age, but we have to dress up. We have to wear suits and ties." That's where it started . . . We were super into the band Louis XIV and they were dressing so cool. We were fans of Vaudeville, Victorian-era dress and all that dapper stuff . . . We were showing up, like, "Look at this blazer I bought!"

SCOTT NAGELBERG: When Fall Out Boy took them out, they were always in character. They wouldn't take the suits off. They'd be driving in the van, ninety degrees outside, no AC, suits on.

SPENCER SMITH: Every band on that tour had a bus, except us. We were in a conversion van with a trailer for our gear.

ALEX SARTI: That tour was built for buses, not vans. It was two months and crisscrossed all over the country.

SPENCER SMITH: It was us pulling in with our ridiculous outfits at these venues where it's semi-truck, semi-truck, semi-truck, bus, bus, bus . . . then our little van.

ALEX SARTI: I can't imagine they were paid more than a couple hundred bucks for each show.

SPENCER SMITH: If you're on a bus and there's a twelve-hour drive through Texas one night, that's fine, because the band will be asleep and the driver's doing his thing. We only had one other dude—our friend who was selling merch—so we had to drive a lot of it ourselves. We would be the last band to show up, just trying to get there before whatever time our sound check was.

ALEX SARTI: Fall Out Boy was exploding and Pete was starting his clothing line, Clandestine. I flew out to Detroit to start the tour, selling merch for Clandestine. I did that for one and a half shows before the Fall Out Boy merch guy called them up saying he needed my help. I was selling like one-twentieth of what Fall Out Boy was selling and that guy was just getting pummeled.

We were in these clubs the tour was way too big for because it had been booked months in advance. We'd play an arena because they moved the show, and then we'd play a seven-hundred-cap room in Boise.

BRIAN DIAZ: They didn't have arena-level production. They just came up there with a backdrop and some amps to play arenas. It was this huge tour, but it still felt weirdly punk rock DIY. Speaking of DIY, we couldn't get their merch into Canada. It was maybe a three-thousand-cap concert and the merch guy for Starting Line got a bunch of white T-shirts, a Sharpie or a paint pen . . . The dudes from Fall Out Boy were back there writing "FALL OUT BOY, TORONTO" or whatever. They sold those shirts and, god, I wonder if anyone has those anywhere . . .

JOSHUA CAIN: In the middle of nowhere on a day off, near El Paso or something, Fall Out Boy was like, "We're all going to a water park!" I think all of us on tour went. People started noticing and following them around. Fall Out Boy was attracting the most attention.

ALEX SARTI: *From Under the Cork Tree* went platinum on that tour.

SPENCER SMITH: You're operating on three hours of sleep, but then you're going onstage, and each night, more and more kids knew the Panic! songs.

LESLIE SIMON: *A Fever You Can't Sweat Out* emerged from MySpace. Those songs were the autoplay songs on so many people's pages. Panic! didn't really come from a scene; the scene they came from was MySpace. That replaced the real-life corner hangout or garage band practice.

JOHNNY MINARDI: There weren't all these sales indicators to let you know what was going to happen back then; all we had to go off of was MySpace numbers, which didn't always translate.

Release day, I'm getting calls at 9:00 a.m. like, "We're already sold out on the East Coast." *What do you mean, your stores opened at seven?* "We're out. We need more." Then comes Central Time, and all the stores are blowing up our distributor. They're like, "You have to greenlight fifty thousand new copies right now."

RANDY NICHOLS: This was the real early days of internet music, looking at PureVolume plays. I was like, "Who's manipulating these numbers? There's no way this is real. This new little band can't possibly have these kinds of numbers."

ELLIE KOVACH: The stations in Vegas, specifically X107.5, I remember being really proud of Panic! and picking it up immediately.

ADAM SISKA: *Fever* came out while The Academy Is . . . was touring the UK, doing a small run of club shows. *Fever* did about ten thousand copies its first week. Jonathan from Crush was with us, and he was celebrating their success; we were happy for Panic! but also a little jealous to see our manager excited about these younger kids.

JOSHUA CAIN: I remember hearing they pressed ten thousand copies. And they sold them all. They literally sold out of their album immediately.

JUSTIN COURTNEY PIERRE: Someone in the band was like, "Oh, we sold this many records? Is that good?"

ALEX SARTI: Scalping was crazy on that tour because every show was sold out. The trajectory of Panic! at the Disco was like pouring gasoline on the fire of that tour.

ADAM SAMILJAN: I remember them sound-checking in St. Petersburg, Florida, and there were so many fans outside singing along.

ALEX SARTI: It was a mad rush to get in the buildings. Panic! was first and every kid knew it.

SPENCER SMITH: As naive and green as we were, what really fuckin' helped is how much of a natural-born performer Brendon is.

MATT SQUIRE: He's a theater kid. If anything was going wrong onstage, you couldn't read it on his face. He was just killing it.

ALEX SARTI: I felt bad for the bands playing after them.

KENNY VASOLI: I liked Brent the bass player a lot because he smoked weed. And he was really the only one from Panic! that would talk to me.

JOSHUA CAIN: We didn't really make friends with the Panic! dudes . . . They were in their own world. And they were also in a van. So I should cut them some slack. They were probably getting out of there as early as possible and driving as far as possible.

JUSTIN COURTNEY PIERRE: The members of Motion City, Starting Line, and Boys Night Out would hang out a lot.

KENNY VASOLI: I loved touring with Boys Night Out and Motion City Soundtrack. *Loved it.* And yeah, the crowds were really big. Fall Out Boy had passes that said, "ALL ACCESS." Everyone else on that tour had passes that said, "SUPPORT." This was the only time this had ever happened on any tour I've ever been on. And it's not like it was just a difference in the passes. That actually restricted you from being able to get your family backstage, being able to get in certain places during the day. It just made it unnecessarily complicated for us to be on that tour. And like, our records came out the same day. *From Under the Cork Tree* and *Based on a True Story*, you can look at the numbers, and you can see how much better Fall Out Boy did. It was meant to be a co-headlining tour between the two of us. And I'm not holding a chip on my shoulder because it wasn't—they obviously should have been headlining. But they could have also remembered where they came from and treated their colleagues as equals and not been fucking rock stars about it.

JOSHUA CAIN: I don't think it was meant as anything; it just came off as belittling and I think people got really upset about it.

KENNY VASOLI: We'd be like, "What's up, support?" We would always say shit like that in the beginning of the day.

JOSHUA CAIN: You could tell Panic! became a big band on that tour, because their attitudes changed. They went from being like, "Hey, we're the new guys," to like, "We should probably not be opening the tour." And rightfully so. They were probably bigger than all three of the middle bands by the end of that tour.

ALEX SARTI: Especially some of the bigger shows . . . I don't want to say the kids were kind of like "whatever" about Fall Out Boy, because that was not the case, but there was definitely the feeling of, "This is the next band. I want to be the first kid to be the Panic! fan. This is the new Fall Out Boy." Panic! was a tractor trailer going down a hill with no brakes.

JOSHUA CAIN: By the end of the tour, their record had been out for two months.

SPENCER SMITH: The reaction of the first show we played to the last was really different . . .

ALEX SARTI: The day before Thanksgiving was the last day of tour.

PETE WENTZ: Was that at a high school gym or something?

ALEX SARTI: That show was in New Jersey, in an arena at some high school. I'd never been to a show there before or after; it was probably one of those places where they had a smaller show booked and moved it to a bigger place.

SPENCER SMITH: In the early days of the band, we would live vicariously through DVDs of bands like the Early November and the Starting Line playing Skate and Surf: "Why doesn't something like this exist where we are?" This was our first real Jersey show.

PETE WENTZ: This was the show where, allegedly, Nick Jonas got busted in the bathroom . . . he was using insulin and there was some kind of security there that thought he was doing drugs.

PATRICK STUMP: After Midtown, I was like, "I don't want to do any of the pranks, I'm good. I don't want to make anybody mad . . ."

PETE WENTZ: We switched Panic!'s intro music . . .

ALEX SARTI: Panic! literally had an iPod they would hit play on, to play along with, for all the samples and drum machine sounds.

SPENCER SMITH: We had this intro thing that we made. The whole thing was probably super cinematic and theatrical.

PETE WENTZ: We switched their intro music to "Everybody (Backstreet's Back)" and thought it was going to be so funny.

People were just psyched, like, "This is awesome." The crowd was so psyched that Backstreet Boys was playing.

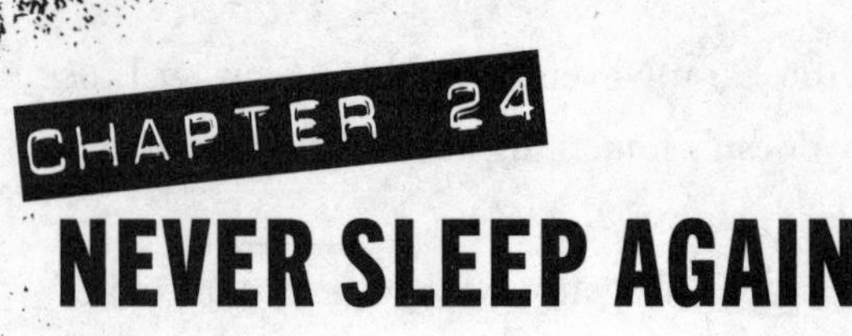

CHAPTER 24

NEVER SLEEP AGAIN

J. T. WOODRUFF: Bands were conditioned to think, "It's all about the gig, it's all about the show." We put ourselves in uncompromising situations to get on that stage.

ELLIE KOVACH: The B-tier of popularity, bands that were not quite MCR or Panic! . . . I feel like the emo scene of the early and mid-2000s was made up of a working class of musicians. People whose take-home pay was like, $24,000 a year, if they were lucky.

JOSHUA CAIN: How do we get to the next level? How do we keep this going? It always feels like it can fall out right under you.

Being in a band on tour is not good for your brain. You're away from your friends, you're away from your family, you're away from that structure.

ANTHONY GREEN: It took me five or six years of touring to learn that I could go to my agent and say, "Could we not play ten shows in a row?" I was having trouble with my voice. Davey Havok from AFI was the first person who was like, "Dude, you should tell your agent. You shouldn't be singing four nights in a row. The way you're singing, you should have a day off." I was like, "Really? I don't know if I can do that. It's gonna lose money . . ."

JOSHUA CAIN: In 2005, I'm pretty sure we played 260-plus shows. It was insane. We were just *in it*.

J. T. WOODRUFF: It's a culmination of all your dreams as a kid coming true.

We were growing at a faster rate than we could even imagine or handle. We were just trying to hang on for dear life. And it wasn't just us. The scene in general was just exploding.

EDDIE REYES: It's not the DIY scene with all your friends anymore. It becomes business and real life.

BUDDY NIELSEN: *Find young bands, prey on how they're willing to do anything to accomplish their dream*—that was a defining trait of a lot of the successful indie label owners in the scene.

Major labels didn't do that, to an extent; they had so much more capital, so much more history. It was really these indie labels that were running Ponzi schemes. There was a level of predatory-ness in that era of music.

MICHAEL GOLDSTONE: We've seen some of the most egregious contracts ever coming from indie spaces.

JEFF SOSNOW: There was a label in Chicago that had a lot of problems with lawsuits . . .

JASON TATE: Every band that has ever been on Victory Records has wanted to be off Victory Records—Taking Back Sunday, Thursday, Hawthorne Heights, Bayside . . .

ANTHONY RANERI: Bayside sold about half a million records there. Our publishing got a good amount of synchs on video games and TV shows. We sold a lot of merch. We never got a single royalty check.

J. T. WOODRUFF: I don't think we were getting any royalties.

SHANE TOLD: Six months after our first record came out, we got a publishing statement from Victory. It said we were owed money, but there was no check.

FRED MASCHERINO: Taking Back Sunday had a record go gold, well beyond gold, and it still didn't recoup, somehow. Meaning, we never got any money for it.

ANTHONY RANERI: You'd hear these stories about how Tony Brummel ran Victory: he owed a band, say, $10,000 in royalties and he didn't want to send it to them, so he'd go to the marketing department and say, "Spend $10,000 by Friday." That way, the band wouldn't be recouped. He'd rather spend the money on selling more records. He felt like giving the money to the band was like burning it.

GEOFF RICKLY: Being the bad guy worked out very well for him; when you're already the bad guy, what can anybody say about you?

ANTHONY RANERI: My first impression of Tony is still my impression of Tony—which is that he's a fucking maniac.

EDDIE REYES: Tony is a special person. That's about as far as I'm going to talk about that. He's a very unique human being. Not many like him.

JASON TATE: There's a reason Victory's logo was a bulldog. Tony wanted to be the bulldog.

ANTHONY RANERI: He looked like a soccer hooligan: Bic'd head, big guy wearing tight Fred Perry polos. An old-school skinhead hardcore guy. Super intimidating.

SHANE TOLD: I later found out that pretty much everything you hear about Victory is true. Honestly, some of the stories were probably under-embellished for fear of repercussions. We were scared. We were threatened.

GEOFF RICKLY: [Did he ever threaten to beat me up?] Not personally. He definitely made allusions, mob boss style, to other people he knew that could be in whatever city we were playing. And I know he had some bands on his label that were fucking no joke. *Noooo joke*, man. I would never start a fight with him. No way.

RANDY NICHOLS: Bands knew what they were getting into. And then many were shocked when they had issues . . .

ANTHONY RANERI: Bayside wanted to be on Drive-Thru, Vagrant, and Triple Crown so bad. But nobody called us back. We didn't pick Victory; Victory were the only people that called.

J. T. WOODRUFF: Victory was like, "Hey, can you come up and do a showcase for us in Chicago?" It was the first time anybody thought of Hawthorne Heights as something that could be better than a local band from Dayton, Ohio, sending in a demo.

We'd never been to Chicago. It was like being sent a ticket to Hollywood, even though we had to pay for the ticket and had to drive in the winter. In Chicago, it's freezing, a cold that I've never felt in my life. And it's in the deepest, darkest rehearsal studio I've ever seen. We had ten minutes to load our stuff, and then the staff is there. We had no time to sound check, our guitars are freezing, they're not staying in tune. We give it everything we have, we flail around onstage, we sing terribly. Ten, twelve people are standing in the back, and after each song there's dead silence.

We packed up all of our stuff, drove home, and we didn't say a word to each other for probably two and a half hours. And out of nowhere I just said, "Fuck. That sucked."

The next day, about 6:00 p.m., I was on a pizza run. I remember the snow everywhere and how miserable it was, back to delivering pizzas. Eron, our drummer, called: "Pull over." I was like, "I am pulled over. I'm about to get out of my car and drop this pizza off." He was like, "Victory's sending over our contract right now. We're going to get signed." I dropped the pizza off, tears streaming down my face.

SHANE TOLD: Silverstein had heard rumblings that Victory was a really hard label to work with and that Tony was crazy. A part of me was like, "Maybe this is a bit of a half-truth . . ."

J. T. WOODRUFF: At our own peril, we gave our lawyer specific instructions: "This is what we want, try and figure this out for us." We were an inexperienced band. We weren't like, "We want this, this, and this." It was more like, "Don't fuck this up." We probably would have said yes to anything, just like any band in that era, in that genre did.

FRED MASCHERINO: If you were one of the Victory bands that got famous, you were gonna get screwed the most. But it was still better than being stuck on Victory and not getting famous . . .

JUSTIN BECK: When bands were complaining about Victory Records, it was like, "Shut the fuck up." If Glassjaw was on Victory Records, we would have been fucking huge. Every band on Victory could be the biggest piece of shit, but you went huge. If anything, I'm more resentful that we didn't sign to fucking Victory, ha, ha. I watch all these shitty bands complain that they're on Victory but it's like, "Bro, you would not have been this big had you not been on Victory."

ANTHONY RANERI: Tony was quick to pull the loyalty card on anybody who ever asked for anything, even when they were owed it. But at the same time, he would do things like shut down bars and rent them out when a bunch of Victory bands were in town, just to hang out. One time some random guys were told they weren't allowed in and thought they were being discriminated against. They tried to fight the bouncers and tried to break into the Sleeping's tour van—they were a band on Victory. They tried to steal the van while Cameron from the band was laying down in the back seat. Tony ripped off his shirt and chased these guys for blocks, down alleyways through Chicago, in the middle of winter.

JASON LINK: The Victory office was weird and uncomfortable. Everyone was salaried, but you had to clock in for work each morning. And the clock-in box was right next to his office.

HEATHER WEST: No sales number was ever enough. It had to be higher, higher . . .

STEPHANIE MARLOW: There was no way to disconnect from work. It'd be the holiday break, I'm trying to have breakfast with my parents on Christmas, and I keep getting messages about a Hawthorne Heights record.

JASON TATE: He read so many CEO jerk-off biographies.

JASON LINK: He read the Steve Jobs book, and then the next day bought everybody New Balances.

HEATHER WEST: The Malcolm Gladwell book that's all about social connectors . . . he was really excited when he read that.

JASON TATE: I think he actually thought he was the Jeff Bezos of indie music. He didn't understand he was nothing without the bands, that he was just a cog in all of this.

ANTHONY RANERI: I'll say it forever—Tony's need to win is a huge part of how we got to where we are. There were times he didn't want to pay anybody royalties. His answer would be, "You want 'em? Come and get 'em. Who's your lawyer? Because I've got a good one." Which sucks, but then he would make a million samplers, buy some vans, and hire people to drive around the country to go to shows and hand them out to make your band bigger.

J. T. WOODRUFF: Other bands in the scene would ask us, "How are you guys everywhere?"
SHANE TOLD: There was all this crazy-intense marketing.
J. T. WOODRUFF: There'd be five Cadillac Escalades with our faces on them, rolling around to other bands' big shows, with people handing out samplers.
SHANE TOLD: They were Escalades, but they were called the Victory Assault Vehicles. *Yes, they were called that.*
ANTHONY RANERI: Sometimes it was good that he didn't take the contracts seriously. We'd have a $5,000 video budget, we'd come up with an idea, and we're like, "Yeah, it's gonna be $25,000." And Tony would be like, "Ah, whatever, fuck it!"
STEPHANIE MARLOW: *Steven's Untitled Rock Show* had interviews and videos and Tony said, "Why don't we do that ourselves?"
ANTHONY RANERI: Before Fuse or MTV2 would play our videos, Tony forced our videos on. He made an infomercial, but it looked like a regular music video show.
STEPHANIE MARLOW: I'd buy infomercial blocks to show Victory bands' videos. They hired a guy to host these hour-long episodes. It was an infomercial, but it looked like actual programming.
JASON LINK: Tony wanted Victory to be an island destination, where there was only Victory music. He didn't want to live in the outside world.
ANTHONY RANERI: Tony was never in bidding wars because he didn't sign bands all the labels wanted to sign. This time period was like Seattle grunge in the nineties where everybody's looking for the next big emo band. Tony wasn't going to compete financially with labels like Fueled By Ramen and all their Atlantic money. He signed bands nobody wanted to sign because he could get them for cheap. His mentality was, "Victory is the best and I can pluck a band and make 'em famous because I'm so powerful and smart."
J. T. WOODRUFF: Victory was releasing everything we liked in the early 2000s, like Thursday and Taking Back Sunday.
ANTHONY RANERI: I think of Victory bands coming in waves. There was the

Hatebreed hardcore wave in the nineties, then Thursday and Taking Back Sunday in the early 2000s. And then us, Hawthorne Heights, and Silverstein signed around 2003. We were all the third wave of Victory successes. It was a big-ass label and a real prime time for them.

STEPHANIE MARLOW: Bayside really fell into their songwriting groove on their self-titled album in 2005. Anthony took charge of writing the lyrics. It sounded so much more confident.

NICK GHANBARIAN: That's also when John Beatz joined on drums.

ANTHONY RANERI: John was into hip-hop and funk. Before joining Bayside, he had never heard Taking Back Sunday or any of our contemporaries. He was playing in a funk band when we met him, so he brought this completely new style into Bayside. Rhythmically, we don't sound quite like any other band in our scene.

NICK GHANBARIAN: John was seven or eight years older than us. He had a wife and they had a house together. I think he knew this was potentially the last opportunity he'd have to play music in a full-time, touring band.

J. T. WOODRUFF: He had this thick New York accent. I always got a kick out of him because I kind of talked like a hick. People think I'm from Ohio because that's where Hawthorne Heights was based, but I grew up in West Virginia.

STEVEN SMITH: Hawthorne Heights was all over Fuse in 2005.

J. T. WOODRUFF: You couldn't turn on MTV and not hear "Ohio Is for Lovers" in a ringtone ad.

JASON LINK: The cheesiness of it; like, why are you screaming, "Cut my wrists and black my eyes?" Who says that? It sounds like a twelve-year-old. But that connected with people. And those Hawthorne Heights songs are bangers. They were able to capture the basic-ness of these screamo bands and write these catchy hooks. If you talked shit on Hawthorne Heights, you'd meet them and realize, "Oh shit, these guys are really nice." Silverstein and Bayside met them and instantly, they're friends.

ANTHONY RANERI: Hawthorne Heights took us on tour right when they were at their peak. Every band on Victory really hated Tony and didn't want to do him any favors, so we hardly ever toured with other Victory bands.

SHANE TOLD: But Hawthorne Heights got huge and they wanted to bring us out on tour, along with Bayside and Aiden. So it became this Victory Records tour.

J. T. WOODRUFF: It was Aiden, Bayside, Silverstein, and Hawthorne Heights. That tour was our first real headliner, at the end of 2005. It was called the Never Sleep Again Tour, because it had so many dates without many off days. Also, because my favorite movie is *Nightmare on Elm Street*.

JASON LINK: Hawthorne and Silverstein were in buses. Bayside definitely wasn't.

NICK GHANBARIAN: Hawthorne Heights was soaring at that point. We were playing in front of 1,000 to 1,500 people every show.

ANTHONY RANERI: Our self-titled record had just come out on August 23, about two months before the tour started in October. We felt we'd made a great record. Getting to play for so many people was a huge opportunity.

JASON LINK: Me and the video guy from Victory rode down in the Victory vans to the first date in Indianapolis, filming everything and passing out samplers.

ANTHONY RANERI: The first show was in Indianapolis and it was probably the most people we'd ever played to. Three shows later, we played Boulder, Colorado.

SHANE TOLD: It was a good show. I remember hanging out at the merch table with Bayside and talking to John Beatz—such an animated personality, always happy. He was telling me how much he loved our song "Discovering the Waterfront." I remember talking to Jack from Bayside about their van and how they weren't too sure about their tires, because they were super old. It was the day before Halloween.

ANTHONY RANERI: The next night's show was in Salt Lake City, Utah. It's impossible to drive from the Denver area to Seattle and play a show the next day, so you have to do that eight-hour Salt Lake City drive overnight. Anyone who's ever toured in a van knows that drive sucks. You have to cross the Rockies. It's treacherous.

J. T. WOODRUFF: Bayside was huddled around, talking after the show. It was pouring snow outside. We were having a conversation: "Look, guys, if it's getting bad, just pull over. If you can't make the show the next day, don't worry about it." Bayside was in a van with a trailer, which is way more dangerous than a bus. A bus has a professional driver, and a lot more weight to it.

ANTHONY RANERI: Our merch guy at the time was driving. I remember going over to the driver-side window before we got in the van. The night before, on our way to Boulder, we hit a deer in the road. This night, everyone was tired.

NICK GHANBARIAN: I was laying down, sleeping in the third bench.

ANTHONY RANERI: I went to the window and said, "Do you want me to drive?" Our merch guy said, "No, I'm good." I was sitting shotgun and fell asleep.

NICK GHANBARIAN: I remember waking up for probably what was under a second, because of the inertia of the van. We weren't moving straight anymore. I just remember bracing myself against the bench in front of me.

ANTHONY RANERI: It didn't feel real. I remember looking back and asking if everybody was okay. We crawled out of the van.

NICK GHANBARIAN: I don't know how much time passed, but I was knocked out, and I woke up on the ground, outside the van. My cell phone had been right next to me on the bench and when I woke up outside, it was beside me, in the exact same spot. And then everything started to happen. I started to see whoever was looking for us. At this point, I was up and walking around. The human body is a crazy thing. My back was broken, but I didn't feel anything for twenty, thirty minutes.

ANTHONY RANERI: We'd hit black ice out in Wyoming, spun off the road, and rolled down a hill on the side of the highway. I only remember bits and pieces of it. I don't remember actually crashing. I remember when we found John . . .

NICK GHANBARIAN: He was truly . . . I mean, I think Jack tried to resuscitate him, but he was . . .

ANTHONY RANERI: It's probably a weird human defense mechanism. It's like that memory is erased from my head. I remember when we found him, but I can't picture it.

NICK GHANBARIAN: An ambulance came, but I have no concept of time. We were in the middle of nowhere in Wyoming. I remember a couple of truckers stopping. They might have helped us get the ambulance.

ANTHONY RANERI: I remember getting annoyed that the paramedics went over to John, and then immediately stood up. I was like, "Why aren't you doing anything?"

J. T. WOODRUFF: Bus drivers would ride together, so Silverstein were just directly ahead of us and came upon it first. I don't know if they got out.

SHANE TOLD: I was in the top bunk. Our driver pulled over and woke up our tour manager. I never sleep, so I was up and I heard the conversation. I got out and I saw it. And I wish I hadn't, man. I wish I hadn't seen it.

J. T. WOODRUFF: I remember our bus driver running into the bus saying someone named John was dead.

SHANE TOLD: Jack from Bayside called John's brother on the phone and I'll never forget that conversation: him crying, telling him what happened. His brother's on the East Coast, where it's the middle of night, you know? Or maybe early in the morning. I don't know. I don't know how long we were at the hospital.

J. T. WOODRUFF: We met up at the hospital, in Cheyenne, Wyoming, or Casper, Wyoming. I can't quite remember. I believe Nick was in surgery. Some of the other guys had concussions and were coming out of the situation not really knowing what had happened.

It was very hard to see them that way. It's something that's always in the back corner of your mind. You compartmentalize these things—just put them in a file and lock it away.

ANTHONY RANERI: I remember sitting down at a table in a hotel restaurant with Jack—Nick was still in the hospital—and the rest of the other bands. I turned to Jack and I was like, "We're still gonna keep going, right?" Immediately we knew we were gonna go home, bury John, and then, we're coming back.

HEATHER WEST: Tony just said, "Whoever wants to go to the funeral, I'm paying." And whoever raised their hands, he bought plane tickets and got hotel rooms and we all went to the funeral to be there with the bands on Long Island.

ANTHONY RANERI: Tony flew out from Chicago for the funeral, but he was in and out. He didn't stay long. It would have been really easy for him to not go, but he came all the way out and only stayed a minute. So instead of thinking, "What a dick, he only stayed a minute," I remember thinking, "That's really human. It feels so much more like he *can't* be here, rather than he doesn't want to be here."

NICK GHANBARIAN: You're talking about someone who not only ran a successful label, but also ripped us off. It's like, "Thank you for paying for the funeral." But it was kind of the least he could do. What about paying for my physical therapy or giving money to John's family?

J. T. WOODRUFF: We missed five shows and started the tour back up in Anaheim.

ANTHONY RANERI: Hawthorne Heights did so much to take care of us. They kept our merch out on the road and sold it for us while we weren't there.

J. T. WOODRUFF: I had our agent ask all the promoters along that tour if they would donate their merch rate to try to get Bayside back on their feet. Every one of them did, except one. When they came to collect the merch rate, it was about the most I'd ever yelled in my life.

ANTHONY RANERI: Our half-hour set was just a dead stage each night.

SHANE TOLD: J.T. and I would go onstage and tell the audiences what had happened. It seems like a weird thing to do now, but at the time, people didn't always know. Information on the internet spread slower then.

ANTHONY RANERI: When we came back out, Silverstein let Jack and I ride on their bus. We played acoustic the rest of the tour.

We got the sense that powering on with the tour is what would have made John happy.

J. T. WOODRUFF: The shows were already sold out, but there was a new energy. When Jack and Anthony performed acoustic on the rest of the tour, it was special. I'm sure it helped them to be able to move forward.

JASON LINK: The last show was [December 11, 2005], at the House of Blues in Chicago.

ANTHONY RANERI: It was heavy. It was really heavy. The whole Victory staff was out.

STEPHANIE MARLOW: Victory staff sitting in the opera box, tearing up.

HEATHER WEST: It was incredibly sad. It would have been incredibly sad if it was anybody, but John was so beloved.

ANTHONY RANERI: When our set was over, I just remember hugging Jack and thinking, "We fucking did it."

What Silverstein did for us, what Hawthorne Heights did for us, we'll be brothers forever. Not a lot of people know this, but at the end of that tour, Hawthorne Heights gave us money to buy a new van and keep us going.

J. T. WOODRUFF: We've always been kind of united, in one way or another.

SHANE TOLD: It really taught us that what we were doing was dangerous. We had just spoken to John. That could have been any one of us.

NICK GHANBARIAN: We were just trying to get to the next show. *Why did this happen to us?* I remember being overwhelmed with that feeling for a long time. We were a bunch of kids trying to do what we love.

PART 5

IT'S AN ARMS RACE

2006–2008

CAST OF CHARACTERS

PART 5

HANIF ABDURRAQIB: author and poet (and Midwest native)

JIM ADKINS: front person, Jimmy Eat World

JOANNA ANGEL: adult film star; cofounder, BurningAngel.com; author (and New Jersey native)

VICTORIA ASHER: keytarist, Cobra Starship

NEAL AVRON: producer, Fall Out Boy

JONAH BAYER: journalist, *Alternative Press;* writer, *Steven's Untitled Rock Show*

JUSTIN BECK: guitarist, Glassjaw; cofounder, Merch Direct

MAX BEMIS: front person, Say Anything

DAVID BENDETH: producer, Paramore

RYLAND BLACKINTON: guitarist, Cobra Starship

AMANDA BRENNAN: meme historian; former head of editorial, Tumblr (and New Jersey native)

SPENCER CHAMBERLAIN: front person, Underoath

IAN COHEN: journalist

JAMIE COLETTA: founder, No Earbuds PR

JONATHAN DANIEL: cofounder, Crush Music; manager, Fall Out Boy, Panic! at the Disco, Cobra Starship, etcetera

ALEX DELEON: front person, the Cab

BRIAN DIAZ: guitar tech, Brand New, Fall Out Boy (and formerly, front person, Edna's Goldfish, the Reunion Show)

SHANE DRAKE: music video director, Panic! at the Disco, Paramore, Fall Out Boy, etcetera

MARIANNE ELOISE: author and journalist

HANNAH EWENS: author and journalist

FAT MIKE: front person, NOFX

MATT GALLE: booking agent, My Chemical Romance, Taking Back Sunday

GLENN GAMBOA: journalist, *Newsday*

AARON GILLESPIE: drummer-vocalist, Underoath

ANDY GREENWALD: author and journalist

TOM HIGGENSON: front person, Plain White T's

ROB HITT: drummer, Midtown (and later, manager, Crush Music)

BEN JORGENSEN: front person, Armor for Sleep

ARI KATZ: front person, Lifetime

MIKE KENNERTY: guitarist, the All-American Rejects

ELLIE KOVACH: blogger and journalist

SARAH LEWITINN: journalist, blogger DJ (alias, Ultragrrrl), cofounder/A&R, Stolen Transmission Records

LIGHTS: musician and comic book artist

ZACH LIND: drummer, Jimmy Eat World

COBY LINDER: drummer, Say Anything

KEVIN LYMAN: founder and producer, Warped Tour; cofounder and producer, Taste of Chaos

FRED MASCHERINO: guitarist-vocalist, Taking Back Sunday; front person, Breaking Pangea
ROB MATHES: producer, Panic! at the Disco
TRAVIE MCCOY: front person, Gym Class Heroes
FINN MCKENTY: vlogger, journalist, graphic designer, zine maker
ANDREW MCMAHON: front person, Something Corporate, Jack's Mannequin
TIM MCTAGUE: guitarist, Underoath
JOHNNY MINARDI: A&R, Fueled By Ramen
JAMES MONTGOMERY: author and journalist, *Spin*, *MTV News*
GRETA MORGAN: vocalist-keyboardist, the Hush Sound
MANI MOSTOFI: front person, Racetraitor
SCOTT NAGELBERG: manager, Panic! at the Disco
RANDY NICHOLS: manager, Underoath, Say Anything, the Starting Line
BUDDY NIELSEN: front person, Senses Fail
JOHN NOLAN: guitarist-vocalist, Taking Back Sunday; vocalist-multi-instrumentalist, Straylight Run
JENN PELLY: author and journalist (and Long Island native)
JOSEPH PEPPER: guitarist, Cartel
JASON PETTIGREW: journalist, *Alternative Press*
CASSADEE POPE: front person, Hey Monday (and later, solo artist and *The Voice* winner)
WILL PUGH: front person, Cartel
ANTHONY RANERI: front person, Bayside
EDDIE REYES: guitarist, Taking Back Sunday (and previously, Mind Over Matter, Clockwise, Inside, the Movielife, Runner Up)
GEOFF RICKLY: front person, Thursday; New Brunswick basement show promoter; producer, My Chemical Romance
JULIO MARTÍNEZ RÍOS: author and journalist
MATT RUBANO: bassist, Taking Back Sunday
KAREN RUTTNER: publicist, manager, DJ
ADAM SAMILJAN: marketing, Fueled By Ramen (and later, day-to-day manager, Paramore)
KEVIN SANDERS: drummer, Cartel
GABE SAPORTA: front person, Cobra Starship, Midtown (previously, bassist, Humble Beginnings)
ALEX SARTI: manager, Crush Music (and previously, merch manager/seller, Clandestine Industries)
NICK SCIMECA: designer, Clandestine Industries (and previously, drummer, 504 Plan)
MARIA SHERMAN: author and journalist
LESLIE SIMON: author and journalist, *Alternative Press*
ADAM SISKA: bassist, The Academy Is . . .
SPENCER SMITH: drummer, Panic! at the Disco
STEVEN SMITH: host, *Steven's Untitled Rock Show*
MATT SQUIRE: producer, Panic! at the Disco
PATRICK STUMP: vocalist-guitarist, Fall Out Boy; solo artist; film scorer
ALEX SUAREZ: bassist, Cobra Starship (and previously, multi-instrumentalist-vocalist, Kite Flying Society)
JASON TATE: founder/blogger, Absolute Punk.net
SHANE TOLD: front person, Silverstein
BRENDON URIE: front person, Panic! at the Disco
KENNY VASOLI: front person, the Starting Line

JON WALKER: bassist, Panic! at the Disco (and previously, guitar tech, The Academy Is . . .)

MIKEY WAY: bassist, My Chemical Romance

PETE WENTZ: bassist, Fall Out Boy (and previously, bassist, Racetraitor; front person, Arma Angelus); founder, Decaydance Records, Clandestine Industries

NICK WHEELER: guitarist, the All-American Rejects

HAYLEY WILLIAMS: front person, Paramore; founder, Good Dye Young

LUKE WOOD: A&R, DreamWorks Records, Interscope Records

DAN YEMIN: guitarist, Lifetime, Kid Dynamite

"BIGGER THAN EMO"

NICK WHEELER: 2005 into 2006 was the pinnacle of this scene. That year, us and Fall Out Boy got to play MTV's New Year's Eve show and watch the ball drop from the *TRL* stage. We were performing together, with Tyson and Patrick trading off vocals. We wanted to play "Don't Stop Believin'"—that song was just starting its resurgence—but I was like, "Guys, that song is so fucking hard, we don't get to rehearse this, we've gotta show up and play on live TV." We wanted to do more of a party song, so we ended up doing "Good Times Roll" by the Cars.

JAMES MONTGOMERY: At MTV, you could tell that there was a real sense of excitement that rock was finally back and there were bands that kids were into, that actually sold records. When I first started writing at *Spin*, it was like, "Garage rock is back." The White Stripes were great, but you had these other bands that never amounted to anything. The appetite to really champion rock and push it to the forefront had always been there. Now you had this perfect storm of social media and fan connection.

AMANDA BRENNAN: In 2006, MySpace was the most visited website in the US.

SHANE TOLD: I remember they added the top eight . . .

LESLIE SIMON: I don't know how anyone got away with ranking friends, without some kind of World War III erupting across the social stratosphere. It was a different time . . .

SHANE TOLD: We had all of our friends' bands in there. I think Silverstein might have been in Fall Out Boy's top eight for a while.

GEOFF RICKLY: After Fall Out Boy had the hit with "Sugar, We're Goin Down," they were headlining Roseland Ballroom in New York—this very prestigious, three-thousand-cap club. I was in the balcony with Jay-Z, and Beyoncé was there. And dude, she knew every fucking word to every song Fall Out Boy played. I could not get over it. I could *not*. I was like, "What the fuck, she knows Fall Out Boy?" Now I'm like, "Of course she did. Those songs are pop classics." It just didn't compute to me that these worlds were crossing.

PETE WENTZ: People will ask about *TRL* or whatever, and I don't even remember most of it. There were too many big, life-changing things crammed into too little time. There's not enough bandwidth. We were just *in it*, every single day.

ANDY GREENWALD: Pete sucked up all the attention and was very happy to be the mouthpiece of the band.

LESLIE SIMON: Patrick was fine letting Pete take the mic, talk to the crowd, and get people excited. At the time, Patrick was still figuring out how to be a front man, an entertainer, and advocate for the band.

ANDY GREENWALD: Patrick is five years younger than Pete, too. I think he was happy that someone could take all the flack, so he could just focus on the music. And Andy was a nice guy who wanted to talk about comic books and was amused that any of this was happening. And Joe was very nice. He was more like Ray or Frank in My Chemical Romance, a guy who was happy to be around for it. There are many successful bands with this kind of dynamic, where someone sucks up the attention so someone else can be a secret musical genius. Pete got so much attention, but Patrick was writing all the music and singing all the words. Even all the words that sounded bad together, he somehow made them work.

LESLIE SIMON: Pete talked in sound bites. I don't know if that's just how his brain worked, or if he was intentionally saying things he knew would make headlines. There are some musicians who want to talk about the music, and then there's musicians who want to tell a story.

ANDY GREENWALD: He was very forthcoming. Maybe this speaks to the social media generation, or at least where Pete was on that timeline, with how easily he was able to package his own stories about pills and potentially almost accidentally intentionally overdosing. There was a lot of vagueness about that; he wouldn't confirm or deny it to me. He was ready to package it into a narrative, the way the editors wanted it. It was already something that was in his rearview mirror, something that influenced these songs. In conversation with me, at least as I recollect it, it never felt like an ongoing concern. Now it's been immortalized in interviews and lyrics: "That's the story of that album, now we're gonna move on to the next thing . . ."

PETE WENTZ: There's no manual anyone gives you, right? Things happen right away. You go to a gifting suite because you're like, "Oh, there's free shit in the gifting suite." You don't realize the gifting suite actually costs so much more money than the thing, because your images are used forever. There's always going to be pictures of you holding that Bratz doll, you know what I mean? You're like, "No one told me that's how I'm paying for this."

JOHNNY MINARDI: Once Fall Out Boy hit the mainstream success of *TRL* and radio, you had the era of Pete in celebrity gossip news.

LESLIE SIMON: Famous people like to hang around with other famous people. Pete and some of the other guys in similar Decaydance bands were more than happy to add people like Paris Hilton, Lindsay Lohan, and Ashlee Simpson to their contacts in their Sidekicks. It was really uncharted territory for these "average, normal, everyday guys" in their twenties to be hanging out with A-list actresses, singers, and models. You couldn't go into a mall, grocery store, or a CVS without hearing "Sugar, We're Goin Down" or "Dance, Dance," so it made sense that the women Pete spent time with had famous last names.

JAMES MONTGOMERY: All of a sudden, Fall Out Boy's on Perez Hilton.

NICK SCIMECA: All of the eyeballs on you can be pretty stressful. It sucks to have lunch at some random place, then leave, and you're like, "Fuck, there was paparazzi behind there, I hope they didn't hear us talking about when the next record's coming out." It felt ridiculous; we started out playing basement shows, you know?

ADAM SISKA: My friendship with Pete suffered when he first reached a new level of fame. He was harder to get on the phone. He did a good job at making you feel like your time wasn't as valuable as his, and that's no fault to him—he went from being like everybody else to being a newly famous guy. I remember he picked me up in LA and was like two hours late to get me for god knows what reason and I definitely didn't call him out because he was my most successful friend and also at the top of our record label. I was a little pissed off, but as soon as I got in the car I was like, "What's up? Good to see you, buddy." We went to Lindsay Lohan's apartment at the Chateau Marmont. I remember playing "Chopsticks" or something on piano with Aaron Carter and some fashion designer. I think Sean Lennon was there. I was just like, "How far have we come from hanging out at fucking Denny's in Schaumburg, Illinois?"

NICK SCIMECA: A bunch of us were at Chateau hanging out with Lindsay Lohan and then we decided we're going to some bar. And she's like, "Well, I need someone to ride in my car," and Pete's like, "Nick, go with her." So it's just me and Lindsay Lohan in her car. She doesn't know who I am. We were talking about the CDs she had in her car. She was totally cool, but it was a bit stressful because now I'm going to be in these pictures. No one knows who I am. And my parents are going to see this and she wasn't . . . she didn't really have a good reputation at the time.

MATT RUBANO: I knew some people in New York that Pete had connected with. I remember thinking, "Wow, if he's friends with them, he must have his eyes on some goals other than music."

GABE SAPORTA: Pete loved doing lots of different shit. He had his clothing line . . .

NICK SCIMECA: We approached Clandestine like band merch: we have this idea that's cool, let's put the words on it, put the Bartskull [*bat, heart, skull*] logo on it, and now it's a Clandestine shirt.

Pete sent me an idea for the Bartskull logo, I started designing it, and I sent it to him like, "Hey, here's the first version of it." I don't hear anything back from him. Next thing I know, he's got it tattooed below his belly button.

MANI MOSTOFI: Pete did a New York Fashion Week show for Clandestine.

ALEX SARTI: It was a real fashion show, at this club called Capitale near Chinatown. There was a runway and press was there. I ended up being in *People* magazine. My mom cut it out. I was so embarrassed.

JAMES MONTGOMERY: "Fall Out Boy Takes on Fashion Week" . . . I must have been there because I wrote that headline for *MTV News*. "Paris Hilton, Russell Simmons Attend Star-Studded Clandestine Show."

ALEX SUAREZ: I put together the audio from the music Pete curated for all the walks. I remember there was Jay-Z and Armor for Sleep. I had to mash those up and it was really tough.

ALEX SARTI: No person that was walking knew what they were doing and the fashion people that were running it just assumed we were real models. They were just like, "OKAY—GO! GO! GO!"

MANI MOSTOFI: It was just like, different versions of hoodies.

ALEX SUAREZ: I'm not your average skinny pop-punk band dude. I'm a little wider and not necessarily muscular. So I got there and the clothes are all extra-small and small, which is not my size. I remember having to wear this tiny cardigan that didn't even fit me and a shirt that was too tight. It was so embarrassing. I was, like, full anxiety doing my walk.

ALEX SARTI: Pete certainly isn't tall enough to be a model. And he definitely walked at the end.

JONAH BAYER: It felt like Pete was a real celebrity who'd transcended the scene.

LESLIE SIMON: I was at my dining room table, either working on something for *AP* or book stuff and I started getting texts, and reading message board posts—the OhNoTheyDidnt LiveJournal was pretty big at the time. There were these nudes of Pete circulating around. Pete was a friend of mine, a pal, and a brother, but this is salacious so I can't not . . . it's like a flesh car crash I can't not look at. So when someone sends me the link or I find the link, download it, and open it, I'm like, "Ohhhh, Pete . . . noooooo." It was very uncomfortable to see. "Why did you keep your face in the picture?" My first reaction was like, "Dude, neck down! You should know this!"

PETE WENTZ: At the time it was just maximum embarrassment, exposure, like the ultimate blending of your private and public life. I feel like the internet the way it is now, it was so different, but it was a changing of the internet at the time. It's just something that's beyond the scope of your control. It's frustrating, so dark. But yeah, looking back on it in the rearview mirror, it's something you wish wouldn't have happened, but at the same time, it is what it is. The world kept moving. My world kept spinning. It didn't end the world.

LESLIE SIMON: A situation like that can either make or break you. And for whatever reason, it didn't break him. I think it made people more interested. I think it gave them something else to talk about. And while I'm sure he was embarrassed and humiliated, Pete has a really tough skin to the public. He wasn't just going to hibernate until the end of time.

ALEX SARTI: He's always thinking of things and ideas. I don't know if he can help himself, but he just has to keep his head moving.

JOHNNY MINARDI: The gatekeeper in the scene really was Pete Wentz, and with Fueled By Ramen, he was on our team.

GRETA MORGAN: We made this first record and it started getting played on MySpace and PureVolume. Apparently, Ryan Ross from Panic! at the Disco heard it and sent it to Pete.

ADAM SAMILJAN: The Hush Sound was one that I thought was incredible. I don't think anyone on Fueled By Ramen beat the sheer musical talent of that band: piano-oriented, jazz- and indie rock–influenced. Very orchestral, very beautiful.

GRETA MORGAN: Pete Wentz came to my house for brunch with my parents, basically to convince my parents to let me go on tour. It was sort of like *Almost Famous*, except instead of being the writer, I was the musician skipping high school to go on tour. So he came to my house and he was so eloquent; my parents were just really impressed. I think his mom was the principal or one of the higher-ups at this really great children's school on the North Shore and his dad is a lawyer. He made a number of promises about putting out our next record: He wanted to have Patrick Stump produce it, Fall Out Boy would take us on tour, and I would still graduate from high school. And he completely followed through.

I loved Pete and Patrick, Brendon and Ryan and Travis. I loved hanging out with those people, but I also felt like such an outsider in that world. When the Hush Sound's record was coming out, the record label came up with this ad campaign where Pete would re-create the nude photos, but instead he would be holding our album in front of his dick. I remember thinking it was so disgusting and tasteless. Also, this was music I wrote from the bottom of my heart, and this is how we're advertising it? All that publicity stunt stuff seemed foreign to my sensibility.

ADAM SISKA: With the ascension of Panic! at the Disco, there was no longer this spectrum of what a popular emo band sounded like. Between Fall Out Boy and Panic!, there became a very distinguishable emo sound. Patrick and Brendon sounded very similar. The lyrical content sort of had this highbrow poetry to it. And I don't think The Academy Is . . . really fit into that. We were tailor-made for VFWs, but we were not an arena act.

ADAM SAMILJAN: Panic! was supposed to open The Academy Is . . .'s first headlining tour, first of four bands. By the time the tour rolled around, Panic! had been bumped up to direct support.

ADAM SISKA: There was a disconnect between how big Panic! was when the tour was announced and a few months later, when it was actually happening.

SPENCER SMITH: A lot had changed for us.

PATRICK STUMP: They were a runaway success. I'd never seen anything like it. The record exploded so fast, they hadn't even decided on a single yet.

JONATHAN DANIEL: Several program directors called me and said, "What's the single off this Panic! record?" I was just like, "Play whatever song you want." We didn't have a single. We hadn't gotten that far. We hadn't made a video. So they all played the first song on the album, "Applause"—I know all the songs from the demo titles—on the album it was called "The Only Difference Between Martyrdom and Suicide is Press Coverage." So when we were going to make a video, the label says, "Okay, you gotta make a video for 'The Only Difference.'" And the band goes, "We don't wanna make a video for that song. We only want to make a video for the songs on side two of the album; those are newer songs and we like those better." On the management side, our favorite song was "I Write Sins Not Tragedies." The band was like, "Cool, we'll do it for 'Sins.'" And the label was very angry: "Are you crazy? You're gonna make a video for the wrong song." But the band drove that. And they were right.

SCOTT NAGELBERG: KROQ started playing it. This was before we were upstreamed to Atlantic; it was just us and Fueled By Ramen doing it. No one was working it to radio, but a bunch of stations started picking up from the buzz. It wasn't top forty at first; it was all alternative. Atlantic came on later, when we were already doing our thing.

ALEX SARTI: Panic! was a freight train you could not stop. Unfortunately, Academy Is . . . got eaten up by that.

ADAM SAMILJAN: MTV was covering the tour and they were treating it like it was Panic! at the Disco's tour, even though they were one of the opening artists.

ADAM SISKA: By the time the tour rolled around, it became very clear that Panic! was probably meant to be the headliner. That being said, tickets sold out very fast. So, it was definitely our fans coming to that tour. In the US, I don't think there was a show that people left before us. The people who bought tickets also turned out to be big fans of this new phenomenon, Panic! at the Disco. So while it could have seemed like this band was eclipsing us, I look at that tour as a major success.

That being said, when we went to the UK headlining over Panic! . . . they smoked us.

SPENCER SMITH: It was a weird thing that shouldn't have been weird and didn't need to be weird, but it was just the nature of what was happening to us. And happening so fast.

HANNAH EWENS: Panic! was being played all the time at HMV, which was our record store over here, on every high street. They had big displays of that album, posters, and merch. I remember coming into school . . . each song is like a long, sassy poem, and people would know all the words.

JOHNNY MINARDI: "Sins" was exploding over there even more than it was in

America. I had a whole tour's worth of merch and by mid-show, day two, I was sold out. I just poured all the money on the table like, "We're done."

ADAM SISKA: There was one UK show in particular, in Birmingham, that I remember watching them play right before us and being like, "Oh, fuck. We're gonna have to go on after them . . ."

ADAM SAMILJAN: Panic! fit perfectly into how the British press works over there, where they're very big into the personalities, trying to get artists to say the key quotes . . .

ADAM SISKA: The UK has always had more of a lane for bands that ride the avenue of glam and makeup. And their sound, especially with the synths, was tailor-made for the UK. Brendon did an interview with *Kerrang!* or maybe *NME* or *Rock Sound*—one of the big magazines there. There was a quote along the lines of how they could feel they were surpassing us on a commercial level and they almost felt bad going on before us. And having known Brendon after all these years, he doesn't have a bad bone in his body; I do think he was misquoted. But all of a sudden, there was this weird energy between our bands.

SPENCER SMITH: We were still trying to figure out who we were and what we wanted to do.

ADAM SISKA: That tour was the very end of Brent. Brent was playing bass for Panic! and having growing pains . . .

MATT SQUIRE: Brent was their friend growing up. I remember he just wasn't really a player; I think Brendon played his stuff on the album.

LESLIE SIMON: The bassist would always wear sweatpants. *Oh buddy* . . . Whenever he was out of costume, he would wear like, the top half of things. Like a toddler who just got home from church. He was sweet. He didn't last that long.

ADAM SISKA: The issue may have been that Brent was partying and the other guys in the band were a year or so shy of letting loose a little bit. So, he kind of alienated himself within the band. In the UK on that tour, he was drinking absinthe on the bus and maybe behaving erratically. That would have been right at home in our band, but for Panic! it was a little too against the grain.

JON WALKER: I was on tour with Panic! as a guitar tech for The Academy Is . . . We met when I fixed one of Ryan's guitar pedals. Within a month, they told me they were thinking of replacing their bass player.

MATT SQUIRE: I'm very punk rock, very chemistry-oriented, so I was conflicted about that. Spencer called me like, "Dude, we're just done with Brent." I was like, "Don't do it, man." Spencer was like, "Dude, we're at a show and he didn't even show up." And I'm like, "Look, you've got a legitimate gripe, I get it. But bringing someone else into this dynamic is gonna be crazy. I don't know if it's gonna be better or worse, but it's gonna be different."

SPENCER SMITH: I had to call Brent and tell him, and it really sucked.

JON WALKER: I learned the bass parts from the record at home. My first gig was the KROQ Weenie Roast in front of 15,000 people. They called me the night before saying their bass player didn't show up . . . I decided pretty quickly I wasn't going to wear eyeliner, but that didn't stop the rest of them.

ADAM SISKA: Jon Walker was definitely cut more from the cloth of The Academy Is . . . We all did hallucinogens and smoked weed by that point, but Panic! on tour was as clean-cut as you could get. The drummer from All-American Rejects had [bought] me a Fleshlight because he told me I wasn't getting laid enough and I remember coming on Panic!'s tour bus in El Paso, tripping on mushrooms and hitting them with it. They were laughing, but I think they were kind of scared.

LESLIE SIMON: I went to Vegas to interview Panic! for their first *AP* cover story. We visited their high school. We drove around, saw a lot of Vegas, outside of the Strip. That's enough Vegas that I ever need to see. I felt very protective of them when I brought them to the magazine; I wanted to tell their story, I wanted to be the one to guide them through the publishing system of, "You start smaller, then you get a feature . . ." They definitely took the fast lane and got to the markers faster than anyone I remembered.

JASON TATE: It was like how people today would say, "You're an industry plant." At the time, people felt like they were skipping a step.

SHANE TOLD: The Panic! at the Disco beginnings were really weird to everybody. Nobody was very accepting of them. We were all really high on this idea of, "You've got to pay your dues." They'd never played shows and they'd already gotten signed and then they practically got as big as Fall Out Boy. There was a lot of jealousy going on, up to the point where I didn't even listen to that record. I just kind of wrote them off.

ADAM SISKA: On Warped Tour in 2006, there was a lot of trash talk directed towards them. It was bands of every stripe, but, I mean, the punk rock bands fucking hated Panic! at the Disco. Funny enough, I remember being in Denver and Panic! came out to Warped Tour to hang out and all the bands that had been hating on them were gathering outside our bus to try to meet them. Lots of jealousy, but they'd kill to open their tour.

JOHNNY MINARDI: Back-to-back months, *Rolling Stone* did covers for Panic! and then Fall Out Boy. Pete had no shirt on.

JASON TATE: In that moment, it felt like Pete Wentz signed off on Panic! at the Disco and they were massive immediately. They'd skipped those steps of paying their dues, even though I think that whole idea is kind of silly. The songs were good and people liked them.

BRENDON URIE: We got thrown into the beef with the Killers' Brandon Flowers out of nowhere. We had no beef with them. Pete and Brandon threw us into that, man! That was unfair, I love both of them. I still am a huge fan of the Killers.

HANIF ABDURRAQIB: Fall Out Boy had a bunch of weird feuds as they ascended.

PETE WENTZ: Us and the Killers shared an A&R, Rob Stevenson. Brandon Flowers said something in an interview like, "It's a bummer we have to share an A&R with such untalented artists," or something. I immediately thought he was talking about us. In retrospect, he probably could have been talking about a bunch of bands.

HANIF ABDURRAQIB: Pete got into it with Brandon Flowers when Panic! came out, which was so fucking weird. I don't think Pete was doing extremely well at that point. But it was this weird thing where Panic! came out and Pete pitted them against the Killers, because of the Las Vegas thing. But it was like, "No, no, no! You don't have to do that! These bands are not making the same music!"

ADAM SISKA: When Panic! did their first big headlining tour, they took out Dresden Dolls, instead of, you know, bringing out other bands in the scene. I think they got so big that they recognized they didn't have to exist in that element. They were bigger than emo.

SPENCER SMITH: The band was taking off and I don't think Ryan's relationship with his dad had really been mended. I think his dad wasn't doing well, health-wise. Ryan leaving and his dad being alone, that was not good. But we were caught up in this whirlwind where maybe I talked to my parents every few weeks, just telling them everything was going really well.

LESLIE SIMON: At that point, Ryan had some really challenging family issues to contend with.

SPENCER SMITH: I don't know how often Ryan was talking to his dad, if at all. But I do remember, on that first headlining tour, we played the Hard Rock in Vegas, and his dad came. And he didn't look great. It was this bizarre experience because, man, the last year and a half had been really rough between them, his dad not approving of what we were doing. He was mad at my parents for encouraging us to do what makes us happy. It was uncomfortable. But his dad's there at the show and he sees three thousand kids cheering and singing every song. I don't know if it had done enough to make him proud of Ryan but . . . it stands out as a weird contrast. I'm glad he got to see that show.

MATT SQUIRE: Ryan's dad passed away when we were on Panic!'s first headlining tour [in July 2006]. I remember getting the call: "Ryan's dad has passed away, and he doesn't have much family, so all of us are going to the funeral to support him." We hopped a plane and went to Vegas.

We flew home for the funeral and thinking back, I don't know if Ryan just didn't deal with it then, or if he dealt with it internally, without really showing it. But I do remember moving on somewhat quickly. A sold-out headlining tour is a really easy way to just remove and distract yourself.

SPENCER SMITH: It's weird, thinking back—it wasn't even like we wanted to be straight-edge vegan kids. It was more because of seeing guys like Pete who didn't do that stuff. I didn't drink. I didn't smoke the entirety of that first album cycle.

PETE WENTZ: They were shooting a video for "Lying Is the Most Fun a Girl Can Have Without Taking Her Clothes Off," and we tried so hard to convince them to be in the video. At the last minute, they were like, "We'll do it, but only if we can have giant fish tanks on our heads."

SPENCER SMITH: We thought all that stuff was great ideas while sober. So that tells you a lot.

ADAM SAMILJAN: "I Write Sins Not Tragedies" was nominated for Video of the Year at the VMAs.

GABE SAPORTA: Not even like, alternative video of the year. *Video of the Year* . . .

JONATHAN DANIEL: Shane Drake, who directed the video, pitched me the video in the hallway at one of the Nintendo Fusion Tour shows. He's very animated.

SHANE DRAKE: I was pitching magicians, weddings, smoke bombs, chaos. We landed on a wedding with two distinctly crazy wedding parties: the Cirque troupe and the mimes.

JONATHAN DANIEL: He was like, "Okay, it's gonna be like a circus! Brendon's gonna have a top hat on!" And then we shot the video cheap—I would say we probably had thirty grand.

ANDY GREENWALD: This might be tough for contemporary audiences to understand, but the VMAs *mattered*. It was like a State of the Union address for pop culture: where we've been, where we're going, what it all means, how it relates to each other . . .

JONATHAN DANIEL: The VMAs were at Radio City Music Hall. Panic! got nominated for five awards. Fall Out Boy had won the year before, so we felt a little like we belonged, but not really. The show opened with Justin Timberlake doing "SexyBack," and he's incredible.

SHANE DRAKE: I got to take my entire team. Back then, the directors were considered almost as high-level as the talent. We did red carpets with the talent, we sat with the talent. I was sat right next to Rihanna. She ended up moving, then Ciara sat down, then she moved, and Lou Reed sat next to me.

SPENCER SMITH: When you're playing a show, at least all the people there know who you are. You're like, "Holy shit, this is amazing, we're all in this together." At the VMAs, it was like, Christina Aguilera has no fucking idea who our band is. And you know, rightly so at the time.

JONATHAN DANIEL: I mean, people knew "Sins." That song was so big everywhere. But yeah, I don't think they knew the band as much. I remember Panic! went to see Kanye in Vegas, and Pete asked Kanye if he had met them and Kanye was like, "No, I didn't see anybody here dressed like the 1800s." So I think they had some idea . . .

SHANE DRAKE: The first couple categories come and go and it's like, "All right, we were up against some pretty huge talent." Then it's like, "We're gonna get Best Rock Video," but we didn't get that. Then it's Best New Artist: "We're bound to get Best New Artist, the band's on the cover of every magazine in town." Boom, we don't get Best New Artist.

JONATHAN DANIEL: Four nominations had gone by and we hadn't won anything . . .

SPENCER SMITH: We didn't know we had won Video of the Year until maybe thirty seconds before they announced it, because they had to bring the camera guy over. And then they kind of tell you—this is within a minute of it happening—"All right, you guys won, so in a second you're gonna stand up, and then you're gonna walk down these steps and go around here . . ."

PATRICK STUMP: I remember them being up against Madonna for Video of the Year.

SPENCER SMITH: It was probably a pretty big upset . . .

PATRICK STUMP: Madonna and MTV. It does not get bigger than that. I don't know how to quantify it.

JONATHAN DANIEL: How much money was spent on the other videos compared to Panic!'s? Ten times more, easy. That was a big win for the underdogs.

PETE WENTZ: That VMA, I remember watching Panic! perform. Ryan and Brendon were at the very end of the stage and I was like, "They kind of look like Steven Tyler and Joe Perry." For the first time, those dudes didn't look like a little baby band. You're looking at this giant rock band.

"EMO PEOPLE *ARE* JUST LIKE US!"

GABE SAPORTA: I learned to dance by going out. Dancing's fun. Dancing's great. Moshing is dancing, too, bro.

LESLIE SIMON: I was going to New York about twice a month to hang out and do work stuff. Every Friday night, two friends of mine, Karen and Sarah, would do a DJ night called Tarts of Pleasure. That would be Friday night's hang, and then on Saturday, we'd all go to Misshapes.

GABE SAPORTA: The Misshapes kids are fucking awesome. They were like scene kids that grew up. They were a little bit closer to my age, like the Midtown-era kids, who were a generation older than the Fall Out Boy kids. They started doing this party called the Misshapes at this club on Varick Street.

ANDY GREENWALD: Misshapes was a little chilly. Those three were good friends of friends of mine, but I never exchanged a word with any of them. I was very intimidated by them because they were so fashionable and wearing black and it seemed a little too cool for school. But it wasn't. Actually, it was pretty fun.

PETE WENTZ: Um, so Misshapes was super dope.

LESLIE SIMON: Misshapes was sort of an anomaly for the emo scene, in that even when emo was huge it wasn't, quote, unquote, *cool.* Peak Misshapes would be Killers, Interpol, the Rapture, the Yeah Yeah Yeahs—bands that were undeniably fucking cool.

KAREN RUTTNER: The Taking Back Sunday guys, the My Chem guys, the Midtown guys, Gym Class Heroes, they all lived in New York or New Jersey. So they were around.

JOANNA ANGEL: The bands are getting older and they're playing to people half their age. So going to those parties, they could be around people their age, doing things people their age do.

SARAH LEWITINN: I would see people from all these bands that you would never think would go to these parties. You'd think they'd be at like, pop-punk parties. But no, they were at these, for lack of a better term, gay parties. The person out at a party every night with like, crazy makeup or a cool outfit was just as famous as a person in a band. Especially if you were in an emo band, you were just as anonymous, or just as famous, as anyone else. You weren't more famous because you were in Midtown or My Chem. It would just be like, "Oh, there's that guy."

KAREN RUTTNER: Gabe was probably the ringleader and would get the other ones to come. Mikey would be at Misshapes, they knew each other because of the Jersey connection.

RYLAND BLACKINTON: I remember taking the train out there, not having any money, buying five-dollar bottles of wine beforehand and just slamming them and showing up with like, fifteen dollars, just trying to buy one drink. But really just being there to listen to the music. That was where you would go to hear the best music. Jarvis Cocker would be DJing. Michael Stipe would be DJing.

ALEX SUAREZ: Yoko Ono, Brandon Flowers, Madonna . . .

ROB HITT: Freakin' Madonna came out!

SARAH LEWITINN: Basically, Madonna was trying to be cool.

KAREN RUTTNER: Madonna was very much like, the mom of the Misshapes. The patron saint, of sorts.

ANDY GREENWALD: So my friend Sarah Lewitinn was like, "Come to Misshapes tonight." This is when it was at Luke & Leroy in the West Village.

SARAH LEWITINN: I probably did my round of text messages to all the people I enjoy hanging out with and seeing at parties and clubs: "Come to Misshapes, Madonna is going to be DJing."

ANDY GREENWALD: I remember going really early, probably nine or nine thirty, and it didn't really pop off till eleven. It was pretty sparse. So a bunch of us went across the street to another bar, Movida.

SARAH LEWITINN: It might have been this night, during the early part . . . I feel like I brought Mikey to the office. People would go to the office at Misshapes and like, that's where the *VI-VI-VI*-VIP room was. It was a tiny little office where they would like, do accounting. There was a hair iron on the table and I remember Mikey picking it up like, "You never know, I might need an emergency hair iron," so dry about it. I was like, "Oh my god, you're so funny."

By the time Madonna finally showed up, it was fairly prompt, but if something's gonna happen at twelve thirty, I tell people to get there at nine thirty. You're gonna be bored, there's only so many cans of Sparks you can drink. So by the time she got there, the place was packed to the brim with, like, gay men and random bands. Maybe even Warped Tour was in town that weekend, you know? There was this wall of emo people and punks and downtown New York City scene kids.

MIKEY WAY: You couldn't really get near Madonna, you know? It was just a mob scene around her and you caught tiny glimpses.

SARAH LEWITINN: I had a record label at the time and one of the bands was called Permanent Me. I was like, "Come to my friends' party, Madonna is going to be performing." They were very sheltered Long Island kids; I took them out to eat sushi for the first time. I was trying to show them a fun time outside of the world they were familiar with.

ROB HITT: The photo that circulates around with Madonna from Misshapes has the drummer from Permanent Me in the background.

ANDY GREENWALD: I went back over to Misshapes as I intended at like twelve thirty, and it was done. I'd missed all of it. The only person still there was Paul Banks from Interpol, on a banquette with like three women.

SARAH LEWITINN: Paul Banks being the last person there sounds about right. The Interpol guys were always good at closing out a club. Also, all those emo bands wish they were in Interpol. I can tell you that much. *They all wish they were in Interpol.*

ANDY GREENWALD: In terms of what these artists represented, the crossover was a strange one.

KAREN RUTTNER: Matt from Taking Back Sunday became friends with the Misshapes folks. Because Matt and I were roommates, we would hang out with them on a friend level, on a brunch level. So they kind of saw, you know, emo people are just like us!

MATT RUBANO: Nightlife shit always made me uncomfortable because I don't really identify as a cool guy. I'd been turned away by doormen so much in my life that I was just like, "All right, enough of this bullshit." When I joined a band and had friends in that world, it felt a little like getting the keys to the kingdom. I learned it as acceptance by association; did I just turn cool? No, I'm friends with the cool kids now. And it was increasingly clearer who was becoming the cool kids over those years. Pete and Gabe Saporta were always involved in nightlife stuff. They saw a bigger picture.

SARAH LEWITINN: Pete would come to Misshapes because Mikey would go, and Mikey would come because I would bring him. I would be like, "Hey guys, I'm gonna be rolling with Mikey from My Chem and Pete from Fall Out Boy," and they'd be like, "Oh shit, can you ask Pete if he wants to DJ?"

PETE WENTZ: "Since U Been Gone" by Kelly Clarkson popped off.

LESLIE SIMON: Pete DJed there a couple times and that kind of started his DJ journey. But his DJ journey, at least when I was shoulder to shoulder with him, was really just pressing play, ha, ha, ha. There wasn't much mixing.

PETE WENTZ: It's very kind of Leslie to say "DJing." I mean, I think I stood next to her while she DJed. I would point at songs and she would play them.

LESLIE SIMON: We had a playlist and went from one song to the next. It wasn't high art. More like a house party where you want to have a good soundtrack. Pete would wear his BAPE parka and some Clandestine fitted hat and make weird snarly smiles, showing those beautiful teeth of his.

SARAH LEWITINN: Leslie was like a teetotaler so . . . she and Pete were pretty, pretty clean.

LESLIE SIMON: We would show up and DJ, or just attend, and it still felt like . . . "Are they gonna kick us out?" I'm not wearing the right stuff,

I'm not looking the right way. And then we would play like, Fugazi. More palatable suburban stuff. But I had illegal amounts of fun there. You just danced your face off, which felt very reminiscent to being at your favorite band's show. It's just that the people on either side of you looked very different. Very, very different!

RYLAND BLACKINTON: I remember seeing Gabe at Misshapes, before we ever really met. Or maybe I met him there . . .

ALEX SARTI: Gabe was really into bands like Phoenix. He loved Kraftwerk.

PETE WENTZ: He was a lot different than my other friends. This is the funniest thing to say about a guy in a punk band, but he was like . . . more cosmopolitan or something. He wore scarves and went to clubs.

GABE SAPORTA: Midtown was done. I came home from the last tour and started working on new music. I was using Reason, which was one of the first production programs.

I wanted to hear what my voice would sound like with a song like "Hollaback Girl." A bit more . . . I wouldn't call it rappy . . . But more rhythmic.

ALEX SUAREZ: The very first piece of music Gabe put out as Cobra Starship was this Gwen Stefani parody, "Hollaback Boy."

GABE SAPORTA: I recorded "Hollaback Boy" and put it on MySpace under the name Cobra Starship.

It started getting some traction on MySpace, and my friend Sophie Schulte-Hillen, who was a writer for *Elle Girl* magazine and part of the scene, got me into Gwen Stefani's fashion show at Roseland Ballroom. I had press credentials, I had this little camera and was filming. Everyone's talking, and I'm like, "Gwen, what do you think about 'Hollaback Boy'?" She's like, "Is that you?" She was kind of laughing, and also kind of like, "This is scary that you're back here," ha, ha, ha. That gave it a little more traction and I don't know what happened next, but all I know is that Jonathan Daniel was like, "There's a movie coming out . . ."

JONATHAN DANIEL: That was all Sisky's idea. Sisky called me and said, "People are talking about this movie called *Snakes on a Plane*."

ADAM SISKA: The Academy Is . . . was on tour and I was reading *IMDb* about this new Samuel L. Jackson movie, *Snakes on a Plane*. The Academy Is . . . had this song called "Black Mamba" and I really wanted to get it on the soundtrack. With all the online marketing, people were talking about this movie six months before it came out, because it looked so crazy.

PETE WENTZ: It's funny to say it like this but our bands were like . . . quote, unquote, *doing the internet*. Other artists weren't making use of it because it was like, too beneath them. So there were all these things you could take advantage of that other people didn't know about. With *Snakes on a Plane*, we knew about the groundswell. You could feel it on the internet.

JONATHAN DANIEL: It turned out my friend Jason was doing the music for *Snakes on a Plane*. He's like, "You really want to put songs on this?" I was like, "I want to do whatever music you'll let me do for this." Gabe was looking for something new to do . . .

JOANNA ANGEL: On Christmas, because I'm Jewish, I'd always wander around New York and see other Jewish people, or people who didn't like their families. I remember seeing Gabe on Christmas at a bar. It was four in the morning, we were waiting in line for the bathroom, and he played me Cobra Starship, that song "Bring It." I was like, "Oh, it's really good . . ."

SARAH LEWITINN: I remember Gabe sent Karen and I his song, and I was just like, "This is so different from Midtown."

"AS MUCH MISCHIEF AS WE COULD"

GABE SAPORTA: I already had the name Cobra Starship. I had rented a house in the Catskills in New York the previous summer and wrote "Bring It" and a bunch of other songs. I had these songs that I thought were awesome and waited a year to put them out. On one hand, it was really frustrating. But on the other hand, I really trusted Jonathan. Finally he was like, "You already have the name Cobra Starship, the movie's called *Snakes on a Plane*, it's all about fucking reptiles in space. It's perfect. It's the perfect launchpad."
JONATHAN DANIEL: I put Gabe in the studio with my friend Sam Hollander, to try and write the song "Snakes on a Plane."
ALEX SARTI: "Snakes on a Plane" was a somewhat different song before. It was just called "Bring It" and had different lyrics.
GABE SAPORTA: At first it had more of a Le Tigre–sounding chorus, but we changed it to a catchy, pop chorus, with long, drawn-out notes. When I first heard it, I hated it. They showed me the lyrics first: "So kiss me good-bye?" How does this fit?
JONATHAN DANIEL: Then it was like, let's try and supergroup it.
PETE WENTZ: Gabe really got—before almost anyone else that I knew—that features and collaborations were at the heart of pop culture.
GABE SAPORTA: They're like, "We're gonna get Maja from the Sounds to sing, William Beckett's gonna sing the chorus, Travie's gonna rap on it." Okay, this is fucking sick.

TRAVIE MCCOY: I got the call from Bob from Crush and he's like, "Hey, listen, there's this movie called *Snakes on a Plane*. It's just Samuel L. Jackson cussing the whole time and killing a bunch of snakes and it's gonna be *the* biggest thing in the world. Gabe started a project called Cobra Starship, blah, blah." I was like, "Okay, where do I fit in?" He's like, "We just need eight bars. And the video's gonna be dope. We got Samuel L. Jackson lined up for the music video." And I was like, "As long as I'm gonna meet Samuel L. Jackson, *I'm in this motherfucker*."

PETE WENTZ: I remember going to the video shoot: *Samuel L. Jackson is going to be in the video*. So we waited for him. And we waited. I think he was in his car outside of the video shoot longer than he was in the video.

TRAVIE MCCOY: We finally got to hang out with Samuel L. Jackson. We talked for a minute. He was really stoked on the movie. He was like, "It is what it is. It's snakes on a motherfucking plane." And I'm like, "Word!"

GABE SAPORTA: *Snakes on a Plane* was meant to be this pulpy, B-movie satire horror flick, like something that would play on *Mystery Science Theater 3000*. I think some people got that, but then other people were really expecting this to be the best movie of all time. The soundtrack launches before the movie, and it's the biggest thing, right?

ALEX SARTI: The soundtrack is basically Crush artists and friends: Fall Out Boy, The Academy Is . . . , the Rejects . . .

GABE SAPORTA: I'm going from Midtown—"No one gives a fuck about you, it's over, you're an emo has-been"—to all of a sudden I'm fucking everywhere: red carpets, *Entertainment Weekly*, whatever. And I don't have a fucking band . . .

RYLAND BLACKINTON: Rewind several months, Gabe was starting Cobra Starship and he needed some band members. He asked me and Alex—Alex Suarez and I went to high school together—if we wanted to join. The music Gabe was making was outside my world at that point. We went to a practice space and played through some demos with Gabe and I liked everybody a lot, but it wasn't really clicking. I was an actor at the time and I wasn't really willing to change my life to join a band. Then some months later, I saw Gabe in a magazine article about *Snakes on a Plane*. I called him like, "Dude, that's crazy. Are you still doing this band thing?" Very opportunist, I'm not gonna try to hide that.

ALEX SUAREZ: Ryland and I both joined as guitar players. Then Alex Sarti, the manager for Cobra, calls us up and he's like, "This band doesn't need two guitar players, I need one of you idiots to play bass." We were outside of this bar Black and White near the East Village. We flipped a coin, I lost, and I became the bass player of Cobra Starship that night.

JONATHAN DANIEL: The week of the movie premiere in LA was so fun. Every station was playing the song, everybody was talking about the movie.

RYLAND BLACKINTON: Okay, maybe this thing's for real . . .

TRAVIE MCCOY: None of us had seen the movie yet.

PETE WENTZ: We went to the premiere party . . .

TRAVIE MCCOY: The premiere for the movie, they went so hard. They had a crashed airplane you could walk inside. There were all these Suicide Girls serving drinks and shit. I'm in fucking sad boy heaven.

All we were told about the movie was like, "It's about a bunch of snakes that get on a plane and people just trying to survive." Within like five minutes of this thing, a dude gets bit on the dick by a snake, and I'm like, "All right, this shit gonna be *stuuuupid*."

GABE SAPORTA: The "Snakes on a Plane (Bring It)" video played in the credits of the movie. We're seeing my face on-screen as we're walking out and I remember a kid doing a double take.

ADAM SISKA: After the *Snakes on a Plane* premiere, we had a party at the Key Club in LA, and Andrew McMahon performed some Jack's Mannequin songs. It was after he had his transplant and got cured of cancer.

JONATHAN DANIEL: Andrew had a remix on the soundtrack album. He did one of his first shows back from being sick.

ANDREW MCMAHON: It was on the eve of what was going to be my one-year checkup, post-transplant. I got to see all my friends. At that point, I was like 118 pounds. I couldn't put on any weight.

ADAM SISKA: He showed up looking sick. He had some sort of rash. He still went onstage and was climbing on his piano as he performed.

ANDREW MCMAHON: I remember almost falling asleep, like passing out onstage performing an acoustic song off the first Jack's Mannequin record. And then at the after-party, I was just pouring bottles of champagne and fucking losing it. For so many years after my transplant, there was this fine line I walked. But everything was a celebration—when I started coming around again, everyone was just like, "YES! You're not dead!"

I couldn't even get home that night. The party itself was close to where I was staying in Westwood, so I had a couple of friends carry me through the front door because I knew I could walk from there to UCLA for my appointment.

GABE SAPORTA: Just as fast as it went up, *Snakes on a Plane* came down right away.

TRAVIE MCCOY: When that shit tanked, I was like, "*UHHH* . . . please take my name off this motherfucker. Please, I don't want to be associated with this shit at all."

RYLAND BLACKINTON: You have to remember, people were talking about it on the internet way before it came out, but I don't think a lot of it was really about the movie, so much as it was the audacity of that working title they ended up keeping.

GABE SAPORTA: People who got the joke were like, "This is fucking hilarious." But because the hype got so big, most people didn't get the joke and they fucking hated the movie with a passion. People felt betrayed by it. They pulled the song everywhere. That song had been blowing up the charts! Everyone's like, "Fuck this movie, fuck everything." But still, when the song was on the charts, I signed to Fueled By Ramen.

In 2006, Cobra Starship was voted "band most likely to disappear next year" in *Alternative Press.* So that's the challenge Cobra had: "Oh, what the fuck, he's putting out an album? Fuck you, Gabe, you're trying to milk this thing?" But hey, if someone's telling you what you're doing isn't real, you can argue with them until your face turns blue. Or you can go out and prove it.

ALEX SARTI: Gabe was going out to a lot of clubs. Cobra Starship just made sense. It was another side of him. I don't think it was a conscious thing to be like, "Let's take advantage of this dance thing." It just kind of happened.

ALEX SUAREZ: The beauty of Cobra was, you were in on the joke, or you're not.

GABE SAPORTA: To me, the joke was, we're these punk rock kids who never really had a shot, no inroads into the music business, and we snuck in through the side door.

VICTORIA ASHER: I ran into my friend Alex Suarez and he was like, "What's going on? I joined this band Cobra Starship, they did the *Snakes on a Plane* movie." And I'm like, "That's funny, I just saw that . . ."

A couple weeks later, I got a phone call from Alex Suarez: "Gabe found your profile through MySpace and he's wondering if you wanted to play keytar in the band." I looked at Cobra Starship's profile, and it so wasn't the scene of music I was interested in . . . when I saw the band performing in the credits of the movie, I was like, "What is this band?" I only knew Maja from the Sounds. But then I met the guys, and Gabe in particular. He took me out for a night on the town in New York to see if I could hang.

GABE SAPORTA: I said, "Can you dance?"

VICTORIA ASHER: We were out till six in the morning dancing and drinking and going to different bars. We literally had a dance-off. Gabe's moves, he always does this thing where he extends his hands out, fingers straight, and he does little hops, but with his hips moving with it, and he walks it, kind of circles. He did it onstage a lot.

GABE SAPORTA: That was an important thing to me with Cobra Starship. I wanted people to dance.

VICTORIA ASHER: I remember him cracking up and hugging me, because I fully went there. At the end of the night, we were both super drunk, and we ended up at this illegal poker place in someone's apartment building.

GABE SAPORTA: That was an underground poker club called the Genoa Club. In between Midtown and Cobra, I had no money. The way I would make money was going to underground poker clubs. They called me the Sneakster, because I played very, very tight. A lot of these guys would just throw money around. I would just wait and wait and wait and wait. I would make six hundred bucks a week playing poker.

VICTORIA ASHER: They scanned my driver's license and had to print out a little ID, to make me a special member to get in. Gabe just handed me a hundred bucks or something and I was like, "Dude, I don't know how to play poker at all, I'm going to lose your money." He was like, "I don't care." I definitely lost his money. I just remember noticing the guy dealing out the cards was so fast, with little nubs for fingers.

GABE SAPORTA: He had no fingers because someone cut his fingers off. It was a gangster place.

ALEX SUAREZ: She could hang with us, you know? She could roll with the punches.

VICTORIA ASHER: That same week, Alex Suarez picked me up and took me to their practice space in New Jersey. We went through all the songs, I played all of them, and I remember them sitting on a couch watching me. I was so nervous. They left the room, came back, and they're like, "You're totally a Cobra. You're in the band." Gabe said, "Do you have any nicknames?" I said, "Vicky T" . . . He's like, "That's totally your stage name, let me see your signature," and started having me sign things to see if I had a good autograph. He's like, "You totally got it down."

GABE SAPORTA: After *Snakes on a Plane*, I went and said, "I have songs I think are good and I'm gonna go play them." We toured for a year, non-stop.

ALEX SUAREZ: In 2006, we started with Gym Class Heroes, doing clubs of five hundred to eight hundred people and sharing a bus with them. Then we went to having our own bus and opening for Thirty Seconds to Mars in 2,500-capacity theaters. And then we jumped right on to Panic! at the Disco's first arena tour, the Nothing Rhymes with Circus Tour, playing to twelve to twenty thousand people a night.

JAMES MONTGOMERY: Panic! at the Disco had one album and had been a touring band for a year.

MATT SQUIRE: Panic! was selling thirty thousand albums a week and selling out arenas.

TRAVIE MCCOY: The first time I'd seen them it was like, *womp womp*. And then the next time it was like, "Holy fuck, what happened, this band is fucking ready for stadiums."

SPENCER SMITH: I remember that period of time just feeling like a fantasy.

Every week management was telling us, "Ten more stations added your song, you sold ten thousand more copies this week than you did the last." Just nonstop good news. And now, you get to headline arenas.

SCOTT NAGELBERG: They basically wanted to bring the set of *Moulin Rouge!*, sketching out windmills, Panic!'s name in lights. They wanted dancers and this narrative story. We went for it. We were like, "This is not normal," but it was worth it to us—let's continue to make these statements. Nobody had ever seen a show like that from a band like Panic! You usually don't see fifteen-foot windmills.

MATT SQUIRE: This far into their record cycle, they're rock stars. They're wearing mismatched designer shoes, like $1,000 on each foot. Ryan was getting a very intricate tree painted on his face every single night by makeup artists.

SPENCER SMITH: Makeup existed in the scene already, whether it was My Chem or Pete; we wanted to do a more exaggerated version of it. We wanted to put on the biggest show—not only in terms of a concert, but a *show* show, like Cirque du Soleil.

MARIANNE ELOISE: They had the big windmills, the dancers, fire breathers, and burning Hula-Hoops. A circus going on. I interviewed Spencer once and he said they couldn't even get half of it through the doors of some of the venues.

RYLAND BLACKINTON: That was the first time I'd ever been on a tour with a band that was clearly spending a tremendous amount of money.

GABE SAPORTA: They made no money because they spent a crazy amount on production.

SCOTT NAGELBERG: Netted 5 percent of what they grossed. Normally you want to be around 50 percent, but to the team, it was an investment, a statement.

TOM HIGGENSON: The Nothing Rhymes with Circus Tour was choreographed to a tee.

SCOTT NAGELBERG: I remember Spencer saying, "I want to play on top of a twenty-foot carousel." We put together this tour—choreographed, scripted, stage-blocking.

STEVEN SMITH: They were green and cute and nice and took the music 1,000 percent seriously.

TOM HIGGENSON: Ryan Ross and his girlfriend would come and watch us play "Hey There Delilah" every night. This was right before the song blew up. Opening an arena tour and playing that song every night I'm sure helped.

RYLAND BLACKINTON: When you spend time on tour with people, the show is only like 10 percent of the experience.

ANDREW MCMAHON: In Jack's Mannequin, we would get big boxes of fireworks and we would light them off from our bus right as we were pulling out, just to get the cops to show up to the arenas. There was a night I think Cobra Starship got the heat. We were causing as much mischief as we could on that tour.

ALEX SUAREZ: Cobra Starship was a party band.

RYLAND BLACKINTON: I remember Panic! being really young and thinking we were really crazy. I don't know if they were straight edge or what, but they definitely weren't partying. We felt like we had to party in secret . . . which is still really fun.

MATT SQUIRE: Far into the *Fever* record cycle, I took them out to dinner in DC after a show, and for the first time in a long time, it was just us. Those guys were superstars, always getting swarmed, but it was just us in a car. They're asking me to play them what I'm working on and I'm playing them Boys Like Girls. And we just had this moment where we all looked at each other: "Yo, in your wildest dreams did you ever think *Fever* was gonna be a big record?" And we all fucking cracked up laughing: "Dude, what is happening to our lives?"

GABE SAPORTA: You didn't have to put out records on an indie first. Going to a major was seen less as selling out. You could do different kinds of music. You could have a contortionist at your show. It was all working.

SPENCER SMITH: Everything was happening in a positive light so quickly and so fast that it was easier to deal with criticism. That being said, as our band went along, we became very aware of the difference in how our bands were viewed, compared to a band like Arcade Fire or even the Killers—bands that were a little more *Pitchfork*-approved. It's funny how you can get very ungrateful for the good fortune; once you win the lottery, the less you look at the big picture. But that's hard to do when you're nineteen years old: "Holy fuck, we're playing in front of fifteen thousand people at this festival," but then being like, "Why don't people think our band is, quote, unquote, *cool*?" It's a weird thing. And it definitely played a part in our second record.

GABE SAPORTA: The first writing session I had for Cobra Starship was with Dave 1 from Chromeo. We were friendly with that [indie dance] world, but we were definitely more on the pop tip. And I think people respected that. Especially because I made efforts to be around that New York dance scene. Those are my friends. I didn't get shit from the hipsters. I got more shit from older scene kids than I got from hipsters. Like, "Cool, you're doing your own thing," you know? I wasn't trying to be a hipster.

KAREN RUTTNER: Sarah and I would mix very popular emo songs in with our traditionally indie, Britpop-sorta set. It was a Friday night party at this place called Orchard Bar. A down-and-dirty, really fun dance party with bad things going on in the bathroom and nonstop energy until 4:00 a.m. I used to torture Adam from Taking Back Sunday; if I saw him walk in, I would play a Taking Back Sunday song in between like, Bloc Party and the Smiths. He would get super embarrassed. I'm like, "No, no, it works!"

SARAH LEWITINN: And it was not an emo party!

KAREN RUTTNER: I don't know if you wanna blame drugs or alcohol, but people *loved* it. People would dance and realize, "I guess you can't hate on a song with a really catchy melody." We closed our set at Orchard Bar every night with "Helena." Four a.m. every night, without fail. The universal anthem of what was perceived to be a cool indie rock party. Whoever was left in that bar would be on the dance floor, screaming "so long and good night."

CHAPTER 28

BRIDGE & TUNNEL

JOHNNY MINARDI: Fueled By Ramen [and Decaydance] were seeing so much success with the more polished pop-emo stuff, where the chorus is big and hooky and the vocalist is out in front. We started paying attention to mainstream radio and festivals. The expectation was wild success, but we would still take a couple shots on hardcore bands, the roots of where the label started . . .

PETE WENTZ: I loved Lifetime. They were one of those bands to me . . .

MANI MOSTOFI: Pete wasn't into Lifetime from the beginning. Around the Racetraitor days, Pete was into moshy, vegan straight edge. He liked Earth Crisis; he liked Chokehold; and he liked Damnation. He wasn't really into the melodic stuff. Pete had cultivated this image of being a bit of a harder street guy, and he's not gonna listen to Lifetime. But a little after *Jersey's Best Dancers* came out [in 1997], that record really changed him.

PETE WENTZ: *Jersey's Best Dancers* was the last record they'd put out. This band has choruses! They're writing music! The melody is catchy!

MANI MOSTOFI: I think *Jersey's Best Dancers* is the most important record for the existence of Fall Out Boy.

I've heard different orders of things from Pete in interviews, but in my experience, it was Lifetime, Lifetime, Lifetime, Lifetime . . . and then the other influences like Saves the Day and New Found Glory came a little later. If you listen to the early Fall Out Boy stuff, it's very Lifetime.

PETE WENTZ: You know when you're talking about evolution, single cell to sea life to whatever, it's rare you can see the moment where the fish grow legs. Lifetime's that for me. Like, it's not a mammal, but it's not in the ocean anymore . . .

ARI KATZ: The universe is weird. We got bigger after we broke up.

CHRISTIAN MCKNIGHT: Lifetime became one of these bands, like Jawbreaker or Refused, these mythological bands that people just worshipped posthumously.

SHANE TOLD: Seeing Lifetime play their '05 reunion in New Jersey . . . I've never cried seeing a band until I saw Lifetime at the Stone Pony. I came out of mosh retirement, and I cried my eyes out watching them play.

PETE WENTZ: I was doing the label and I put out Panic!, Gym Class . . . I think the singer Ari from Lifetime originally reached out to me about them maybe doing some new music.

ARI KATZ: I don't think we would have thought about doing it without someone asking us. Our booking agent was like, "Don't you wanna look around or . . ." Honestly, I didn't know one Fall Out Boy song.

DAN YEMIN: I had met Pete a couple times before he was famous, because he was in Racetraitor in Chicago. So we'd crossed paths.

ARI KATZ: Pete was like, "I'll pay for whatever you guys need. I just would love to have another Lifetime record in the world." And we're like, "Well, that sounds pretty fucking good."

PETE WENTZ: Like, we could try to get this on *TRL* or we could just put it out. I just wanted more Lifetime music: "Whatever it takes, you guys pick . . ."

DAN YEMIN: No disrespect to Pete—he was great to us—but I think if I had more of an understanding of what kind of phenomenon was happening, I might have been more inclined to keep my distance. But ultimately, he was a straight shooter. He basically said, "I love the band, I want to be involved in what you're doing next. I understand you guys are grown-ups with jobs. You can do whatever you want." We were starting to have families and there's a lot of labels that will give bands money to record, but expect you to tour full-time. Pete was just like, "I'm excited you guys are doing a record. You guys can do whatever you want to do." So that seemed like a good proposition to us.

MANI MOSTOFI: When Pete put out the Lifetime record, it was kind of like, "This was the band that created Fall Out Boy."

SHANE TOLD: I remember so many people hating on that, because they just looked at Pete Wentz as like, MTV Pete Wentz.

PETE WENTZ: I hosted the red carpet at the MTV Movie Awards and I'm in a Lifetime shirt, sitting next to Rihanna.

DAN YEMIN: I would go into the waiting room of my office and him and his girlfriend would be on the cover of *People*.

SHANE TOLD: Yes! Use this money to bring us another Lifetime record!

ARI KATZ: I think they offered us more money than we took. I think the offer was bigger and we were like . . . it was kind of dumb, looking back. We probably should have taken as much money as we could.

DAN YEMIN: With Lifetime's previous records on Jade Tree, there's a couple of employees. I could drive to their office in half an hour if I wanted to talk about artwork or complain about something that didn't go the way we wanted. Pete's label was an offshoot of Fueled By Ramen, and dealing with them wasn't so much fun. That was more like dealing with a big company. I didn't enjoy that.

It became clear that Fueled By Ramen was connected to Warner Bros. In punk music, there's a long history of staying away from doing business with major corporations. That was always one of the values that felt really important—being connected to a viable and vibrant underground. We'd been assured that Pete's operation was entirely independent, but after the record came out, I started getting invoices that said "Warner Bros." on them. It was confusing, and it felt a little underhanded.

ARI KATZ: I'm definitely proud of it, but it's not my favorite [Lifetime album]. It was hard to make. I had little babies at the time and I was driving to record vocals after work. It wasn't as easy and fun as the first few. Although they weren't fun, either . . . I guess they were all hard to make. Lifetime is always hard to make records.

MANI MOSTOFI: I expected more Fall Out Boy fans to get into Lifetime as a result of that record. But I went to some Lifetime shows after it came out, and I didn't notice it in a crazy way. But I'm sure they drove some.

FRED MASCHERINO: That Lifetime record, I probably only heard it once, to be honest. I wasn't so much a fan as I was a peer. With my old band [Brody] in the nineties, I played bars with them with like fifty people there—the bad bar afternoon matinee shows where you're trying to sneak your friend in because it's eight dollars and that's too expensive. That's how I remember Lifetime. So when the young kids started liking Lifetime, they were already gone.

AMANDA BRENNAN: Those Lifetime reunion shows were wild because that was a band I literally never thought I would see. "Theme Song for a New Brunswick Basement Show" was my entire college experience: that unsure feeling of being a weird punk kid was best expressed in my brain through Lifetime lyrics. At this point, I'd seen some good reunion shows, and I'd seen some bad reunion shows . . . Let's put it that way. But with Lifetime, I was like, "This band is on fire. This must have been what it felt like when this band was playing before."

STEVEN SMITH: I was at Bamboozle [2006] doing interviews. We had 'em booked to give each band fifteen minutes. The reason we were going so fast was because Lifetime had reunited and we all wanted to go see them. We were jumping through questions and Chris Conley was like, "I get it, I get it!"

DAN YEMIN: At the Stone Pony, they put up this tiny little barricade six inches from the stage to keep people from stage diving, and we're quibbling with the management about it. Then you're at Bamboozle and between the barricade and the bouncer, you're like, fifty feet away from the audience.

That year we played right before Taking Back Sunday, which was a pretty cool spot.

STEVEN SMITH: Adam has Lifetime lyrics tattooed on his elbow.

FRED MASCHERINO: There were a bunch of bands besides us playing Bamboozle, who were all watching Lifetime's set side stage. I remember the singer Ari said, "I want to thank all the other bands playing tonight." I don't know if he mentioned anyone specifically, but somehow I knew he was talking about all the bands that were sitting on the side of the stage drooling, watching them. He goes, "Without you guys, we wouldn't be here today."

I wasn't sure if he was being sarcastic or not. Was he was being grateful, saying they wouldn't have reunited if all these young bands didn't love them so much? Or was he saying, "None of you fuckers would be here today without my music influencing you"? He said it, he didn't look at anyone, and I was like, "Was that an insult or a compliment?" And then they played their last song, and that was that.

MATT RUBANO: When TBS went from *Tell All Your Friends* to "MakeDamnSure," that was a big jump, and I never really got the sense we lost people. Our fan base had grown and changed, but I don't think we had any old-school protestors.

JOHN NOLAN: When *Where You Want to Be* came out in 2004, it was not that long after I had left the band; Straylight Run's album came out at a similar time. I tried to not pay attention at all because there was no way I could listen to Taking Back Sunday's music as a normal listener, you know? Everything was so tied up in my experience with everybody that I didn't feel like I was going to get anything positive out of listening.

By *Louder Now*, time had passed, and I wasn't quite as emotional anymore. And the band was really blowing up, so it was getting harder to avoid. "MakeDamnSure" was everywhere. That was the first one after I left where I had to be like, "Yeah, this is good." I had to give it to 'em.

JUSTIN BECK: I didn't get them when they had their old lineup. I never saw them perform till they had their new lineup with Matt Rubano and Fred. I remember watching them like, "Wow, these guys are fucking legitimate. They're a real fucking rock band."

EDDIE REYES: "MakeDamnSure" was our biggest single. "Cute Without the 'E'" is just as popular, but "MakeDamnSure" was the one that broke us.

AARON GILLESPIE: I still think they're the best ones from the era—better than My Chem, better than the Used, better than Fall Out Boy. The best. The absolute best. The Fred, Matt Rubano era of Taking Back Sunday. The best scene band, fact, hands down, bar none, in my opinion. Fred's interplay with Adam was so different than anything, the way Adam was all over the stage, and how tight the band sounded. Fred and Adam just had a thing. I know that there was social stuff, they couldn't get along. But those two, man. They just had a thing.

To be honest, I wasn't into all the theatrical shit. Even with Panic!, I thought the songs were good and I liked the guys, but that wasn't my thing. I liked that Adam wore cowboy boots, didn't give a fuck, and swung his microphone around.

GLENN GAMBOA: The Long Island show from the *Louder Now* tour is one of the most memorable shows I've ever been to. They headlined the Nassau Coliseum and were able to sell it out.

EDDIE REYES: That was like, our peak. We did it. We finally made it.

MATT RUBANO: I mean, as a Long Islander, I fucking saw Billy Joel there six times as a kid.

GLENN GAMBOA: There weren't any seats on the floor; it was all general admission. What the Coliseum people didn't know was, Taking Back Sunday fans like to mosh. And they're kids, generally, so they're going to try and get to the mosh pit. You had to have special tickets to be in the GA area, so kids were leaping over the barriers, and they'd get caught, and security would send them back to their seats. But at some point, they realized, "While security runs over to *this* side to stop people from jumping over, *that* side can jump over." Eventually there were like five thousand people on the floor. The security was just like, "Well, we don't know what to do."

And it was very emotional for the band. Adam got choked up because he was talking about how years ago, he used to deliver sandwiches just down the street. And Eddie is a Long Island guy. For him to sell out the biggest Long Island venue is a big deal.

EDDIE REYES: When something's exciting like that show, it goes by way too quick. You want it to last forever, and it doesn't.

JUSTIN BECK: Taking Back Sunday just took off in that moment. And Brand New, those guys just went fucking massive. I wasn't upset, just bitter, that

Glassjaw had no fucking commercial success. These shitheads . . . I was actually so psyched for 'em, I can honestly say that. It was nice to see something, for better or worse, come out of Long Island and these guys have success.

JASON TATE: Brand New had a gravity unlike anything I've ever covered before or since. Anything around the band potentially being in the studio was guaranteed to immediately have people obsessing over every little detail.

JASON PETTIGREW: Taking Back Sunday were bringing the decibels and the melodies. And they were really likable dudes. Brand New were so incredibly difficult with dealing with at nearly every level at *Alternative Press*.

There was a series called "Idol Worship" where somebody from a new band interviewed somebody from an old band in *Alternative Press*'s history that they were a very big fan of. Someone was like, "Jesse wants to talk to you about this." He was like, "I'm not really interested in doing this. I'll only do it if it's Morrissey."

MAX BEMIS: *Deja* was kind of cool because at least there is a self-hatred in there. *Devil and God* is so self-serious I can't listen to it anymore.

LUKE WOOD: To get *Devil and God* out, they went through a lot of soul-searching. They went to the Hamptons, ha, ha, ha, for about six months, lived out there and recorded every day. They recorded so many songs, and a lot of them leaked, ultimately. The leak was super devastating.

JASON TATE: I got a message from someone on the AbsolutePunk.net forum saying, "I have new Brand New music." I was like, "There's no way. Prove it." He sent me a .zip file. I remember listening to the first song and going, "Sounds like Jesse." I called up their manager and held the phone up to the speaker. He goes, "Ahh, that's 'Brother's Song.' How the fuck do you have that?" And I was like, "You're about to have a very bad week." He's like, "You gotta tell me where this came from," and I told him I could only tell him the kid that messaged me. I remember him calling the kid and the label got involved. They were like, "We need you to sign an NDA that you're not going to give these away to anybody." And I was like, "Dude, they leaked online. They're everywhere."

LUKE WOOD: It was weird to me, as I was going through the demos—and I really understood math rock!—but I kept getting so frustrated and confused. Like, "You want to turn into math rock? You want to turn into Slint? I thought you were going to be like Bruce Springsteen!"

I had a lot of equity in Interscope at the time and I was working really closely with Jimmy Iovine. I was having success and I chose to spend that equity on Brand New. So I wasn't gonna let them feel any of the heat, but they felt some of it, of course, because we had some raw conversations. Jimmy tried to explain to them his John Lennon, Bruce Springsteen, Tom Petty point of view on making music. Patti Smith had been in the same room with him and gone through the same questions, and Patti Smith didn't think "Because the Night" would be "Because the Night," you know what I mean? But it was a beautifully crafted record and once she had a hit, she was on the cover of *Rolling Stone*. In terms of any negativity or weight on the band, I shielded them a lot.

MIKE KENNERTY: Brand New, those guys seemed so up their own ass. Except the drummer, who was always very nice, very normal. But the rest of those guys, man. That's the only band I've ever vocally talked shit on because they were so like . . . They really thought they were fucking *artists*, and they're making important art that's so much better than everyone else.

The major label intervention on *Devil and God* . . . I'm not even saying that was a bad thing, because people love that record. So I think it was warranted—Luke being like, We signed you based on the strength of these things you've done before and you're just not delivering something as strong.

Brand New portray themselves in such an artful, weird way, when that record is the epitome of what everyone talks shit about with major label interference. You did not get to make the record you wanted! You had to continually keep making it until they were finally like, "Okay, this works."

LUKE WOOD: There wasn't a music video, there wasn't even a photo shoot. There wasn't a bio. They wanted none of it. They were retreating from the commercialization of the genre they came from. They were like, "Okay, everybody else is this, we're gonna be that."

There was no twisting of the arm, because they were way more sophisticated than that. And in transparency, I was very close with them, and I stayed that way, so we were aligned, we were friends. They're smart people. I couldn't bullshit them with, "Hey, just give me a half-day shoot!" None of that bullshit was gonna work. They knew everything. They did do one TV appearance, where they played "Jesus" on *Conan*. We agreed to that.

JASON TATE: After Brand New released *Devil and God*, you'd see all these bands that had been playing pop-punk make their attempt at a rock opus. Usually very badly.

LUKE WOOD: Rock music is always exciting as an area of urgency and discovery and opposition. When something has so much broad commercial appeal, it can become a trope, or a meme.

ADAM SISKA: Around 2006, there was a big clash between the early 2000s emo and everything that was gonna come after.

CHAPTER 29

THE BLACK PARADE

MIKEY WAY: At Madison Square Garden, me and my brother saw the Smashing Pumpkins on the *Mellon Collie* tour in 1996. I nudged him and said, "Gerard, this is what we're gonna do. We're gonna play this room someday." And he said, "I think you're right."

LESLIE SIMON: Being at *AP*, and seeing how people reacted to My Chemical Romance for the *Three Cheers* era, versus *The Black Parade* era, it was like a Niagara Falls of possibilities.

HANIF ABDURRAQIB: *The Black Parade*, as it stands, is a concept album that has a story arc, and listeners were left to their own devices because the band was too busy playing out the story arc in real time.

MIKEY WAY: The album was initially called *The Rise and Fall of My Chemical Romance*. That was the working title, the code name, taking a nod from Bowie. We wanted it to be a concept album. We wanted to tell this grand story. But we didn't want to have a title like that, because it would detract from the art we were making. Too tongue-in-cheek. Gerard came up with the concept of *The Black Parade* and had costumes and characters immediately, just drawing them in his notebook. I heard the title and it was one of those moments . . . like that shot in *Jaws* when they zoom in on Roy Scheider—you know the one I'm talking about. When Gerard told me the title of the album and showed me the picture, I remember feeling very similar to Chief Brody from *Jaws*.

JASON PETTIGREW: There was no middle ground. I thought *Black Parade* was going to be an absolutely magnificent realization of the My Chem vision, or a failure.

MIKEY WAY: It was like getting hit with a bolt of lightning. We knew we were doing something very risky. You know when you're in Las Vegas and you're betting everything on something? We were betting everything on this, and it was a gamble, a huge gamble, doing something so left of center from what we were known for and celebrated for. But we knew we were doing something that we loved. And that was more important.

LESLIE SIMON: It wasn't just that they were an emo band, it was that they were an arena rock band, with personality. Which we hadn't had in a really long time.

MIKEY WAY: We wanted to be a rock band. At the time, we were at odds with the term "emo" and we did everything we could, kicking and screaming, to get away from it. Even if it meant risking everything.

ANDY GREENWALD: I interviewed My Chemical Romance for a *Blender* cover story in 2006. Gerard was very nervous. That was my main takeaway. I think he doesn't think of himself as naturally a front man or a singer. The whole story was that he had to dress up and become a character to do this. And breaking away from that, doing the things that he wanted to do in the band artistically and musically without the drugs or alcohol was terrifying to him. So he was in a place of new and delicate sobriety. But he was also extremely excited. Not that he was manic, but I think he was getting a high from what was at his disposal: getting the comic book artist James Jean to paint *The Black Parade* artwork, getting Liza Minnelli to sing on the record. Things like that were the most exciting to him. I think he was in a very delicate and sensitive place, feeling the potential of what this could be if he approached it with a clear head and clear eyes.

GEOFF RICKLY: Whereas his brother was more of a recluse, Mikey was somebody I thought was totally equipped for it.

ANDY GREENWALD: They talked a lot about recording in LA, in the Paramour mansion, in the *Blender* story. And partly because they believe in ghosts. So, here's exactly . . . I just found my interview with Mikey from then. He's talking about his anxiety and how it was building and building: "I just chalked it up to being one of those months that got worse as we got closer to leaving for LA. It got worse and worse. You take all these factors, mixed with the follow-up for a multi-platinum, super-successful album. We're all scared. If you got that stuff on your mind, you factor that and it keeps adding and adding. You roll a snowball down a hill and eventually it becomes an avalanche. I tried to get in a positive frame of mind about LA, how it was gonna rule, it will be just what I need and so much fun. And then we got to LA. I saw the house. Just picture in your head, a horror movie and some sort of old-style Hollywood mansion in a horror movie. You can draw the Paramour: a huge gate, top of a hill, people didn't know where it was, like a hidden place. You walked in, you're in a different world. No cell phone, no heat, no TV. It almost killed us. It's famously haunted. And one of my biggest fears is ghosts."

He wasn't doing well . . . I think it was more of people who didn't have the equipment, you know, to deal with that. They didn't understand the language of what he was going through or how to talk to him or what kind of help to give him. And they all credit Stacy Fass, who was their attorney, for saving Mikey's life and saving the band in the process. Because she was an adult who could step in and see that he needed serious help.

MIKEY WAY: Being in a band illuminated that I need to take care of my mental health. And it made me work diligently to conquer a lot of the demons that I had.

MATT GALLE: I was in LA the day that they finished *Black Parade*. The producer Rob Cavallo wanted to celebrate and he took us, me and the band—they asked me if I wanted to come—to Vegas on a private plane. That was the first time I had ever been on a private plane. We stayed at the MGM at these crazy suites that had a basketball court. Like, we saw it on *The Real World* one time.

GEOFF RICKLY: I lost my mind when I heard *Black Parade*. I was like, "*This is it*. If you want to leave your mark on the world, *this is it*." I knew that no matter what happened, it was a massive cultural step. Even if everybody hates it, I just knew. It was just too good. This dark, cheeky, theatrical nature of it—it's when somebody matches their music exactly to their personality, and you just think, "This is who you are. I was waiting for this one."

MATT GALLE: I remember listening to the finished version of *Black Parade* in the parking lot of Long Beach Arena. Taking Back Sunday was playing there and My Chem came out and played it to us on the bus.

FRED MASCHERINO: *Louder Now* came out and we're like, "Oh man, we crushed this. No one can touch 'MakeDamnSure' or 'My Blue Heaven!'" And then they played us *Black Parade* and it's just like . . . *motherfucker*.

MATT RUBANO: "These guys have leveled up. These guys have grown into a punk Queen . . ."

FRED MASCHERINO: There's something transcendent about My Chemical Romance's music. I feel like Taking Back Sunday made great rock records, done in a way other emo bands didn't do. Timeless rock records. But My Chemical Romance has some kind of magic you can't put your finger on . . .

MATT RUBANO: Anytime somebody drops a concept record, and nails it, it's like, "Oh boy . . ." Artists versus, you know . . . a bunch of dudes in a band.

MATT GALLE: Everybody was just like, "This is insane, this sounds so huge."

CHRISTIAN MCKNIGHT: They played on the Top of the Rock during the VMAs; that's the first time they all wore the black costumes. Two or three days later, I saw Frank at a Converge show at Webster Hall. I was like, "You guys are gonna be the biggest band on the planet." He didn't know what to say. Frank was just going to shows, just hanging out.

MIKE KENNERTY: The night *Borat* came out, Gerard rented out a movie theater to stay open after the show—we played a show near Philly with them—and Gerard invited all the bands to come and watch *Borat*. I had just listened to *Black Parade* and I remember being at the theater talking to him about it: "Hey, man, that's a good record you guys did." And he was like, "Thank you, I'm really proud of it."

JASON TATE: They'd started blowing up with *Three Cheers* and there's this group—myself not included—that were like, "Okay, they've gone beyond what they were, is it cool to like this *Black Parade* album?" If you go back and read some of the reviews on AbsolutePunk at the time, it's the writer dealing with this debate of, "This band is so popular, is it cool for me to admit that this is good? Is it too teenybopper-ish?" Questions about selling out and all that sort of nonsense we were thinking back then. Now you look back and it's just ridiculous, because *Black Parade* is a stone-cold classic album.

HANIF ABDURRAQIB: I think critics warmed to them. The critics didn't feel like they were doing a Queen impersonation; they felt like they were doing an updated version of what Queen could have been.

ANDY GREENWALD: *Black Parade* blew people's minds, because no one had that ambition. We were so used to bands doing it the, quote, unquote, *right way*, meaning the R.E.M. way, which didn't really exist anymore. So when I wasn't writing about bands like My Chemical Romance, I was writing about bands like Death Cab, because people were like, "They're doing it the right way." You know, the indie labels, the lack of drama, blah, blah, blah. And then there were bands like the Strokes or whatever who came from an indie or punk ethos where it's like, "You're not supposed to wear makeup or sing in character." And then My Chemical Romance fucking did it.

GEOFF RICKLY: They took us out on their first big tour of the record, which was in England, because they were even bigger than they were here. Every single one of those shows was in a stadium. We played Wembley Stadium, sold out, back-to-back dates. Just being an opening act on those, the crowd was so supercharged. I would say something and it would echo around the stadium in a way I knew people couldn't understand what I was saying, but the whole place would just erupt, like they're just so excited about the idea they got to finally scream. And then My Chem came out.

HANNAH EWENS: MCR were inspired by Queen. In the UK, we're very used to that operatic rock sound. We have a penchant for the performative, especially men being performative. We really love that.

GEOFF RICKLY: When we were in London with My Chem, if we went to get food or something, My Chem would wear hats and sunglasses. If people spotted them, you'd hear, "IT'S GERARD!!!" You'd see a stampede of people, like *Hard Day's Night* . . . or *Night of the Living Dead*.

HANNAH EWENS: More girls than boys were into MCR, that's definitely true. They got a big male fan base on the first record, then all the girls jumped in on record two. Men are starting to filter off and then by *Black Parade*, this is a heavily female fan base.

GEOFF RICKLY: Gerard's just not the most social person by nature. When he was signing stuff, I think Gerard's most common expression was laughing and backing up at the same time, ha, ha. If it's not this staged moment of somebody crying and freaking out, like sitting and talking with fans one-on-one before a show, I've seen him be very open and warm. But a line of people treating you like a product is a very awkward situation to be in. Even if you end up being one of the biggest stars in the world, if that's not your personality, it's just not a natural fit. That's part of why Frank's really important to that band. He's doesn't wanna be the star, but he's very good at putting people at ease. So if somebody was crying about meeting Gerard, he'd be the one that's like, "It's okay, come over here and talk to me." The vibe was kind of like, "You're afraid to meet Santa? Here, I'm the helper!"

These kids thought about this person every day, obsessively. They have pictures in their locker. They get made fun of for liking them. And finally, it's their one moment . . . what are they supposed to say? It's so much pressure.

MIKEY WAY: I'm lucky to have had those experiences with people, however short they may be.

Kids were really appreciative of what our music did for them. "You saved my life" became a big keystone. We would flip it back at them: "*You* saved *your* life," because it's the truth. We didn't really do anything, you know what I mean? Maybe we made them realize they could save their life, in whatever way they meant it. There were kids that didn't have direction in life, and then there were people that were like, "You saved my life," in the respect of, they were going to end theirs. A lot of kids said that and it's a heavy thing to hear. But I always felt they did it themselves. Maybe we just made them realize they could.

HANIF ABDURRAQIB: I don't think they became a great band onstage until *The*

Black Parade. And they had to. It was so visceral that it required them to match that visceral nature onstage.

MATT GALLE: Behind them onstage was a fifty-foot *Black Parade* set piece. Gerard was rolled out as the Patient on a gurney and there was pyro, costume changes, with this operatic, Broadway feel. They took elements of artists that they loved like Queen and David Bowie that had awesome production—Gerard's always thought that way from his drawings and storylines. It was fucking exciting, dude.

HANNAH EWENS: As their career went on, they became less accessible to straight male fans, because they were becoming more operatic. The level of drama is just very feminine, right? *Black Parade*, they're literally doing a musical. From what they were wearing, to the visuals, the sound, the lyrics . . .

ELLIE KOVACH: My Chem is really the band from this world that comes to mind as feeling really protective of the queer kids and young women in their audience. Which is why, even today, they still feel set apart from a lot of their peers.

MIKEY WAY: "Don't ever let some shitty dude tell you you have to do anything for a backstage pass." That's something my brother said onstage for most of our career. This is a decade before #MeToo, you know what I mean?

JASON PETTIGREW: Gerard would be up there asking guys to take off their shirts, which is kind of like a fuck-you to the mentality of, "Hey, girls, show us your tits!" "What's the matter? You're too cool to give me your shirt?!"

The fact he wasn't drinking or on drugs, he just got sharper, more fearless. Not in a way of, "Kiss my ass, don't you know who I am?" But the guy who in the past maybe claimed he was fearless was now bona fide un-fuck-with-able. And that rubbed off on everybody in the band; they felt like a street gang. That was the by-product of coming clean.

STEVEN SMITH: They played the album all the way through on that tour.

MATT GALLE: We're booking the *Black Parade* tour in arenas and we're like, "We're gonna step this up." We were scared to do full arenas but we knew we could play bigger rooms and scaled-down arenas with closed sections, to start. And we did cheap tickets, like thirty to thirty-five bucks in arenas, which is hard. They're not making much money, but they're from basements and punk rock. And I remember putting them on sale, and opening up section after section. Then Madison Square Garden sold out.

MIKEY WAY: We ended the *Black Parade* run there. We sold it out in the round, like every ticket. And everyone we ever knew was in that room.

SARAH LEWITINN: I remembered Mikey telling me this story of going to see Smashing Pumpkins at Madison Square Garden and someone giving them like, primo seats because Gerard looked like Billy Corgan.

Watching them onstage at Madison Square Garden, I was thinking there's probably someone in the crowd who pushed their way to the front, and how this was going to shape their life.

HANIF ABDURRAQIB: I saw the Black Parade Tour multiple times. I'm not someone who often catches bands multiple times on the same tour, but with the Black Parade Tour, it was so fulfilling and so layered that it felt like seeing it once, you hadn't seen the whole thing, even though you had. It's like, am I missing something here? You didn't get a lot of over-explanation, because they were so insistent on being in character.

JASON TATE: The confidence of Gerard . . . From the very beginning I knew that dude was going to be a rock star. Meeting people at a younger age, I felt that a couple times in my life: "This person knows who they are, they're confident and they are going to see their dreams come true."

STEVEN SMITH: I asked Gerard on their tour bus before I saw the show: "Hey, how are you gonna do the Liza Minnelli part?" He's like, "I'm gonna do it."

HANIF ABDURRAQIB: The theatrics of *The Black Parade* get the headlines, but what is interesting about *The Black Parade* is how thoughtful it is about grief and loss and fear. Because it's My Chemical Romance, and because it's Gerard, you can't really separate the theatrics from the concept. But I don't think the organizing principle of the album, conceptual as it was, was about the theatrics. I think it was using theatrics as a vehicle to explain the otherwise unexplainable process of death and grieving.

People don't know what death is like. We don't know what waits for us when we die, if there's anything. I think approaching that with some understanding is frightening. And I appreciated *The Black Parade* for trying to, in a high-concept way, not be very comforting about the fact we're all gonna die. So I don't feel really comforted by *The Black Parade*, but I do feel comforted by the vision and the goal—understanding that, if there is something that waits for us after we die, it could be artfully articulated with the human imagination.

IN DEFENSE *OF THE* GENRE

HANNAH EWENS: I remember coming home from school one day and going to a newsagent to get sweets, seeing the newspapers lined up. The *Daily Mail* has always been a very right-wing paper. I remember reading, "No child is safe from the sinister cult of emo."

I went home and was like, "Oh my god, why are they saying this about . . . *my people*?" Obviously that part is funny, but I found it quite horrible and also scary, because it's saying this music is encouraging people to self-harm. Just massively stigmatizing and, ironically, a very hysterical piece of editorial about how hysterical emo was making teenage girls.

In the week that followed, my grandma was a *Daily Mail* reader and she cut out this article and brought it over to my parents' house: "This is what Hannah's been listening to."

MARIANNE ELOISE: A young girl who was thirteen, she was the same age as me, she took her own life. And because she was a My Chemical Romance fan, a lot of the newspapers in England picked up on that and said emo was a death cult.

HANNAH EWENS: British fans of My Chemical Romance arranged to protest outside the *Daily Mail* offices in London. A lot of people went, a lot of girls went—people there estimated it was between 150 and 200. When you think about how young the girls are and how big the UK is, it's kind of astonishing how many turned up. I remember sitting at home and looking for updates on social media, wishing I had been there.

I think the main reason girls were angry was because they were worried they would be stopped from doing what they loved doing. They were worried that parents were going to tell them to stop listening to this music and change how they were dressing. When you're a teenager, your love of music has been activated in a way that can only happen when you're a teenager. Girls knew they had to defend their right to participate in this fandom.

MARIANNE ELOISE: My Chemical Romance ended up doing an open letter like, "Obviously we're against suicide. That's not what we're about."

MIKEY WAY: We knew the tradition of tabloids in their culture, and we knew the tabloids were using it to sell papers. It's a game they play. We were offended. We defended ourselves when asked about it, because it was very much untrue.

JULIO MARTÍNEZ RÍOS: I remember one news anchor around 2006, 2007, sending to the commercial break and saying something like, "When we're back from the commercial, I will tell you all about emo kids, *the ones who enjoy suffering*."

JASON TATE: The mainstream press would have their freak-outs around self-harm and exploitation, like, "Kids should not be listening to this."

HANNAH EWENS: Being a British emo, the fandoms were super intense, super rabid.

MARIANNE ELOISE: I used to get beaten up all the time. In England, it was kind of bad. We all got bullied. There was a lot of gendered hate, a lot of homophobic hate with emo.

There was one issue of *NME* from 2006 where they interviewed boys at a Panic! at the Disco concert, like, "Why are you here?" So many boys were like, "I heard it's a great place to meet girls." And then some of them were there with girlfriends.

SPENCER SMITH: We played a show in 2006 for MTV's Spring Break in Panama City, Florida. This part of Florida is like . . . in the Panhandle, so it's a bunch of ridiculousness, a weird mix of people. I was walking from the bus to the venue and there's all these kids on line to go to the show. There was a girl there to see us and her boyfriend, who was obviously just being dragged along. We had on our fucking skinny jeans. And I mean, this is not a good word to say, but I remember the guy going, "Hey, nice tights, faggot." Like, holy shit, that dude's in line for our show.

PETE WENTZ: There was bending of pronouns within lyrics, which was pushing boundaries, at the time. Now it's just not, but I will say we were pushing boundaries with makeup and clothes.

BUDDY NIELSEN: It was always a constant topic in those days: "These fucking emo bands wearing fucking girl jeans, fucking painting their nails . . ." I mean, it's playful in nature but it definitely falls into the gender thing, the "you should be a man" . . . which is funny because punk was always like, "Go against the system!" "Okay, cool, I'm gonna dress like a girl." "No, no, no, no, no! NO. That's not what we meant."

On those Warped Tours, it wasn't even necessarily coming from bands. It was like, the fucking stage guy giving me shit for wearing girl jeans. I'm about to go out and play in front of ten thousand people with girl jeans on, and you're talking shit to me while you're loading the fucking trailer. Kinda seems a little weird to be giving me shit! Clearly wearing girl jeans has gotten me here, so I guess it's not *that* bad.

KAREN RUTTNER: A lot of people that were not in that scene didn't take it seriously. When it was more underground, it was easier to adopt, because it was just this cool thing bubbling up. And then once it did bubble up . . .

IAN COHEN: *Pitchfork* was at the height of its powers and had gone from just completely shitting on all these bands to not covering them at all.

Every now and again, maybe we would get a conversation about a new Paramore record or Fall Out Boy . . . In 2006 or 2008, there was maybe a conversation about My Chem. But as I recall, it just wasn't even considered.

MAX BEMIS: I think Fall Out Boy was the dividing line, where everyone in the scene younger than Fall Out Boy was willing to run with it. But the people who had preceded Fall Out Boy, even some of my favorite bands like Saves the Day and the Get Up Kids, were like, "Oh shit, we've really got to make some fucking indie rock music. We're just getting made fun of by *Pitchfork* and *Vice*." And they were driven away because emo was all they knew and they were sick of it. But for me, it felt kind of like betrayal: "Okay, but this is really important to all these people . . ." So basically anyone who invented it started to become disenfranchised with it, because emo was reviled by so many people. And because it was popular, it was no longer cool.

I felt Say Anything . . . *Is a Real Boy* kind of focused on what was not redeeming about emo. *In Defense of the Genre* was about what I felt was redeeming.

ELLIE KOVACH: Gerard Way could write in character, but he couldn't do music journalism inside a song like Max could.

MAX BEMIS: Emo had become popular, so there's a backlash to this kind of music, because society is trying to promote misogyny and feelingless-ness . . . My theory—and I still believe in it—is that it was just a reaction to the innocence in the music. People couldn't handle the innocence. I remember someone saying to me, "I can't listen to emo, it's too sincere." Like, dude, *what*?

RANDY NICHOLS: The name of the album, *In Defense of the Genre*, sums it up perfectly. Like a lot of us, Max in that era felt like there was this target on our back, like the genre doesn't matter. You wouldn't get the press coverage, you wouldn't get the radio stations playing it, compared to all these other bands who didn't have nearly the same meaningful impact on people's lives as bands from that scene. That record was Max's attempt to say, "We're important."

HANIF ABDURRAQIB: I love how sprawling *In Defense of the Genre* is and how it's a monument, a statement album.

ELLIE KOVACH: Max was trying to prove something with that album's ambitiousness. Trying to prove that this genre is something that could sustain a double album, an album of that length and thematic depth.

RANDY NICHOLS: Max came to me and he's like, "Here's a list of all the people I want to guest on this record." And I'm like, "Oh my god. How am I going to make this happen . . ."

MAX BEMIS: The people we couldn't get for that album were mostly people who were not emo at all. But we were on a major label, so let's ask fucking Scott Weiland or Rivers Cuomo!

Jesse Lacey told us he couldn't do it but wanted to, but then I think he told other people that he'd turned us down, ha, ha, ha. He had to play it like he turned us down.

COBY LINDER: We're on Warped Tour, we had a list of people, and they all sent their parts over in one or two days . . . Hayley Williams, Anthony from Bayside, Jordan and Chad from New Found Glory, Chris from Saves the Day, Gerard Way . . .

MAX BEMIS: He was always a friend and [My Chemical Romance] was one of those few bands that took us under their wing. We opened for them several times when we were first on tour, so it was an easy call to make. Getting Gerard to sing on the title track, his performance was incredible.

PARKER CASE: It was perfect timing because you almost could not make that record again. I mean, Dave Grohl can get whoever he wants, but there was something about this particular cast of characters that all fell into this web, this common thread.

MAX BEMIS: I was always of the mentality to like people who were not too cool for emo, and the scene. I wasn't one of these people who was like, "YEAH, STAY TRUE TO THE SCENE, MAN!" Like, I already knew it was kind of a joke. But just because it's kind of a joke doesn't mean that you shouldn't take responsibility and own what you like in life.

RANDY NICHOLS: There's so many weird things that went on in that moment. It was like high school, where different people dated at different periods of time, different bands had different relationships. It was almost like you had the jocks and the cool kids.

BUDDY NIELSEN: You were dealing with bands that were generationally different, the coming together of two separate generations.

FAT MIKE: I don't know what an emo band is. I don't know what makes one. Younger kids that don't have a very good sense of melody, I guess. Except for My Chemical Romance.

KEVIN LYMAN: In 2006, Warped Tour was coming off that giant year of 2005.

I was really worried I alienated our core fan base, that there were too many pop radio kids that came out and screwed up the festival for the people who came to Warped Tour every year. So I came back with a really hardcore lineup. It was NOFX, Helmet, Underoath . . . Underoath was probably one of my top five bands in 2006.

AARON GILLESPIE: '06 was the one, you know? *Define the Great Line* came out that June, debuted at number two [on the *Billboard* 200] and sold 100,000 copies its first week. We were still a Christian band.

Warped Tour '04 was fine for us. [In] '05 it kind of started to get bad. It didn't really get bad until Warped Tour '06.

RANDY NICHOLS: Everyone got together every summer for Warped and not only was it a place where all these bands connected, but it was that high school thing. You have the old punkers—Pennywise, NOFX, Bad Religion, Rancid—they were one group. And then you have the screamo kids, the pop-punk kids, and there's crossover between some of the groups, but the old punk rock guys kind of looked down their nose at everyone, most of the time.

FAT MIKE: NOFX hung out with the older bands: Joan Jett, Bad Religion, the Bouncing Souls, Less Than Jake. It's not like I went around watching Warped Tour bands. I went around taking drugs and hanging out in my blow-up pool. Warped Tour was hot. I would also golf four, five hours a day. And have dance parties on my bus.

KEVIN LYMAN: Some of the members of Underoath were very, very adamant, with a strict interpretation of Christianity. And other people were questioning certain facets.

FAT MIKE: Someone told me they were a Christian band. So one by one I . . . I like to introduce myself to a lot of the younger bands. So I met Aaron. Nice kid. He told me he didn't believe in dinosaurs.

SPENCER CHAMBERLAIN: It was getting weird within Underoath. There were a lot of internal conflicts over spiritual beliefs.

AARON GILLESPIE: We just didn't get along. Spencer got into all kinds of drugs and bullshit and half the other guys were pretty religious. I was really religious.

SPENCER CHAMBERLAIN: I was already dabbling before we made *Define the Great Line*, in late '05.

RANDY NICHOLS: Spencer was going through a drug problem at the time, and he'd actually opened up to a couple of people about his problem. He'd stopped for a minute right before Warped Tour.

SPENCER CHAMBERLAIN: They were having Bible studies on Warped Tour. That was another huge rift. I never went to them but some of the guys in Underoath were going to the Bible studies. I was private about faith; I wouldn't sit around and talk about it with a bunch of people I didn't know. Chris, Tim, and Grant from Underoath went for sure. Aaron might have gone to one or two.

AARON GILLESPIE: We had a Bible study on the tour with Emery and Paramore, and Fat Mike would show up, fucking hammered on pills and just talk shit.

FAT MIKE: I wanted to watch what these weirdos fucking do at night. A lot of people just kept saying how bad they felt because they coveted women, because they wanted to be with women, and they knew it was bad. And I'm like, "What the fuck are you people talking about?" I mean, if you're in a relationship and it monogamous, it's bad. But why do you feel bad about getting with a woman?

STEVEN SMITH: Oh yeah, the Bible study, Fuse shot it. I've seen the footage of Mike going, "What about dinosaurs?"

AARON GILLESPIE: Dude, it was a mess. It was so fucked up. Every time he showed up, he would be wearing a kilt and was like, fucked up on pills and drinking. We would bring a beer to Bible study and he'd be like, "You drink? How are you a Christian?"

FAT MIKE: At the time, the Mormons were really going after gay marriage. You know, Proposition 8 . . . I talked to Tim and he said he was against gay marriage. That's when everything clicked in my head and I go, "You know what, I don't want to be on fucking tour with a band that's homophobic."

TIM MCTAGUE: Even if there was a position that was held, it was never an anti-anything. It was just like, "Oh that's not for me."

KEVIN LYMAN: Mike's always looking for a reaction. If he's not getting a reaction from me, he's looking for a reaction from someone else.

AARON GILLESPIE: He would just come and sit by our bus and try to shock us with all these *shocking stories* because he knew we were a Christian band. He would tell us how they had a dominatrix on their bus, and she would beat the shit out of them while they all fucked her. NOFX are all ten years older than we are, we knew they were all married with kids. I don't even know if any of those stories were true.

Why Fat Mike chose to fuck with us, in hindsight, was because we were the band to watch that summer.

FAT MIKE: They always had a huge crowd. A lot of those bands would outdraw the punk bands in smaller cities. When you got to LA, San Francisco, or Chicago, it wasn't like that as much. But if we're playing Kansas City, all the newer bands drew more, because radio and shit.

RANDY NICHOLS: NOFX was always a Warped staple, but they weren't necessarily ever the biggest band on Warped. They were tying the tour back to its roots, keeping it still punk rock, and then you kind of had the trend bands that came and went. Not to say that Underoath was a trend that came and went, but they were the next cool thing. They were most likely the biggest band that summer.

FAT MIKE: I started going after them onstage, saying mean, yet funny, things.

AARON GILLESPIE: It was part of his schtick: "I'm the funny guy from the punk band." And we took it to heart. We kind of let it burn us down.

KEVIN LYMAN: Mike has a way of dividing and conquering. So when he starts hanging out with certain members of the band . . . It was much more a public rivalry than a *fuck you* rivalry backstage.

SPENCER CHAMBERLAIN: One night I hung out by their bus and drank a few beers, and Fat Mike offered me drugs. I said, "Nah, I'm good, I don't really do that on tour."

Then he joked about it onstage the next day and that's when it all hit the fan.

FAT MIKE: The next day onstage, I go, "Hey! I was hanging out with Spencer last night. You know what, he's a good kid. He didn't even want to do any cocaine!"

RANDY NICHOLS: The story spun and twisted . . .

TRAVIE MCCOY: Fat Mike called them out. He was like, "You guys like Underoath? Those guys are super Christian! I was up doing blow with Spencer all night!" I was like, "Ohhh shit, son!"

SPENCER CHAMBERLAIN: It was funny—I went the whole summer without doing drugs and I got kicked out of the band for doing drugs because I told the guys I was scared that I had a problem. I told our A&R rep at the time, hoping there would be some sort of community or love or help, but instead it was your biggest fear . . .

RANDY NICHOLS: Spencer opened up to a few people about his problem, one of them their A&R Chad Johnson. Chad, being this hardcore, fundamentalist Christian at the time—or still is—didn't really think through the right way to deal with it. His job was selling Underoath records and he broke Underoath up, because he felt his faith called him to.

SPENCER CHAMBERLAIN: Chad flies out, tells your manager, you walk on the bus and they're waiting to scream and kick you out of the band.

AARON GILLESPIE: Spencer doing drugs with Fat Mike, that didn't happen. But we believed it. It's so funny now in hindsight. We were like, "YEAH, MAN, YOU DID DRUGS WITH FAT MIKE, WE'RE SUPPOSED TO BE EXAMPLES, WE'RE SUPPOSED TO BE GOOD PEOPLE!"

SPENCER CHAMBERLAIN: There were a lot of Bible verses screamed at me.

AARON GILLESPIE: We just imploded. And we just left the tour. Kevin was like, "Wait, *what*?"

KEVIN LYMAN: I walked on that bus and I was like, "This band will not be a band anymore if they don't go home."

RANDY NICHOLS: Spencer called me telling me things were getting bad and that they were going to go home from Warped Tour. They were in Pittsburgh. I'm like, "Can you get everybody to wait till I get there?" While I was on the phone with him, I literally drove to the airport, called my assistant, and asked her to book me a flight, which I'd never done before in my life, I always booked my own travel. There's thunder and lightning, the flight's delayed, and I'm sitting there for four hours on the runway. I convinced Underoath to at least wait for me in Pittsburgh at the venue. When I finally got there, the Warped Tour parking lot is empty, there's nothing left, except for one bus, which was them.

KEVIN LYMAN: It was something you couldn't fix on the road. They couldn't fix it within their bus. It was only going to get worse and worse and worse.

RANDY NICHOLS: They were one of the biggest bands on the tour, but Kevin was like, "This band needs to go. It's the right thing for them." Things are pretty bad if Kevin is saying they should go home . . .

SPENCER CHAMBERLAIN: The shit those guys said was worse than what I was doing, you know? Telling an addict that you're wrong and there's no hope for you and you should be ashamed of yourself is not the best thing to do. You're supposed to get someone help. That could have ended really badly.

FAT MIKE: I had absolutely no idea about the addiction stuff until I heard about it later, after they already quit.

AARON GILLESPIE: The band was over, in our brains.

RANDY NICHOLS: I rode the bus home with them. Nobody was really talking for most of the ride. At one point, I was in the bunk talking to Spencer. We thought we were alone, but Aaron was in his bunk, unbeknownst to us. And Spencer said something to me—I can't remember the details anymore—and Aaron's head pops out of his bunk and just replies, "If you said that yesterday, we wouldn't be driving home right now." Right in that moment, the two of them clicked, and they were back seeing eye to eye.

AARON GILLESPIE: Randy and Chad Johnson—who was a big linchpin in the whole thing falling apart—helped us put it back together.

RANDY NICHOLS: Chad and I flew to Florida weekly for a month, having meetings with them. And each trip, we kind of won over one band member. Tim was one of the last to come around.

TIM MCTAGUE: That was probably the most selfish I've ever been. I remember going, "I don't even care if the band goes on, I'm done." I'm taking my ball and going home.

RANDY NICHOLS: The last meeting I was like, "I thought you guys were different. I thought you were different than what I thought of all super-religious Christians, but you have a friend who needs help and you don't want to help him." I was like, "You know what, all that shit Fat Mike jokes about from stage every day? He's right. I'm disappointed. I'm out of here." I gave everyone a hug goodbye, got on a plane, and flew home. Tim called me three days later, in tears saying like, "You were right." He said, "That hug you gave me goodbye was the angriest hug I ever got." He's like, "You're right. I have as much of a problem as Spencer does. Spencer has a problem with drugs. I have a problem not being open-minded to understand other people." That opened things up to a whole other level and led to the band coming back together.

KEVIN LYMAN: A couple months later, they were a band again.

AARON GILLESPIE: I felt like we had been given everything back.

KEVIN LYMAN: I don't think it was 100 percent fixed, but it was fixed enough that they could deal with each other in a different way.

RANDY NICHOLS: Underoath came back to Warped Tour in 2007.

FAT MIKE: I wasn't playing Warped Tour, I just went to it. Spencer or Aaron came up to me and gave me a shirt that said, "UNDEROATH: We Do Believe in Dinosaurs." And there was an image of a dinosaur with blue hair, which was clearly me. That was awesome. I loved that. That's a good one, you got me. I am a fucking dinosaur.

RANDY NICHOLS: I don't know if I've told this story in public before, but I feel like enough time has passed. I'm with Underoath on Warped Tour in Connecticut and the band would always pray before they went onstage back then. Mike knew that, and came over, talking and fucking with them to see if he could distract them long enough so they wouldn't have time to pray. Typical Fat Mike—being a dick, but a friend dick, you know what I mean? There's two minutes to go onstage and Chris from Underoath was like, "Guys, we gotta pray. Mike, do you want to pray with us?" You should have seen the look on Mike's face. He's like, "Fuck yeah, Underoath just invited me to pray with them!" He's kinda laughing, just being in it. And Chris turns to him and says, "Is there anything you want us to pray for, Mike?" He had mentioned at the time that he was going through a divorce. Chris says something like, "God, I hope that whatever happens is best for Mike, his wife, and his child."

Mike's demeanor completely changed. Mike's perception was that he was going to pray for everything to be fixed, for the family to be together, and all this crap everyone believes Christianity should be. Instead, Chris is standing there going, "Man, I hope your life gets better."

CHAPTER 31

"IT WAS *A* RECKONING *TO* HAVE THIS YOUNG WOMAN OVERTAKE *THE* SCENE"

GRETA MORGAN: The first time I met Hayley was at Bamboozle festival in 2006. We were both finishing high school by correspondence. She was like, "Isn't it such a bummer when you have to do homework before the show? My parents won't even let me go on tour without them. My parents are on tour with us right now." I was like, "Oh, wow, that's crazy. I'm lucky my parents let me go on tour by myself. But I gotta go home and take my final soon."

HAYLEY WILLIAMS: We were just kids before *Riot!* came out. In fact, we were kids for a long time after that!

I have a distinct memory—in fact, somewhere there's a video—of all of us, Taylor, too, hanging out at the park. It was springtime 2007, and we were literally playing in a field together. How much more innocent can you get? In many ways, it was the last uncomplicated season for us as friends.

JAMIE COLETTA: Hayley was cool. She looked like someone I'd want to hang out with, straight up.

PATRICK STUMP: Hayley was just this other thing entirely. I think she spoke to young women in a way that, not being a woman, I don't think I could ever understand.

HANNAH EWENS: A lot of being an emo fan was about the fashion and suddenly you had a woman—besides scene queens and other women on

MySpace—who was a style inspiration and an actual musician, a really cool front woman.

JAMIE COLETTA: It was all dudes, everywhere. Every band was all dudes. For me, it was this connection where, for the first time, it wasn't *that*. Hayley was awesome. She had orange hair, she was just so cool and fun. It was like, "I back this shit. Almost a little bit more than everything else . . ."

PATRICK STUMP: Hayley's really good. It's very easy to manufacture things, but you can't manufacture that.

PETE WENTZ: Whether it was Patrick, Brendon, or Hayley, those were the bands I thought stood out from our scene—bands where the singers had some serious pipes. You didn't need any smoke or mirrors.

ADAM SAMILJAN: I think John at Fueled By Ramen was smart about not going to radio too early. Not even entertaining that conversation on the first Paramore album was important.

JASON TATE: When *All We Know Is Falling* came out in 2005, it was not a thing where everyone was like, "Oh, this is the next big thing." That record for them was *Riot!*

In those days, it was always a big deal for them to make it not all about Hayley. There were so many rumors all the time: "This is just a launching pad for her solo career, they're just doing this now to give her industry cred, and then she's gonna go solo." So they spent so much time pushing back against that: They had the "Paramore Is a Band" T-shirts. That was a meme for a while. They wanted to say, "We are a *band*. That is what we are."

JOHNNY MINARDI: I remember getting a Paramore demo from John. It was called "Mexico," because they recorded it onstage during a sound check in Mexico. That song became "Misery Business."

ADAM SAMILJAN: We were all in a very small office in Tampa. John would be playing it from his office. I thought the first Paramore album was good, but when I first heard that demo . . .

JOHNNY MINARDI: I remember sitting there, probably on my first-generation iPod, and it was "Paramore Mexico Demo," or something like that. I played it a hundred times over the weekend. I remember going into John's office on Monday like, "I'm obsessed with this song."

ADAM SAMILJAN: Such a different vibe from the first album. The chorus felt huge. Hearing that very rough demo, you could tell, this album is going to be a huge step up.

DAVID BENDETH: Right before we started preproduction, we all went Christmas shopping at the Short Hills Mall [not far from my studio] in New Jersey. We were in these fancy stores and they were like, "Why are we here? We can't afford any of this." We ended up in Macy's, because that's always a good hit to buy Christmas presents. I remember walking back to the car and thinking, "I wonder if this band will be like others I've worked with, where they could never go back to walking around a mall."

HAYLEY WILLIAMS: There was an excitement around it that we knew was different from anything we'd experienced up until then. Of course, we'd only put out one other album at that point . . . but I want to say that we were confident that people—or at least, the right people—would get it.

DAVID BENDETH: Hayley took over this part of my studio in the storage area. There's a little ladder and it goes into this tiny loft. It has candles, it's away from everything, you can lock the doors. There was no question she was gonna make that her home.

I put it into the band's mind that we were going to write songs in the studio. Some of the sixteen songs they came in with were not finished yet. We had a lot of work to do. So when Hayley wasn't writing in that loft, she was in the TV room with the TV off, sitting on a couch. She was drawing and writing a ton of poetry and stories. She would put them up online anonymously to get feedback from other literary people, whether they were adults or not. When I saw that I was like, "This isn't just another person who writes lyrics."

ELLIE KOVACH: Hayley bypasses a lot of what we think of as stereotypical emo lyricism, that post–Chris Conley school of wordplay and metaphors. She does a bit of wordplay, but she's much more direct about what she's saying.

IAN COHEN: The lyrics were not as self-consciously clever or celebrity gossip-ish as Fall Out Boy was. It seemed more approachable and less whiny, like,

"Oh, this sounds like *Bleed American*." "That's What You Get"—that's the one for me.

JOHNNY MINARDI: While *Riot!* was getting recorded, we were getting songs from the band, like "That's What You Get." I think that's my favorite Paramore song ever.

STEVEN SMITH: While Paramore recorded *Riot!*, they asked *Steven's Untitled Rock Show* to come by the recording studio and hang out. They asked me to do gang vocals on "That's What You Get," so I'm listed in the liner notes as "Steven Untitled Smith." If you see the footage, I look real nervous. Like, "Ahhhhh, this is forever . . ."

SHANE DRAKE: Upstreaming was the goal. You were always hoping to get upstreamed to the major label affiliate. The worry is, "Will they service the band with the same integrity, energy, and enthusiasm as the independent affiliate?"

DAVID BENDETH: The head of Fueled By Ramen loves *Riot!* and they bring it into a meeting and they play a couple of songs. Lyor Cohen, the president of Warner Bros., thinks the record needs a hit . . . He's signed Nickelback and they're on fire, Lyor and Chad Kroeger . . . So he says, "Let me phone up Chad Kroeger and get him to write a song for Hayley Williams." I love Chad Kroeger, he's a great songwriter. I know people hate that band, but it doesn't really matter because the guy's so good. So, Chad Kroeger writes a song, sends it to Lyor, who then sends it to me. I listen to the song, and it's fantastic. It's a girl singing. And it's a little less rock.

They give me the task of talking to the band, to Hayley, and seeing if she likes the song, so we can cut it. The manager is not there. The A&R person's not there. It's just David Bendeth and the band. I tell them we played the record for the label and Lyor Cohen wants them to record this track. Hayley runs out of the studio, goes in the loft, locks herself in it, and I can hear her crying.

There's no words said. I call the A&R person saying this is a problem. I'm sure Hayley called her manager, as she should. And then Lyor Cohen got angry, because I'm sure he didn't want to be made a fool of with Chad

Kroeger, because he'd asked him to do this as a favor. And the song was great; you couldn't argue with it. Was it right for Paramore? We never really got the opportunity to go there.

JAMES MONTGOMERY: There was this question of whether Paramore were, quote, unquote, an *authentic band*, or put together by a label. All of their records are driven by that desire to prove people wrong.

DAVID BENDETH: It ended up getting ugly for a week. And I think it was really Fueled By Ramen that reasoned with Lyor Cohen. They'd played the music for some radio stations and felt quite confident that we had a good leadoff with "Misery Business." And I don't think Lyor had bad intention. But I don't think he knew the artist very well, hadn't spent a lot of time with them or knew what they were about.

"Misery Business" came out. I heard it on Top 40 radio and almost crashed my car into a wall: "What's that song doing on Top 40?"

JASON TATE: I remember the producer David Bendeth messaging me on Facebook, saying something along the lines of, "We're getting really good early numbers for this record." And then "Misery Business" becomes massive as the lead single.

JOHNNY MINARDI: It was like Panic! with *Fever*, where you heard the record three months before release and you were like, "Oh fuck. There's no chance of nonsuccess. This thing is going."

HAYLEY WILLIAMS: A few months before the record came out, we were headed to play a show at the Underworld in Camden and we were all looking out the window of the car we were in, and I saw the word "RIOT!" spray painted on the side of one of the buildings, ways away from the venue. I knew it was for us because it was done in the same sort of scribble, almost exactly like what was on the album cover. I said out loud, "People get it! This is the best sign we could ever have . . . that other people are making it their own."

ADAM SAMILJAN: On Warped Tour 2007, they ascended to the main-stage spot they really deserved. I remember the big amp stacks with "RIOT" spelled out on them.

DAVID BENDETH: I knew that this was going to be the beginning of a voyage.

KENNY VASOLI: Warped Tour 2007. Everybody was flipping out because they'd just released *Riot!* and *Riot!* fucking rocks. Live, it was ridiculous. They were the tightest band on that tour. It was a reckoning to have this young woman overtake the scene. It was beautiful.

HAYLEY WILLIAMS: The first big tour we did during the *Riot!* cycle was in the fall of 2007 . . . A lot of beautiful theaters that we'd opened shows at but never headlined. A lot of new fans had come along and we wanted to show them all that there was more to us than what they'd seen on MTV. There was depth and there were roots beyond some poster of us with MySpace hairdos . . . We covered a song by Sunny Day Real Estate on that tour. They were one of our favorites. It was about a six-minute-long song and every night we knew only a handful of people would know it. It turned out to just be a good reminder for me each night that, even as things were getting crazier, all of this started one day after school, at the Farros' house or in the Yorks' basement . . . just learning songs and bonding over bands we loved.

JIM ADKINS: When we toured with Paramore [in 2008], Hayley would ask a lot about the days of us touring with Mineral. She knew her stuff with the early days of our scene. She would come out and sing the high harmonies on the chorus of our song "Always Be." And kill it.

KENNY VASOLI: Touring with Paramore in the *Riot!* cycle, right away you could tell there's this real generosity to that band. I'd be coming out of smoking weed and drinking with my band and Hayley would still be out there signing shit for kids, right after she'd come offstage from this hour and ten-minute set. And there were a lot of kids.

JONAH BAYER: I remember Paramore would just go on the bus and eat tons of candy. There was candy everywhere. That was sort of their vice. Everyone was hanging out eating candy.

I was out with them for three or four days, writing a cover story for *Alternative Press* while they were on that tour with the Starting Line. We'd pull into venues with kids just lined up around the block in the morning, hours before doors. My impression was Paramore was even surprised by how many people were there.

JASON TATE: Paramore did a chat on AbsolutePunk.net and crashed the website immediately because we got hit by hundreds of thousands of people from Brazil. I'm not sure why they were such a massive band in Brazil. But they took down my servers.

ZACH LIND: When I watched them live, I thought, "Man, if these kids can keep their shit together, they're gonna be really good." They were already a really good band, and you could tell there was some talent and good musical instincts in the mix. You could also tell that they were very young.

JIM ADKINS: The advice I remember giving them is that you've got to protect the place the music comes from. You need boundaries on some personal levels, because with what was happening with them, they were gonna get pushed, and it's gonna be up to them to decide how far that goes. It really isn't the end of the world if your record doesn't break in Chile, you know? You gotta be smart about opportunities that come by, but if you're just killing yourself and don't want to do this anymore, what's the point?

ZACH LIND: You could tell there was a lot of drama with them. I think the problem was the business arrangement. The way the band existed, in a legal sense, was really just a solo project with hired people, to be in a band that supported Hayley and whatever contract she had with her label. That's how they were on paper, but in real life, they existed as a band, not dissimilar to how we operate. I think Hayley preferred being in that type of arrangement, and fostered and participated in it. But the unfortunate thing was that wasn't reflected in how the band was compensated.

For Jimmy Eat World, every dollar we get is split four ways: I get twenty-five cents, Jim gets twenty-five cents, Tom gets twenty-five cents, Rick gets twenty-five cents. And that is a direct reflection of how we operate and how we started. So I was always like, "You guys need to have a conversation about how you want to operate as a group, and then make sure your legal and business arrangements reflect how you operate in real life." I talked to them a lot about that: "Hey, you're always going to run up against this because your legal framework doesn't reflect how you guys operate."

KENNY VASOLI: I think you could sort of see the writing on the wall.

JONAH BAYER: That lineup did not last a super-long time, even though *Riot!*

was such a successful record. But my perception was that everyone was having fun. Like I said, I just remember them hanging out, eating candy.

HAYLEY WILLIAMS: What I take from that season of life is that we all have this one golden summer of life—which *Riot!* truly felt like—that we can try and mine out of forever . . . or we can appreciate it for what it was and carry on. We have to find our other summers. Those other definitive seasons in our lives that make us feel like we're exactly where we're supposed to be. If you're always turning around, facing the direction you came from, how can you appreciate where you're standing today? You have to give yourself a chance.

CHAPTER 32

TAKEOVER

MANI MOSTOFI: February 2007, the Chicago Bears were in the Super Bowl, so it was a big deal for us Chicago boys. Pete got this corner booth at the 40/40 Club—Jay-Z's club—in New York City, and it's packed with all these in-crowd, New York people, and we were just these dudes sitting in a booth. It's Pete, me, some of the road crew, maybe his friend Charlie, who was a kid from the hardcore scene who was Pete's bodyguard for a while. The only reason we were there is because Pete's famous and sorta knows Jay-Z. So we're sitting there and the waitress keeps coming and asking us to order more. She's supposed to be generating thousands of dollars from Super Bowl weekend at this corner booth. People should be ordering Cristal, and we're all these vegetarian and vegan straight-edge kids. Pete's the only one of us that had any money. We're trying to come up with stuff to order. A couple of us drank some beers. We're like, "Let's get ten baskets of fries!" Halftime rolls around and the waitress comes up to us like, "Look. I need to be making a shit-ton of money. I got all these Wall Street guys over here that are dying to sit at this booth and they're gonna be ordering $1,000 bottles of champagne. I really need this booth, guys." I don't think she knew that Pete was famous, because at the time, Pete was famous to fifteen-year-olds. Pete went back to the hotel and I watched the second half in my friend's dorm room on this thirteen-inch TV.

LESLIE SIMON: Before *Cork Tree*, Fall Out Boy were so hungry; they hadn't tasted what fame was beyond the Midwest. Then "Sugar, We're Goin Down" was such an exponential jump. To know there's even more potential out there . . .

PATRICK STUMP: I can pinpoint the moment that I decided, "Oh, I should learn how to sing." The band was nominated for a Grammy, and we were close to the stage—four rows back—because they want you on camera if you win. I'm sitting behind Chuck D, across from Elvis Costello, and twenty feet in front of me, Alicia Keys presented an award to Stevie Wonder, who sang a little something. Right then I was like, "I shouldn't be walking around being like, 'Oh, I'm not really a singer.'"

The label wanted "Sugar" Part Two and I was like, "Fuck this, this is the last time I can guarantee someone's going to pay for strings, horns, and anything I can dream of. This is it." So I threw everything at the wall. Absolutely everything.

"This Ain't a Scene, It's an Arms Race" started out as a beat I made Gym Class Heroes that they didn't want. I thought, "What if I made this a rock song?" I just started singing the "this ain't a scene" part with Pete's lyrics.

PETE WENTZ: It was just a little group of bands, then all of a sudden, people are on *TRL* . . . It felt like a nuclear buildup.

NEAL AVRON: Pete would email Patrick: "Here's some cool lines I think belong together." And Patrick would edit those together into a song. You could email Patrick some words, and he hears melody in those words. He can sing you where the melody should go up, and where it should go down. It was like Elton John and Bernie Taupin.

PETE WENTZ: "Arms Race" is a weird fucking song. It's got a middle bridge that's kind of based on Justin Timberlake, but then a super-punk chorus.

JONATHAN DANIEL: I don't think the label thought "Arms Race" was a pop single, which it probably isn't. But their manager Bob McLynn thought it was the right move.

PATRICK STUMP: He was like, "I've never been more proud and scared to promote a single to radio."

JONATHAN DANIEL: And he was right. Coming off the back of *Cork Tree*, "Arms

Race" became a giant pop hit. And we all felt very good about "Thnks fr the Mmrs" as a follow-up. It's such a great pop song. I remember making the video with the monkey playing chess with Patrick. And I can't remember what actress we were supposed to get, maybe Lindsay Lohan or Paris Hilton . . .

PETE WENTZ: I was friends with Christina Milian and I reached out to her. She was like . . . Her mom didn't want her to do it. In retrospect . . . well, maybe she didn't want to be in a video with a bunch of dudes in a band and real, live monkeys. Maybe she was just being nice about it by being like, "My mom says I probably shouldn't do this video."

JONATHAN DANIEL: Pete was like, "Well I know this girl Kim that could do it." It was Kim Kardashian. Pete's like, "I know her, she's cool."

PETE WENTZ: That was definitely the last time I would be in a picture with her where we'd be in any way equally famous, you know what I mean?

She was super focused, showed up early, did whatever it was: "Oh, will you stand next to this monkey?"

SPENCER SMITH: Pete Wentz always had a Jay-Z-esque spirit in him, of being bigger than just the bass player in Fall Out Boy.

MANI MOSTOFI: The emo and pop-punk scenes were really white. And I think because Pete can be white-passing if the magazine cover does the hues and the saturations in a certain way, Pete's identity and background were hidden. But not if you were paying attention.

ANDY GREENWALD: One thing that came out of one of my Fall Out Boy cover stories is that Pete's related to Colin Powell. There was a picture of Colin Powell at his family's house. I don't know if it was by choice or not, but Pete's biracial background and heritage was never a part of the conversation about the band.

Patrick knows a lot about all kinds of music, but Pete adored hip-hop. I think he adored the swagger, the brand-building, the myth-making. He had no allegiance to the remnants of the nineties where you should be ashamed about wanting to promote yourself. He was in tune with people like Pharrell, people in that moment who were brand-building while making hits. Pete's willingness to be upfront with that set Fall Out Boy apart.

PETE WENTZ: Jay-Z had gone into retirement and he was president of Def Jam. Fall Out Boy was on Island, part of the same label group, so we were like, "Why don't we call in all the favors we possibly could?" What if we had Jay-Z intro *Infinity on High*? That was the big wish.

At the time we didn't really understand critics, so we were like, "What if we whispered all the reviews and then Jay-Z intro'd the record?" We told the label and they're like, "We'll see."

NEAL AVRON: The album was done. We were getting ready to master, so it was very much the end of the process. Pete called me and said, "Jay-Z might do this."

PETE WENTZ: We got a phone call that it was gonna happen: "He's in Australia, his tour manager is gonna call you, and then you'll call him." So we're sitting there, talking about it: "How do you ask for Jay-Z? Do you say Jay-Z or Mr. Carter?"

We called the tour manager and while we were waiting, Jay-Z just answered: "Whuddup, this is Hov." We were like deer in the headlights. He was like, "What do you want me to say?" And we were like, "*Uhh*, pretty much anything you say will be cooler than what we ask you to say." So the "Thriller" intro, he did a whole take over the entire song. There is a mega-take somewhere but we ended up cutting it down to what was at the start of the album.

NEAL AVRON: In retrospect, I wish I mixed Jay-Z a little louder.

ALEX SUAREZ: *Infinity on High* came out and Fall Out Boy were freaking massive. Those guys were superstars.

JONATHAN DANIEL: Everything became, "How do you do something big?" And that's Pete's forte. Going bigger, bigger, bigger . . .

SPENCER SMITH: They actually opened a bar.

ANDY GREENWALD: On the East Side, Angels & Kings.

RYLAND BLACKINTON: On Avenue A and Eleventh Street, in the East Village. It was an area we were always hanging out anyways, close to Gabe's apartment.

GABE SAPORTA: Angels & Kings was like having our own clubhouse.

SARAH LEWITINN: Finally, a club was made by the emos, for the emos, where they could listen to Depeche Mode.

GABE SAPORTA: Internally, we used to call it AK47, because Pete really wanted to call it that. He wanted there to just be a neon sign of a gun at the door, which I thought was dope. Then we decided to call it Angels & Kings—out of honor to the Crush founders Jonathan and Bob; Jonathan had been in a band called Electric Angels and Bob had been in a band called the Step Kings.

SARAH LEWITINN: You wouldn't see Interpol there, you know? You would see Taking Back Sunday and Armor for Sleep there. It was kind of like, when Planet Hollywood opened, a kid might imagine Tom Cruise was gonna be there all the time. He was never actually there, but with Angels & Kings, Pete Wentz was always there. So it became an attraction . . . a tourist attraction for emos.

PETE WENTZ: A lot of what we tried to do with Angels & Kings was based off Misshapes.

NICK SCIMECA: Pete invited me to New York for the opening. I remember sitting on the stoop outside, it was me and Travie from Gym Class, and Jay-Z and Beyoncé walk in. We're just like, "What is happening right now?"

RYLAND BLACKINTON: Pete introduced me to Jay-Z there. I was like, "Nice to meet you. Can you pass me my jacket?" My jacket was just to his right. Afterwards I was thinking, "Wow, that's the conversation I had with Jay-Z? Can you pass me my jacket?" I remember shaking hands with him. I could fit like seven of my hands in his, and I have big hands.

JAMES MONTGOMERY: The crowd was a lot of hoodies, a lot of bangs. They really tried to make it a straight-up rock bar: good records, good drinks.

MATT RUBANO: It wasn't a nightclub; it was one room with a bar and a couple of booths. There would be kids—and by kids, I mean, underage fans—outside like paparazzi. You'd go up to the door, and the door person knew who was who, I guess. Inside, it was everybody standing, nuts to butts, and still a bunch of scene kids and fans, with digital cameras taking pictures of the whole room.

ALEX SUAREZ: A lot of rowdy sing-alongs and a lot of people drinking canned beer.

MATT RUBANO: I remember Will Forte from *Saturday Night Live* trying to pick up my girlfriend, no fear about it, and being like, "That's so cool. Will Forte's here!" Fans and artists and socialites and random New York City nightlife people all crammed into the same room, where everyone was having a pretty different experience.

ALEX DELEON: Smaller touring bands couldn't afford to go out and pay twenty dollars for Manhattan drinks, so we'd all go to Angels & Kings because we could drink and party for free. That's where everyone ended up. It was just what you did in New York.

SARAH LEWITINN: Karen and I did our party there when it first opened.

KAREN RUTTNER: It was just because we were friends with Gabe and the Crush crew. And like, by default, Travie McCoy. They bought the bar and they wanted to have cool parties there, so they asked us if we would move our party to Angels & Kings.

SARAH LEWITINN: It was a place they could feel famous, you know? They could go Misshapes, but no one's gonna know who they are. They go to Angels & Kings, they're going to get treated like a fucking angel and king.

ALEX SUAREZ: All the main guys had this Knights of the Round Table thing going on between them: Pete, Travie, Gabe, William Beckett.

TRAVIE MCCOY: Everybody thought me and William Beckett were a couple. They called us Treckett, they thought we were gay together. We would always get drunk and kiss . . . We loved each other; it was a brotherhood, you know what I'm sayin'? I'm not about that life; I don't knock it, though.

ADAM SISKA: I definitely have a photo of Gabe and William from The Academy Is . . . kissing each other in New York City. I think at one point in time it could have broken the internet. Now I think everyone kind of knows that sort of thing was going on. I never did hear of anything beyond that happening between the bands. But I wouldn't be surprised.

KAREN RUTTNER: You didn't see that at Angels & Kings. They were not hanging around in the corner booth making out with each other.

ADAM SISKA: Usually, it would be on a walk from the bar to a hotel, or something like that, when everyone's really liquored up and goofing around.

And usually it would probably be because some women were hanging around, and somebody like Gabe was trying to get a rise out of everybody.

GABE SAPORTA: Remember, in context, we were pretty rambunctious. We weren't tough guys or dangerous, but Pete was getting into fights regularly, you know? There were news articles coming out about fights happening around us. We came from the hardcore scene, right? So I think some of us saw ourselves as having the personality of not backing down from a fight. Juxtaposing that with kissing each other, for me, came from as a kid, seeing Nirvana perform on *Saturday Night Live*, and Kurt kissed Krist Novoselic onstage. That didn't feel edgy for the sake of edgy. It was pushing the envelope, in certain ways. I don't really know how to explain it, but I hope it was a positive thing.

ADAM SISKA: There were rumors that Bowie and Mick Jagger had sex with each other. Maybe this was part of stoking the fire of wanting the fans of the bands to have this ambiguously sexual relationship between the front men. Definitely a presence online of fan fiction involving all sorts of guys from that Decaydance scene. There was some story about me and Ryan Ross being lovers, which I always thought was hilarious.

GABE SAPORTA: I think the kissing was a bit for both the shock value and the normalization of it. It was not something we saw a lot normally in culture. I don't know if we were consciously trying to normalize it, but we were always very much pro-everyone feeling welcome.

It was never like, behind closed doors. It was always on camera, in front of whoever. So it was more about making some kind of statement. What that statement is exactly, I'm not sure how to put into words.

LESLIE SIMON: I don't remember the kissing feeling real, versus, "Oh my gosh, two guys are kissing!" Like, I don't really remember William Beckett sucking face with Travie, you know?

PETE WENTZ: The only time I kissed any of those guys was a picture that's somehow on the internet where Gabe grabs my face and kisses me, and I was like, "What is happening right now?"

GABE SAPORTA: [Who was the best kisser?] Definitely Pete. Maybe tied with William Beckett.

PETE WENTZ: There were a couple of years where we all hung out and we would meet up all around the world. I know it's the cheesiest thing to say, but it was just like the Avengers or something.

TOM HIGGENSON: Fall Out Boy always had a great sense of A) what was cool. And B) who their audience is, and would spoon-feed that to them.

JAMES MONTGOMERY: I was cohosting a show with Pete on MTV called *FNMTV*. It was every Friday of the summer, big video premieres. They were trying to make videos important again.

PETE WENTZ: Lil Wayne came on the show. I was a superfan of him when he had the mixtapes, before he got super crazy in pop, but everybody in hip-hop knew. I gave him my bass, this signature bass I had with Fender.

JAMES MONTGOMERY: The 2007 VMAs in Las Vegas, at the Palms, MTV gave Pete his own suite . . .

PETE WENTZ: They were like, "We're doing this thing in Vegas, you guys get a suite and you can just do whatever you want."

ALEX SUAREZ: There were performances in each of the suites.

JONATHAN DANIEL: We had Fall Out Boy, Panic!, Gym Class . . .

VICTORIA ASHER: Before the performances during the day, we just got to go to all these gifting suites. It was a total *Spinal Tap* moment, no one knowing our names. "Who is it? Cobra Starfish?" But then we're suddenly picking out all this stuff you can get for free.

RYLAND BLACKINTON: I think I got an Xbox that night. Gifting suites were outrageous back before they attached tax liabilities to them.

JAMES MONTGOMERY: Jay-Z was hanging out in Pete Wentz's suite. Gym Class Heroes were there and Babyface was around.

PETE WENTZ: I remember rehearsing with Lil Wayne, because we were gonna do the "Arms Race" remix with him. And he's a true savant, right? He's walking around and you're like, "I don't know if this guy knows where he is." Then the music starts going, and every time he does a verse, you realize he's making it up on the spot, because he's rapping about people in the room. Like, "Wow, this guy is actually genius level."

TRAVIE MCCOY: That was the first time I kicked it with Lil Wayne. We kicked it on the bus. And that was a really dark time for me because I was heavy on pills and shit and I knew Wayne had the purple drink, you know what I mean? So I was like, "Wayne, I know you got some of that purple." He gave me a bunch of weed and I was like, "Nah bro, that *purple* purple." His man poured me half a Gatorade bottle full of promethazine. It was the thickest . . . It was the illest shit you can get. You don't need much to get wasted and I'm just guzzling that shit. So before they call us to do the "Arms Race" remix, I'm in the chair getting my hair done, like falling out and shit. And they're like, "Yo! Five minutes and you're performing!" So I pop up and we do the "Arms Race" remix with Fall Out Boy.

ALEX DELEON: Pete gave me a backstage pass. I remember just being a kid wandering the hotel rooms at the Palms and meeting Rihanna. Pete was like, "Oh, this is Rihanna, we're performing ['Shut Up and Drive'] with her."

PETE WENTZ: Fall Out Boy ended up being Rihanna's backing band. It was interesting because the way she looked at the time, we really looked like we could be her backing band.

ALEX DELEON: Then I walk down the hall and meet Dave Grohl and Lemmy from Motörhead.

TRAVIE MCCOY: That VMAs was a fuck show. It was in all these different rooms . . .

RYLAND BLACKINTON: The whole thing was crazy, just on a TV production level. Big bundles of cabling running across every hallway, just tremendous AV bandwidth required to make this happen. It was really hot in the room when we performed.

PETE WENTZ: The whole thing was so poorly thought through. You had to take an elevator down to the award show from the suites when the awards came up, but there were no elevators that could get you down there. I guess they were so busy that there was no elevator for it. So we just ended up doing the awards in our room. I remember walking through the suite, just trying to find a place to hide and hang out, and seeing the Gym Class VMA before it was announced and thinking, "Damn, that's fucking really special." They were such an outlier, they didn't fit in anywhere.

JONATHAN DANIEL: I think Travie was a reluctant pop star.

SHANE TOLD: This was Gym Class Heroes blowing up with "Cupid's Chokehold."
TRAVIE MCCOY: They were like, "All right, we gotta get you over here because they're announcing Best New Artist." It was Jamie Foxx and Jennifer Garner. This is the fucked-up part, man, this is one of the biggest moments of my career and Jennifer Garner's stupid ass . . .
PETE WENTZ: "And the award goes to . . . Gym Class Fall Out."
TRAVIE MCCOY: "Gym Class Fall Out." I was like, "WHAT?!?! YOU HAD ONE JOB! ONE JOB!!!"

I celebrated by guzzling more promethazine and codeine. "Thanks, guys, fucking Gym Class Fall Out." But yeah, we got a Moonman out of that motherfucker.

ALEX SUAREZ: Crush was like, "We're gonna get you guys on at the end in the credits . . . *Go!* Get in there and play 'Snakes on a Plane'!" There's maybe ten seconds of Cobra performing in that hotel suite.
SHANE TOLD: For the afterparty, we were on the top of the Palms and there was a balcony and these hot tubs. There were hot chicks in the hot tubs, and they were repping Skyy vodka or some vodka brand. It was the most kind of mainstream rock star thing I'd ever seen.
TRAVIE MCCOY: Another funny story at that VMA . . . Mind you, I'm fucking sedated out of my brain, and I bumped into . . . remember that chick Lil Mama? That song "Lip Gloss"? I bumped into her, and she was dressed like a baby: a bonnet, a silk pacifier. I went to shake her hand, she has a pacifier in her mouth, and she just looked at me and rolled her eyes. I'm like, "You're dressed up like a baby right now, how are you gonna diss me?"
RYLAND BLACKINTON: That night, Brent from Mastodon got into some kind of fight and got put in the hospital. [Mastodon had been playing in the Foo Fighters' suite.] I bumped into Brent in the hallway. He had been drinking a lot. Randomly, he was like, "Hey, man, come with me." I followed him into a limo and Brent was like, "The Four Seasons." I don't even think there is a Four Seasons in Vegas. The limo driver was really confused. We drove through Vegas until the driver found out it wasn't Brent's limo and neither of us had any cash. We got kicked out somewhere in the middle of

Vegas. I remember a couple of really intense moments where he was like, "Look at me, look at me," like he wanted to hold really intense, sustained eye contact.

SHANE TOLD: It seemed weird that there was this bender going on. I talked to Gabe Saporta about Cobra Starship that night, we had a conversation for quite a while. Just a crazy, crazy Las Vegas party at the top of the Palms. We stayed up very late.

RYLAND BLACKINTON: What a fucking eclectic mix of genres and people. It makes me think of Aerosmith and Run-DMC, when Wayne started really fucking with guitars hard.

TRAVIE MCCOY: There's always something alternative, bro.

PATRICK STUMP: Travie was an MC, who could also sing. It sounds stupidly simple to talk about, but that was a novel idea at the time. There wasn't a lot of that.

TRAVIE MCCOY: Wayne was really stoked on Gym Class.

PETE WENTZ: A year later, I saw Lil Wayne in the Kevin Rudolf video for "Let It Rock." And he's playing that Pete Wentz Fender bass I gave him.

THE BAND *IN A* BUBBLE

MATT RUBANO: As the shows stopped being underground-y, it seemed like people were getting choosy about their punk and hardcore ethics. I mean, Taking Back Sunday was on a fucking Denny's menu. We did a Denny's promotion for cash, where we made a menu item with a Denny's chef. We went to one of their test kitchens. We had little Denny's chef's coats. We did a photo shoot for it and we got to create an item that was on the menu. There were some other bands that did it: the All-American Rejects, Eagles of Death Metal, Plain White T's, Sum 41, Good Charlotte.

I'll tell you one that we turned down: I forget which company it was, but it was a manufacturer of hot dogs, and they offered us a bus. I don't remember if it was a hot dog–shaped bus, or a vinyl advertising sticker wrapped around the bus. The company was like, "We'll absolve your bus fees for the tour if you roll in these." You go, "Wow, we could cross off buses on our touring budget? That's kind of cool." Then somebody luckily speaks up and goes, "Yeah, that's cool. You know what's not cool? Getting off of a gigantic hot dog every day outside a venue."

WILL PUGH: It's like the Steve Buscemi meme, "How do you do, fellow kids?" That's what corporate America will do. You can completely turn your back to it as an artist, or you can look at it as an opportunity: "Okay, we'll take your corporate dirty money and we're gonna use you right back."

JASON TATE: I thought Cartel was headed for superstardom. I thought, "This could be the next Fall Out Boy."

WILL PUGH: The era we came from was sort of a transition from bands like New Found Glory, Saves the Day, My Chem, and Fall Out Boy. Fall Out Boy had much more of a grassroots, underground following in Chicago. The scenes those bands came out of were bigger, so it granted them a lot more relevance. Where we came from, Atlanta, it was just like, "Oh, weird. A scene band from Atlanta that blew up."

KEVIN SANDERS: Florida hardcore was a big thing, and Atlanta had a big hardcore scene; those bands would do tours in the Southeast all the time.

WILL PUGH: We caught a lot of shit for being poppy in a scene dominated by hardcore bands, but we were all friends with those guys: "Yeah, sure, give us our fair share of hell." That was kind of the joke.

KEVIN SANDERS: New Found Glory was one of our biggest influences, mainly because Will's voice was so similar.

ALEX DELEON: Will was a great singer, with a super-pop voice. No matter what the genre, he could sing.

KEVIN SANDERS: Our first album, *Chroma*, was released October of '05, by the indie label the Militia Group.

WILL PUGH: We blew up on MySpace in '05, '06.

JOSEPH PEPPER: After *Chroma*, we were playing Warped Tour in 2006 on the Ernie Ball Stage, this side stage that wasn't even the second largest stage. The crowds went out past the sound tent and through the areas around other bands' merch tables. That pissed off the merch people because they couldn't make any sales. We had been playing smaller venues, house shows up till that point. That's when I started being like, "Oh shit, we got something here."

KEVIN SANDERS: By summer '06, we were on Epic and they wanted to rerelease *Chroma*.

LESLIE SIMON: Will was considered heartthrobby. They also kept their noses clean. They were pretty well-behaved; they didn't make waves. They didn't do or say bad things.

JOSEPH PEPPER: Will looked a lot like Aaron Carter, when he was younger.

WILL PUGH: "Yes, for the fifty thousandth time, I know I look like Aaron Carter. We have the same little black streak in our hair, we happen to be blond, we're white guys with some jawline . . ."

JOSEPH PEPPER: There's a story, he was chased by a mom and her daughter because the daughter thought he was Aaron Carter. They were honking and almost ran him off the road.

WILL PUGH: "ARE YOU AARON CARTER?" "Nope." "ARE YOU SURE?"

MARIA SHERMAN: Cartel already has their hit song "Honestly," with a video that parodies MySpace.

WILL PUGH: When we signed to Epic, they wanted us to reshoot the "Honestly" video. Epic decided I needed to look more done-up in the video.

The original version of the video had the traditional shot of the band playing in a room, and had all these different people sitting in front of computers, going through online profiles, taking selfies, posting them, being very flirtatious and dressing up, but then they'd see each other on the subway or out in the street and just cower. It was kind of an early introspective on online dating. I had the typical emo-ish hair. Little bit of bangs. It wasn't dyed or spiked at the time. I wasn't wearing a lot of makeup. Epic was like, "We don't want to push this video to MTV with you looking like last year's version of yourself." We were like, "We're not gonna reshoot the entire video." They're like, "No, no. We just want to reshoot the live performance."

The night before the shoot, in my hotel room—no, in a different hotel room in the same hotel—they hired a stylist to come in and cut my hair with five people from Epic standing around saying things like, "Yeah, just a little more like this . . ." The haircut was fine, it looked normal but like . . . very detailed. "We need to style it exactly like this, and he's got to cowlick it there . . ." The next day, we reshot the entire live performance for $20,000, because they wanted me to change my haircut. They didn't give a shit about anything else. That's the story of the $20,000 haircut.

KEVIN SANDERS: You've got a Top 40 hit, you've got some success, but you're playing in the major leagues now. You've got to be bigger than the thing you just did.

WILL PUGH: It didn't get any bigger than MTV.

JOSEPH PEPPER: When *Band in a Bubble* got brought up for the first time, our manager was like, "There's this idea MTV's pitching to the label and we want you guys to do it."

WILL PUGH: Our A&R guy's like, "Yeah, we've got to do this. It'll be on MTV. You go into isolation, and it's like *Real World* meets a recording studio."

JOSEPH PEPPER: *Real World* and *Road Rules*, all those old reality shows I enjoyed growing up in the nineties, there was a lot more realness to it. There wasn't much intervention between the producers and the people involved, you know? By 2007, reality shows were a little more calculated.

LESLIE SIMON: At that time, MTV was looking for cred because Fuse had become the default home base for up-and-coming bands. Fuse was a bit more of a trusted source; it wasn't as commercial. So a lot of people would defer to doing things with Fuse, though still, you knew you made it when you were on MTV.

KEVIN SANDERS: You're trying to compete with big names. You're trying for something that makes people go, "That band's got a fucking reality TV show, they must be big." Like, did Fall Out Boy get bigger because of their songs or because Pete Wentz was fucking Ashlee Simpson? You almost have to be a starfucker, one of you needs to date someone famous. It's this weird notoriety ladder you're climbing, and it exists outside the scope of music. That's where *Band in a Bubble* sits.

JASON PETTIGREW: I think the first band they went to was Motion City Soundtrack, and Motion City Soundtrack was like, "No, dude, sorry."

JASON TATE: I know it was presented to Motion City Soundtrack and to Andrew McMahon for Jack's Mannequin, and both of those bands turned it down.

JOSEPH PEPPER: At first, there was a lot of talk about, "Should we do this? Bands don't do this stuff, we're gonna lose fans, blah blah blah."

It was pitched to us like, "You're in this house, there's cameras there, and you guys record your next album. You guys can just do what you normally do in a studio but we'll pay for the studio and everyone can watch." Okay, great! That sounds awesome.

WILL PUGH: Through the label, we found out Dr Pepper was sponsoring it. We didn't think soft drinks sponsoring stuff was anything strange. You've got people with Red Bull and Monster sponsorships. Dr Pepper, who cares? We wished it was Coca-Cola because we're from Atlanta, but oh well, we'll take it.

KEVIN SANDERS: How bad can it be?

WILL PUGH: As well received as *Chroma* was, we were already starting to get some crap for being too catchy. We were like, "We're not a pop band, we're not a boy band, we're a rock band." We had already written songs for the next album, self-titled, which were darker, more melancholy. We were all like, "Yeah we get it, MTV is corporate, but what better place to launch our vision of what the band could be?"

JOSEPH PEPPER: Eventually it was like, "Fuck it. Who cares?"

WILL PUGH: We asked for a shit-ton of money, which we probably got laughed at for asking. We asked for $1 million, because why not?

JOSEPH PEPPER: We quickly learned that's not how it works.

WILL PUGH: MTV was like, "No way is that going to happen. We're actually not going to give you any money. We're going to give money to your record label and publishing, and you guys will get killer publicity. And when you tour in the fall, after being on an MTV show, you're probably going to sell three times as many tickets."

JOSEPH PEPPER: Once we signed on, there was stuff in the contract that said MTV could change anything and we'd still have to agree to the contract. That's when they put it in a glass house on Pier 54 in Manhattan with hidden cameras everywhere. That's when they started getting all the other sponsors . . .

WILL PUGH: The night we drove in, we saw the signage outside the bubble for the first time. It was Dr Pepper, and these other brands I guess you could call sub-sponsors. We didn't know KFC was a sponsor. We didn't know Taco Bell was a sponsor. We didn't know Walmart was a sponsor. Too late . . .

KEVIN SANDERS: They drove us in a black car up to a red carpet. They did the whole shebang.

WILL PUGH: The actual living space was like a giant fucking igloo.

KEVIN SANDERS: Twenty days, make a record, then we get out. But you're able to watch this whole thing like we're zoo animals, livestreaming twenty-four hours a day.

MARIA SHERMAN: You would buy Dr Pepper, and inside the cap there'd be a code that would let you go online and watch them. It was so Big Brother, so surveillance-y.

JOSEPH PEPPER: The furniture wasn't real furniture; it was something out of a Playskool house, like beanbag chairs. During the first interview, you can see us kind of looking at each other, smirking and laughing, like, "Oh, what are we doing . . ."

WILL PUGH: The producers were amping it up like, "We do the *Real World*. These people come in and it's all cool, but after a couple of weeks, people start getting mad, shit starts to hit the fan! *Are you guys prepared for that?!*"

KEVIN SANDERS: They wanted a drama.

JOSEPH PEPPER: They thought if they fed us booze all day we would end up fighting. But it's like, we've been touring for years. We know how to drink around each other. Any fights we could have gotten in, we've already gotten in. Now, everything is just fun. So yeah, just endless amounts of booze.

WILL PUGH: We'd open the fridge and the camera would show two-liters of Dr Pepper sitting in the door. We didn't really drink it at all. We're not really soda people.

JOSEPH PEPPER: We had to drink everything out of Dr Pepper cups.

WILL PUGH: They were those giant plastic souvenir cups. They're thirty-two ounces and you're pouring a twelve-ounce beer in. You're just like, "This is sad."

JOSEPH PEPPER: I'd be sipping on whiskey out of this giant cup that was one-tenth of the way full.

WILL PUGH: Once we agreed to do the show, we were like, "All right, here's the thing: We smoke a lot of weed."

JOSEPH PEPPER: So, one of the first things we did when we got in the bubble was see where the cameras were, and any blind spots they had. Someone would sit on the toilet, the rest of us would go online, and we'd go, "Okay put your hand out and move it." And then we'd draw a line on the wall so we could say, "Okay, if you're taking a shit, they won't see you if you sit *like this*. The cameras in the showers only see you from the chest up." And in the back hallway, we found there was a three- or four-foot-square area where no cameras could see you at all. So we talked to production, "Hey, we're gonna smoke weed here."

WILL PUGH: That was where we put our microphones on in the morning and took them off at night. Production made a little vent where you'd flip a switch and this little fan just shot the smoke outside, over the Hudson River. Obviously, no one wants us smoking weed on camera. But we're making a record. They were like, "All right, we get it. There just can't be more than one of you back there at once."

KEVIN SANDERS: Weed was "drumheads." We'd tell catering, "We need some more drumheads." We had this guy in New York we'd known. They'd wait till the pier closed down and they'd walk him down with his little backpack. I think we spent $2,500 on weed in twenty days.

WILL PUGH: That was another smoke-and-mirrors thing—how are you going to write and record an album in twenty days? Anyone who knows anything about making music . . . are you fucking kidding me?

JOSEPH PEPPER: Yeah, the whole record was pretty much recorded before we went inside. The only thing we did was a couple of vocals, some drums that weren't tracked, and there was a guitar solo that we actually did write in the bubble.

WILL PUGH: They brought livestock in. We'd wake up with roosters sitting on our chests and we'd have to shoo out all the animals into New York. They had some TV fitness lady show up at seven in the morning and make us do jumping jacks and stuff after we'd been drinking all night.

JOSEPH PEPPER: They brought in New York Knicks cheerleaders because they thought it would make us look awkward, like, "These band guys don't know how to talk to girls!"

KEVIN SANDERS: I have a fucking girlfriend and she's gonna watch this!

WILL PUGH: Our A&R Peter Malkin came on the show saying something like, "We need sonic weapons!" or whatever it was about singles. That dude I've never seen wear a suit one solitary time in my life, and he walks into the bubble wearing a suit. Like, "Peter! They got to you, man!"

MATT RUBANO: A girl I was dating at that time was friends with a girl who was dating one of the Cartel dudes. She was like, "So-and-so wants us to go over and visit and then I think we can be on the show." And I was like, "Oh, that feels a bit gross . . . No, I don't really wanna do that."

JOSEPH PEPPER: Cobra Starship showed up on the show. They couldn't wait. Gabe's kind of a ham, right? He definitely likes having the camera on him.

GABE SAPORTA: I was on that?

WILL PUGH: Probably the biggest sellout move was when the show ordered us fucking KFC for lunch. The colonel brought buckets of KFC and delivered them inside.

JOSEPH PEPPER: Ugh, just the worst food . . . I mean, we ate it. That mashed potato mix and the biscuits. We were drunk, so we're eating anything, stuffing our faces and being disgusting. We shook his hand and made a joke of the whole thing. But then a couple days later, Kevin asked, "Can we get the colonel to come back?"

WILL PUGH: We never got Taco . . . ah, maybe we did get Taco Bell? I don't remember. I mean, it's Taco Bell. It's not that memorable. And they don't have a mascot to deliver it to you.

KEVIN SANDERS: It's like, "This show is already getting panned . . . careful." And so you're like, "Well, if it wasn't a joke, now it is."

WILL PUGH: You're getting feedback in real time, and you can put two and two together pretty quickly. Especially if you've had the favor of online comments. When you're on the other side of that, you know rather quickly.

JASON TATE: I think *Band in a Bubble* went over poorly on AbsolutePunk.net because like . . . Dr Pepper, are you kidding? And doing a reality show with MTV had such a negative connotation to it.

JASON PETTIGREW: This generation of listeners—and every subsequent generation—they actively enjoy being marketed to. So they can either show their interest, or flex their cynicism.

GABE SAPORTA: Was that a jump-the-shark moment for the scene?

FINN MCKENTY: It did help Cartel, but not as much as they wanted it to. It was a base hit, at best. I mean, that's the reason why people remember Cartel now, right? So it didn't have zero impact. But if the goal was to make them the next Fall Out Boy or whatever, that didn't happen.

STEVEN SMITH: On the last episode, you know when the glass broke when they came out? That kind of glass doesn't make a sound when it breaks. Nothing. So they used the sound of glass breaking from the beginning of a Billy Joel song. I could be wrong but I think it was "You May Be Right." I was like, "Oh, did you steal that from Stone Cold Steve Austin?" They were like, "No, Billy Joel."

JOSEPH PEPPER: There was a breaking out of the bubble party at some bar in New York. We got out of the bubble and they put us up in this really nice hotel, the Bowery. We got to have a real shower for the first time in twenty days, got dressed, and met downstairs to get carted over to this place. On our way, they made it a huge production, with walkie-talkies, saying stuff like "I have the band" and "ten-four." We got to the bar and we're like, "This is lame. We're gonna go to Angels & Kings."

KEVIN SANDERS: That record, Cartel self-titled, was kind of dead in the water the moment it came out. Epic thought the show was going to be all this free promotion, really kind of do the work for them. And that wasn't the case.

LESLIE SIMON: At the time, there was a lot of Atlantic, Warner Bros., Interscope; Epic didn't have a ton of emo irons in the fire.

JOSEPH PEPPER: Epic moved on. I think Shakira had something coming out, so they were focused on her instead.

JASON TATE: Self-titled came out and I was like, "This is fine." I didn't have the hyperbolic take of like, "This is garbage!!!" It was the wrong album for that time period, when you look at 2007 with albums like *Infinity on High*. And there wasn't a massive single on it.

KEVIN SANDERS: It was going to be tough to listen to that record unbiased. You weren't going to listen to that record outside of what you perceived the bubble to be—gimmicky, cheesy, stupid, selling out, or whatever you want to call it.

WILL PUGH: Maybe we shoulda had some PR going on so people didn't think, "Oh, they're millionaires now." Ha, ha! I wish.

KEVIN SANDERS: We got panned from a sellout perspective. And then people got to run rampant with what they thought we were making. And I was like . . . If I was making what you think I'm making, I wouldn't even be worrying about your comment.

WILL PUGH: We were going on a headlining tour in the fall and we couldn't find bands who were willing to go on tour with us. I think a lot of it was because we crossed over into MTV land and the bubble got a bad rap.

In a lot of places, we still ended up selling more tickets than we did for the *Chroma* tour. But the shows were booked in venues that were too big, so it didn't look great. Selling 1,700 tickets is nothing to sneeze at, but when you put 1,700 people in a 4,000-cap venue, it doesn't look very good.

MARIA SHERMAN: It feels kind of eerie . . . in the future, we would get unparalleled access to artists, bands, whomever. Just not with the Dr Pepper caveat.

KEVIN SANDERS: MTV felt habitually influential. We were so used to MTV having an influence, though we weren't sure what was next. I think everyone saw the writing on the wall with *TRL* getting past its prime, and it was gone [in 2008]. I think *Band in a Bubble* skirted in before a shift. With MTV, we didn't know what was next. But we knew things were changing.

THE END OF THE EARTH

PETE WENTZ: So I'd moved out to California but I was pretty lonely, so I would just take Ambien and stay up and stuff. I would send out bizarre, super-tripped-out emails. I sent one to my manager that was like, "Yo, let's be the first band to play on all five continents."

He was like, "There's seven continents." I was like, "Oh, tight."

JONATHAN DANIEL: I don't even know what to say about it. It was such a great, big idea.

PATRICK STUMP: The only reason I do a band, the only reason I sing, is so I can write music. That's the only thing I wanna do. We were in this grind where we'd make a record, then tour on it for two years. We'd been touring so much, we almost broke a world record.

JAMES MONTGOMERY: They were trying to go to Antarctica because they wanted to set a Guinness World Record, becoming the first band to play on every continent.

PETE WENTZ: We'd just played South Africa a few months before. Antarctica was the hardest one.

BRIAN DIAZ: We did one show in Chile, in Santiago, at some theater. It ended . . . it was a mess . . . Pete threw a drum in the air or put his bass . . . He wrecked a drum. The band's long gone and me and the tour manager are fighting with the rental company we got the drums from.

The guy was trying to take our money and then he was like, "I called the police!" Like, "No! We have to go to Antarctica in two days! You can't call the police!"

Anyway, we sort that out, and we take off for Punta Arenas, Chile, the southernmost inhabited city in South America . . .

PETE WENTZ: We flew past the end of the Patagonia region, to basically the last inhabited part of Chile. We were gonna go to the Chilean base on Antarctica. We brought an adjudicator from *Guinness World Records.*

JAMES MONTGOMERY: You'd have to get on an aircraft carrier to a cargo plane or some sort of military plane to the research facility in Antarctica. This was the only place you could get a flight.

BRIAN DIAZ: Fly in there, go to this little base, set up in this rickety rec room, play a show, make it official.

PETE WENTZ: This was the end of the time of year where you could fly in Antarctica, so it was very tricky. You'd have to fly in, play, and fly out because they can't keep extra people on the base. Every day we would just look at the runway. There was a live cam of the runway and we would just hope there was not that much snow. We would watch it every day in the hotel room, all day.

BRIAN DIAZ: Their manager Bob was like, "Look at that! It looks like we can do it, call Captain John!" And we're making jokes like, Captain John's not even in Antarctica, he's in fucking Palm Springs somewhere going, "Oh, yeah, it's snowing. Sorry!"

JAMES MONTGOMERY: We just hung out in a room and dicked around. They had the benefit of having a guy from *Guinness World Records* there, so they were brainstorming the most ridiculous world records they could set, and never did any of them. Like, "Hey, dude, we're gonna set a record for trying to throw the most pieces of furniture out of a hotel room."

PETE WENTZ: It would be like, eat the most saltine crackers anybody can eat in a minute! And you're like, "Dude, I can eat like, four hundred." No you can't. You can eat like, seven.

I think we ended up doing this one our label probably convinced us to do, where we did the most radio interviews in twenty-four hours . . . Like, this just sounds like you're trying to get a bunch of pop radio ads . . .

JAMES MONTGOMERY: Every teenager in this town and all the surrounding towns knew this famous rock band was there, so they were just camped outside the hotel twenty-four hours a day.

PETE WENTZ: There wouldn't be a band in this town, you know what I mean?

JAMES MONTGOMERY: Me and a photographer would leave, walk the street, and turn around and there'd be a hundred teenage girls following us. Like, "We're not the band!" We'd go to restaurants in town and they'd be like, "Oh, you eat for free!"

BRIAN DIAZ: On the third day, we're like, "Fuck! Let's go see penguins!" We go on this long-ass ride to some bay, it's beautiful, there's penguins everywhere. Drive back into town, and now shit's crazy because people saw us leave and know we're back. We basically can't get out of the vans. There's so many people, they're banging on the windows. Patrick is freaked out. I'm like, "Okay, here's what we're gonna do: We're gonna open it up, I can speak Spanish, I'm gonna scream at all these people to get the fuck outta the way, we're gonna barrel through."

As we go through, some kid jumped on Patrick's back. We shake everyone off, get to the hotel, lock the doors, and Patrick's like, "I wanna go home." We still hadn't gotten to Antarctica but he's just like, "I don't feel safe, I got shit to do at home." Patrick was closing on a house or something, I think Pete was hosting an award show in LA. There were a lot of life things going on.

PETE WENTZ: We found out we weren't going to clear the runway. And three days before we left, I found out I was having a kid.

JAMES MONTGOMERY: Pete would leave to go and talk on the phone with Ashlee for a long time.

PETE WENTZ: So we flew back.

JAMES MONTGOMERY: When it was clear they weren't going to get to Antarctica, they spirited us away in the middle of the night in these unmarked vans, just to get back to the airport. It was a week where I was technically supposed to be on assignment with this band, just trying to write things when there's nothing to write about. They printed up shirts for the world record and then they didn't get to actually set the world record.

PATRICK STUMP: We were touring just absolutely relentlessly, and not getting to make new music. And for me, that was just not worth it.

"THEY TOOK *THE* EXCLAMATION POINT OFF THEIR NAME"

PETE WENTZ: I've heard this quote where Bono said, "My best advice to a band is don't make an interesting second record."

JONATHAN DANIEL: It's hard to follow up a juggernaut like *A Fever You Can't Sweat Out*. That record was so big and so unique and Panic! didn't have the preparation that Fall Out Boy had. Fall Out Boy, to the outside, might have seemed like an overnight success, but it wasn't. Panic! was.

PETE WENTZ: Panic! is a weird one. They got so famous when they were so young that it was inevitable *Fever* was not going to be the entire DNA of the band. There's no way the songs they made when they were seventeen, eighteen years old were going to become the basis of what the band is. Back then, I was just kind of wondering what it would be.

SPENCER SMITH: *Pretty. Odd.* went through a lot of different . . . uh . . . the making of that album had a lot of false starts and scrapped ideas.

MATT SQUIRE: They knew that if they went back in the studio with me they were going to hear the word "no." They would have to collaborate and do the things we did that made *Fever* into *Fever*.

I got a call from Jonathan Daniel that was like, "Look, we can't really talk to the band right now. It blew up overnight. They're huge rock stars." He gave this school analogy: "They want to have their summer now. And we kinda want to let them do whatever they want, because they earned it. They're the ones who put the circus makeup on. They're the ones who engineered a lot of the marketing of *Fever*, and they did an amazing job." Then Jonathan was like, "Bro to bro, they're gonna do the next album with someone else. They're gonna do it with a string arranger. They're not really gonna have a producer."

It was difficult to hear, but I respected it. It wasn't until much later that I realized, "Oh, they're in trouble. They're not in a good headspace."

SPENCER SMITH: Back when we did *Fever*, there were forced deadlines, which can sometimes be helpful. This was sort of the opposite. No label or A&R person understood why *Fever* got so big, so they were just like, "Seems like these kids know what they're doing! I guess we'll just let them do whatever they want."

JOHNNY MINARDI: There's the rumored cabin record Panic! did that never came out . . .

ALEX DELEON: Panic! said, "Come to our cabin up in the mountains in Mount Charleston." I was the biggest fan of these guys and I'm like, "Come to your cabin?"

SPENCER SMITH: We'd rented this cabin in this place called Mount Charleston, which is like forty minutes outside of Vegas.

ALEX DELEON: They're like, "Bring your band and just come to our cabin. Let's hang out and we'll show you our new album."

ROB MATHES: This has been the question I have been asked seven billion times, and boy, I wish I had the answer everyone wants. Everyone is dreaming and believing, and I think, some of the band, but not the whole band, have wanted to keep the idea alive that there's a whole masterpiece living somewhere called *Cricket and Clover* . . .

SPENCER SMITH: We initially wanted to make an album that would have been like a Danny Elfman score, a concept album that told a story. It was very theatrical and Baroque. The problem was we lost sight of what makes songs good. We were deliberately not doing verse-chorus-verse-chorus, just so we could say we did it, and not realizing, this also can make a song unlistenable.

ALEX DELEON: The album had this whimsical aspect to it. The verses would be super beautiful, with major chords, and then this really menacing part would come in, like a villain was walking into the room. It was almost like Panic! at the Disco scored a Tim Burton movie, or *Cinderella*.

PETE WENTZ: I have to say, I felt like an outsider. This was a very insular project. They weren't coming to me or Crush saying, "Here's the demo we did today."

SPENCER SMITH: This was also the first time that, you know . . . me and Ryan didn't drink or do anything in high school. We were not teenagers that were getting fucked up and partying, so when we first went on tour, I think we felt a bit younger and more immature. But during the writing and recording of this album, me and Ryan definitely started to make up for lost time. We were isolated deliberately out there and we were smoking weed, trying mushrooms.

ALEX DELEON: The experimentation that was going down in the cabin in the mountains was wild. I saw things I had never seen before in my life.

SPENCER SMITH: We were a bit lost. I remember Bob and Jonathan from Crush coming out to the cabin and listening to the songs and I don't know if they said it to our faces, but knowing them now, I would imagine they probably left in the car and looked at each other like, "What the fuck is going on?"

JAMES MONTGOMERY: I would love to hear that record, the one they scrapped before they made *Pretty. Odd.*, when they were just stoned in a cabin for like six months. I would kill to hear that one. I interviewed Panic! a lot back then and I remember Ryan would say things like, "It's gonna be an orchestral fantasy romance album, like *Nightmare Before Christmas*." All this shit. He had big hopes for it. I wonder if the album they wanted to put out was kind of insane and the label was like, "We can't do this."

GABE SAPORTA: I remember Crush being so pissed off, talking about these guys being out in the desert just drinking. They were like, "They're not fucking writing shit, they're not being serious." There was a lot of that. Like, "What kind of music are they making? What the fuck is this?"

I knew that Ryan Ross was seen as the problematic figure by Crush. They thought Ryan was trying to take the band in a direction that didn't make sense. I wasn't involved, but those were the things I would hear.

ALEX DELEON: Ryan was such a mad scientist that I wouldn't be surprised if he was like, "Let's do this super whimsical movie score album," and then one day woke up with an epiphany like, "Nope, we're doing this instead." You listen to the lyrics on *Fever*, and his mind was all over the place, dude. It was Wonderland up in that head. I don't know why they pivoted away, but I remember being super surprised because I was there for a lot of the recording process in the cabin and they spent so much time on the songs.

JONATHAN DANIEL: At some point, I'm pretty sure I gave Ryan two Beatles compilation albums, the red and blue ones. If it wasn't me, somebody did. And he started getting into the Beatles.

ROB MATHES: Abbey Road is my home away from home. I would bring whatever I could to Abbey Road. Then Panic! happened. The band wanted to channel Brian Wilson's *Smile*, *Magical Mystery Tour*, that whole flower power Carnaby Street, Baker Street, London late sixties thing on *Pretty. Odd.*

SPENCER SMITH: I knew all that stuff, but Ryan really hadn't. His dad didn't really listen to music. The music they would have listened to would have probably been sixties country. Discovering the Beatles totally shifted what Ryan wanted to do. And that's why *Pretty. Odd.* sounds the way it does, influenced by late sixties stuff like the Beatles and the Zombies. When you're influenced by something you heard yesterday for the first time, it's in some ways . . . a naive, pure influence.

JAMES MONTGOMERY: Ryan was a rock retro-ist and he wanted to do this Spector-esque wall-of-sound production, things like that. Jon Walker, the bass player, was with Ryan in that camp. And then Brendon is more of a theater guy, more of a pop-oriented dude. I think those two started butting heads.

JOHNNY MINARDI: In marketing meetings, the band was so adamant about certain things: "We don't care about 'I Write Sins,' we don't care about hitting that exact fan base. This is what we are, this is what we're doing." And it was so delicate because a multimillion-selling debut record is very rare. So, to then almost spit in the face of that, it was delicate to navigate things like, "What's the first song? How are we going to roll it out? Are people gonna freak out and hate the band? Are you gonna fall off the face of the earth?"

ADAM SISKA: The Academy Is . . . were doing something in LA and we went to Panic!'s hotel to hear *Pretty. Odd.* They were done making it and we all smoked a joint. We were in disbelief that Panic! had turned into these . . . kinda bad boys. We all got stoned and listened to the record. I thought Brendon sounded cool. He even played some bass on it. I thought the single "Nine in the Afternoon" was really good. Jon Walker had played that on our bus when he worked for us as a guitar tech; he cowrote that song.

JOHNNY MINARDI: Was one of those *Pretty. Odd.* songs going to break number one on pop radio? Probably not, not even close. "Nine in the Afternoon" probably just went to alternative radio. It had its success based on the back of "I Write Sins" and that was it.

JASON TATE: *Pretty. Odd.* was perceived two ways: One was everyone who liked the first album being like, "What the hell is this? This is your weird Beatles jerk-off session." And then there was a group of people that used it as a way to say, "See? We told you these guys were great all along. Look at all this musicianship!"

ADAM SISKA: *Pretty. Odd.* shows you that desire to shed the emo signature. They took the exclamation point off their name.

JAMES MONTGOMERY: I had to write about fifteen stories about that.

SHANE DRAKE: In the original lineup, the most vocal members were always Spencer and Ryan. Brendon participated in those creative discussions, but Spencer and Ryan were the main voices. By the time we did the "Nine in the Afternoon" video, Ryan's voice had become the loudest in the band.

HANIF ABDURRAQIB: I will say I never liked Panic!; I liked Ryan Ross. And so that means I liked *Pretty. Odd.* a lot. I still think *Pretty. Odd.* is good. I think the reason *Pretty. Odd.* is good is because it channeled their obsession with excess and extravagance into something that felt manageable and thoughtful. I get the stuff people make fun of: "Did drugs once and listened to *Sgt. Pepper's*!" But it worked for me. It was dialed down. The theatrics were gentler.

JASON PETTIGREW: The day I interviewed them for their *Alternative Press* cover story, they were playing some undersell club show. The show was kind of like watching *New Year's Rockin' Eve* when they're like, "AND LIVE, WE'VE GOT PANIC! AT THE DISCO!" And there's a bunch of people who don't know who Panic! at the Disco are, trying to get their friends' attention holding up their drinks like, "I GOT YOU A DRINK!" while these guys are trying to play "Nine in the Afternoon." It was a bunch of people who were probably told to be there because they got on a list, or because they knew somebody who worked for the bar. It felt like there were maybe fifteen Panic! fans planted there because they'd got in through a fan club or something like that. But that didn't seem exactly like the crowd the band was trying to impress, either. So I think all that probably tapped the accelerator on Ryan Ross's discomfort.

SPENCER SMITH: On the first tour for *Pretty. Odd.*, as openers, we had the Hush Sound and Phantom Planet, who Fueled By Ramen had just signed. That was the beginning of the different friends, Ryan and Jon wanting to be associated with a different scene and different groups of people.

LESLIE SIMON: They started to take sides, which seems like a pattern for a lot of these bands . . . You had Spencer and Brendon on one side, and then you had Ryan and Jon on the other.

ADAM SISKA: Most other bands were fixated on trying to tap into something really deeply personal, and almost spiritual. And I don't think Brendon's artistry is built around trying to get to the core of emotional depth. Brendon's an entertainer. And I don't mean that in a bad way. Brendon just had his eyes on the prize.

JAMES MONTGOMERY: I think Ryan is much more of an artist, whereas Brendon is more of a "let's get this shit done" person.

SPENCER SMITH: Throughout that touring cycle, we were diverging. When you're spending almost every day together, gradual changes are happening. You're growing apart creatively, even as friends. It wasn't all wrapped up in one blowout fight. It was this thing we were all aware of, almost unspoken.

MATT SQUIRE: I didn't realize until the *Pretty. Odd.* arena tour. Usually if you go backstage, it's crazy, right? Hangers-on, industry people, usually this crazy energy. And I remember on *Pretty. Odd.* they took out Plain White T's as direct support. "Hey There Delilah" was huge at the time. Backstage in LA at the Staples Center, Plain White T's' dressing room was that kind of insanity. Then I go knock on the Panic! door, and it's just me, Jonathan Daniel, and the band. And they were the headliner. Something felt just wrong, you know what I mean? And sure enough, something was really wrong. I wasn't in the mix enough to speak with any authority on it, but I was definitely concerned. And then I started hearing stories about Ryan. It's just so sad, man.

HANIF ABDURRAQIB: I get why Ryan Ross and the band split. I think it wasn't a healthy environment for anyone. So even glorifying *Pretty. Odd.* feels rough.

JONATHAN DANIEL: The band ecosystem is very unusual. You get in a band and you're like, "If we could just get a record deal, everything would be great!" But a few years go by, and success and money and decisions are tied to it. You're like, "I don't know if these are the right guys to spend the rest of my life with. I don't know if I want to make this kind of music." I think that was a big thing for Ryan. I remember doing a radio show with The Academy Is . . . in Chile, and the host asked the kids, "Do you love Fall Out Boy?" *YAY!* "You love Panic!?" *YAY!* "You love Academy?" *YAY!* "You love Cobra?" *YAY!* "You love Paramore?" *YAY!*

I went outside and I called Ryan. I was like, "Oh my god, I think I figured out why you're so depressed." I was like, "You hate me. Not me personally, but you hate what I represent. And you hate Fueled By Ramen and you hate Panic!" And he's like, "I didn't sign up for any of this shit. I didn't know what I was doing. I don't want to be forced into wearing eyeliner and things." It was just a real moment. That really was the end of that era of Panic!, that phone call.

"WHEN YOUR FANS START DRESSING LIKE YOU, YOU GOTTA FIND *THE* NEXT THING"

LESLIE SIMON: So you've got *Riot!*, which was a sensation for the Hot Topic crowd; the look, the feel, the sound—super signature 2007. And then there's this small vampire movie that a soundtrack is being made for. And it's being released by Atlantic and the first song is going to be by Paramore . . .

ADAM SAMILJAN: Hayley saw how big that soundtrack could be just by seeing how excited her fans were about the books.

LESLIE SIMON: *Twilight* had such a stranglehold of the zeitgeist, that for Paramore to be the face of the soundtrack, "Decode" took them to the stratosphere. Like, "Do not pass go, do not collect two hundred dollars, you're just going to lap everybody a few times."

MARIA SHERMAN: I always valued young women as tastemakers in alternative and popular music, and the way they adopted so much of this music shows that power. Without women, this shit wouldn't have blown up to the size it did.

HANNAH EWENS: Unlike some of the other bands . . . if you were a Paramore fan, you really followed Paramore from the beginning to the end. And I think a lot of that is because of feeling super obsessed with Hayley Williams and her look, everything to do with her.

JENN PELLY: Being in these male-dominated spaces where there were only men onstage—I only ever saw one woman onstage, maybe two—made me think about power structures and what it meant. Why I felt uncomfortable about the fact people would treat me like I was just going to shows because I wanted to meet boys or something. I was really serious about being a music fan.

VICTORIA ASHER: Every single interview Cobra Starship did, the guys would get asked tons of questions, and the only question I would get was, "What's it like being the only girl in the band?"

LESLIE SIMON: Just like it was not easy to be a woman working in the scene, it was even more difficult to be promoted as a woman working in the scene. Which never made sense to me, given the demographics.

JASON TATE: It became even harder for any female-fronted band to be embraced in the scene because they immediately got pigeonholed as trying to rip off Paramore.

JOHNNY MINARDI: Hey Monday never had a lot of mainstream success, but they could have, no question.

CASSADEE POPE: The overall goal for branding and marketing us was that we were the sunny side of Paramore. And at the time, I hadn't listened to Paramore. And then I kept getting compared to Hayley, so I started to get kind of bitter: "Well, now I don't want to listen to them, because then I'm gonna be singing differently." They were very aware that we were going to get pinned against each other, so they were like, "Let's take you over here on the poppier side." They were also very adamant about me showcasing my vocals, belting every song at the top of my range.

We were just automatically compared to Paramore because I'm a girl. I don't think Hayley's voice and my voice are similar. I think we sounded more similar to Fall Out Boy or Blink-182, and I didn't hear people comparing us to them. All the publications would just compare us to Paramore and think it was a compliment. And it obviously was a compliment, but it was also underhanded sexism.

MATT SQUIRE: I do wonder if Paramore took the lane, and we only had the one slot, as a community.

ALEX DELEON: The Cab and Hey Monday did the *AP* tour together. We both got the cover of *AP* for their 100 Bands You Need to Know issue.

JOHNNY MINARDI: Fueled By Ramen had great relationships with radio people and with synch departments. We were getting songs all over the place—on *Gossip Girl*, *The Hills*. If we signed a band, and they don't fit the formula of going to radio, MTV, or these shows, we were underutilizing our strengths.

CASSADEE POPE: I think our album not getting huge had a lot to do with the fact we didn't really have a grassroots approach.

GABE SAPORTA: For something to be huge coming out of the scene, you needed the grassroots. The Cab and Hey Monday, these bands were accepted, no one was saying, "You can't be here." They were great writers, great singers, great performers, great people. But it didn't feel like they came from the scene. The scene got so big that there was this overlap of scene kids who loved reading about these bands on MySpace, AbsolutePunk, and then there's the mainstream kids. What made our scene so big was the mesh of both. But some bands only had the mainstream kids, and without the fervor of the scene kids, it's hard to really break.

ANDY GREENWALD: At a certain point, there are fans, and then there are *fans*. There's only a limited number of people who will live every second of an album and get the Thursday dove tattooed on them.

CASSADEE POPE: Hey Monday didn't really have the thing where you're a band for a few years in your hometown, word gets out, and you have a more organic build. It was organic, but in a different way. It was fast. We accumulated these fans fast. And I've kept a lot of them, so I will say they're loyal, but if a fan gets on board when you're already at a certain level of success, I don't know they feel as responsible to help keep you there. I think we should have taken it slower. We often didn't have time to nurture the fans that we had, who we should have spent more time with after shows. So much of the time, I was either losing my voice or hadn't gotten a lot of sleep because all of the press they were having us do.

ADAM SISKA: By 2008, 2009, it was like if you're not selling a million records, you're kind of a failure.

MATT RUBANO: Once these dudes get a little bit of money, they change. All of a sudden, you have a bit of freedom to move around and do stuff, but I just remember seeing so many dudes behave so stupidly. And like, especially around the *TRL*, MTV-ization of that whole scene. No offense to anyone, but like, *TRL* is fucking wack. Like, yes, it was basically the *Ed Sullivan Show* of that generation but culturally, artistically, it was horseshit. It was *Billboard* on television. It was never cool.

CHRISTIAN MCKNIGHT: Because people saw the massive bands, they were like, That's what I wanna do. It wasn't, "I wanna be in a band because I want to be part of a scene"; it was, "I wanna be in a band because I wanna be a rock star." I was still doing some local shows, and the bands with the big followings were rich kids, because their parents could pay for really good gear.

ADAM SISKA: It was all about the swoop cut and the eyeliner. It was pop culture to be an emo band.

NICK SCIMECA: Skinny jeans started to become a normal thing. You could go to Hot Topic or Levi's, even, and get a pair of skinny jeans.

BUDDY NIELSEN: When your fans start dressing like you, you gotta find the next thing.

SARAH LEWITINN: Angels & Kings got corny and directionless. If you're a place for emos to listen to music that's not emo, but then people who listen to emo go to see people who are emo, then you have to play music for them. And that was not the bands' original intent. It turned into a snake eating its tail.

VICTORIA ASHER: Some nights, Angels & Kings just felt like a meet and greet.

JOSEPH PEPPER: There was a lot of, "Hey, sign this! Can I get a selfie?"

KAREN RUTTNER: Kids would come up to the DJ booth and they would only want to hear Fall Out Boy songs. Travie used to come and ask us to play his music. It was kind of like, "Yes, we know this is your place but . . . not really sure how Gym Class Heroes works into this mix?"

Fall Out Boy was the main request from kids, because it was the Fall Out Boy bar, but it was Panic! at the Disco, too. And then there was, "Can you play the Red Jumpsuit Apparatus and Cute Is What We Aim For?" Band names that would make me heave onto the decks.

BRIAN DIAZ: No disrespect . . . Cute Is What We Aim For is a band that toured with us. I don't know anything about Cute Is What We Aim For. They were on tour with Fall Out Boy, couldn't name a single song, couldn't name a member of the band. But when you have a thousand Cute Is What I Aim Fors, it dilutes everything. You don't have one band that's doing something really well; you have a thousand bands that are just doing a thing.

BEN JORGENSEN: There was so much emo fatigue.

JAMES MONTGOMERY: I don't really know where a lot of these bands went, post-MySpace . . .

WILL PUGH: Cartel had a *tooooooon* of MySpace plays before it went down. I think "Honestly" had like ten million streams, which wasn't monetized, so we got screwed on that. Around 2009, Spotify really started to go, so our success between '06 and '09 was sort of skipped over in the transition from MySpace to Spotify and Facebook. We're kind of lost in the void.

JASON TATE: MySpace never evolved in the way it should have or could have. They also sold to the Murdochs—good for them, they got paid—but they sold out so quickly, there was no incentive for the company that took it over to try to innovate. And so, MySpace just became known for horrific ads—you know, those punch-the-monkey ads—and being a garbage, outdated platform.

FRED MASCHERINO: I didn't see the beginning of the hair metal movement in the eighties, but I was fully aware of it by 1987, 1988, and I was there for its downfall; I was a high school senior in '92, right when Nirvana hit. The more emo got into the haircuts, the more it mirrored the eighties hair metal, and that worried me: *This is all gonna come crashing down soon.* Fall Out Boy started to disassociate themselves from our scene by using more pop elements. I was like, "Shit, people are fleeing the building."

PETE WENTZ: People would get in my car and they're like, "This dude just listens to Lil Wayne. I thought he listened to scene bands all day!" I think my ears were just shredded from that stuff all the time.

NEAL AVRON: During the making of *Folie à Deux*, Pete and Ashlee were getting chased by paparazzi nonstop. We were doing preproduction at my house and Pete and Ashlee decided to stop by. I opened up the gate, and the paparazzi started following them up the driveway. I told them to get the fuck off my property, and then they all just stood at the edge of the gate the whole time Pete and Ashlee were in there. There was even a woman—she was following the paparazzi because I think she wanted to be famous—she was standing outside on top of the limo, fully naked. Just a crazy fucking scene I'll never forget.

LESLIE SIMON: Fall Out Boy had been sprinting for a good five years by this point: tour to tour, record to record. And yet, they still had personal lives; some of them were getting married and some were having children. I think they were getting older, and they were tired, and they needed a break. From the outside, it appeared that what started as a really tight-knit gang of friends turned into a functional group of coworkers. That's not to say their friendship wasn't intact, but in my opinion, they were going in different directions.

NEAL AVRON: There was more bickering towards the last record that I did with them, *Folie à Deux*. I didn't see as much of Pete around the studio as I did in prior records. He came in to do his parts and then he'd come down occasionally to hear things. He was a little less involved in the day-to-day.

JAMES MONTGOMERY: You could tell there was some sort of dissention in the group, so that was the first time it was really only Patrick speaking on behalf of the band, taking me through the songs. I think *Folie* showed his influence more than Pete's. I think Pete was a little checked out at that point, so for better or worse, *Folie* is more of a Patrick Stump record.

NEAL AVRON: Pete and Patrick were on the phone one day, going back and forth. I think it was one of those long phone calls where they were kind of pissed at each other. After, Patrick came up with the whole riff and concept for "I Don't Care." I think it all came out in that song.

MARIANNE ELOISE: With Patrick, his influences are pop music. It's Michael Jackson, Elton John, Elvis Costello . . .

MIKEY WAY: What always struck me about Patrick was I would go on the Fall Out Boy bus, and he'd be listening to Prince. He loved R&B. It felt like he was able to embrace that more.

PATRICK STUMP: I don't keep a journal for my personal thoughts. I don't really communicate that way. Honestly, I don't think the world needs to hear my thoughts. That's not how my mind works. I'm not burning to share something with anybody. I think most of my thoughts are dumb. But music is where . . . I don't really know how to put it into words . . . but I put a lot of myself into that music.

NEAL AVRON: Fall Out Boy likes to poke fun at themselves, kind of a meta way of referencing themselves. I think that was the idea of "What a Catch, Donnie" . . .

PATRICK STUMP: I was feeling pretty down about something, which is on brand for me. I sat down and I found these lyrics of Pete's. And this doesn't happen often—I'm not a big connecting-with-lyrics guy—but something about those lyrics felt like what I was feeling at the time, and I wrote the song.

I had a sense in the studio that we might not keep going. I think we all did. I think we all had a sense of . . . except for Pete. Pete was very frustrated about it; the rest of us were like, "I think maybe things are winding down." The front half of the song is just me being miserable, and putting that into song. And the back half of the song became a celebration of the band, and what we had been, up to that point. So it's very self-referential, interpolating all these melodies from other Fall Out Boy songs. And we asked a bunch of our friends to sing them.

NEAL AVRON: Let's have different artists come in and sing a line, make a real "We Are the World" moment out of it . . .

ALEX DELEON: I remember going to the studio and he's like, "I have this idea. We wanna take some of our friends, some of the guys on the label, have them pick a part of a Fall Out Boy song they like and sing it." I did "Thnks fr th Mmrs." They also got William Beckett, Brendon Urie, Travie, Gabe . . .

GABE SAPORTA: Did it feel like a goodbye kinda thing? A hundred percent. It felt like this was it.

NEAL AVRON: I'll tell you a funny story . . . The na na na's at the end of the song . . . That's all Patrick. I printed out a picture from the "We Are the

World" session and we were looking at all the different musicians in it. We must have done twenty tracks of Patrick singing the na, na, nas, and each track is him doing it in a voice of someone from "We Are the World." There's one in a Bob Dylan voice. There's one in a Bruce Springsteen voice. There's one in a Cyndi Lauper voice.

PATRICK STUMP: I've been doing Elvis Costello impressions for so long. To this day, I haven't met Elvis Costello, and I don't want to, because I'm a big fan, and I want to keep that separate. He was going to come in and record his guest part on "What a Catch, Donnie," but he got sick, so he couldn't fly out. But he ended up going into his studio, laying down one vocal line. He knocked it out. I remember listening to it and it took me a good three seconds to be like, "Oh, that's not me!" That was the first time I realized how much, either on purpose or by accident, I really tried to sound like him. I put a lot of his inflections in the way that I sing, or certainly used to.

JONATHAN DANIEL: *Folie* got a bit screwed up because people at the label had changed. And we had a great plan. We were rolling out this thing that Pete had done called Citizens for Our Betterment, which was tied to the 2008 election with a mixtape.

JOHNNY MINARDI: They kinda piggybacked the Obama stuff with the mixtape.

MANI MOSTOFI: Pete's embrace of Obama was partly a Chicago pride thing, and partly because he's related to Obama. He had a very similar background, in some ways.

If you were paying attention to some of the causes Fall Out Boy raised money for, like child soldiers in Uganda, part of that was rooted in Black culture and Black politics of the nineties. Because of where he grew up and who his parents were, Pete wasn't always 100 percent within that, but from my perspective, he kept an eye on it. It was part of his life, because it was something he related to. And it definitely got lost in the story of Fall Out Boy.

TRAVIE MCCOY: Everybody put out samplers—Fueled By Ramen, Victory, Equal Vision—so we said, "Let's take it to another level and add a hip-hop layer to it." Around that time, mixtapes were the way to go because you didn't have to worry about getting sample clearances and you could just do whatever the fuck you want.

JOHNNY MINARDI: Borrowing from the hip-hop world with mixtapes, you could leak alternate versions of songs, clips, and demos.

GRETA MORGAN: Oh my god, the Hush Sound made a song for that mixtape that was like, "We believe in Barack Obama! He loves you and he loves your mama!"

GABE SAPORTA: Katy Perry "I Kissed a Girl" was kind of revolutionary at the time, and the mixtape had Cobra Starship "I Kissed a Boy." I think I wrote that on Warped Tour. There were a lot of pictures circulating on the internet at the time of me kissing other dudes, so that was kind of our way to address it . . . I'm trying to remember the lyrics, "I kissed a boy just to start shit . . ."

JONATHAN DANIEL: Yeah, that mixtape . . . it was all kinds of Pete shenanigans, it was great. But I don't think the label really understood what we were doing. They kept thinking it was all about the radio for Fall Out Boy. So they moved the album back. And it kind of took momentum away from that thing.

JAMES MONTGOMERY: *Folie à Deux* was supposed to come out on election day, and they pushed it back. They had some sort of stunt planned, or some alternate reality game. I think you could sort of tell that nobody was really telling them no. No one was stepping in and saying, "That's a bad idea. We can't do that." But then, no one was holding them accountable to follow through on the plans they had. So Wentz would say they were gonna put out an album on November 4, and the week before it was clear it wasn't coming.

NEAL AVRON: I don't know if this is 100 percent true, but I heard this about "I Don't Care," the lead single from *Folie à Deux*: The label had done research on how it was reacting at radio, and the data looked not good. So they pulled the single off the radio, and the album kind of got shelved. And I heard that shortly after they decided to pull support for the single, they realized they had read the data wrong, and it was actually doing incredibly well at radio. Like, they had moved a decimal point into the wrong place. But at that point, you can't go back to radio with a single. That was the story I believe I heard from a marketing person, definitely from somebody in the band, and maybe even from somebody in management. But that was really the death knell for that record.

PETE WENTZ: Popular music at the time went to four-on-the-floor dance music, like Lady Gaga. You just couldn't get songs on . . .

RYLAND BLACKINTON: The late 2000s club-pop thing, that huge-ness—Akon, Lady Gaga, whatever . . . It was one of the most maximalist times.

ALEX SUAREZ: The pop scene was changing greatly. That's when mega stars like Rihanna and Britney Spears were continuing to be huge. You had these big female pop stars rising and electronic music becoming a big factor. People's tastes were evolving.

ANDY GREENWALD: December 2008, *Folie à Deux* comes out, and that's my favorite album by Fall Out Boy by a long margin. I still listen to it all the time. "Disloyal Order of Water Buffaloes" is their best song.

A lot of these bands were hitting their natural point of evolution. I also think a couple other things shifted. Broadly speaking, the Obama era was different than the Bush era, in terms of national mood. I have a playlist I love called "Obama Era Triumphalism," and it's all like, The-Dream tracks. Very propulsive, celebratory pop. "Live Your Life" by Rihanna, you know? The mood changed.

BUDDY NIELSEN: One reason I think 2000s emo got so big was because it was kind of inappropriate to have party music as the background to two wars and probably the deadliest terrorist attack in American history. The response was music that captured the energy of the youth, which was this fucked-up world we're living in . . . In 2008, there's a generation of kids that may not remember 9/11 in the same way, and it switches to a different style of music that reflects the zeitgeist. It's just what happens with popular music.

MARIA SHERMAN: If it's music that's tied to young people—which is all popular music—at a certain point, it falls out of vogue, because a new generation comes in. There's a new sound, someone's innovating. Hip-hop was becoming the dominant musical force. Indie rock was bubbling up near mainstream consciousness.

I also wonder if people who are loyalists to this music—ride or die Warped Tour every year—I imagine at a certain point they were sick of seeing bands they love blow up to an enormous size and no longer feel like their own. Not that you have to be younger to have that experience but . . . there's such a feeling of ownership over this music that you connect to deeply. And after a while it's like, "Okay, well it got too big. *I'm out.*"

LIGHTS: I went to a movie with Tom—I wanna say it was *Avatar*. This was after he'd gracefully checked out of MySpace. It was towards the end, when MySpace was on its last legs. We met up in LA: a friend of his and this girl—I can't remember her name—she was an artist who came up on MySpace: "You gotta meet her, maybe you guys can collab." Tom was a very low-key guy. We watched the movie, and I remember the whole thing was very low-impact. He was showing me photos he took in Laos and Cambodia, these beautiful places he was traveling to. Hangin' with Tom! But at a point where it was not that relevant anymore, because he was already out of MySpace. It was strange. And kind of normal.

CHAPTER 37

"TOTAL, COMPLETE TRANSFORMATION"

ANDY GREENWALD: The story of emo was always that boom and very quick bust. It's never actually sustained itself like My Chem and Fall Out Boy. They were the ones. They were the princes who were promised. They were the ones who were going to inherit the ground that had been won by previous generations and then go pop.

HANIF ABDURRAQIB: I think both bands set interesting bars, and I think My Chemical Romance set a bar that was maybe too high to even be met. Here's the thing . . . So much of the genre, for better or worse, is self-centered. It relies on the self in order to be propulsive. The whole *Black Parade* project specifically was to be severed of their selves and create something else in their own image. I think a lot of bands in that scene weren't willing to push that way. They didn't have the patience. They weren't ego-less enough. And My Chemical Romance was.

GEOFF RICKLY: We talked a lot on the *Black Parade* tour about where My Chemical Romance could go from there. That was one of the big topics: "Well, you got here, what can you even do?" Gerard is a big David Bowie fan and he was about total reinvention. Coasting on something that's working does not work for Gerard. That's not him. He likes total, complete transformation. So it was exciting to talk to him about it. Because he knew . . . he knew it was the pinnacle. He knew that *Black Parade* was like, "We're never gonna live this one down."

AMANDA BRENNAN: *Black Parade* is this monolith.

ANTHONY RANERI: It's just a fucking triumph. The pinnacle of the scene.

NEAL AVRON: It felt like My Chemical Romance had gone from album number one to album number five in one album cycle.

There wasn't a lot of room to grow after *The Black Parade*, as far as, "Let's add more, let's make a bigger production out of this." It was the ultimate production.

ANDY GREENWALD: My Chemical Romance were at a place that a lot of bands find themselves in when they reach or exceed their dreams. They literally poured everything of themselves—certainly Gerard did—every part of ambition that he's ever had—whether it was songwriting, or comic books, or performance—they poured everything into it, and connected on a global scale. They pulled it off.

Any successful artist struggles with what to do next when you can do anything. With My Chemical Romance, there's such a clean trajectory from the scrappy first album, breakthrough second album, to globe-crushing third album. And then it's like, well, *we could do anything*. Warner Bros. will write a check if we want to make a reggae album, you know? They might not like it, but we can do that. So what *do* you do?

GABE SAPORTA: The more successful you are, the more you're going to be touring and sharing, and just working. It's hard to carve out time to think about your next move, to be creative again. All of this success also takes a toll on your personal life. Any semblance of normalcy—being with your family, your partner, whatever it is—starts to disappear.

PATRICK STUMP: It was very much a personal rejection when *Folie à Deux* was hated as it was. But I really tried. I had a vision, I had creative dreams on that record of what songs would sound like and visions of . . . I have very light synesthesia and I had these images of things I wanted the record to sound like. It was a very personal record.

NEAL AVRON: I'm sure they were all bummed; as I recall, Patrick put a lot of the onus on himself. Maybe even more so than *Cork Tree* and *Infinity*, Patrick really explored the depth of what he could do as a musician and a singer.

BRIAN DIAZ: You're not selling records, morale is low, too many bands are doing the same thing. The scene had run its course. That version of the scene had run its course.

PATRICK STUMP: It wasn't just that *Folie* failed commercially, because who cares about that. The failure was a new experience for us. That was the first time people would pay to go to a show, stand in line for hours, watch a couple other bands, and then boo us: Here's an old song, YAY! Here's a new song, BOO! That was a new thing for me. Personally, I mean, it's stupid; I think of that Meg Ryan line from *You've Got Mail*: "You poor, sad multimillionaire, I feel so sorry for you." But it was really personally devastating, to put yourself out there and have it be received that way.

I remember a show in Tinley Park, outside Chicago, at an amphitheater they called the World Music Theatre when I was a kid. It was the coolest place, where all the biggest bands in the world played. We were getting booed the whole time by the front row. I don't wear my glasses onstage; they're the only ones I can interact with. And they were vicious. You're rich and famous, you're in some band, *boo-hoo*, but there's really not enough money and prestige in the world to make that not feel devastating. Unless you're a wrestling heel. Then that's the plan, to have people come out and boo and throw things at you.

PETE WENTZ: I think everybody was ready to do their own thing. So that was the spirit we went into the Blink-182 tour with [at the end of the album cycle].

Those shows were kind of fun because it's Blink's show, you know what I mean? We were just there to be a good appetizer. It's interesting, because at the time the emo thing was still a thing for people, you know what I mean? There were fans there that were just like "fuck these guys" or whatever, fans who were mad Blink didn't just play a two-and-a-half-hour show. I think we were kind of fine with it. In some ways, I think that's where we thrived the most. And that probably comes from hardcore, honestly.

We used to make all kids of bets and deals back then. I think I told Mark Hoppus he could shave my head if they took us on the tour.

PATRICK STUMP: That last show of the tour . . . I remember Mark coming up and cutting Pete's hair. I remember being really crabby about everything. I was kind of checked out.

JAMES MONTGOMERY: I wrote an article for *MTV News* . . . "Blink-182 Bassist Shaves Pete Wentz's Head Onstage at Madison Square Garden." Wow, I was there. "Pete Wentz, Mark Hoppus Declare 'Death of the Emo Haircut.'"

PETE WENTZ: Shaving the head was like a rebirth, a baptism through fire kind of thing. Mark said at the time he was like the grandfather of a million bad haircuts and it was like . . . "I don't really want to be a haircut," you know what I mean? It's like you're working at a company and the company is your hair. Like you're a Halloween costume. The look can't get any bigger than being a Halloween costume.

So I was like, "This is cool." He shaved it. I remember one of my managers following Mark around with a plastic bag and saving the hair because he was gonna put it in a limited vinyl, or something. I was like, "What the hell is happening?" But in some weird ways it felt like the close of an era. In so many ways, for me personally, it felt like, "Let's be done with that." I don't know how to explain the feeling because I didn't know what was next. I was pretty sure Fall Out Boy wasn't gonna exist anymore in the incarnation that it did. It was just freeing.

GABE SAPORTA: When you're creating music, you're making something out of nothing. You're in your head, envisioning playing this for thousands of people. Then it starts to happen, and once it starts happening, there's so much going on. There's so many moving pieces you almost have to feel like it's happening *to you*, whereas in the beginning, it's very self-directed. When it explodes, you have to let go of the reins.

PART 6

EPILOGUE

Kids grow up, they do.

Talk all you want about Fall Boy Boy's hiatus, MySpace's downfall, Hot Topic's "less dark" rebrand, kids losing interest in guitars, the EDM boom, Sonny Moore changing his name to Skrillex; emo's pop era fizzled out because kids got older. A kid who saw one of the first *Black Parade* shows in 2006—let's say they were sixteen . . . by the time MCR released its next album, that kid would have been twenty. It's no one's fault, really: *Danger Days* is a neat record, and the American teenage brain goes through a lot of wild shit between buying a ticket to junior prom and your first legal drink. You want to assert yourself as a young adult. You've earned freedom from the high school bell and your parents' car keys. You might start denying ever enjoying My Chemical Romance and telling people at college parties your favorite band has always, always been Joy Division. You might've found a new identity in the 2010s through Tumblr, Urban Outfitters, HBO's *Girls*, or a job. You might even be listening to Swedish House Mafia right now.

But emo never went away. In the mid-to-late 2000s in places like Scranton, Pennsylvania, and Fenton, Michigan, far off as they seemed, new scenes bubbled up and produced an array of exciting, new bands. If there was one common thread through these so-called Emo Revival bands, it was sounding way different than the previous wave of emo. The passion of the Hotelier, the twinkle of Algernon Cadwallader, the drive of Tigers Jaw . . . free from any mainstream expectations, these bands could get delicate, intense, and vulnerable in ways the old guard wasn't willing to, or just couldn't. "Emo music was cool because you could touch it," says Will Yip, the Philly-based producer of bands like Title Fight and Balance and Composure, who's as responsible as anyone for revitalizing the genre through the 2010s. "The swoopy hair era, you couldn't touch, you know what I mean? Bands wanted to make that music that you could touch again."

While traditional, guitar-based emo headed underground in the 2010s, Gen Z rap culture snapped up some of the genre's old touchstones. Lo-fi production, moody guitars, and yearning, singsongy hooks were in style again, with artists like Juice WRLD and Lil Peep on the verge of pop breakthroughs. Juice WRLD, a Chicago native, cited Fall Out Boy and Paramore as influences and became a star with 2018's emo-rap anthem "Lucid Dreams." Lil Peep, a Long Island native, rapped over Brand New and Mineral samples, and possessed incalculable star power beneath his introverted veneer. Emo purists scoffed at the new movement, with its trap beats, sampled guitars, face tattoos, and complicated embrace of drugs like Xanax and Percocet. Tragically, both Lil Peep and Juice WRLD died of drug overdoses, in 2017 and 2019, respectively, shortly after their twenty-first birthdays. Years later, emo feels increasingly embedded in rap's DNA, in large part to their growing legacies.

As for the bands that ruled 2000s emo, the shifting landscape of the early 2010s presented a daunting crossroads. Some acquiesced to playing much smaller crowds; others broke up. Fall Out Boy's hiatus lasted into Obama's second administration and My Chemical Romance called it quits around the same time. With most of the scene clawing back to its punk roots, the aughts' most famously contrarian band, Brand New, saw its legend grow exponentially. Self-releasing sporadic projects and touring with indie rock bands like Modest Mouse, they avoided "I used to like them in high school . . ." status like no one else from their era. Their legacy, however, is impossible to untangle from the accusations against Jesse Lacey that surfaced in late 2017.

"That was a moment where I noticed a generational shift," says Ellie Kovach, a moderator of emo's subreddit page at the time. "Most of the people I knew who followed Brand New since the 2000s were like, 'That sucks, but I'm probably still gonna listen.' Whereas, there was this younger generation of kids that were still discovering Brand New, latching on to them with such fervent intensity. They were burning their records or getting their tattoos covered." The cancellation of Brand New's 2018 arena tour and reassessment of Lacey's legacy felt part of a much larger discourse. This era of emo no doubt fostered other, much less famous, yet just as harmful offenders, who took advantage of their elevated platform in a male-dominated scene. For the genre to maintain its relevance, this reckoning must continue. "As I got older, I stepped away from emo because of the misogyny I felt in the air at those shows during that era," says writer Jenn Pelly. "I've always been interested in emo and hardcore as music, and it seems more enlightened today than it was when I was thirteen, which has made me more interested in keeping up with new bands. When something can be critiqued and grow and change from that critique, that's positive."

In reviewing the bands covered in this book, Paramore feels especially unique. They were the only famous band with a female vocalist, yes, but Paramore deserves so much more recognition than that. 2010's *Brand New Eyes* is just as good as 2007's *Riot!* and their 2013 self-titled album is even better. Look around the scene in 2013, at where this class of 2000s bands was at, and almost no one else even comes close. It's more impressive when you consider the constant Paramore sideshows: the Farro brothers finally quitting the band in 2010, bassist Jeremy Davis suing Williams on his way out in 2016, etcetera. Paramore's 2017 album *After Laughter* was loved by critics in a way I could not have fathomed for any band of this scene ten years prior. The rest of the decade saw a new wave of nostalgia and appreciation for 2000s emo, but I don't think so many ships would have been lifted without the rising tide of Paramore.

During my seven years as a staff writer at *Billboard*, perhaps the wackiest thing I ever got to do was cover three Paramore cruises—sailing from Miami to the Bahamas with about three thousand fans, as Paramore performed on the ship's deck. A long, long way from seeing them play Randolph, New Jersey, in 2006 to a couple hundred people. There's a good chance, I think, that some other kid from that crowd was somewhere on board, too. On the 2018 cruise, I interviewed the band atop the ship somewhere in the Atlantic Ocean. With nothing but blue all around,

Hayley Williams thought back to the mid-aughts days of Paramore.net: "We've found a lot of people out in the crowd are the same people from the early years. It's this tangible, multicultural thing—people are coming from all over the world—and yet we're part of a real community. I'm really proud of that—in 2018, it's hard to imagine the internet did something so pure."

—Chris Payne, Brooklyn, New York, October 2022

WE'LL CARRY ON

HAYLEY WILLIAMS: If we didn't have all that stupid fucking drama for all those years, would people even fucking know who we are anymore? Did that or did that not help us during some of the slower years? I don't know. I'm not trying to go back and fix it.

ADAM SAMILJAN: Paramore self-titled in 2013 was a scary one. There were some major lineup changes with the band. I think fans were hesitant and curious to see what the band would do after Josh and Zac left. I don't think people were expecting them to go in the direction they did, especially from how dark and heavy parts of *Brand New Eyes* were. It was awesome seeing it pay off with the Grammy win for "Ain't It Fun." The band grew well beyond what their roots were.

LESLIE SIMON: Hayley is the iconic alt-rock flower that continues to bloom a different color every season.

ADAM SAMILJAN: *After Laughter* in 2017 is probably my favorite Paramore album.

HAYLEY WILLIAMS: *After Laughter* was such a sweet time. Especially for me and how depressed I was. We enjoyed each other, we talked about this stuff. Zac was able to talk to us about where he was when he quit. I didn't talk to him for six years.

The first time I talked to him was when we were playing a headline show in Auckland during self-titled [2013]. Zac was living in New

Zealand. We were in his territory. I was trying to take inventory of how that felt in my body. I wasn't mad anymore. As I'm sitting in my hotel room thinking about it, a commercial for a festival comes on and Zac's band HalfNoise is on. I was surprised I felt so proud. Out of nowhere. Six years had gone by, but I was like, "Fuck, yeah, that's my boy Zac." I remembered him making GarageBand demos in the van, and now he was playing a festival in New Zealand on his own. I looked up his email address, and I wrote him: "You just came on my TV. All I wanna say is that I'm so proud of you." That's when the ice was broken.

He was so sweet, like, "I can't come to your show, but I'm so proud of you and I miss you." We didn't end up hanging out for a while. It wasn't until we got into the studio for *After Laughter*. I was nervous to hang with him again. It was so life-affirming. Me, Taylor, and Zac sitting in a room again. They were the guys I hung out with when we were younger.

ADAM SAMILJAN: *After Laughter* is such an interesting creative concept: very sad, personal, dark lyrics over some of the band's most upbeat, poppy music. Just a lot more musicality that you certainly didn't get on their first album. So much more going on.

HAYLEY WILLIAMS: There was a period of time after we wrapped touring for self-titled where I really feared my best days were behind me. It felt a bit like a death. When we finally had demos that excited us, I wasn't so hopeless anymore. I really credit Taylor for giving me whatever courage I had during that time.

ADAM SAMILJAN: I think Taylor really came into his own as a producer and songwriter. I think that Hayley's better than she's ever been on *After Laughter*.

LESLIE SIMON: I wonder what the Hayley from the early Paramore years would think about the Hayley now, because they seem so different. I mean, the core human is the same. But with all the stops and starts and relationships and heartbreaks, I don't know if she would have thought this is where she would be. I say that without judgment; I would love to know, what would your younger self think of you today? Would she have started a hair dye company? Would she have released a solo record? All these things that have happened over time and feel very gradual. Looking back at the tiny human she was, it feels so much bigger once you fast-forward through the years.

AMANDA BRENNAN: In the mid- to late 2000s, that's when MCR, Fall Out Boy, Panic!, and Paramore all had that moment. I call it Hot Topic Emo, the more well-packaged and easy-to-sell stuff. I feel like it all had this ebb and flow; it was super popular when it first happened, then it kind of ebbed, and then it had a second moment once another set of fifteen-year-olds found it.

ELLIE KOVACH: More than any of these bands, Paramore appeals to the widest variety of people.

LESLIE SIMON: The more campy qualities of the music and lifestyle, as demonstrated by Paramore and Hayley and Panic! and Brendon, that was not something during the aughts that the scene intentionally highlighted or pushed to the crowd. Unfortunately—and I'm just speaking for myself—it's disappointing to look back and not realize sooner that this was not a diverse and inclusive scene. This was not a scene where people felt comfortable being themselves if you were different. You could see that by the representation of those playing the instruments and singing the songs. And also by the faces in the crowd. There were some exceptions but again, in the 2000s, there were not many people of the BIPOC community in the scene. There were not many open, out members of the LGBTQ community. It was noticeable, though not often brought up in conversation.

I don't think Brendon could be the lead in *Kinky Boots* in 2009. I don't know if Brendon could have sung a song about loving yourself unconditionally in 2007. I don't think the scene was ready. I think the change has been forced because the people in it are different.

CASSADEE POPE: It makes so much sense that Brendon did *Kinky Boots*. He's got such a theatrical brain . . .

JOHNNY MINARDI: The *Pretty. Odd.* drop-off was so drastic for Panic!'s career. Now, obviously, we get to hear the redemption story.

AMANDA BRENNAN: High, high hopes!

SPENCER SMITH: Brendon's the best natural performer of anybody in any of these bands.

ADAM SISKA: Touring behind their 2018 album *Pray for the Wicked*, I went to see them play in Chicago. And they played *one* song from *A Fever You Can't Sweat Out*.

Brendon rode his fucking piano around the United Center, the place Michael Jordan jumped through the air and dunked. Brendon was way higher than MJ, playing his piano for crying girls. When he landed by the soundboard, he saw me and goes, "What's up, Siska?" Because he's so down to earth.

MATT SQUIRE: There's something about Brendon and Ryan Ross together that just would have been Queen or U2, and still could be. Honestly, I believe that. I've had that conversation with J.D. in the past couple years. I was just like, "Dude, Ryan Ross. What a visionary." And he was like, "*Yeah*, one of the biggest visionaries I've ever seen."

JONATHAN DANIEL: I sent Ryan *Pretty. Odd.* when it went platinum [in March 2019]. He got a good laugh. That was the last time I talked to him. He did a couple shows . . . Gabe organized some thing, and Ryan played a couple songs. I'm not sure what he's up to, but I'm sure it's interesting.

If you wonder why Fall Out Boy took a break or why Panic! split in two, it's so they didn't lose their minds. Everything can't solely be based on a careerist perspective.

BERT MCCRACKEN: I had this moment for myself, that I'm sure Gerard had, where I was like, "This is not sustainable." He's a little bit older than I am; maybe he just saw the light before I did. I wasn't able to quit on my own.

TRAVIE MCCOY: We used to go *hard* hard. Bert was a trip. Then I saw him while he was getting clean and they were taking the whole minibar out of his hotel room.

BERT MCCRACKEN: I needed to go to rehab and get full-blown professional help. I sincerely hope, looking back, that I didn't put a bad taste in people's mouths forever. But if I did, that's the way it had to go down, I guess. I was such an intoxicated mess back then.

TRAVIE MCCOY: I was a full-blown heroin addict; I'll keep it a buck. It was bad. It was really bad.

People that helped me get out of that . . . Pete for sure. When I first went to real, thirty-day rehab, Pete was there. I stayed with him for four months in Hollywood Hills. He held me down. Also Sia. She would send me songs every week, like little sketches. Like, that's where my song "Golden" featuring Sia came from. There's another one called "I Won't Go Down." She sent me that shit in rehab. I had a solid fucking foundation. If I didn't have that, I wouldn't be here now.

PETE WENTZ: Mental health wasn't spoken about in the public in the same way it is now years ago. I mean, I think I was going to do some kind of mental health campaign, and there was a big talk from management and PR people about like, "Is that showing weakness?" I appreciate how much has changed. What really helps is people like Jay-Z and sports figures. I don't think anybody thought any of our bands were like, normal bastions of strength or something, but when I see someone like Jay-Z talk about these things it's like, "I guess everybody goes through things like this."

With the kind of personality I have, I would just know about every drug, and I mean, not illegal drugs. I would know about like, any benzo. I would just kind of be like a drugstore cowboy and take stuff. And it really was at that time, that particular era, really easy to acquire things.

The generation after us, you know, Peep and Juice WRLD, it was a generation where . . . I don't know. I have regrets about not being able to reach out to those guys. I feel like that's a place where I could have probably reached out and had some relatable experiences.

MARIANNE ELOISE: I interviewed Lil Peep . . . I'll cry if I talk too much so we're not doing that . . .

HANNAH EWENS: I was very, very, very into Lil Peep. Intensely into him.

MARIANNE ELOISE: I was like, "Well, this is the future of emo, this is great." This is a way it can exist in 2016 . . .

ADAM MCILWEE: When I first met him, he was just on the cusp of blowing up . . . This would be 2016, or so.

WILL YIP: Emo-rap . . . Adam [as Wicca Phase Springs Eternal] had taken the most accessible elements in two genres and mashed them together. People love emo music because of the melodies and lyrics; people love hip-hop because, obviously the lyrics as well, but it's so agreeable—hip-hop beats are consistent, they bang.

ADAM MCILWEE: I met a lot of these kids on Tumblr. Cold Hart would send me beats. He sent me a beat called "GothBoiClique" and I was like, "This should be the name of a group."

Mackned joined GothBoiClique, Lil Tracy joined JPDreamthug, Fish Narc, and Yawns . . . It was all Twitter, Tumblr, and then iPhone group chats. Then Peep came into the picture. He was just a kid on the internet.

This scene—whatever you want to call it—there was a sound. And then Peep was just like, "Oh okay, this is the sound, I can perfect this."

HANNAH EWENS: Lil Peep was the first thing I'd listened to in years where I had that very teenage, obsessive, falling-in-love experience. I listened to *HELLBOY* on SoundCloud and I don't even really use SoundCloud. I dyed my hair pink because he had pink hair at that era. I had merch and stuff and like, that wasn't something I did as an adult woman anymore. I only bought merch for old artists. He and his music definitely weren't for me, a twenty-seven-year-old woman, but I was sold on everything about him. He was like emo Kurt Cobain or something in terms of how he looked.

ADAM MCILWEE: Peep's sound naturally lent itself to the mainstream. He was amazing at writing choruses. He had a carefreeness in his delivery. It sounded effortless. It captured all the parts of this scene that would make it marketable: cool, kind of edgy, kind of drugged out. Which is, unfortunately, a major part of this scene.

MARIANNE ELOISE: You saw emo resonating in the most mainstream ways in a really long time. The older people around him had fucking dollar signs in their eyes and needed him to be a huge star and didn't think about the support he needed. It was this fucking insane new life he was not prepared for.

HANNAH EWENS: I interviewed him once over the phone for *Kerrang!* It was really sad, actually, because I knew he was into Xanax and drugs. That was part of the whole narrative around him, and the things he rapped about. He was so intoxicated when I interviewed him. I wish it was in person because it was hard to have a good interview. I remember sitting at my dining room table in the flat I rented with my friend and during the interview, I swapped from my little mic earpiece and put him on speakerphone because he was so fucked up that I was worried it wasn't going to record properly. I was writing down what he was saying as he spoke, and I'd never done that before in an interview. The surprising element of it was he sounded like a baby. It was like I was having a conversation with a four-year-old, honestly. He was just so softly spoken and sounded like a mix of scared and confident, giving these one-, two-, three-, four-word answers.

In another industry if you're engaging with someone with bad addiction or mental health problems, you could just tell your manager or whatever. It was just a short interview; I wasn't gonna write that he seems intoxicated. You do your little piece, you hand it in, you talk to your editor or you might say something to PR but it's like . . . I don't know. You just feel kind of helpless, slash, it's not your business to do anything about it.

ADAM MCILWEE: It's a weird, slimy thing. Who's gonna tell him no? When Peep is the one making them money and he's telling them he needs Xanax or Percocet to work, they're not gonna say no. Or if they're offering him this stuff to get him to work, he's not gonna say no. He's a kid.

HANNAH EWENS: When he died, my friend and I found out at work, and we both had to go outside. We were crying outside of work, in floods of tears. We'd met him and interviewed him and it just felt really surreal, like losing . . . Not like losing a friend but, it did kind of feel like losing someone you know. And it just felt so avoidable.

MARIANNE ELOISE: It was a big deal for me. Like, my first tattoo was a *Crybaby* tattoo. I went out to New York for a memorial. It was an album listening thing, with friends and family.

HANNAH EWENS: We see the influence through artists like Lil Peep. It's emo as emotion, emo as feeling, rather than any specific genre. That's why we can speak about emo in such a loose way now. It was already loose in the

2000s mainstream emo era, but especially now, the way these influences have trickled down, it's like emo is literally just the feeling. The feeling of emo music. Not anything to do with the lyrics, the sound, the visual identity of emo. It's just emotions. But it's still so powerful.

WILL YIP: These kids, your Peeps and Juice WRLDs, RIP, your Post Malones and your Halseys, I'm grateful they helped make the genre not a dinosaur, you know what I mean? The second I heard Halsey, I was like, "Oh, she listened to fucking My Chemical Romance." You can tell by the shapes in her melodies, her storytelling. Same thing with Post. And Adam and GothBoiClique, they helped make this genre not a dinosaur. You've seen rock niches come and go. You've seen grunge come, it went, it comes back in a way, but outside Nirvana becoming a pop band because they're so fucking popular, it didn't evolve into a viable mainstay. I don't care what you say about grunge music, grunge music will never always be there. I fucking love grunge music, but it's not always gonna be there on Top 40 radio. Because of these younger artists, emo is a mainstay in popular music and modern popular culture. And because of that, emo bands will always have a place to live—the *band* bands, you know? Not just emo rap music. And that's really fucking cool.

ANTHONY RANERI: Now, the bands who are left standing are the ones who had staying power. They've been able to maintain a career . . .

JIM ADKINS: I'll get phone videos all the time from friends saying, "Hey, man, I'm at this place and guess what? This dude's covering 'The Middle.'" It's a trip.

I mean, "The Middle" still is us. "The Middle" is the idea that your self-worth doesn't come from external validation. That's a lifelong thing to figure out. It's a constant theme over all our records.

JOHN NOLAN: Mark O'Connell brought up the idea of Shaun and I coming back to Taking Back Sunday. Right off the bat, I was skeptical. But he was talking about how he didn't feel like the band was in a good place. He wasn't happy and he didn't feel like anyone was happy. He could picture this scenario where Shaun and I came back . . .

NEIL RUBENSTEIN: I remember . . . should I tell this story? All right, fuck it.

I was working with John Nolan when Brand New's *Daisy* came out. We were like, "Oh, that's a good record." John liked it, but he didn't know about the screaming. He was like, "I don't know if at thirty I can muster up to be screaming about stuff anymore." And then the next thing, he rejoins Taking Back Sunday and he's screaming his balls off, ha, ha, ha, ha.

FRED MASCHERINO: When it's this nostalgia thing, it's a strange phenomenon . . .

MATT PRYOR: The first time I went on tour with Max Bemis . . . I didn't know that Max was this Get Up Kids super fan. I had to be like, "Hang on, stop. You can ask me about one song a day. I can't keep doing this for this whole fucking tour. I appreciate you, I love you, I can't keep just psychoanalyzing every single one of my lyrics every single day with you."

AARON GILLESPIE: I'm a spiritual person, for sure. If I had to carry a label, that would be Christianity, but I don't really carry a label. I'm emotionally and socially wounded from my upbringing. I don't think I'll ever recover. I spent a lot of time working on that.

SPENCER CHAMBERLAIN: Finally, in '09, we decided to not be a Christian band. We weren't preaching the gospel in our songs. We were singing about how fucked up it is.

AARON GILLESPIE: Finally, it was like, "Let's just say it."

And then, for Spencer, he was navigating all his stuff. He stayed on drugs about ten years after 2006 Warped Tour. Finally, he came to me around 2015, 2016, like, "I need help." And that's when he figured it out. But that took a long time.

SPENCER CHAMBERLAIN: Getting the band back together in 2015 was the start of getting my life back on track.

RANDY NICHOLS: Underoath all liked George W. Bush back when he was running for office. And now, they're very liberal. They became Bernie Sanders guys later in life.

The thing I really love is that, even though they don't identify as one, they are still, in a sense, a Christian band. But in the best possible sense. They were taught from the churches they were in that certain things were bad, but they met people and realized, "That's not bad." They live the way Jesus says. Love everybody.

BUDDY NIELSEN: I decided to define as queer because it seems the most vague. It doesn't mean straight, but I am in a straight relationship.

Senses Fail put out a couple records in the 2010s that were heavier and more aligned with hardcore. Those records were me coming out and dealing with a lot of anger. We created these shirts that said "QUEER HARDCORE" and people really liked them. People are always asking for them.

CHRIS CARRABBA: The scene that I'm from, you get lifelong friends. You get a sense of family.

ANTHONY RANERI: On Bayside's most recent tour, I remember that Denver to Salt Lake drive. We're sitting in the front lounge of our bus and it's October, coming up on the anniversary of John Beatz's death. We've driven past the site a hundred times since it happened. And now when we do, we tell stories about John, fun stories about those days. We're happy to have known him.

J. T. WOODRUFF: Hawthorne Heights is working on getting our platinum plaques for *The Silence in Black and White*. It's owned by Concord now; we deal with them since Victory sold to them. That's all cool. That milestone stuff is what dreams are made of. That's why I can't focus on the negativity. We beat the odds. We have gold records hanging on our walls. And we came from DIY rental halls.

ALEX DELEON: Why are all these people from the scene so successful? It was a grind, man. It was playing shows three hundred days a year. The work ethic prepared you for anything.

PATRICK STUMP: The response to my solo record was even worse than *Folie.*

MATT RUBANO: It's a shame, because that *Soul Punk* record has some badass music on it.

TOM MULLEN: I saw Patrick open for Panic! and Foxy Shazam at Starland Ballroom in Sayreville, New Jersey, in 2011. Patrick's set was cool. He did a Phil Collins cover and he did "Let's Dance." I liked it. I'm not trying to pick on him, but I'm telling you, no one gave a flying fuck. No one cared. I go, "Is that because they only want to hear 'Sugar, We're Goin Down'? Has the fan base moved on? Or is this just because it's a Tuesday?"

PETE WENTZ: When me or Patrick gets bummed and reaches out, we kind of put aside the way the band is supposed to work and try to figure it out for each other. I'll give you a frickin' scoop here, man . . . when I was going through my divorce, I was fucked up emotionally and Patrick reached out, and we wrote some songs together. This was in 2012. We wrote these lost songs that I'm pretty sure will never see the light of day. I don't even have them. I'm pretty sure they suck, ha, ha. It wasn't the intent of them being Fall Out Boy or not being Fall Out Boy; I think Patrick just tried to make me feel better.

PATRICK STUMP: I was in an interview with *Spin* and I was talking about the solo record. And they really weren't interested in the solo record. They wanted to ask about Fall Out Boy, and I'm like, "I don't have any news on Fall Out Boy!" They kept pushing and pushing and I go, "You know what? For the purposes of this interview, just pretend I'm not in Fall Out Boy for this interview." And that got snipped to "I'm not in Fall Out Boy." And that became the headline the next day.

Pete read that headline and was really upset. So now, all of a sudden, I'm not in the band anymore. All of a sudden, I accidentally broke up Fall Out Boy.

Pete called me up and goes, "Hey, I know that the band's not working out right now." At this point, he thinks I quit the band because I gave a shitty interview. He goes, "We should still be friends. Like, it's fucked up that you don't know my kid." And I was like, "Yeah, that is kind of fucked up. I'm sorry." But the thing is, for me to hang out, we have to do the music thing. That's the way that you hang out with me. I'm a weird guy. I've kind of struggled with it. The truth is, I don't really have friends in the normal sense because I'm so consumed with my hobbies. I don't get dinner. I don't watch the game. So Pete's like, "If that's the way you hang out, let's get together and do music stuff." And we did.

ALEX DELEON: They came back. "My Songs Know What You Did in the Dark" was one of the biggest songs of their career.

PATRICK STUMP: It's weird, because in the annals of Fall Out Boy history, it's, "And then they surprised everybody with a record, they had this whole plan, this amazing rollout, blah, blah, blah." We didn't know any of it. We didn't know we were going to do a record. We put out a song. We approved the music video the morning we put it up.

We played a show that night in Chicago. The song had been out six hours and everyone sang along with it. Everyone knew all the words. I was like, "Well, that's new!"

That day, I remember it feeling like when we released *Cork Tree*. I thought about telling my parents, "I'm just going to see where this goes, and when it fails, I'll go back to school." Historically, bands don't come back. You don't really get a second act.

PETE WENTZ: It's interesting the way time changes things.

PATRICK STUMP: And there we were. It was like 2005 all over again. Maybe bigger.

JONAH BAYER: When I was interviewing Fall Out Boy for an *AP* cover story in 2015, they did an in-store signing at Vintage Vinyl in New Jersey. It was girls and guys, but I remember these girls were crying. They would be like, "Fall Out Boy's my favorite band." And I would be like, "When did you get into them?" And they're like, "Two and a half years ago."

MANI MOSTOFI: If Racetraitor plays a show and somebody says to me Racetraitor's the first hardcore band they ever listened to, you 100 percent know they were a Fall Out Boy fan. There's no other way we were their gateway into hardcore. We're ten layers deep into hardcore. We're a cult band of a cult genre. If some twenty-something comes up to me and says "Racetraitor's the first hardcore band I was ever into," it's like, "Oh, this is someone who loved, loved, *loved* Fall Out Boy."

SPENCER SMITH: For the longest time, to the writers of *Pitchfork*, *Noisey*, or whatever, our bands were not cool. They wouldn't write about us, or if they did, it would be some snide, sarcastic thing. Then all of a sudden, like four years ago, I started noticing a different tone. The story would be like, "Here's my afternoon with Pete Wentz!" And it wasn't a *wink, wink* thing; it was sincere. Like, that's kind of nice! This is a new feeling! You know, all the twenty-five-year-old writers at these places were fourteen when our bands were coming out.

PETE WENTZ: All our bands used to hate being called emo because at the time, it felt like a disclaimer: "This band's not really a rock band; they kind of suck; but emo bands are big, so we kind of have to cover them." A lot of us ended up with this weird mental scar that we carried forever. People will come up to me like, "Dude, you're such a fucking emo legend!" And I'll like, cower, because I'm like, "Oh my god, is this person making fun of me right now?" And they're like, "No, no, you're so fucking cool."

MATT PRYOR: I've come to terms that, similar to the term "punk," emo is in the eye of the beholder. So is emo Rites of Spring and Sunny Day Real Estate, or is emo My Chem and Fall Out Boy? And the answer is "yes." It is whatever it is to you. And since I've never self-identified as emo, it means very little to me, ha, ha, ha.

ANDY GREENWALD: Fall Out Boy and My Chemical Romance, they're nice people and wish each other well. But I also think, just knowing them personally and watching them up close . . . they're supercompetitive. Even if they don't admit it publicly, they are. I think on some level, Fall Out Boy either distrusted or, depending on whether we're talking about Pete or Patrick, either distrusted or envied My Chemical Romance's patina of artistic purity. And I don't know if that went in the other direction. Was there a moment, when Fall Out Boy came roaring back on the charts in 2014, when Frank Iero looked up from picking up his kids at daycare like, "Motherfucker, why couldn't we have just held it together and written another hit?!" I don't know that moment ever existed. With Gerard, it didn't, because he immediately just started doing comic books and scripts.

PATRICK STUMP: When My Chemical Romance's hiatus happened, at the time, I didn't really think anything of it. But in retrospect, I really missed them. When you look at the bigger, successful bands—and I'm not comparing myself to this at all—but you know, the archetype of how the Beatles and Beach Boys used to rush out and get each other's records and be like, "Ah, why didn't I think of that?" They were friendly, but they had competition with each other. I realized that was something I did with My Chem. And then when they stopped, I was like, "Fuck, what do I react to?"

ANDY GREENWALD: Gerard's rare, in terms of rock and roll musicians, where he legitimately has other avenues. You know, this is relevant to what we're talking about here . . . In 2018, I reached out to Gerard because my friend Julio was turning forty and I wanted to get him a really special present. I was like, "I hate bugging you with this . . ." but I explained the comics my friend was into and was like, "Could you just scribble on something to make it special?" Gerard was like, "Come over."

So I went to his house—not a mansion, but like, a cool LA house—and his wife was there and I met his daughter. He and his wife are out in the back studio where his comic books are, smoking cigarettes. He literally is living the dream. He's writing his own line of DC comics at this point. He has a back house full of comic books and instruments. He had just made his solo single "Baby You're a Haunted House," which was my favorite song of that year, and *Umbrella Academy* was being developed for TV. He's friends with Grant Morrison. All of his dreams had been checked off. And it felt so reasonable and healthy—except for the smoking!—and such a success by any metric, other than, "What were your follow-up sales to your last major record?" Gerard was like, "Ray and Mikey were over here for a barbecue last week, you know, Mikey played on my song." He said they would probably play shows again at some point, but who knows, and then he busted out a one-of-a-kind *Doom Patrol* thing and signed it for my friend. But anyway, all of this is to say I've always felt that they broke up because they could.

And it's almost perfect, isn't it? That the band that was obsessed with dying at the end of things, the only band of that era I think people would have believed if they said they were never going to reform, emerges from the ashes like a glorious, black hair–dyed phoenix.

JAMES MONTGOMERY: At their first show back in 2019, it was amazing, seeing the fans queued up ahead of time [at the Shrine Expo Hall in LA], just waiting and waiting and waiting. There were a lot of people in full *Black Parade*, lots and lots of spooky brides and grooms like the cover of *Three Cheers*.

GABE SAPORTA: The great thing about it was the kids in the front. A lot of times with these reunion shows, the crowd just gets older. But there is a whole new generation of kids that love My Chem, never got to see them, and are excited about them as if they were a brand-new band. I remember Michael from 5 Seconds of Summer going crazy.

MATT GALLE: They broke the record at the Shrine for most merch ever sold there. They broke Billie Eilish's record, like $250,000 or something.

ANDY GREENWALD: It was like a high school reunion of everybody from the scene seeing each other for the first time in god knows how many years. Like, "Oh, there's Chris Conley and Geoff Rickly hanging out," and all of these people who had washed up from Jersey and Long Island.

AMY FLEISHER MADDEN: There wasn't a vibe of jealousy or, "I wish my band had gotten this big." It felt like when the good guys win.

GABE SAPORTA: I caught up with Geoff, hadn't seen him in a while and we were just talking. It felt like no time had passed.

SARAH LEWITINN: It was like a class reunion. Frankie was like . . . I fucking love Frankie. He's so sincere and bright-eyed, just a wonderfully happy person. To see it on his face, the joy he felt from seeing the crowd, performing the old songs, seeing all his friends backstage . . .

MIKEY WAY: You know the movie *It's a Wonderful Life*? It felt a little bit like that.

ANDY GREENWALD: The show itself was just exultant.

AMY FLEISHER MADDEN: I'll never forget when their banner dropped: this flowy, silk, gigantic iconographic thing falling from the sky and the loudest crowd I've ever heard.

JULIO MARTÍNEZ RÍOS: Each song felt like it was a living thing going through the building.

MIKEY WAY: I remember the adrenaline kicking in. I couldn't feel my hands for the first few songs. It didn't feel real while it was happening. I didn't know if we would ever do that again. We weren't sure we would ever do that again.

AMY FLEISHER MADDEN: Relentless crowd participation. Which, I'm used to because of Dashboard Confessional being so much of my DNA, but it was audibly different, shouting the entire show.

JULIO MARTÍNEZ RÍOS: I remember Gerard asking if anyone was there seeing MCR for the first time, and many hands raised.

ANDY GREENWALD: It really came down to, "Let's do it now, while we won't embarrass ourselves." Because they wanted their kids to see them onstage.

MIKEY WAY: I was a dad and I was sober. And that was a beautiful thing, to be extremely happy and present. For the first time in my life, I felt safe.

GEOFF RICKLY: Mikey had a bass solo; he played them off. And he could, 'cause he's that good now.

ANDY GREENWALD: The show was an incredibly validating moment. Not just for people like me, who always believed in the band, but for anyone who'd ever been affiliated with the scene. There had been a journey, there had been an arc, and it had led to something.

JULIO MARTÍNEZ RÍOS: When we were leaving the show, I remember a circle of very young people sitting outside; I don't remember which song they were singing, but they were singing an MCR song.

ANDY GREENWALD: There were kids, just like there had been kids at my first My Chem show, god knows how many years before, sitting on the sidewalk, sitting in circles, doing the thing that teenagers do where you wear all black and you sit huddled together and you whisper things. They were still high on the show. I don't think they were sitting there because they expected Gerard to like, come out and hail an Uber. I think they just didn't want the night to be over.

JIM ADKINS: For someone growing up and experiencing all the things of being a teenager or someone in your twenties, the idea that a scene of music could be a window into thinking that how you feel is okay . . . Nothing on classic rock is telling you that. Nothing was telling me that. Now, here's an environment where that's okay.

For me, that's the core of punk rock. Everyone is accepted, you know? We'll meet you where you're at. And you can come along for the ride.

CHRIS GETHARD: When UCB launched their new theater, [owner] Matt Besser, who had punk roots, had his flight from LA to New York get delayed because of a blizzard. They were doing this big show at UCB they'd done on Sunday nights for many years, called Asssscat, where they have somebody come in and tell stories and the comedians improvise based off them. I've done shows where Chevy Chase did that, where the news anchor Brian Williams did that. Besser said it would be a dream to get Ian MacKaye and the booker somehow reached out to him and got Ian MacKaye. But Besser's flight had gotten turned back. Amy Poehler goes, "Gethard! You like punk rock, right?" And I'm like, "Yeah, I came up in the punk scene." She goes, "This guy, Ian . . . Besser was really the only one who knew him . . . He's kind of just sitting there by himself in the green room, it's getting kind of awkward because he seems a little shy or a little uncomfortable in this environment . . . Could you just sit with Ian MacKaye and just like, talk to him and make sure he's feeling good?"

So it's just me in a room with Ian MacKaye off in a corner. I was able to ask this dude every question that anybody who came up liking punk stuff would be able to ask, and all the major crossovers in my interests, like when Fear destroyed the set at *SNL* in 1981. He's like, "Oh yeah, here's the stories that have never showed up on the internet from that night . . ." So I got to talk to Ian MacKaye because of my famous people connections. I don't really give a shit about famous people. I'm not trying to sound cool. But coming up in the punk scene led me to a night where I got to sit in a greenroom with Ian MacKaye and lead the discussion with him for stretches where I was the only person he was shooting the shit with. I go, "Dude, I used to run a fanzine in New Jersey. We sent out copies to different labels we loved and the only people who bought an ad for issue two was Dischord Records. My friend I ran it with, our jaws were on the floor: Dischord Records just sent us like thirty bucks!" Ian goes, "Yeah, when we were getting local zines asking for so little we would go, 'Man, this is clearly just a kid, let's fucking throw them thirty bucks and maybe their ten friends buy some records and we make up the thirty bucks and let them know they're doing a good thing.'"

Twenty years in comedy, it's one of those nights that meant the most to me. It's one of the small joys of working as hard as I did to a point where I was invited into that situation: to be able to look one of your heroes in the eye and thank them for helping you survive.

ACKNOWLEDGMENTS

This book could not have existed without the many, many interview subjects who generously gave me their time and trusted me to tell their stories. To everyone who spoke with me over the past two years, my sincerest thanks. You'll always have a special place in my memories. Furthermore, a book of this scope could not have come to fruition without the interviewees who helped me even further by connecting me with their friends and colleagues. I want to give special thanks to a handful of master connectors: Anthony Raneri, Adam Siska, Mike Doyle, Rob Hitt, Gabe Saporta, Alex Saavedra, Randy Nichols, Mike Marquis, Andy Greenwald, Chris Carrabba, Christian McKnight, Ricky Saporta, Mike Dubin, Christine Morales at Epitaph, and everyone at Big Picture Media, especially Dayna Ghiraldi, Katy Cooper, and Natalie Schaffer. Check out Mike Doyle's podcast *This Was the Scene* for an even deeper dive into late '90s and early 2000s punk lore; check out Rob Hitt's Instagram account Bodega Cats of Instagram if you like cats.

This book started out as a DIY project, just me and my laptop alone in my apartment after being laid off during the pandemic, but it never could have become what you're holding in your hands without the team that helped me along the way: my agent, Alyssa Reuben, who fought for this project time and time again, alongside the help of Mike Marquis, who together brought me to Dey Street Books. Thank you to Matthew Daddona, for taking on my book at Dey Street, and for steering me through a first-time author's many challenges; thank you to Kate Napolitano for guiding this book toward the finish line with your incisive editing skills and uncanny Jersey instincts; thank you to Stuart Roberts for seeing it through to publication. And thanks to the rest of the Dey Street team, especially Carrie Thornton, for believing in the book, Andrew Jacobs for the legal read, and Rosy Tahan and Chelsea Herrera, for your tireless work behind the scenes.

Thank you to Mom, Dad, and Alex; thank you to Madeleine for all the love and support. You were all there for me time and time again when this project felt kind of impossible. Turns out, it wasn't! But you knew that all along. And Grandma and Grandpa Payne; Grandma and Grandpa Zamorski, and Aunt Janet. This book belongs to all of you. A very special thanks to Uncle Howard, for everything.

Thank you to my roommates, Shen and Erin: I'll never forget popping that bottle of champagne together, in the middle of Pandemic Winter, the night I sold this book and signed my contract. Thanks to Dana Kandić for taking my author photo; thanks to Justin for the haircut. Thanks to my fellow writers and editors who were kind enough to help with my proposal and the ins and outs of pitching a book: Andrew Unterberger, Matthew Ismael Ruiz, Amanda Dissinger, Ross Scarano, Maria Sherman, Marissa Moss. Thanks to Lizzy Goodman for hopping on the phone with me before I'd even done my first book interview; all that advice meant the world to me, and still does. Thanks to all the editors who believed in me over the years, especially: Bill Canacci at the *Home News Tribune*, my first-ever editor, who helped show me I could be a music journalist, as a high schooler in 2004. Jillian Mapes and Jason Lipshutz, who hired me as an intern at *Billboard*. Tye Comer and Jessica Letkemann, who brought me on staff at *Billboard*. And Andrew Unterberger and Ross Scarano, who helped nurture my writing craft immeasurably over my time at *Billboard*; I often heard your voices over my shoulder as I fine-tuned the pages of this book. Thank you to my therapists over the years: Lou, Christina, and Jesús. Thank you to my best friends Jason, Pat, Dom, and Dave (though Pat needs to stop telling people this is a book about pop-punk). And there's no way I could write this section without shouting out all the kids I used to go to shows with in high school, especially Dave Destro, Greg Scalera, Fred Ilac, Rich Moy, Chris Pajonk, Danielle Sweeney, Zuzanna Sitek, Jason Goncalves, Rich Alberto, Janette Lawrence, Ashley Grabowski, Jimmy and Stevie Lynn Quartuccio, and anyone else I might have forgotten. It's been a long time since Bamboozle in Asbury Park.

INDEX